MCSD: Visual Basic® 5 Companion CD-ROM

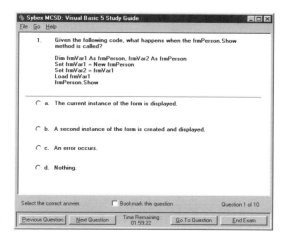

For Windows 95, 98, and NT 4 users, this *autoplay* CD-ROM automatically displays the set up for the Sybex Test Engine. Just pop it in the CD-ROM drive and let the autoplay CD boot the Sybex Interface. You'll find the following software products on the CD:

The Exclusive Sybex MCSD Test Engine. All the questions and answers in this book are included on the Sybex MCSD ExamReady Test Engine, an easy-to-use program for test preparation.

VB5 Code. Try your hand at tweaking the examples and demos created by the author for this Study Guide.

MCSD Offline Update. The latest Microsoft information on the MCSD certification program. NOTE: Internet Explorer 4 is required to run this HTML-based document.

Internet Explorer 4.01. This powerful browser includes everything you need for accessing the Net.

MCSD on the Web. Popular MCSD Web sites listed in order of importance to MCSD students.

Using the Sybex MCSD ExamReady Test Engine

The Sybex test engine is an autorun test engine created exclusively for the Sybex MCSD Study Guides. To prepare for the real exam:

1. Close all active and minimized applications.
2. Put the CD in the CD drive and wait a few seconds until the MCSD test engine setup screen appears.
3. Follow the installation prompts to install the ExamReady engine. At the end of the install, **reboot your PC**. Afterward, the ExamReady test engine will start.
4. If you choose not to run the program after it installs, you can start it by clicking on Start, Programs, Sybex Study Guide, ExamReady2228.
5. When the main screen appears (shown on this page), click on name, enter a name. Then, click on Exam, Timed Exam to begin the timed MCSD practice exam.

To access other elements of the CD, use Windows Explorer (File Manager).

MCSD: Visual Basic 5
Study Guide

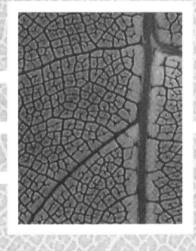

MCSD: Visual Basic® 5 Study Guide

Michael McKelvy

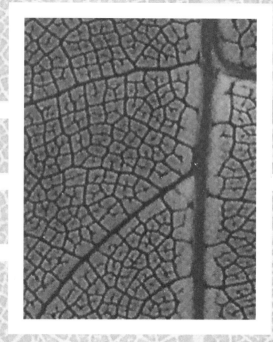

San Francisco • Paris • Düsseldorf • Soest

Associate Publisher: Gary Masters
Contracts and Licensing Manager: Kristine Plachy
Acquisitions & Developmental Editor: Peter Kuhns
Editor: Lawrence Frey
Project Editors: Ben Miller, Michael Tom
Technical Editor: Don Hergert
Book Designers: Patrick Dintino, Bill Gibson
Electronic Publishing Specialist: Bill Gibson
Production Coordinators: Duncan Watson, Amy Eoff, Rebecca Rider
Indexer: Ted Laux
Companion CD: Molly Sharp and Ginger Warner
Cover Designer: Design Site
Cover Illustrator/Photographer: Design Site

Screen reproductions produced with Collage Complete.

Collage Complete is a trademark of Inner Media Inc.

Library of Congress Card Number: 98-85643
ISBN: 0-7821-2228-0

Manufactured in the United States of America

10 9 8 7 6 5 4 3 2 1

November 1, 1997

Dear SYBEX Customer:

Microsoft is pleased to inform you that SYBEX is a participant in the Microsoft® Independent Courseware Vendor (ICV) program. Microsoft ICVs design, develop, and market self-paced courseware, books, and other products that support Microsoft software and the Microsoft Certified Professional (MCP) program.

To be accepted into the Microsoft ICV program, an ICV must meet set criteria. In addition, Microsoft reviews and approves each ICV training product before permission is granted to use the Microsoft Certified Professional Approved Study Guide logo on that product. This logo assures the consumer that the product has passed the following Microsoft standards:

- The course contains accurate product information.
- The course includes labs and activities during which the student can apply knowledge and skills learned from the course.
- The course teaches skills that help prepare the student to take corresponding MCP exams.

Microsoft ICVs continually develop and release new MCP Approved Study Guides. To prepare for a particular Microsoft certification exam, a student may choose one or more single, self-paced training courses or a series of training courses.

You will be pleased with the quality and effectiveness of the MCP Approved Study Guides available from SYBEX.

Sincerely,

Holly Heath
ICV Account Manager
Microsoft Training & Certification

MICROSOFT INDEPENDENT COURSEWARE VENDOR PROGRAM

Software License Agreement:
Terms and Conditions

The media and/or any online materials accompanying this book that are available now or in the future contain programs and/or text files (the "Software") to be used in connection with the book. SYBEX hereby grants to you a license to use the Software, subject to the terms that follow. Your purchase, acceptance, or use of the Software will constitute your acceptance of such terms.

The Software compilation is the property of SYBEX unless otherwise indicated and is protected by copyright to SYBEX or other copyright owner(s) as indicated in the media files (the "Owner(s)"). You are hereby granted a single-user license to use the Software for your personal, noncommercial use only. You may not reproduce, sell, distribute, publish, circulate, or commercially exploit the Software, or any portion thereof, without the written consent of SYBEX and the specific copyright owner(s) of any component software included on this media.

In the event that the Software or components include specific license requirements or end-user agreements, statements of condition, disclaimers, limitations or warranties ("End-User License"), those End-User Licenses supersede the terms and conditions herein as to that particular Software component. Your purchase, acceptance, or use of the Software will constitute your acceptance of such End-User Licenses.

By purchase, use or acceptance of the Software you further agree to comply with all export laws and regulations of the United States as such laws and regulations may exist from time to time.

Software Support

Components of the supplemental Software and any offers associated with them may be supported by the specific Owner(s) of that material but they are not supported by SYBEX. Information regarding any available support may be obtained from the Owner(s) using the information provided in the appropriate read.me files or listed elsewhere on the media.

Should the manufacturer(s) or other Owner(s) cease to offer support or decline to honor any offer, SYBEX bears no responsibility. This notice concerning support for the Software is provided for your information only. SYBEX is not the agent or principal of the Owner(s), and SYBEX is in no way responsible for providing any support for the Software, nor is it liable or responsible for any support provided, or not provided, by the Owner(s).

Warranty

SYBEX warrants the enclosed media to be free of physical defects for a period of ninety (90) days after purchase. The Software is not available from SYBEX in any other form or media than that enclosed herein or posted to www.sybex.com. If you discover a defect in the media during this warranty period, you may obtain a replacement of identical format at no charge by sending the defective media, postage prepaid, with proof of purchase to:

SYBEX Inc.
Customer Service Department
1151 Marina Village Parkway
Alameda, CA 94501
(510) 523-8233
Fax: (510) 523-2373
e-mail: info@sybex.com
WEB: HTTP://WWW.SYBEX.COM

After the 90-day period, you can obtain replacement media of identical format by sending us the defective disk, proof of purchase, and a check or money order for $10, payable to SYBEX.

Disclaimer

SYBEX makes no warranty or representation, either expressed or implied, with respect to the Software or its contents, quality, performance, merchantability, or fitness for a particular purpose. In no event will SYBEX, its distributors, or dealers be liable to you or any other party for direct, indirect, special, incidental, consequential, or other damages arising out of the use of or inability to use the Software or its contents even if advised of the possibility of such damage. In the event that the Software includes an online update feature, SYBEX further disclaims any obligation to provide this feature for any specific duration other than the initial posting.

The exclusion of implied warranties is not permitted by some states. Therefore, the above exclusion may not apply to you. This warranty provides you with specific legal rights; there may be other rights that you may have that vary from state to state. The pricing of the book with the Software by SYBEX reflects the allocation of risk and limitations on liability contained in this agreement of Terms and Conditions.

Shareware Distribution

This Software may contain various programs that are distributed as shareware. Copyright laws apply to both shareware and ordinary commercial software, and the copyright Owner(s) retains all rights. If you try a shareware program and continue using it, you are expected to register it. Individual programs differ on details of trial periods, registration, and payment. Please observe the requirements stated in appropriate files.

Copy Protection

The Software in whole or in part may or may not be copy-protected or encrypted. However, in all cases, reselling or redistributing these files without authorization is expressly forbidden except as specifically provided for by the Owner(s) therein.

To my wife, Wanda, and my children, Laura and Eric, for their love and support, and for their patience during the long hours of the project.

Acknowledgments

A book like this is not the effort of a single individual, it takes a talented team of people to create a book that is useful for the reader and is a quality publication. I would like to thank all the members of the team that helped me put this book together. Peter Kuhns, who got me started on the project and helped me get the outline and intent of the book right. Michael Tom and Ben Miller, who coordinated the project and persisted in making sure that all the material got where it was supposed to be, and got there on time. Lawrence Frey who handled the editing and made sure my explanations made sense, and Don Hergert, the technical editor who made sure that what I told you in the explanations was right. Finally, I would like to once again thank Fred Slone, who first got me started in the great adventure of writing books, and who recommended me for this book.

Contents at a Glance

Table of Contents

Appendices

Table of Exercises

Introduction

These days, almost every job requires some level of computer literacy. You will even find computers being used in most restaurants to handle order processing, a task that was previously done by hand. For all the tasks that are being performed by computer, someone needed to write the software to handle the task. This is the role of the software developer. Finding qualified software developers is a major issue for many companies today.

But how is a company supposed to determine who is qualified and who is just a computer user with a few elementary programming skills? Determining the qualifications of people is difficult when there are so many who claim to be computer experts, even if their expertise was setting up their own Web page. To help with the task of determining who is qualified and who is not, Microsoft developed its Microsoft certification program to certify those people who have the skills to work with Microsoft products and networks.

For developers, this certification is in the form of the Microsoft Certified Solution Developer. This certification establishes that a person is familiar with the inner workings of Windows and has skills in working with multiple programming languages or development environments. Visual Basic is one of the languages in which you can be certified on your way to becoming an MCSD. Even if MCSD is not your goal, being Microsoft certified in Visual Basic can make it easier for you to get a programming job or to command a higher salary for the job.

The purpose of this book is to make it easier for you to pass the Visual Basic certification exam. After working through the book, you will understand the objectives covered by the test and will know the types of questions to expect on the test.

Your Key to Passing Exam 70-165

This book provides you with the key to passing Exam 70-165, Developing Applications with Microsoft Visual Basic 5.0. You'll find all the information relevant to this exam, including hundreds of practice questions, all designed to make sure that when you take the real exam, you are ready for even the picky questions on less frequently used options.

Understand the Exam Objectives

In order to help you prepare for certification exams, Microsoft provides a list of exam objectives for each test. This book is structured according to the objectives for Exam 70-165, designed to measure your ability to create applications in Visual Basic.

At-a-glance review sections and more than 200 review questions bolster your knowledge of the information relevant to each objective and the exam itself. You learn exactly what you need to know without wasting time on background material or detailed explanations.

This book prepares you for the exam in the shortest amount of time possible. To be ready for the real world, however, you need to study the subject in greater depth and get a good deal of hands-on practice.

Get Ready for the Real Thing

More than 200 sample test questions prepare you for the test-taking experience. These are multiple-choice questions that resemble actual exam questions, some are even more difficult than what you'll find on the exam. If you can pass the Sample Tests at the end of each unit and the Final Exam at the end of the book, you'll know you're ready.

Is This Book for You?

The target audience for this book is the programmer who has some experience with Visual Basic but needs to understand the topics covered in the exam objectives. While the explanations and exercises are written to be easily understandable, a certain level of Visual Basic programming background is assumed. If you are not familiar with the basics of programming in Visual Basic, you would probably do well to take an introductory class or read an introductory book before continuing toward certification.

Understanding Microsoft Certification

Microsoft offers several levels of certification for anyone who has or is pursuing a career as a professional developer working with Microsoft products:

- Microsoft Certified Professional (MCP)
- Microsoft Certified Systems Engineer (MCSE)

- Microsoft Certified Solution Developer (MCSD)
- Microsoft Certified Professional + Internet
- Microsoft Certified Systems Engineer + Internet
- Microsoft Certified Trainer (MCT)

The one you choose depends on your area of expertise and your career goals.

Microsoft Certified Professional (MCP)

This certification is for individuals with expertise in one specific area. MCP certification is often a stepping stone to MCSE or MCSD certification and allows you some benefits of Microsoft certification after just one exam.

By passing one core exam (meaning an operating system exam), you become an MCP.

Microsoft Certified Systems Engineer (MCSE)

For network professionals, the MCSE certification requires commitment. You need to complete all the steps required for certification. Passing the exams shows that you meet the high standards that Microsoft has set for MSCEs.

The following list applies to the NT 4.0 track. Microsoft still supports a track for 3.51, but 4.0 certification is more desirable because it is the current operating system.

To become an MCSE, you must pass a series of six exams:

1. Networking Essentials (waived for Novell CNEs)
2. Implementing and Supporting Microsoft Windows NT Workstation 4.0 (or Windows 95)
3. Implementing and Supporting Microsoft Windows NT Server 4.0
4. Implementing and Supporting Microsoft Windows NT Server 4.0 in the Enterprise
5. Elective
6. Elective

Some of the electives include:

- Internetworking with Microsoft TCP/IP on Microsoft Windows NT 4.0
- Implementing and Supporting Microsoft Internet Information Server 4.0
- Implementing and Supporting Microsoft Exchange Server 5.5
- Implementing and Supporting Microsoft SNA Server 4.0
- Implementing and Supporting Microsoft Systems Management Server 1.2
- Implementing a Database Design on Microsoft SQL Server 6.5
- System Administration for Microsoft SQL Server 6.5

Microsoft Certified Solution Developer (MCSD)

MCSD certification shows that you have an understanding of the Microsoft Windows system architecture, as well as an understanding of programming languages. To obtain this certification you must pass two core exams and two electives. The core exams for the certification are:

- Microsoft Windows Architecture I (70-160)
- Microsoft Windows Architecture II (70-161)

For your electives, you have the choice of several programming languages and database systems:

- Implementing a Database Design on Microsoft SQL Server 6.5
- Developing Applications with Microsoft Visual Basic 5.0
- Developing Applications with C++ Using the Microsoft Foundation Class Library
- Microsoft Access for Windows 95 and the Microsoft Access Developer's Toolkit
- Programming in Microsoft Visual FoxPro 3.0 for Windows

Microsoft Certified Trainer (MCT)

As an MCT, you can deliver Microsoft certified courseware through official Microsoft channels.

The MCT certification is more costly because, in addition to passing the exams, it requires that you sit through the official Microsoft courses. You also need to submit an application that must be approved by Microsoft. The number of exams you are required to pass depends on the number of courses you want to teach.

For the most up-to-date certification information, visit Microsoft's Web site at www.microsoft.com/train_cert.

Preparing for the MCSD Exams

To prepare for the MCSD certification exams, you should try to work with the product as much as possible. In addition, there are a variety of resources from which you can learn about the products and exams:

- You can take instructor-led courses.

- Online training is an alternative to instructor-led courses. This is a useful option for people who cannot find any courses in their area or who do not have the time to attend classes.

- If you prefer to use a book to help you prepare for the MCSD tests, you can choose from a wide variety of publications, including test-preparedness books similar to this one.

For more MCSD information, point your browser to the Sybex Web site, where you'll find information about the MCP program, job links, and descriptions of other quality titles in the Network Press line of MCSD-related books. Go to http://www.sybex.com and click the MCSD logo.

Scheduling and Taking an Exam

When you think you are ready to take an exam, call Prometric Testing Centers at (800) 755-EXAM (755-3926). They'll tell you where to find the closest testing center. Before you call, get out your credit card because each exam costs $100. (If you've used this book to prepare yourself thoroughly, chances are you'll only have to shell out that $100 once!)

You can schedule the exam for a time that is convenient for you. The exams are downloaded from Prometric to the testing center, and you show up at your scheduled time and take the exam on a computer.

After you complete the exam, you will know right away whether you have passed or not. At the end of the exam, you will receive a score report. It will list the six areas that you were tested on and how you performed. If you pass the exam, you don't need to do anything else. Prometric uploads the test results to Microsoft. If you don't pass, it's another $100 to schedule the exam again. But at least you will know from the score report where you did poorly, so you can study that particular information more carefully.

Test-Taking Hints

If you know what to expect, your chances of passing the exam will be much greater. The following are some tips that can help you achieve success.

Get there early and be prepared   This is your last chance to review. Bring your Test Success book and review any areas you feel unsure of. If you need a quick drink of water or a visit to the restroom, take the time before the exam. Once your exam starts, it will not be paused for these needs.

When you arrive for your exam, you will be asked to present two forms of ID. You will also be asked to sign a piece of paper verifying that you understand the testing rules (for example, the rule that says that you will not cheat on the exam).

Before you start the exam, you will have an opportunity to take a practice exam. It is not related to Windows NT and is simply offered so that you will have a feel for the exam-taking process.

What you can and can't take in with you   These are closed-book exams. The only thing that you can take in is scratch paper provided by the testing center. Use this paper as much as possible to diagram the questions. Many times diagramming questions will help make the answer clear. You will have to give this paper back to the test administrator at the end of the exam.

Many testing centers are very strict about what you can take into the testing room. Some centers will not even allow you to bring in items like a zipped-up purse. If you feel tempted to take in any outside material, be aware that many testing centers use monitoring devices such as video and audio equipment (so don't swear, even if you are alone in the room!).

Prometric Testing Centers take the test-taking process and the test validation very seriously.

Test approach As you take the test, if you know the answer to a question, fill it in and move on. If you're not sure of the answer, mark your best guess, then "mark" the question.

At the end of the exam, you can review the questions. Depending on the amount of time remaining, you can then view all the questions again, or you can view only the questions that you were unsure of. I always like to double-check all my answers, just in case I misread any of the questions on the first pass. (Sometimes half of the battle is in trying to figure out exactly what the question is asking you.) Also, sometimes I find that a related question provides a clue for a question that I was unsure of.

Be sure to answer all questions. Unanswered questions are scored as incorrect and will count against you. Also, make sure that you keep an eye on the remaining time so that you can pace yourself accordingly.

If you do not pass the exam, note everything that you can remember while the exam is still fresh on your mind. This will help you prepare for your next try. Although the next exam will not be exactly the same, the questions will be similar, and you don't want to make the same mistakes.

How to Use This Book

This book is designed to help you prepare for the MCSD exam. The book reviews each of the exam objectives and explains to you how to accomplish the objectives. The explanations include exercises that help you understand how to implement the programming concepts.

Each chapter of the book contains review questions to help you make sure you understand the material in the chapter and to prepare you for the exam itself.

For each chapter:

1. Review the exam objectives list at the beginning of the unit. (You may want to check the Microsoft Train_Cert Web site to make sure the objectives haven't changed.)

2. Review your knowledge in the Study Questions section. These are straightforward questions designed to test your knowledge of the specific topic. Answers to Study Questions are listed in the Appendix at the back of the book.

3. When you feel sure of your knowledge of the area, take the Sample Test. The Sample Test's content and style matches the real exam. Set yourself a time limit based on the number of questions: A general rule is that you should be able to answer 20 questions in 30 minutes. When you've finished, check your answers with the Appendix in the back of the book. If you answer at least 85 percent of the questions correctly within the time limit (the first time you take the Sample Test), you're in good shape. To really prepare, you should note the questions you miss and be able to score 95 to 100 percent correctly on subsequent tries.

At this point, you are well on your way to becoming certified!
Good Luck!

PART

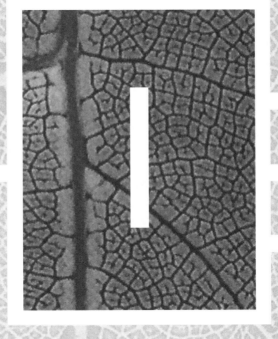

I

Review of Basic
Concepts

CHAPTER

1

Creating an Application
with Forms and Controls

One of the key areas covered in the Visual Basic certification exam is the ability to design and create forms. Typically, you think of designing forms and creating the visual interface of your program by adding controls to the forms of your program while you are in design mode. The exam is not concerned with your ability to arrange the controls of your form in an aesthetic manner; however, it is concerned with your ability to control the functions of the forms and controls of your program through properties, methods, and events.

This chapter will start with a brief review of how you create the visual interface of your program, then move into the areas of controlling the behavior of the forms and selecting the right events for given situations.

Review of Form and Control Basics

Most programs that you create in Visual Basic contain at least one form, which in turn contains a number of controls. About the only programs that do not contain a form are ActiveX servers, which will be discussed in a later chapter. The forms and controls of your programs are the only parts that your user sees. Therefore, much effort is expended by programmers to ensure that the interface created by the forms and controls is intuitive to use, visually pleasing, and makes it easy for the user to accomplish the desired task. This is true whether you are writing a custom database program to handle membership tracking (like the program shown in Figure 1.1) or a simple game as shown in Figure 1.2.

F I G U R E   1 . 1

The interface of a data entry program may be quite complex...

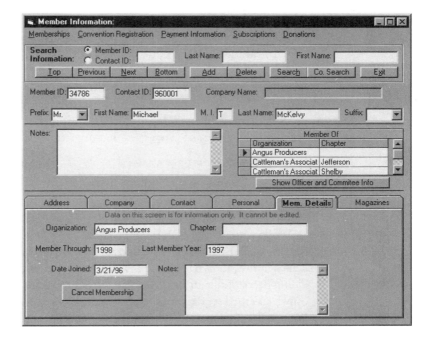

F I G U R E   1 . 2

whereas a game interface may be quite simple.

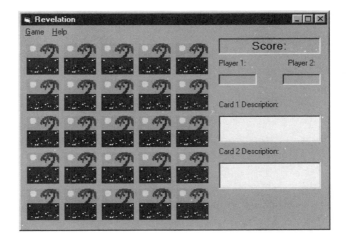

Working with Properties

As you add controls to the forms of your program, you control the behavior and appearance of these controls, and of the forms themselves, through the properties of each control. Properties such as Left, Top, Height, and Width determine the size and position of each control. These four properties, along with the Name property, are common to every control you use. The other properties available will depend on the specific control you are using. There are three categories of properties that are available for each control:

- Properties that are available only at design time
- Properties that are only available at run time
- Properties that can be set any time

While you are in design mode, you change the properties available at design time through the properties window of the Visual Basic design environment. This window, shown in Figure 1.3, allows you to easily set the properties by providing descriptions of the properties, drop-down lists for properties that have only a specified set of values, and even dialog boxes for some properties such as Font or ForeColor and BackColor. All these elements are designed to make it as easy as possible for you to create your programs.

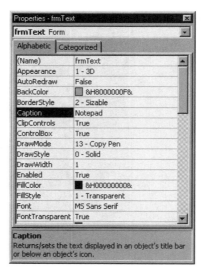

FIGURE 1.3

Visual Basic's properties window allows easy access to control properties.

To further facilitate the design process, many controls (especially third-party controls) have a Custom button in the Properties window that brings up a set of Property Pages for the control. These property pages help you set up all the necessary properties of a control. The Property Pages are particularly useful for complex controls such as ImageList or TreeView. The TreeView Property Pages are shown in Figure 1.4.

F I G U R E   1.4

The Property Page for the TreeView control

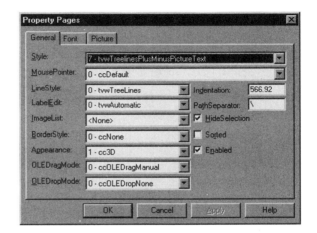

While you will work most with the properties of the form and controls while in design mode, there are times when you will want to change the appearance and behavior of controls while your program is running. A typical case is changing the Enabled property of controls as program conditions change. The Enabled property determines whether the user can interact with the control. To change a property in program code, you simply use an assignment statement to set the new value of the property. This statement, like the one shown below, specifies the name of the control, the name of the property, and the new value to be set.

```
cboFieldName.Enabled = True
```

Some properties, such as the Name property, can only be set at design time, but most properties can be set with program code. This manipulation of properties will make up a large portion of the Visual Basic code that you write.

Writing Code for Events

The properties of the forms and controls determine their appearance and behavior, but it is code that you write for the events of the forms and controls that really make your program perform tasks. You can have the most well planned, perfectly designed user interface, but without program code. It looks good, but it won't get you anywhere.

Events are actually Visual Basic's way of notifying you that the form has received a Windows message from the operating system. These messages can indicate that the user has pressed a key, clicked a mouse button, or taken some other action. The events can also be triggered in response to system events or control events, such as having a specified amount of time elapse. While there are a large number of events available for each control and for forms (take a look at the form event list in the code window), your program will only respond to events for which you have written program code. All other events will be ignored.

Program code can be divided into two major categories:

- **Assignment statements**   Assignment statements are used to set the value of a control's property or of a variable. You saw such a statement earlier in this chapter.

- **Control statements**   Control statements, as their name implies, control the flow of a program. These statements include For...Next loops, If...Then...Else...End If structures and others. You will learn more about controlling program flow in Chapter 2.

You should be familiar with writing event procedures; Exercise 1.1 provides a brief refresher for those who aren't. The code takes the input from two text boxes, performs a calculation, and displays the results in another text box. The code will be executed when a user clicks the Command button on a form.

EXERCISE 1.1

Writing an Event Procedure

1. Open the code window by clicking the code button on the project window.

2. In the object list, select the command button (named cmdCalculate). The Click event is the default event and the header and footer for the procedure will be automatically created for you.

3. You can go directly to this event procedure from your form by double-clicking the command button.

4. Enter the following code in the code window:

```
Dim iNumber1 As Integer, iNumber2 As Integer
iNumber1 = txtInput1.Text
iNumber2 = txtInput2.Text
txtOutput.Text = iNumber1 * iNumber2
```

You can omit the Text property from your code. Most controls have what is called a "Value" property, which is the default property for the control. If you do not specify a property name, the default or Value property is assumed. Text is the default property of the TextBox control.

Design Considerations

You know that creating a user interface for a program can be as simple as placing controls on a form. Add program code for specific events, and you have a working program. We all know that creating a good program is more involved than this, however, and many design issues can make a program either a good one that users will use or a bad one that users will avoid. While we won't cover a large number of design issues (whole books have been devoted to the subject), there are a few key areas of which you should be aware.

Because the MCSD exam uses multiple choice questions, you will not find questions specifically related to design. The exam is designed, however, to measure your ability to apply programming theory and to test your experience. These design considerations are an integral part of the practical application of programming theory.

Tab order One of the first areas is Tab order, the order in which controls on your form are accessed as the user presses the Tab key. The tab order of controls is determined by the TabIndex property of each control. As you add controls, the TabIndex of each control is set to one greater than the last control on the form. If you design a form perfectly, tab order will not be a problem. However, many programmers add all the labels to a form first, then the text boxes, then other controls. While this makes it easy to initially set up the controls, it plays havoc with the tab order.

The most desirable tab order starts at the top left of the form and moves left-to-right and top-to-bottom on the form. Because this is the way most users read, it is a logical order in a form. To set the tab order, start with the control you want your users to hit first and set its TabIndex to 0. Then proceed in the order you want for the tab order, setting the TabIndex property of each control to the next available number.

Visual Basic does not have a built-in tool for easily setting tab order, but several third-party products (such as Sheridan's VBAssist) do a nice job of helping you with tab order.

Another key design issue is keyboard navigation for your forms. Setting the tab order allows a user to move through the form in a logical manner; however, users may often have a need to go directly to a specific control. They can do this by clicking on the control with the mouse, but a good design will allow them to move directly to a control without moving their hands from the keyboard. You already know how to use hot keys (Alt+key) to enable command buttons and menu options, but you can also provide this functionality to other input controls. Exercise 1.2 shows how to enable a text box for keyboard navigation.

EXERCISE 1.2

Allowing a User to Move Directly to a Text Box

1. Place a text box on the form.

2. Place a label control near the text box. Set the TabIndex property of the label to 0. This will automatically increment the TabIndex of the text box to 1.

3. Set a hot key in the Caption property of the label using an ampersand (&).
   For example, &Name.

4. Add some other controls to the form.

When the user presses the hot key combination for the label, Visual Basic will try to set the focus to the label. However, because a label cannot receive focus, the control next in the tab order (the text box) will receive the focus. The KeyBoard.vbp project on the CD shows how this is implemented.

Creating Applications with Multiple Forms

Microsoft ✓ ***Exam Objective***   **Create an application that adds and deletes forms at run time.**

You can create some very useful programs with a single form, but most of the programs you create will involve multiple forms. Many large projects can have fifty forms or more. You will have to have a way to create and display other forms from within your program code, because Visual Basic will only load a single form on startup.

Displaying Forms in a Program

You create all the forms of your program in the design environment. The key to using these forms is to display them in your program at the proper time, typically in response to user actions. Visual Basic provides a form method and a command to allow you to display additional forms in your program. The simplest way to handle displaying a form is to use the Show method, which loads the form into memory and displays it on-screen. Exercise 1.3 provides a simple example of this method.

Displaying a Second Form in a Program

1. Start a new project in Visual Basic.

2. Add a second form to the project by choosing the New Form item from the Project menu or by clicking the New Form button on the toolbar.

3. Place some controls on the second form.

4. Return to the first form.

5. Place a command button on the form.

6. In the Click event procedure, place the following statement:

   Form2.Show

7. Run the program.

The Show method handles all the work of displaying the second form. An optional parameter can also be specified with the Show method, which allows you to make the form *modal*; that is, the user cannot move to another form in the program until this form is hidden or unloaded. Modal forms are often used for dialog boxes that you want to have the user complete before moving on. To display a form as modal, use the following variation of the Show method:

Form2.Show vbModal

If you can display a form, you also want to be able to hide it. The Hide method removes the form from the display, but does not remove it from memory. The Hide method is used as shown in the following line:

Form2.Hide

In addition to the Show and Hide methods, there are two commands that are used in manipulating forms:

- **Load**   The Load command places the form in memory but does not display it on the screen.

Because a form is automatically loaded when the Show method is invoked, why would you want to use the Load command? Often, a large form takes a long time to load. If you have one or two large forms in your program, you can use the Load command to load them into memory during program startup when users are more tolerant of delays. Then, issuing the Show method quickly displays the form. You can also use the Load command if there are a number of options that needed to be set by your program code before the form is displayed.

- **Unload** The Unload command is used to remove the form from memory, freeing up most of the memory used by the form definition. The Load and Unload commands are shown in the following lines of code:

```
Load Form2
Unload Form2
Unload Me
```

The last code line shows the use of the Me keyword to refer to a form. This keyword tells a command to operate on the form that contains the code line. Using the Me keyword to internally refer to a form helps avoid any problems that can arise from renaming a form after it is originally created. You will also find that it is essential in properly using object variables to manipulate forms and in creating MDI applications, which are discussed in the next sections.

Using Variables to Manipulate Forms

Using the Load, Show, Hide, and Unload commands and methods with the name of a form allows you to work with a single instance of each form that you create in your program. Because forms are Visual Basic objects, however, you can use object variables to work with forms. This allows you to create multiple instances of any form you have designed.

To use a variable to handle form operations, you need to declare a variable for the form to be used. You can then use the variable in place of the form name in any form operation. By using the New keyword in either the variable declaration or in the Set command that assigns a form to the variable, you can create multiple instances of the form. Exercise 1.4 illustrates how to create two instances of a form using object variables. An example of this technique is contained in the FormObj.vbp project on the CD.

EXERCISE 1.4

Creating Multiple Form Instances

1. Create the primary form for your project. This form should contain a command button for creating and displaying the instances of the second form.

2. Create a second form to be used as a template for your form objects. For the example, name the form frmPerson.

3. Open the code window for your main form (the first one you created).

4. Place the variable declarations in the Declarations section of the form. The variables are declared using the following code:

```
Dim frmVar1 As frmPerson, frmVar2 As frmPerson
```

5. In the Click event of the command button, place the code to create and display the form instances. The Set command with the New keyword creates a new instance of the frmPerson form. The Show method applied to each form variable displays the form.

```
Set frmVar1 = New frmPerson
Set frmVar2 = New frmPerson
frmVar1.Show
frmVar2.Show
frmVar2.Move 500, 500
```

6. Run the program. When you click the command button on the main form, two instances of the frmPerson form will be created. Each of these instances is independent of the other.

WARNING   When you are creating multiple instances of a form, you should always refer to them by the variable that you used to create the instance of the form. Attempting to refer to either form using the form name (that is, frmPerson.Show) will not affect either of the instances assigned to variables, but will create an additional instance of the form.

Creating MDI Applications

The most common method of using variables to create multiple instances of a form is in the creation of an MDI (multiple-document interface) application. You made use of MDI applications when you worked with multiple documents in a word processor. Also, the interface for Visual Basic 5 is an MDI application, placing each form and each code window in a separate child window of the main form.

In an MDI application, there is a single parent form that contains a menu and optionally contains toolbars that allow you to create, arrange, and work with the child forms. The MDI parent form does not contain any standard controls. Each child form provides an interface with which you can work on a document, a spreadsheet, a data entry form, or any other type of program interface. Each child form is contained within the borders of the parent form, but each child form is capable of independent operation.

A typical example of an MDI application is a notepad or simple word processor. Without going into all the details, Exercise 1.5 illustrates the basics of creating an MDI application.

EXERCISE 1.5 ·

Creating an MDI Application

1. Start a new project in Visual Basic.

2. Add an MDI form to the project using the Add MDI Form item of the Project menu.

3. Make the MDI form the startup form for the program. To do this, select the Properties item from the Project menu, then select the MDI form in the Startup form drop down list.

4. Using the original Form1 that was created when the project was created, change the name to frmText and set the MDIChild property to True.

5. Add a text box to this form to allow the user to input text.

6. On the MDI form, add a menu item called File and a sub menu called New. (Menu creation will be discussed in detail in Chapter 4.)

EXERCISE 1.5 (CONTINUED)

7. In the Click event for the New menu item, place the following code:

```
Dim frmVar As frmText
Set frmVar = New frmText
frmVar.Show
```

8. Run the program. Each time you select the New item from the File menu, a new instance of the child form will be created within the MDI parent.

Events in a Form

Microsoft
✓ *Exam*
Objective

Add code to the appropriate form event, such as Initialize, Terminate, Load, Unload, QueryUnload, Activate, and Deactivate.

Properties control the appearance and behavior of a form and method allows the form to perform tasks, but it is the events of the form that tell it when to take action. If you look at the event drop-down list in a form's code window (see Figure 1.5), you will see that there are a number of events that a form recognizes and to which it can respond. All these events can cause action to be taken, but only the events for which you write code will actually perform any functions in your program. If you have no code in the procedure for an event, the event is ignored.

This section will not examine each event to which a form can respond. Rather, it will look specifically at some of the events that occur when a form is loaded and when it is closed. You will also see the sequence in which some of these events occur. Knowing the sequence of events is important in knowing where to place your code to get the desired results.

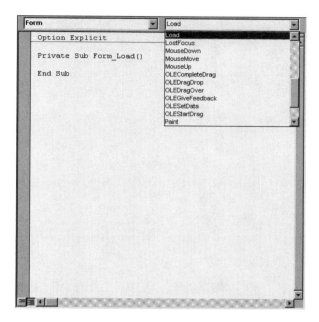

Events Occurring when a Form Loads

There are several key events that occur when a form is loaded for the first time. These events are summarized below. Table 1.1 lists these startup events and when they are triggered. Figure 1.6 shows how some of these events are used in an actual program.

TABLE 1.1	Event	When Triggered
Event and Trigger	Initialize	When the form is first referenced in any manner by your program
	Load	When the form is first placed in memory using the Load statement or Show method
	Activate	When the form receives focus as it is shown or the user moves back to the form from another form or application
	Resize	Whenever the user or the program changes the Height, Width, or WindowState properties of the form
	Paint	Whenever any part of the form needs to be refreshed

FIGURE 1.6

Multiple events may
be accessed when a
form loads.

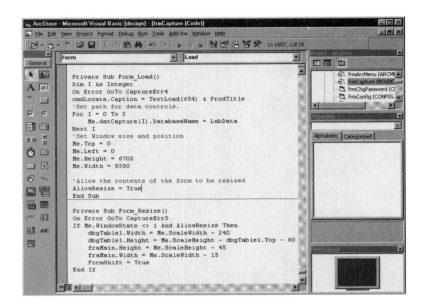

The Initialize event   The Initialize event is triggered only once during the lifetime of a form. The Initialize event is triggered by one of the following actions:

- When a property or method of the form is referenced by another part of the program.

- When an object variable is used to create a new instance of the form. (This was covered in the section "Object variables for form manipulation.")

- Automatically when the form is loaded by the Load command or the Show method.

   The Initialize event can be used to set initial values of custom properties that you create for a form. Giving them an initial value ensures that a valid value will always be available for the property.

The Load event   Like the Initialize event, the Load event is triggered only once during the lifetime of a form. The Load event is triggered by one of the following actions:

- When the Load command is issued to load the form into memory.

- Automatically when the Show method is used to display a form that was not previously loaded.

The Load event is often used to set the initial properties of the form itself and of the controls contained by the form. Most control properties can be set from the Load event.

The Resize event   The Resize event occurs when the form is initially loaded or whenever the form changes size. If you have controls, such as a grid, that need to be sized to match the dimensions of the form, the Resize event is the location for that code.

The Paint event   The Paint event is another event that occurs when a form is initially displayed. It also occurs whenever a part of the form needs to be refreshed, such as, when the form is initially loaded or after it has been covered up by another form.

The Paint event is where you place code that prints on the form or draws graphics on the form. For example, if you are printing labels instead of using the label controls, you place the code in the Paint event to assure that the labels get reprinted whenever part of the form has been covered.

The Activate event   The Activate event occurs whenever the form receives focus from another form or another program. It is also triggered when the form is initially shown using the Show method. This event may be used to initialize the state of a form each time it is shown. For example, you may place code in the event to set the focus to a particular control, so the user always knows where to start. Also, some initial settings, such as the Record-Source property of a data control, cannot be set during the Load event and must be initially set in the Activate event.

Sequence of Events

It is important to know which events are good for specific tasks, but it is also necessary to understand the sequence in which these events occur, because the code in one event may be dependent on code in other events. For example, the code in Figure 1.6 sets a variable in the Load event that determines whether controls on the form will be moved or sized in response to the Resize event. The Load event is the proper location for this assignment because it occurs before the Resize event.

For the first four events listed earlier, the proper sequence is

1. Initialize

2. Load

3. Resize

4. Paint

If you want to experiment with the sequence of other events, simply place a message box in the event procedure for each event of interest. Then, as you perform operations on the form, you can see the order in which events occur. A sample program is contained in the FormEvent.vbp project on the CD.

The Activate event will also occur between the Load and the Paint events, but it is not triggered if your program has code for the Resize event.

Events Occurring when a Form is Unloaded

In a manner similar to loading the form, there is a series of events that occur when the form is unloaded. The three key events are

1. QueryUnload

2. Unload

3. Terminate

The characteristics of these three events, as well as the Deactivate event, are summarized below.

QueryUnload event The QueryUnload event occurs when the form is closed using the control menu, the Close button or the Unload command. The QueryUnload event allows you to determine the method by which the form was closed. The QueryUnload event occurs before the Unload event; it can be used to determine how the form was closed and to cancel the unload if desired. The UnloadMode argument of the QueryUnload event procedure tells you how the form was unloaded. The argument can have one of five values as listed in Table 1.2.

TABLE 1.2	**UnloadMode Value**	**Cause of Unload action**
UnloadMode Value	vbFormControlMenu	The Close option of the control menu (upper-left corner of the form) was chosen or the Close button (upper-right corner) was clicked.
	vbFormCode	Your program code issued the Unload statement for the form.
	vbAppWindows	The user is shutting down Windows.
	vbAppTaskManager	The application was closed by the Task Manager.
	vbFormMDIForm	The child form is being closed because the MDI parent form was closed.

Unload event The Unload event occurs when the form is unloaded by any of the means specified in Table 1.2. This event is used to close objects, such as recordsets, that were opened within the form. It can also be used to return a program to the same state it was in before the form was loaded. The Unload event always occurs after the QueryUnload event.

Terminate event The Terminate event is unique in the closing events of a form. The Terminate event always occurs after the Unload event, but it occurs only when all references to the form are destroyed either by being set to Nothing or by an object variable going out of scope. The Terminate event typically is used for clean-up code to handle tasks such as releasing memory used by form variables, resetting a program state, or other similar tasks.

Deactivate event The Deactivate event occurs when the focus is transferred to another form or program. This event can be used to ensure that certain operations are completed before the user leaves the form.

To illustrate how these events might be used in a program, Exercise 1.6 demonstrates how to prevent a user from closing a form using the Control menu or the Close button.

EXERCISE 1.6

Preventing the User from Using the Close Button

1. Start a new project.

2. Place a command button on the form and set the caption to Exit.

3. Open the code window for the form.

4. Place the statement "Unload Me" in the Click event of the command button.

5. Select the QueryUnload event of the Form object.

6. Use the following code to check for the method by which the form was closed and cancel the unload if the close button was clicked.

```
If UnloadMode = vbFormControlMenu Then Cancel = 1
```

Control Events

Like forms, controls are also capable of responding to events. And, like the events of a form, control events occur in a specific order. Control events are too numerous to list here, but a few worth special mention are outlined in this section because questions about them may appear on the certification exam.

Almost all controls respond to the user pressing a key. For these controls, there are three events of importance:

- **KeyDown**   Occurs as the user presses the key.

- **KeyUp**   Occurs when the user releases the key.

- **KeyPress**   Occurs between the KeyDown and KeyUp events.

These events not only detect keystrokes, but also can tell you what key was pressed and allow you to modify the keystroke if you want. The KeyPress event tells you only the ASCII code of the key that was pressed, making it useful for limiting input, for example, making sure that the user only enters numbers. The KeyDown and KeyUp events are also capable of telling you whether any shift or control keys were being held down while the key was being pressed.

The other action that almost all controls respond to is the mouse click. Like a keystroke, there are three events that occur whenever the user clicks the mouse on a control (in order of firing):

- MouseDown
- MouseUp
- Click

If the user double-clicks the mouse, these three events are fired, followed by the DblClick event and a second MouseUp event. Because of this sequence, you can see why it is necessary to be careful what code is placed in an event. The double-click not only fires the DblClick event, but also fires the Click event and the MouseUp event twice. The Click event only detects that the left mouse button was clicked. The MouseUp and MouseDown events tell you which mouse button was clicked, whether a shift key was pressed, and the position of the mouse cursor, making these two events useful for handling functions such as context sensitive pop-up menus.

Extending Forms through Custom Properties and Methods

Y ou are familiar with the built-in properties and methods of forms. The properties of a form control its appearance and behavior, and the methods of the form handle perform tasks in your programs. However, you are not limited to using only the internal properties and methods of forms; you can create your own, enabling you to pass data back and forth between forms and extend the functionality of forms.

Creating a Property in a Form

The properties that you create for a form are really variables of the form that have a public interface; that is, they can be accessed from other parts of your program. The capability of accessing custom form properties allows you to do more with forms than is possible with the built-in properties alone. For example, a program could use the same form to allow a user to input information about customers or employees. Because both functions require the input of a name, address, and phone number, using a single form makes sense. However, suppose you wanted the form's Caption and some of the command buttons to have a different appearance depending on whether a customer or employee was to be input. The solution to this problem is to create a property in the form that could be set before the form was loaded. Then, code in the Form_Load event would set up the form based on the value of the property. The code for this is shown below:

```
Private Sub Form_Load()

' This will be loaded from 2 forms; Security &
' Customer.  The form title will vary based
' upon the calling form.

On Error GoTo AddUserErr1

'Use TextLoad function to load language appropriate captions, etc.
'   Captions for this form will be in the range of 151 to 175
If AddType = 1 Then
    'Called from Security screen
    frmAddUser.Caption = TextLoad(151)
    lblAddUser.Caption = TextLoad(153)
    'Add button is default, called if user presses Enter
    cmdAddUser(0).Caption = TextLoad(156)
    txtNewUser.MaxLength = 20
Else
    'Called from Customer screen
    frmAddUser.Caption = TextLoad(152)
    lblAddUser.Caption = TextLoad(158)
    'Add button is default, called if user presses Enter
    cmdAddUser(0).Caption = TextLoad(159)
    txtNewUser.MaxLength = 50
End If
'Cancel button is default, called if user presses Esc
cmdAddUser(1).Caption = TextLoad(157)

Exit Sub
```

```
AddUserErr1:
LogError "AddUser", "Load", Err.Number, Err.Description
Resume Next

End Sub
```

There are two methods of creating a property in a form:

- Declaring a Public variable in the declarations section of the form

- Using Property procedures

We will look at both of these methods, but using Property procedures is recommended for reasons that will be covered later.

Going Public with a Variable

The first and simplest way of creating a property in a form is to declare a Public variable in the form using a statement like the one below:

```
Public iFormType As Integer
```

Using this statement, you create a variable that can be accessed from any-where in your program by specifying the name of the form and the name of the property (variable) using the same dot notation as you would for built-in properties. In fact, if you are using the "Autolist Members" feature of Visual Basic, you will see your Public variable listed right along with the built-in properties of the form in the member list.

Using a public variable is the easiest way to create a property, but it has two major drawbacks. First, it is not possible to validate the values that are set by other parts of the program or by your users (if you are basing the value of the property on user input). With a public variable, the user can set any value regardless of what values may be appropriate for the form. Second, you cannot use the variable for information only. That is, other parts of your program will always have the capability to modify the value of the variable.

Creating a Property through Procedures

The second and preferred method of creating a property in a form is through the use of Property procedures. These procedures allow your program to per-form validation on the values passed to the property to assure that the values are appropriate for the function. Also, you can restrict the property to be read-only, which allows you to use the value within the form and provide access to the value of the property to determine the state of the form. There are three types of Property procedures that you can create:

- **Property Let**   Used to set the value of a property that is stored as a standard variable type (an integer, floating point number, string, and so on).

- **Property Get**   Used to retrieve the current value of the property.

- **Property Set**   Variation of the Property Let procedure. Property Set is used to set the value of properties that are objects. For example, you could use a Property Set to pass a recordset to a form.

Typically, you create a Property Let and Property Get procedure together to allow read/write capabilities for the property. However, you can create a read-only property by omitting the Property Let procedure. Likewise, you can create a write-only property by omitting the Property Get procedure. Exercise 1.7 demonstrates how to create a read/write property using both the Property Let and Property Get procedures.

EXERCISE 1.7

Creating a Property

1. Open the code window of the form in which you wish to create a property by clicking the code icon in the Project window or double-clicking the form itself.

2. In the Declarations section of the form's code, create a Private variable of the same type as the property you are creating. This variable will be used internally by the form code to reference the value of the property.

3. Select the Add Procedure item from the Tools menu in Visual Basic to bring up the Add Procedure dialog box shown here.

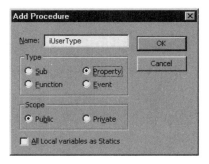

4. Specify a name for the procedure, choose the Property button in the Type group, choose the Public button in the Scope group, then click the OK button in the dialog box. The skeleton code for a Property Let and a Property Get procedure will be created in the code window, as shown here:

```
(General)                          iUserType [PropertyGet]

Option Explicit

|

Public Property Get iUserType() As Variant

End Property

Public Property Let iUserType(ByVal vNewValue As Variant

End Property
```

5. Change the type specification of the variable in the Property Let procedure to match that of the internal variable you created in step 2.

6. Change the type specification of the Property Get procedure to match the variable in step 2.

7. In the Property Let procedure, set the value of the internal variable to the value passed to the procedure. The Property Let procedure is where you will place the validation code for the property. For example, the following code verifies the input and sets the value of the internal variable.

```
If iInptType < 0 Then
    iFormType = 0
ElseIf iInptType > 10 Then
    iFormType = 10
Else
    iFormType = iInptType
End If
```

8. In the Property Get procedure, set the value of the Property to the internal variable to allow other parts of your program to determine the current value of the property. For example,

```
PersonType = iFormType
```

9. The complete code for the PersonType property is shown here.

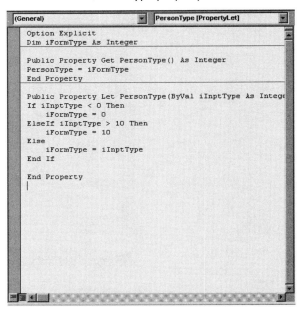

```
(General)                                    PersonType [PropertyLet]

    Option Explicit
    Dim iFormType As Integer

    Public Property Get PersonType() As Integer
    PersonType = iFormType
    End Property

    Public Property Let PersonType(ByVal iInptType As Intege
    If iInptType < 0 Then
        iFormType = 0
    ElseIf iInptType > 10 Then
        iFormType = 10
    Else
        iFormType = iInptType
    End If

    End Property
```

As with the property created using a public variable, properties created with these procedures behave like the built-in properties of a form. The following code line shows how the type of form is set from another part of the program.

```
frmPersonInfo.PersonType = 1
Load frmPersonInfo
```

Creating a Method in a Form

Custom properties help you pass data to a form, but custom methods help you extend the functionality of a form. Methods can be used to handle simple tasks such as centering the form, or more complex tasks such as populating a grid with database information. A properly written method makes it easier to maintain your code and to create reusable forms that can be used in multiple projects.

A custom method of a form is simply a Sub or Function procedure that has a public interface. You will learn more about procedures and functions and their scope in Chapter 2. Exercise 1.8 shows you how to create a method that centers the form.

EXERCISE 1.8

Creating a Method to Center the Form

1. As with creating a Property procedure, open the code window for the form.

2. Select the Add Procedure item from the Tools menu in Visual Basic.

3. Specify the name of the procedure (CenterMe), choose the Sub button in the Type group, choose the Public button in the Scope group, then click the OK button in the dialog box to create the skeleton of the procedure in the code window.

4. Add the following code to the procedure to perform the actual operation:

```
If Me.WindowState <> 0 Then Exit Sub
Me.Top = (Screen.Height - Me.Height) / 2
Me.Left = (Screen.Width - Me.Width) / 2
```

The CenterMe method can now be called like any of the built-in methods of the form. You can call the method from within the form's code to center the form, such as after a resize event. You can also call the method from other parts of the program. Also, the method will show up in the member list just as if it were a built-in method. This is illustrated in Figure 1.7 where the method is called to center a form after it is initially shown.

FIGURE 1.7

Custom methods
behave just like built-in
methods.

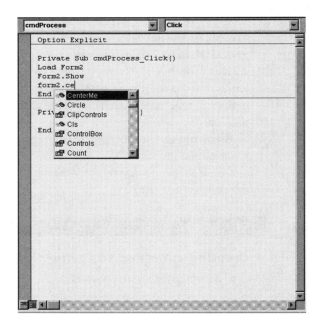

Summary

In this chapter we have reviewed a number of aspects of programming the forms and controls that make up your programs. The chapter has provided you with some of the basic information that you will need to create most of your Visual Basic programs, including how:

- Event sequences can have an impact on your programs.

- Choosing the right event will allow your program to perform the tasks that you want it to.

- Multiple instances of a form can be created by using object variables.

- The functionality of forms can be extended by creating your own properties and methods.

An understanding of these topics will help you meet these Microsoft Certification exam objectives:

- Create an application that adds and deletes forms at run time.

- Add code to the appropriate form event, such as Initialize, Terminate, Load, Unload, QueryUnload, Activate, and Deactivate.

Also, and perhaps more importantly, understanding these topics will prepare you for the real-world test of creating professional programs to meet real needs. Now it is time to put your knowledge to the test. The following questions are typical of those you might find on the Visual Basic Certification exam.

Review Questions

1. What is the sequence in which the following events are triggered when a form is loaded?

   A. Initialize, Resize, Paint, and Load

   B. Load, Initialize, Resize, and Paint

   C. Initialize, Load, Paint, and Resize

   D. Initialize, Load, Resize, and Paint

2. What is the sequence of events when a form is unloaded?

   A. Unload, QueryUnload, and Terminate

   B. QueryUnload, Unload, and Terminate

   C. Unload only

   D. QueryUnload and Unload

3. How can you keep the user from exiting a form using the Close item on the Control menu or by clicking the Close button?

   A. Place code in the Unload event.

   B. Place code in the QueryUnload event.

   C. This can only be done using a Windows API call.

   D. This cannot be done in Visual Basic.

4. How do you create a read-only property in a form?

   A. Create a Property Let procedure.

   B. Create a Property Get procedure.

   C. Create both a Property Get and Property Let procedure.

   D. Declare a Public variable in the declarations section of the form.

5. Given the following code segment, how many instances of the form are created and displayed?

```
Dim frmVar1 As frmPerson, frmVar2 As frmPerson
Set frmVar1 = New frmPerson
Set frmVar2 = frmVar1
Load frmVar1
frmVar2.Show
```

   A. None

   B. 3

   C. 1

   D. 2

6. Given the following code, what happens when the frmPerson.Show method is called?

```
Dim frmVar1 As frmPerson, frmVar2 As frmPerson
Set frmVar1 = New frmPerson
Set frmVar2 = frmVar1
Load frmVar1
frmPerson.Show
```

   A. The current instance of the form is displayed.

   B. A second instance of the form is created and displayed.

   C. An error occurs.

   D. Nothing.

7. Which event(s) allow you to determine which key was pressed by the user? (Check all correct answers.)

   A. Click

   B. KeyPress

   C. KeyDown

   D. KeyUp

8. Which event(s) allow you to determine if a control or Shift key was pressed by the user? (Check all correct answers.)

   A. Click

   B. KeyPress

   C. KeyDown

   D. KeyUp

9. When is the Terminate event of a form triggered?

   A. When the user moves to another form or program

   B. When the form is unloaded

   C. Never

   D. When all references to the form are deleted

10. Which event is triggered when the user moves to another form?

   A. Unload

   B. Deactivate

   C. Terminate

   D. Load

CHAPTER

2

Basics of Writing Visual Basic Code

Microsoft Objectives Covered in This Chapter:

- Declare a variable.

- Declare a Variable—Use the appropriate declaration statement.

- Define the scope of a variable by using the Public, Private, and Static statements.

- Write and call a Sub or Function procedure using named arguments or optional arguments.

- Write and call Sub and Function procedures that require an array as an argument.

- Call procedures from outside a module.

In Chapter 1, we took a look at the visual interface that you create for your programs using forms and controls. However, the bulk of the work that you will do in creating a program is not in creating the visual design, it is writing the program code that is behind the forms and controls. This is where your program actually does work and where you will spend the bulk of your development time. Chapter 1 briefly introduced you to programming code and to procedures (remember the event procedures for a control). This chapter will take that discussion further.

Program code is made up of a variety of programming statements. These statements can be broken down into two main classifications:

- **Assignment statements** Used to assign a value to a variable or to a property of an object.

- **Control statements** Used to conditionally execute a section of code or to execute it multiple times. These statements include If...Then...Else...End If, For...Next, and Do statements.

While these control and assignment statements are important to your programs, they are not specifically called out in the Certification Exam Objectives. Therefore, the reader is referred to other books, such as *Visual Basic 5: No Experience Required*, also by Sybex, to learn more about these statements.

This chapter will focus on those basic programming elements that are covered by the Microsoft exam objectives, including:

- Define the scope of a variable by using the Public, Private, and Static statements.

- Use the appropriate declaration statement.

- Write and call Sub and Function procedures by using named arguments or optional arguments.

- Write and call Sub and Function procedures that require an array as an argument.

- Call procedures from outside a module.

A Review of Variables

If you write any but the most simple of programs, you will encounter the need for variables. Variables are memory locations that store information temporarily for use in your programs. You can think of a variable as sort of your program's scratch pad, where numbers and other information are jotted down before being used in another calculation or task. Variables have different lifetimes within your program, but all variables have two things in common:

- Their values can be changed within the program.

- The values are not stored permanently.

The value of any variable is lost when it either goes out of scope (we will look at scope shortly), or when your program is shut down.

Variables can be used to store any type of information, from simple numbers to long strings of text. Variables can even be used to store references to program objects such as forms or instances of a class.

Comparison of Variables and Constants

There are actually two ways to store information in memory for your program to use. The first way is to use a variable. The second is to use a constant. Constants and variables are very similar in their uses within a program, but there are several key differences in their behavior:

- Variables can be assigned new values anywhere in the program. Constants can only be assigned a value when they are declared.

- The evaluation of a constant is handled during compilation of the program. The evaluation of a variable occurs while the program is running.

Constants are really programming tools that allow a programmer to define a value once and use it multiple times within the program. For example, if you need to use the conversion of miles to feet several times in your program, it is easier to define the constant once, then use it multiple places, rather than remembering the value of the constant. Using constants also makes your code more readable. This use of a constant is shown in the following listing. The first listing shows the use of the constant; the second listing shows the same calculation using a literal value. Notice how the first listing is more readable from a code maintenance perspective.

```
Const MilestoFeet As Long = 5280 'Conversion of miles to feet
Private Sub Command1_Click()
Dim lInptMiles As Long, lOtptFeet As Long
lInptMiles = txtMiles.Text
lOtptFeet = lInptMiles * MilestoFeet
txtFeet.Text = lOtptFeet
End Sub

Private Sub Command1_Click()
Dim lInptMiles As Long, lOtptFeet As Long
lInptMiles = txtMiles.Text
lOtptFeet = lInptMiles * 5280
txtFeet.Text = lOtptFeet
End Sub
```

The first listing above shows both the use of a constant and how to define it. To define any constant, you use the Const keyword followed by the name of the constant, its data type, and finally the value that is assigned to the constant. This declaration is illustrated in the following code line. It is also good programming practice to use a comment to define the constant, as shown in the code below.

```
Const KWHtoBTU As Integer = 3409.52   'Energy conversion factor
```

Constants can be used to store any type of information that will be used frequently within a program. In addition to the constants that you define, you will find that Visual Basic has a number of internal constants to help you with values for everything from colors (vbRed, vbBlue) to values used in setting up dialog boxes (vbExclamation, vbYes, vbModal, etc.).

Constants can be defined in the declarations section of any module or form, or within a procedure. Constants that are defined within a procedure are local to the procedure only; they cannot be accessed by any other code in the form or module. Constants that are defined in the declarations section of a form or class module can be used anywhere with the form or class, but cannot be accessed from other parts of your program. Only constants that are defined in the Declarations section of a standard module can be made accessible from anywhere in your program, and only by declaring the constant to be Public. (We will discuss the concept of Public and Private scope later in this chapter.) Exercise 2.1 demonstrates how to create such a Public constant.

EXERCISE 2.1

Creating a Constant That Can Be Used Anywhere

1. Start a new project in Visual Basic.

2. Add a standard module to the project by choosing the Add Module item on the Project menu. You will be placed in the code window for the module as shown here.

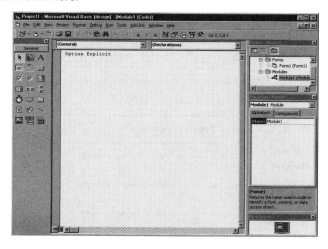

3. Enter the constant declaration in the code window as indicated in the graphic above. An example declaration is shown below.

```
Public Const AuthorName As String = "Michael McKelvy"
```

Understanding Data Types

It is true that variables in Visual Basic can store any type of information, but you will find that it is best to tell Visual Basic in advance what type of data will be stored in a particular variable; this provides you with several benefits:

- Defining the proper variable type can avoid certain types of errors, such as overflow errors.

- Defining the variable type forces your program to treat a variable in a specific manner. For example, storing "1" in a string variable forces your program to use the character, whereas storing "1" in an integer or single variable forces the program to treat it as a number. Without variable typing, the program would have to guess how the variable is to be used, and may guess wrong.

- Using specific variable types saves memory. Each un-typed variable uses a minimum of 16 bytes of data whereas an integer type only uses 2 bytes.

Visual Basic supports a wide variety of data types. These data types and their storage capabilities are summarized in Table 2.1.

T A B L E 2.1 Data Types and Storage Capabilities	**Data Type**	**Stores**	**Range of Values**
	Byte	Whole numbers	0 to 255
	Integer	Whole numbers	–32,768 to 32,767
	Long	Whole numbers	–2,147,483,648 to 2,147,483,647
	Single	Floating-point numbers	+/– 1E-45 to 3E38
	Double	Floating-point numbers	+/– 5E-324 to 1.8E308

T A B L E 2.1 *(cont.)* Data Types and Storage Capabilities	Data Type	Stores	Range of Values
	Currency	Special decimal number with up to 15 places left and four places right of the decimal point	+/–9E14
	String	Characters and text	Up to 65,400 characters for fixed-length strings and up to 2 billion characters for dynamic strings.
	Boolean	Logical values	True or False
	Date	Date and time data	1/1/100 to 12/31/9999
	Object	Form references, instances of a class, OLE objects	N/A
	Variant	Any of the above defined data types.	N/A

Declaring Variables

Microsoft ✓ *Exam Objective*

Declare a variable.

Visual Basic is a very flexible language, which makes it easy for you to create programs. One of the flexibilities of the language is that variables can store any type of data and do not have to be declared before they are used. That is, you can create a variable in your program by simply assigning a value to a variable name. While Visual Basic is capable of handling this operation, it is very poor programming practice and will lead to problems in any but the simplest project.

Declaring variables allows you to define the type of information that they will store and provides you with a list of all the variables used in a particular procedure or module. You can also use comments in the declarations section to make your code self-documenting, as shown in Figure 2.1.

FIGURE 2.1

Using comments to make your code more readable

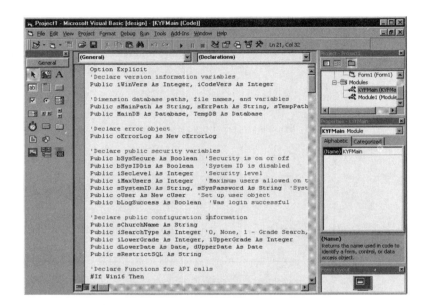

 You can place comments anywhere in your code, but having a commented list of variables at the beginning of a procedure or module makes it easier to remember what the variables were if you later have to perform maintenance on your program or someone else's program.

Forcing Variable Declaration

Visual Basic, by default, does not require you to declare all your variables, but it does provide an option that you can use to force yourself to declare all variables. The main advantage of forcing variable declaration is that Visual Basic will check to see that any variables used in your program are declared before they are used, helping you eliminate some of the most common programming errors, such as:

- Typographical errors where the name of a variable is misspelled

- Variables that are defined as the wrong scope. You will learn more about scope later in this chapter in the section "Scope of Variables."

To force variable declaration, follow these steps:

1. Select the Options item from the Tools menu to bring up the Options dialog box shown in Figure 2.2.

FIGURE 2.2

Editor Options allow you to force variable declaration.

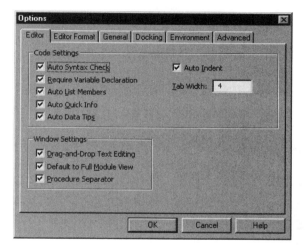

2. On the Editor page of the dialog box, check the box next to Require Variable Declaration.

3. Click the OK button on the dialog box to add the "Option Explicit" statement to all new forms and modules you create in your project, as shown in Figure 2.3.

Any forms or modules that are already part of a project are unaffected by a change in the Require Variable Declaration option.

FIGURE 2.3

How the Option Explicit
statement is added
to code.

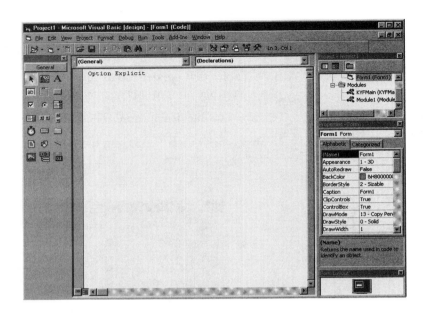

FIGURE 2.3

How the Option Explicit
statement is added
to code.

Declaring Specific Variable Types

Microsoft ✓ *Exam Objective*

Declare a Variable – Use the appropriate declaration statement.

The simplest form of a variable declaration statement uses the Dim keyword to define the variable, as shown in the following code:

```
Dim iMyVar
```

This type of declaration statement tells Visual Basic that you are setting aside a name for a variable. It can be used inside a procedure or in the Declarations section of a form or class module. Other forms of a declaration statement allow you to specify the scope of the variable. In its simplest form, the Dim statement does not provide information about the type of data that will be stored in the variable. Therefore, programmers typically use a more detailed form of statement to declare a variable. There are two forms of declarations that define the type of data a variable will hold, explicit declaration and implicit declaration.

Explicit Declaration

Explicit declaration of a variable uses an optional clause of the Dim statement to specify the data type of the variable. This clause uses the As keyword and one of the data types listed in table 2.1 to declare the variable. The general form of this statement is

```
Dim iMyVar As Integer
```

The above statement declares a variable as an integer. To declare a variable of a different type, simply replace the word "Integer" in the above statement with one of the other data types listed in Table 2.1. An example of a number of variable declaration statements is shown in Figure 2.4.

FIGURE 2.4

Samples of variable declarations

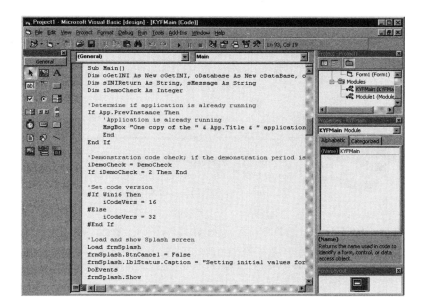

You probably noticed in the figure that there were variables declared that were not the standard data types of integer, string, single, and so on. These declarations create object variables. The variables are used to reference objects such as a form, an instance of a class, a database or recordset for database operations, or even an instance of an OLE object such as Microsoft Excel or Word. Object variables are declared the same way as data variables and have the same scope as data variables, as described later in the chapter.

Implicit Declaration

For a number of the standard data types, explicitly assigning the variable type is not the only way to tell Visual Basic what information the variable can store. The most common variable types also can be specified through the addition of a special character at the end of the variable name. Using this approach is called implicit declaration. Implicit declaration has two advantages over explicit declaration for the variable types that support it:

- The symbol at the end of the variable provides a visual cue as to the contents of the variable.

- You save some typing in the declaration statements.

The disadvantages of using implicit declaration are:

- Not all data types can use implicit declaration.

- You cannot declare object variables implicitly.

- If you omit the symbol later in your code, Visual Basic will generate an error, because it assumes the name without the symbol is a new undeclared variable.

If you are forcing variable declaration, you still have to use the Dim statement to declare the variable with implicit declaration. You just don't have to include the As clause of the statement.

Table 2.2 shows the various data types that support implicit declaration and the corresponding symbol for each type. The code after the table shows how these symbols are used in the declaration statements.

	Data Type	Symbol
TABLE 2.2 Symbols used in variable declarations	Single	!
	Double	#
	Integer	%
	String	$
	Long	&

```
Dim iNumStudents%
Dim sStudentName$
Dim lStudentID&
Dim sngGrade!
Dim dAverage#
```

Variable Naming Conventions

If you look carefully at the variable declaration statements that have been given in the examples, you might deduce that there is a pattern to the names of the variables. Each variable name gives you an idea of what the variable is used for and what type of information the variable is designed to hold. Naming variables in this manner helps to make your code self-documenting. That is, another programmer, or yourself at a later time, will have an easier time figuring out what the program does because the variable names provide some of the explanation. This concept is so important that there are guidelines on variable naming. Before we look at the naming conventions, however, let's take a quick look at variable naming in general.

Older programming languages often placed severe limits on the size of a variable's name (due to compiler or operating system constraints), leading to two problems in program maintenance. First, the variable names were very cryptic, such as I1, I2, TotCst, and so on. Second, variable names were often reused for different tasks in the same procedure. Visual Basic (and most current programming languages) do not have these severe restrictions on the size of variable names. In fact, there are only a few restrictions that Visual Basic places on the names you can give your variables:

- Names must start with a letter.

- Names cannot contain a period (due to the period being used as part of dot notation).

- A name must be unique within the scope of the variable.

- Names must be less than 255 characters in length.

What this means for you is that you can use very descriptive names for your variables, such as TotalCostofProductsinShippedOrder. The general rule is to make the name long enough to be descriptive, but short enough to make it easy to type.

Now for the naming conventions. Naming conventions recommend that you specify the type of information contained in the variable and the scope of the variable by using prefixes on the base name. Following a naming convention provides you with several benefits:

- You have an indication of the scope of the variable, which can help avoid errors caused by an undeclared variable.

- Knowing the scope of the variable makes it easier to know where to look when a variable contains a value that causes problems in your program. This is part of program debugging.

- Knowing the data type of the variable helps avoid Type Mismatch errors in your program.

The following tables summarize the variable naming prefixes that are recommended by Microsoft in the Visual Basic documentation. Table 2.3 shows the data type prefixes and Table 2.4 shows the scope prefixes. Figure 2.5 shows some of these prefixes in use.

T A B L E   2.3

Variable Data-Type Prefixes

Data Type	Prefix
Boolean	bln
Byte	byt
Collection	col
Currency	cur
Date/Time	dtm
Double	dbl
Error	err
Integer	int
Long	lng
Object	obj
Single	sng
String	str
User-Defined Type	udt
Variant	vnt

Scope	Prefix
Global	g
Module	m
Local	(None)

T A B L E   2.4
Variable Scope Prefixes

F I G U R E   2.5
Using Prefixes to
Identify Variables

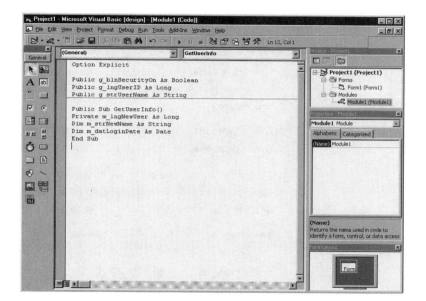

 Microsoft's recommendations are just one naming convention. While it is not critical that you follow their naming convention, it is very important that you establish and follow a naming convention, particularly in multiple developer projects.

To put all this information together, let's walk through the creation of the variables necessary for a procedure to calculate the area and perimeter of a room. This procedure could be part of a program that is used to calculate the amount of wallpaper necessary for a decorating job. Exercise 2.2 shows you how to do this.

EXERCISE 2.2

Declaring Variables

1. Start a new project.

2. Add four text boxes and a command button to the form.

3. Open the code window of the form.

4. Place the code Option Explicit as the first line of the declarations section of the form. This forces the variables to be declared before they are used.

5. Open the event procedure for the Click event of the command button. You can do this by selecting the name of the command button from the object list on the left of the code window.

6. Use the following statements to create the variables for calculating area and perimeter. These statements should be placed at the top of the event procedure.

    ```
    Dim sngRoomLength As Single, sngRoomWidth As Single
    Dim sngRoomArea As Single, sngRoomPerimeter As Single
    ```

7. Place the following code in the event procedure to perform the calculation. (Note, one of the variable names is intentionally misspelled to illustrate how forced declaration helps you.)

    ```
    sngRoomLength = Val(Text1.Text)
    sngRoomWidth = Val(Text2.Text)
    sngRoomArea = sngRoomLength * sngRoomWidth
    sngRoomPerimeter = 2 * (sngRoomLenght + sngRoomWidth)
    ```

8. Run the program and notice the error message that occurs. (The error may not occur until you click the command button.)

Scope of Variables

Microsoft ✓ ***Exam*** ***Objective*** | **Define the scope of a variable by using the Public, Private, and Static statements.**

Now that you know all about naming variables and assigning data types, it's time to turn our attention to the subject of variable scope. Put simply, *scope* defines the area of your program in which the variable can be accessed. You can think of variables as being similar to a paging service. If you buy one type of pager, you can receive messages around town, but you are out of luck if you leave the area. Pay a little more, and you can get regional service that lets you receive messages within your state or geographic region. Pay even more, and you can get nationwide paging. The coverage you have depends on how your service is defined and set up for you.

The scope of a variable in Visual Basic is similar to the coverage area of a pager. While you do not have to pay more for variables with broader scope, the scope is determined by how and where you set up the variable. There are three levels of scope in Visual Basic:

- **Local**   The variable can only be used within the context of the procedure in which it is defined.

- **Module**   The variable can be used anywhere within the form or class module in which it is defined.

- **Global**   The variable may be used anywhere within the program.

Setting the Scope of Variables

As just stated, a variable can have one of three scopes—Local, Module, or Global. The scope of any variable is dependent on two things:

- Where you declare the variable

- Which declaration statement you use to create the variable

Let's look more closely at the three possible scopes of a variable and how Visual Basic's four declaration statements are used to set the scope.

Local Variables

Local variables are the easiest to deal with. To create a local variable, you use the Dim statement to declare the variable within a procedure. These statements are located in the procedure where the variable will be used and are typically placed at the beginning of the procedure. The following code shows some typical declaration statements in a Visual Basic procedure. Variables declared within a procedure cannot be used outside of the procedure. Figure 2.6 shows you a variable declared within a procedure, and the comments in the code show you the areas where the variable can be used.

```
Dim intCount As Integer
Static blnBeenHere As Boolean
```

FIGURE 2.6

Usage of Local variables

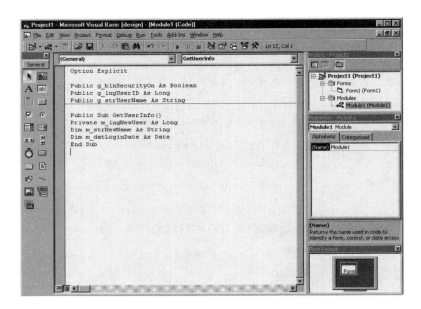

You cannot use the Public or Private statements within a procedure.

If you look closely at Figure 2.6, you will notice that the Dim and Private statements were not the only ones used to declare a variable. The Static statement that was used to declare a couple of the variables is a special case of a local variable. Typically, when you declare a local variable, its value is only retained while the procedure is executing. Once the procedure finishes, the value is lost. A Static variable can only be used within the procedure in which it is declared; however, it retains its value between procedure calls, allowing you to maintain persistent data within a procedure without creating a module level or global variable.

Module level variables

Module level variables are those that can be used anywhere within a form or class module but cannot be accessed from outside the module. These variables are created in the Declarations section of the form or class module using either the Dim or Private statements. Figure 2.7 shows some examples of module level declarations.

FIGURE 2.7

Declaring a Module Variable

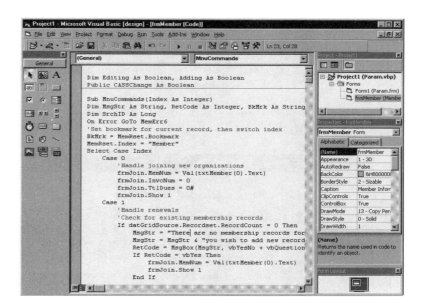

You cannot use the Static statement for module level variables.

Global variables

There are two types of global variables that you can create in Visual Basic. Both of these variable types are created using the Public statement, and both types of variables are accessible from anywhere in your program. The difference in the two types of global variables is where they are created and how they are accessed in the program. These two types can be referred to as Global variables and Public Form variables.

To create a true Global variable, you must first create a Visual Basic standard module in your project. Then, you use the Public statement in the declarations section of the module to define the variable. The following line of code shows how this is done:

```
Public sMainDatabaseName As String
```

Once declared in this manner, the variable can be used anywhere in the program simply by referring to its name. The following two statements show examples of using the variable in statements.

```
sMainDatabaseName = "Nwind.mdb"
Set MainDB = DBEngine.WorkSpaces(0).OpenDatabase _
(sMainDatabaseName)
```

Exercise 2.3 walks you through the complete process of creating a global variable.

EXERCISE 2.3

Creating a Global Variable

1. Start a new project.

2. Add a module to the project by selecting the Add Module item of the Project menu. You will be presented with a dialog box that asks if you want to add a Module or an Add-in. Choose the Module option. (The dialog box is shown here.)

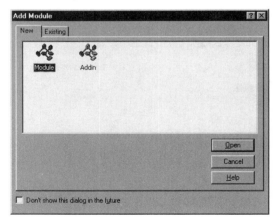

EXERCISE 2.3 (CONTINUED)

3. Open the code window of the new module.

4. Create a variable using the Public statement as follows:

```
Public bErrorTracking As Boolean
```

Public Form variables are declared the same way as global variables, using the Public statement; however, this type of variable is created in the Declarations section of a form or class module. Within the form or module, you can use the variable by simply referencing its name. This works the same way as a global variable. The difference comes in when you want to access the variable from another part of your program outside the form in which it was defined. In which case, you must specify the name of the form and the name of the variable, as shown in the following line of code:

```
IntComplete = frmMembership.intCompletionCode
```

Review of Procedures

The first part of this chapter looked at the creation of variables. This section looks at a related topic, Procedures. You may be wondering what procedures and variables have in common. For our purposes, both variables and procedures

- have to be declared in your program,

- have their scope determined by the type and placement of the declaration statement, and

- are restricted by the same naming rules of variables such as size and allowed characters.

In addition to looking at creating procedures, this section will also look at how you pass information to a procedure in the form of arguments. You will also see how to call procedures from various parts of your program.

Types of Procedures

Before getting into the actual creation of procedures, we need to quickly review what procedures are. A *procedure* is a segment of code designed to perform a specific task. You have seen procedures in the form of event procedures that perform tasks in response to an event of a form or control. These procedures have all the same elements as the procedures you can create in your code. All procedures have a declaration statement that identifies the name, type, and scope of the procedure, and they all have program code to perform their task.

There are three types of procedures:

- **Sub procedures** Perform a specific task, such as opening a database or updating information. A Sub procedure uses its own internal variables and any information that is passed to it in the form of arguments. A Sub procedure does not return a specific value.

- **Function procedures** Are similar to Sub procedures. They use internal variables and passed arguments to perform a specific task. The key difference between a Function and a Sub is that a Function does return a specific value.

- **Property procedures** Are designed to set or retrieve the value of a property of a form or class module. There are two property procedures, Property Get and Property Let. You will learn more about these in the chapter on classes.

Creating and Calling Procedures

Before you can begin creating a procedure, you need to decide two things about it. You need to know the type of procedure to create (Sub, Function, or Property) and the scope that is required for the procedure.

The scope of a procedure is similar to the scope of a variable. Like a variable, the scope of a procedure is determined by the declaration statement used and the location of the procedure. There are three elements of Visual Basic that can contain procedures—forms, standard (.BAS) modules, and class modules. For the purposes of determining scope, class modules and forms behave the same way.

Procedures in a Form or Class Module

There are two statements you can use to create a procedure, Public and Private. The Public statement creates a procedure that can be called from anywhere within the form and can be accessed from outside the form. In fact, a

Public procedure of a form or class actually creates a method of the form or class. The Private statement creates a procedure that may only be used within the form. A private procedure cannot be accessed from other locations in your program. The following statements show you several procedure declarations for a form.

```
Private Function AddNums(intNum1 As Integer, intNum2 As _
Integer) As Integer
End Function

Public Sub UpdateGrid()
End Sub

Sub ShowEditMode()
End Sub
```

Hey, wait a minute! We talked about the Public and Private statements, what about the last statement in the preceding code; it doesn't contain either keyword. This type of declaration is perfectly valid. In a form or class module, if you do not specify the scope of the procedure, it is assumed to be private.

Creating Procedures in .BAS Modules

The other location for creating procedures is in a standard (.BAS) module. Like the procedures created in a form, you can create a procedure in a standard module using either the Private or Public statement. In a module, a Private procedure may be accessed from anywhere in the same module, but may not be accessed from outside the module. The Public statement produces a global procedure. This procedure can be accessed from anywhere in your program.

Procedures and variables that are defined within a form can only be referenced within the form or must be referenced with the form name and procedure or variable name. The only way to create global variables and procedures is to place the definitions in a .BAS module, allowing the variables and procedures to be accessed from anywhere in your program.

In a module, you can also create a procedure without using either keyword. However, in the case of a procedure in a module, the default is a Public procedure, which means that if you omit the Public or Private keyword, Public is assumed and the procedure can be accessed from anywhere.

Using the Procedure Dialog Box

The simplest way to create the skeleton of a procedure is through the use of the Procedure dialog box. This dialog box, shown in Figure 2.8, is accessible by choosing the Add Procedure item from the Tools menu. The dialog box lets you specify the name of the procedure, the type of procedure to create, and the scope of the procedure. Using the dialog box is the simplest way to assure the proper syntax of the declaration statement for a procedure.

FIGURE 2.8

Creating a Procedure with the Procedure dialog box

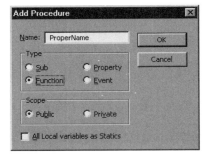

There is one other option on the Procedure dialog box that needs explanation, the check box marked All local variables as Static. You know that a static variable is one that retains its value between procedure calls. One way to create a static variable is through the use of the Static keyword in a declaration statement. If you desire, you can make all the variables in a procedure static by including the Static keyword in the procedure declaration, as shown here:

```
Private Static Sub DisplayStats()
```

Passing Arguments to a Procedure

Because procedures are self-contained segments of code, they need a way to get information from other parts of the program. There are two ways that a procedure can communicate with the rest of your program, through the use of global variables and with arguments. It is possible to use global variables to pass information to a procedure, but it is not good programming practice to create a large number of global variables. The key problems with this approach are:

- The values of global variables may be changed in unexpected ways that can cause problems for your program.

- Global variables take up memory until your program finishes, even if the variable is not being used.

Using Arguments

The best way to get information to a procedure is through the use of arguments. The arguments are a list of variables that are defined in the procedure declaration. These variables provide a means of passing information to a procedure and from the procedure back to the calling routine. The following code shows the declaration of a procedure using arguments and the line that calls the procedure from another area of the code.

```
Sub CalcSum(intNum1, intNum2, intSum)
intSum = intNum1 + intNum2
End Sub

Private Sub Command1_Click()
Dim intTotal As Integer
intTotal = 0
CalcSum 5, 8, intTotal
Text1.Text = intTotal
End Sub
```

As you can see in the code, three arguments were created for the procedure in the declaration statement. Then, in the calling statement, a value or variable was assigned for each of these arguments. Typically, you will need to have a one-to-one correspondence between the arguments defined in the procedure declaration and the calling statement.

Defining the Argument Type

The declaration shown above simply identified the variables that were used as arguments of the procedure. As you may remember, if a variable is not specifically assigned a data type, Visual Basic automatically makes it a variant data type. For most of your procedures, you will want to assign the data type for each of the arguments by adding the As clause to the declaration of each variable. This is similar to the clauses used in regular declaration statements. The following line shows the modification of the above declaration needed to assign data types to each argument.

```
Sub CalcSum(intNum1 As Integer, intNum2 As Integer, intSum _
As Integer)
```

Passing Arguments ByVal or ByRef

When arguments are defined as shown above, the procedure can modify the information in the argument; then that information is passed back to the calling routine. For example, the variable intTotal in the calling routine above was modified when the procedure changed the value of the argument intSum. This type of assignment is known as passing a value by reference. In this case, the calling routine passes the address of a memory location to the procedure. The procedure then uses this memory address as the location to store the value of the argument. Changes to the argument are then reflected in the original calling variable.

While this operation does give a procedure a way to send information back to the calling routine, there are times when you do not want the contents of your original variable to be modified. In such a case, you want to pass the actual value of the variable, not its address. Visual Basic allows you to do this through the use of the ByVal keyword. When you specify ByVal, a copy of the original variable, or literal data, is passed to the procedure and stored in a separate location, and the original value cannot be changed. The following line shows how to use the ByVal keyword to pass arguments to a procedure.

```
Sub GetAverage(ByVal iNum1 As Integer, ByVal iNum2 As Integer)
```

Notice that you have to use the ByVal keyword with each argument that you want passed by value. If you do not specify ByVal, by reference (ByRef keyword) is assumed.

Use ByVal unless you need to pass information back from the procedure to eliminate a number of potential errors that can occur from changing the value of variable. The errors would typically show up as unexpected results in your program.

Now that we have discussed the basics of creating a procedure, Exercise 2.4 will walk you through the process of creating a function that returns a person's full name, with the first letters capitalized.

EXERCISE 2.4

Creating a Function

1. Start a new project.

2. Open the Code Window of the Form.

3. Start the New Procedure dialog box by choosing the Add Procedure item from the Tools menu.

4. Specify the name of the Function as ProperName. Select the Function option of the dialog box, and specify the Private option. After you have filled in the information, click the OK button. The skeleton of the function is created for you as shown here.

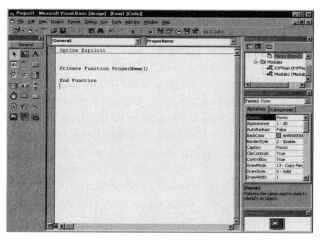

5. Add the variable declarations to the function by placing the following code between the parentheses of the function declaration:

```
ByVal sLastName As String, ByVal sFirstName As String
```

6. Assign a data type to the function by placing the following statement after the parentheses in the function declaration:

```
As String
```

7. Place the following code in the body of the function. This code sets up the full name and assigns it to the function return value.

```
Mid(sLastName, 1, 1) = UCase(Left(sLastName, 1))
Mid(sFirstName, 1, 1) = UCase(Left(sFirstName, 1))
ProperName = Trim(sFirstName) & " " & Trim(sLastName)
```

Using Optional Arguments

Microsoft ✓ **_Exam_** **_Objective_** | **Write and call a Sub or Function procedure using named arguments or optional arguments.**

Most of the time, you will call a procedure with the same number of arguments each time you call it. However, there are occasions when you may want to only pass a minimal amount of information. As an example, consider Visual Basic's MsgBox function. The only information that you are required to pass to the function is the text to be displayed as the message. If you are happy with the default button and no icon, you can omit the rest of the parameters. Other times, when you need the additional functionality, you will want to pass some or all of the optional parameters to make the function do more.

You can also create optional arguments for your own procedures. Using optional arguments, you can establish a default behavior for the procedure and add enhancements if the argument is passed.

Declaring the Optional Argument

Creating an optional argument is accomplished by simply placing the Optional keyword in front of the declaration of the argument. The Optional keyword works with either ByVal or ByRef calls and works with any variable type. The only restrictions on the use of the Optional keyword are:

- Optional arguments must be placed at the end of the argument list. Required arguments cannot follow an optional argument.

- Optional arguments cannot be used if you are using the ParamArray.

The following code shows how to include an optional argument in a procedure declaration:

```
Public Sub DatatoForm(frmData As Form, oFrmRset As cRSet, _
Optional sFldSkip, Optional iSkipType)
```

Determining if the Argument was Passed

Obviously, if you have optional arguments in a procedure, you will want to know if the arguments were passed to the procedure. Visual Basic includes a function called IsMissing that will let you determine if a value was passed to the procedure. Typically, you use the IsMissing function to set a default value of the argument if one was not provided. The following code checks the value of an optional argument and assigns a value if one is not present.

```
'Set initial values for missing parameters.
If IsMissing(sFldSkip) Then sFldSkip = ""
If IsMissing(iSkipType) Then iSkipType = 0
```

Creating Default Values

Another way of making sure that the optional argument has a value is to define a default value as part of the declaration statement by adding the value assignment at the end of the variable declaration (following the type assignment). Creating the default value assures that the argument will always have a value. If the calling program passes a value for the argument, the passed value is used. If the calling program omits the argument, the default value is used. The following declaration shows how to create a default value for an optional argument.

```
Sub DBNavigate(rsNavigate As Recordset, Optional iMoveType _
As Integer = 1)
```

Exercise 2.5 shows how to add an optional argument to the function created in Exercise 2.4.

EXERCISE 2.5

Adding an Optional Argument

1. Open the project containing the ProperName function created in Exercise 2.4. Then open the code window of the form.

2. In the declaration of the ProperName function, add the following code to allow the optional specification of a middle initial:

```
Optional ByVal sMiddle As String
```

3. Replace the last line of the existing procedure with the following code. This code uses the IsMissing function to determine if the middle initial was passed in, then takes the appropriate action.

```
If IsMissing(sMiddle) Then
    ProperName = Trim(sFirstName) & " " & Trim(sLastName)
Else
    sMiddle = UCase(Left(sMiddle, 1))
    ProperName = Trim(sFirstName) & " " & sMiddle & ". " & _
    Trim(sLastName)
End If
```

Passing Arrays to a Procedure

Microsoft ✓ ***Exam*** ***Objective***   **Write and call Sub and Function procedures that require an array as an argument.**

Finally, there are times when you need to pass an entire array of values to a procedure. These procedures may handle functions such as sorting the array or getting the sum or average of all the elements in an array. To pass an array to a procedure, you must create an array in the argument list. However, you cannot set the dimensions of the array. You must create a dynamic array as the argument. Within the procedure, you can use the LBound and UBound functions to determine the bounds of the array. Then you can set up your procedure to process all the elements of the array. The following code shows how you can set up an array as an argument of the procedure and calculate the average of all the numbers of the array.

```
Private Function CalcAverage(sngNums() As Single) As Single
Dim iLower As Integer, iUpper As Integer, I As Integer
```

```
Dim sngSum As Single
iLower = LBound(sngNums)
iUpper = UBound(sngNums)
sngSum = 0
For I = iLower To iUpper
    sngSum = sngSum + sngNums(I)
Next I
I = iUpper - iLower + 1
CalcAverage = sngSum / I
End Function
```

Calling Procedures

Microsoft ✓ *Exam* *Objective*

Call procedures from outside a module.

Creating a procedure is only half the task of using it. The procedure by itself does nothing unless some other part of your program calls the procedure. How you call a procedure depends on three things:

- The type of procedure

- Where the procedure is located

- Where the calling program is located

Calling Sub Procedures

There are two basic ways to call a Sub procedure:

- Specify the name of the procedure followed by the arguments required for the procedure.

- Use the Call statement.

If you specify the name of the procedure, the arguments of the procedure are listed following the procedure name. These arguments should appear in the order in which they are defined in the procedure declaration. Each of the arguments needs to be separated from the others by commas. Also, you do not enclose the argument list within parentheses. The following code shows an example of this type of procedure call:

```
FormtoData Me, oChRset
```

The other method is to use the Call statement. In this case, you specify the Call keyword, followed by the name of the procedure with the argument list enclosed within parentheses. This method of calling a procedure is shown in the following line:

```
Call FormtoData(Me, oChRset)
```

The two methods shown in the code samples work for calling global procedures, or for calling a module or form procedure from within the same form. If you have declared a form procedure as Public, you can call it from elsewhere in your program; however, you will need to specify the name of the form as well as the name of the procedure. The following code calls a procedure on a form that updates a grid on the form. The call is made from another part of the program.

```
FrmResults.GridUpdate
```

Notice how this manner of calling a public procedure is the same as calling a built-in method of the form.

Calling Functions

Because a function returns a value to the calling program, the manner in which a function is typically called is different from that of a Sub procedure. A function is typically called from the right side of an assignment statement or as part of a control statement (such as an If or Do statement). The following two statements show how this is done.

```
Text1.Text = CalcAvg(5, 7, 3, 8)
If CalcAvg(5, 7, 3, 8) > 6 Then
```

In older versions of Visual Basic, this was the only way that a function could be called. However, now, you can also call a function the same way that you call a Sub procedure. You can do this with a function that performs a task in addition to that of generating a return value. For example, you might have a function that opens a file and reads data, then assigns a return code to let you know the success of the operation. If you do not care about the return value, you can call the function as a Sub procedure.

Summary

In this chapter, you have learned about the scope of variables, how to declare a variable, and how to create procedures. These concepts are the cornerstones of the programs you will create with Visual Basic, because the user sees the visual interface, but the real work is done in code. Several of the key Microsoft exam objectives were covered in this chapter. Specifically, you learned how to use declaration statements for creating variables and you learned how to properly set the scope of a variable. In addition, you learned how to write and call different types of procedures and how to pass information to the procedures. These topics will help you with the following Microsoft exam objectives:

- Declare a variable.
- Define the scope of a variable by using the Public, Private, and Static statements.
- Use the appropriate declaration statement.
- Write and call Sub and Function procedures.
- Write and call Sub and Function procedures by using named arguments or optional arguments.
- Write and call Sub and Function procedures that require an array as an argument.
- Call procedures from outside a module.

Review Questions

1. How can you create an integer variable in your program? Check all that apply.

   A. Assign an integer value to a variable.

   B. Use the As Integer clause in the declaration statement for the variable.

   C. Make sure the variable's name begins with int.

   D. Add the % symbol to the end of the variable name.

2. All of the following statements are true about variable names except:

   A. Names must start with a letter.

   B. Names can be any length.

   C. Names cannot include a period.

   D. Names must be unique within the scope of the variable.

3. What are the advantages of using variable naming conventions? Check all that apply.

   A. The name of the variable forces its data type.

   B. The name indicates the data type of the variable.

   C. The variable names help with code documentation.

   D. The names indicate the scope of the variable.

4. How do you create a global variable?

   A. Declare the variable with the Public statement anywhere in the program.

   B. Use the Dim statement to declare the variable in a standard module.

   C. Use the Public statement to declare the variable in a standard module.

5. What are different types of procedures? Check all that apply.

   A. Sub

   B. Public

   C. Function

   D. Property

6. Which of the following are true of creating an optional argument for a procedure? Check all that apply.

A. You must include the Optional keyword.

B. You must pass the argument ByVal.

C. You cannot specify the data type of the variable.

D. The argument must follow all required arguments.

7. Which of the following is the proper declaration for a procedure to which an array is to be passed?

A. Sub ArraySort(sArray As Array)

B. Sub ArraySort(sArray)

C. Sub ArraySort(sArray() As Array)

D. Sub ArraySort(sArray())

CHAPTER

3

Creating User Interfaces with
Windows Common Controls

Microsoft Objectives Covered in This Chapter:

- Implement user interface controls in an application.

- Display information by using the StatusBar control.

- Provide controls with images by using the ImageList control.

- Create toolbars by using the Toolbar control.

- Display data by using the TreeView control

- Display data by using the ListView control.

Developers, particularly Microsoft, seem to always be adding new interface features to their programs. For example, a menu used to be the main interface mechanism for handling tasks. Now, programs have not one, but multiple toolbars for providing easier access to tasks. Another feature is the addition of the status bar, the area at the bottom of the program window that keeps the user informed as to the state of the program. There are even interface shifts such as the TreeView and ListView elements that make up the Windows Explorer interface. This is a change from some older ways of presenting data. And most recently, the interface is shifting toward the browser interface, where many applications either are or look like an extension of a web browser.

Fortunately for Visual Basic developers, the development tool has kept pace with many of these new design features. For most features, if you see it in Microsoft's programs, you will probably see a way to implement it in the next version of Visual Basic. And if you can't wait for the next version, third party vendors will come out with tools that let you implement the features.

Implement user interface controls in an application.

One such set of controls was added to Visual Basic 4 and 5 as the Windows Common Controls. This set of controls includes eight controls that let you implement various new design features:

- **TreeView**   Displays information in a hierarchical tree, like the left panel of Windows Explorer.

- **ListView**   Displays information in a multi-column list, like the right panel of Windows Explorer.

- **Toolbar**   Lets you create the push button toolbars that you see in most programs.

- **StatusBar**   Allows you to present information to the user in a concise manner.

- **ProgressBar**   Allows you to keep the user informed of the progress of a long operation.

- **ImageList**   Provides an easy way to manage the images that are used by several of the other controls.

- **TabStrip**   Allows you to create multiple pages on a single form, with each page being accessible by pressing a tab.

All these controls are contained in a single OCX file that comes with Visual Basic. To use any of these controls, you have to add them to the toolbox. You can do this through the Components dialog box accessible by choosing the Components item on the Project menu. To add the controls, check the box next to Microsoft Windows Common Controls 5.0 in the dialog box. The dialog box and the toolbox with the controls added are shown in Figure 3.1.

In this chapter you will learn how to use the TreeView, ListView, ImageList, Toolbar, and StatusBar controls. The chapter focuses on these specific controls out of the ones in the Windows Common Controls, as these five controls are specifically called out in the Microsoft exam objectives.

FIGURE 3.1

The Windows Common Controls let you add advanced interface elements to your programs.

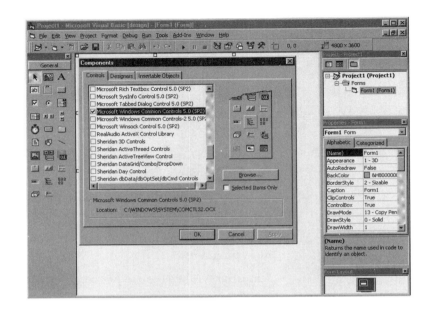

Keeping the User Informed

Most users want to have constant information about the status of the program they are using. For example, your word processor keeps up with the page number you are currently working on, the total number of pages in the document, the position on the page, the status of several options, and whether there are any spelling errors in the document. The purpose of status information is two-fold:

- First, the user should be able, at a glance, to determine what options are in effect and where they are in a program. This location can be the record number of a database application, the cell of a spreadsheet, or the page information in a word processor.

- The second purpose of status information is to let the user know the progress of a long operation. Keeping up with the status lets the user know that the program is still working, and is not hung for some reason.

Visual Basic provides two controls for handling the different jobs of status information. The StatusBar provides an easy way to provide the user with information about the current state of the program. The ProgressBar provides the user with information about the progress of a long operation. We will look at both of these controls in this section.

Creating a StatusBar for Your Program

For most applications, the StatusBar is a thin bar at the bottom of the screen that contains information about the program. This bar typically contains a variety of panels that are used to display various bits of information such as the state of toggle keys, like Caps Lock and NumLock, date and time information, short messages about current operations, and location information as described above. A typical StatusBar is shown in Figure 3.2.

FIGURE 3.2

A StatusBar to keep the user informed

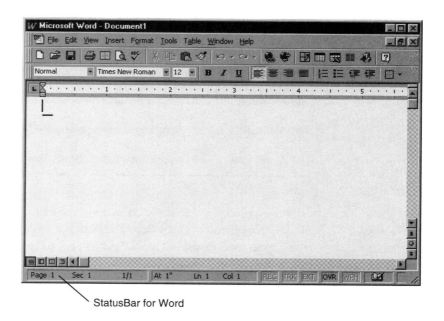

StatusBar for Word

Microsoft ✓ Exam Objective

Display status information by using the StatusBar control.

For most of your applications, you will design the basic StatusBar setup in the design environment, then update the information through the use of code. However, you can handle the complete setup of the StatusBar with code if you desire (other than creating the instance of the control). We will cover both of these techniques.

Creating the Panels of the StatusBar

The first step to creating a StatusBar is, of course, placing the control on your form. When you first place the control on the form, it will default to a position at the bottom of the form and will expand to cover the full width of the form. This is the default behavior and is the one that you will use for most programs. If you wish to use a status bar position other than the default, you can choose from one of five options. These options are assigned to Visual Basic constants as described in Table 3.1.

	Constant	Where the Control is Positioned
T A B L E 3.1 Visual Basic Assigned Constants	vbAlignNone	Allows the control to be placed anywhere on the form.
	vbAlignTop	Positions the control at the top of the form.
	vbAlignBottom	(Default) Positions the control along the bottom of the form.
	vbAlignLeft	Positions the control along the left side of the form.
	vbAlignRight	Positions the control along the right side of the form.

After you have placed the control on the form, you are ready to start adding panels to the StatusBar. The panels are objects that actually contain the information displayed in the StatusBar. To create the panels in the design environment, you simply access the Property Pages of the control. You can do this by selecting the Custom property in the Properties window and clicking the ellipsis button, or by right clicking the control and choosing the Properties item from the popup menu. Either way, you will be shown the Property Pages dialog box, as illustrated in Figure 3.3.

FIGURE 3.3

The Property Pages of
the StatusBar control

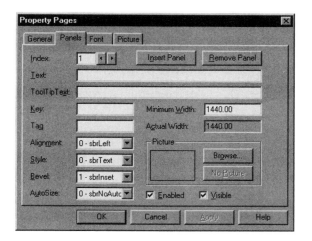

To start creating the panels, click the Panels tab of the dialog box. You will see that the first panel object is created for you; you only have to set the properties. To create more panels, you simply click the Insert button on the dialog box. As you create each panel, you will need to set the properties to control what information is displayed and how it is displayed. Let's take a closer look at these properties.

One key property for each panel is the Style property. This property determines whether the panel will show text that you assign to the panel or will automatically display status information about key states or dates and times. There are eight possible settings of the Style property:

- **sbrText**   Allows you to insert the text to be displayed. The panel will display the information contained in the Text property of the panel object or will display the bitmap contained in the Picture property. This is the only setting that allows you to modify the information in the panel.

- **sbrCaps**   Displays the text "CAPS" in the panel. When Caps Lock is on, the text is shown in normal text. When Caps Lock is off, the text is displayed dimmed.

- **sbrNum**   Similar to the sbrCaps option, except that this panel style displays "NUM" to indicate the status of the NumLock key.

- **sbrIns**   Similar to the sbrCaps option, except that this panel style displays "INS" to indicate the status of the Insert key.

- **sbrScrl**   Similar to the sbrCaps option, except that this panel style displays "SCRL" to indicate the status of the ScrollLock key.

- **sbrDate**   Displays the current date.

- **sbrTime**   Displays the current time.

- **sbrKana**   Similar to the sbrCaps option, except that this panel style displays "KANA" to indicate the status of a special setting used for handling Katakana characters in Japanese language programs.

If you are creating a sbrText Style panel, there are two properties that determine what appears in the panel—the Text property, which contains any text to be displayed, and the Picture property, which determines if a bitmap will be displayed, and which bitmap. Each panel is capable of handling both the text and a bitmap simultaneously.

The relative position of the text and the picture depends on the Alignment property. If Alignment is set to Left (the default), any picture will appear at the left side of the Panel, followed immediately by the text. With Alignment set to Right, the picture will appear at the right edge of the Panel immediately preceded by the text, and if Alignment is set to Center, the picture will appear on the left side of the panel, with the text centered in the remaining space of the panel.

There are also several other properties that you can use to control the appearance of the panels of the StatusBar:

- **ToolTipText**   Specifies the text to be shown if the user rests the mouse cursor on the panel.

- **Key**   A text string that uniquely identifies the panel in the collection.

- **Bevel**   Determines whether the panel has a raised, indented (default), or flat appearance.

- **MinWidth**   Specifies the minimum width of the panel.

- **Autosize**   Controls how the panel will be sized, while observing the minimum width constraint. This property has one of three settings:

  - **sbrNoAutoSize**   Causes the panel size to be set to the size specified in the MinWidth property.

  - **sbrSpring**   Causes the panel to occupy the remaining space in the status bar after all other panels have been sized. If more than one panel uses the sbrSpring setting, the remaining space will be shared equally among these panels.

- **sbrContents** Causes the panel size to be adjusted to fit the contents of the panel, whether text or picture or both.

Exercise 3.1 shows how to set up a simple StatusBar that keeps up with key states, the current date and time, and provides a space for other information.

EXERCISE 3.1

Creating a StatusBar

1. Start a new project.

2. Add the Microsoft Common Controls to your toolbox.

3. Add a StatusBar control to the form. Name the control stbSample.

4. Access the Property Pages of the control and select the Panels tab of the pages.

5. For the first panel, set the following properties:

Property	Value
Text	Sample Text
Styles	sbrText
AutoSize	sbrSpring
Key	CurStatus

6. Click the Insert button to create another panel in the StatusBar. For the second Panel, set the Style property to sbrCaps, and set the MinWidth property to 700.

7. Repeat the process in Step 6 to add four more panels. Set the style properties of these panels to sbrNum, sbrIns, sbrDate, and sbrTime, respectively. For the Date and Time panels, set the AutoSize property to sbrContents.

8. Accept all the panels by clicking the OK button in the Property Pages. Then, run the program. Your status bar should look similar to the one in Figure 3.4.

FIGURE 3.4

The StatusBar of the exercise

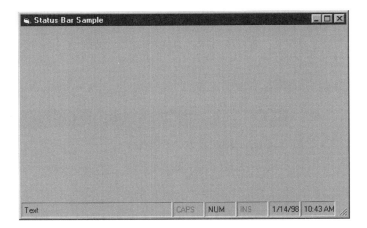

Modifying the Status Bar with Code

As you can see, you can set up the entire status bar from the Property Pages. However, you will still need to make use of code to handle changes in the status of the program. Because the sbrText Style panel is the only one that allows you to modify the contents, we will look at how to access this panel in code. The other types of panels have their information updated automatically, based on the conditions of the computer and the system date and time.

To modify the contents of the panel, you will need to access the Text property of the panel object. This is handled through the Panels collection of the StatusBar. You can work with a specific panel by listing its index number in the collection or by using its key property. For the text panel created in Exercise 3.1, you can change the Text property using either of the following lines of code:

```
stbSample.Panels(1).Text = "Text"
stbSample.Panels("CurStatus").Text = "New Text"
```

The index numbers of the Panels collection start with 1 instead of 0 as is customary for other collections. If you try to access a Panel object with an index of 0, an error will occur.

In addition to being able to modify the contents of the Text property, you can actually set up the entire StatusBar from code. The following code shows how to create the same status bar that you created in Exercise 3.1. The code uses the Add method of the Panels collection to add new panels to the control.

```
Dim pnlNew As Panel
With stbSample.Panels(1)
    .Text = "Text"
    .Key = "CurStatus"
    .AutoSize = sbrSpring
    .Style = sbrText
End With
Set pnlNew = stbSample.Panels.Add
pnlNew.Style = sbrCaps
pnlNew.MinWidth = 700
pnlNew.AutoSize = sbrContents
Set pnlNew = stbSample.Panels.Add
pnlNew.Style = sbrNum
pnlNew.MinWidth = 700
pnlNew.AutoSize = sbrContents
Set pnlNew = stbSample.Panels.Add
pnlNew.Style = sbrIns
pnlNew.MinWidth = 700
pnlNew.AutoSize = sbrContents
Set pnlNew = stbSample.Panels.Add
pnlNew.Style = sbrDate
pnlNew.MinWidth = 700
pnlNew.AutoSize = sbrContents
Set pnlNew = stbSample.Panels.Add
pnlNew.Style = sbrTime
pnlNew.MinWidth = 700
pnlNew.AutoSize = sbrContents
```

You can learn more about working with collections in Chapter 6.

Working with the ProgressBar

The StatusBar provides one method of giving information to the user. The ProgressBar control is designed to allow you to display the percentage of progress of a long operation, such as a database search or a file copy. You have probably seen the progress bar when you are copying large files or when you are connecting to the Internet or retrieving e-mail. What the progress bar provides to the user is an indication that the program is still working and is not hung up. It also provides the user with some indication of how much time is remaining until the completion of the operation.

The ProgressBar is quite easy to set up. The only properties you need to set to make it work are the Min, Max, and Value properties. The Min and Max properties specify the numbers that make up the range of the ProgressBar. The Value property is a number between the Min and Max properties that indicates the relative progress of the operation. The ProgressBar will represent the Value as a percentage fill based on the range of the Min and Max properties. For example, if you set the Min property to 0 and the Max property to 500, you could set the Value property to 100 to indicate that an operation is one-sixth complete. This would show up in the ProgressBar as one-sixth of the space being filled, as shown in Figure 3.5.

FIGURE 3.5

The ProgressBar in operation

Exercise 3.2 shows you how to create a ProgressBar. The exercise uses the Timer control to provide an event for updating the ProgressBar's Value property.

EXERCISE 3.2

Creating a ProgressBar

1. Start a new project and add the Common Controls to the toolbox.

2. Add a ProgressBar to your form and set its Name property to prgSample. Set the Min and Max properties to 0 and 100, respectively.

3. Add a Timer control to the form and set its Name property to tmrProgress.

4. Place the following code in the Timer event of the timer. This code updates the Value property of the ProgressBar and stops the timer when the Value property reaches 100.

```
prgSample.Value = prgSample.Value + 10
If prgSample.Value >= 100 Then
    tmrProgress.Interval = 0
    cmdStart.Enabled = True
End If
```

5. Add a command button named cmdStart to the form. Set the button's Caption property to Start. This button will be used to start the timer and set the initial value of the ProgressBar.

6. Place the following code in the Click event of the command button.

```
prgSample.Value = 0
tmrProgress.Interval = 1000
cmdStart.Enabled = False
```

7. Run the program.

Setting Up the ImageList Control

Among the Windows Common Controls, the ImageList is unique. The ImageList control is not accessible directly by the user. Instead, it provides a repository for images that are used by several other controls—the Toolbar, TreeView, and ListView controls. The ImageList control adds images to the control through the design environment or through code, then reference the index of the image to use it in another control.

Microsoft ✓ *Exam* *Objective*	**Provide controls with images by using the ImageList control.**

In this section, we will look at both methods of setting up the ImageList control. How the control is used with the other controls will be covered in later sections.

Working in the Design Environment

For most of your applications, you will want to set up the ImageList control from the design environment. The reason for this is that once it is created in the design environment, all the images associated with the control are included as part of your application. You do not need to distribute the bitmap files in addition to your application. Setting up the ImageList from the design environment is simply a matter of choosing pictures and specifying one or two optional properties.

The ImageList control maintains the images in a collection of ListImage objects. (The collection name is ListImages.) Each ListImage object has three key properties:

- **Picture**   Contains the actual image that is stored for the ListImage object.

- **Key**   A text string that uniquely identifies the image. The Key property can be used to refer to the image instead of having to use the Index of the collection.

- **Tag**   Allows you to associate other data with the image. The property is not used by Visual Basic itself, so you can set the value to anything that would be useful to you in your program.

Exercise 3.3 shows you how to set up an ImageList control from the design environment.

EXERCISE 3.3

Setting Up the ImageList Control

1. Start a new project and add the Microsoft Windows Common Controls to the toolbox.

2. Add an ImageList control to the form and set the Name property to imlToolbar. (We will use this ImageList in the Toolbar creation exercise later.)

3. Open the Property Pages of the ImageList control and select the Images tab of the Property Pages. This page is shown here.

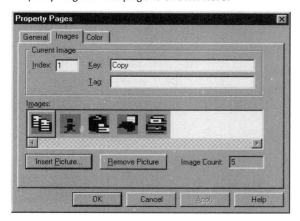

4. To add the first image to the control, click the Insert Picture button at the bottom of the dialog box to bring up the Select Picture dialog box shown here.

5. For the first image, select the Copy.bmp file from the Tlbr_w95 folder. This folder is located in the Graphics\Bitmaps folder of VB.

6. After the image is selected, it is added to the Images window of the Property Pages. At this point, you can set a value for the Key property to make it easy to access the ListImage object from code.

7. You can add additional images in the same way. Click the Insert Picture button, choose the image from the dialog box, and set a value for the Key property. Using this procedure, add the following bitmaps for use in the Toolbar exercise: Cut.bmp, Paste.bmp, New.bmp, Open.bmp, Save.bmp, Print.bmp, Bld.bmp, Itl.bmp, and Undrln.bmp. Once you have added these images, the Property Page for the image control will look like the graphic below.

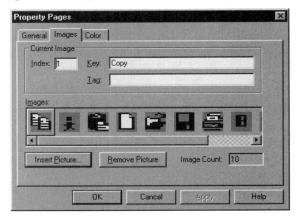

In addition to being able to add images to the ImageList control with the Property Pages, you can also delete pictures from the control. To do this, simply select the picture by clicking on it, then click the Remove Picture button.

You cannot modify an ImageList using the Property Pages after the control has been bound to another control. You can however, add pictures using code.

Adding and Deleting Images with Code

As with most other controls, the ImageList control can be modified by code. The main task that you may want to handle in code is the addition or removal of pictures in the ImageList, using the ListImages collection. Like most collections, the ListImages collection has three key methods:

- **Add**   Adds a new ListImage object to the collection.

- **Remove**   Deletes a ListImage object from the collection.

- **Clear**   Removes all ListImage objects from the collection.

To add pictures to the ImageList control, you use the Add method and specify

- the index of the picture (optional parameter),

- the Key property, which specifies a unique identifier for the picture (also an optional parameter), and

- the picture to be included.

The picture source can be the Picture property of another control, such as an Image or PictureBox, or you can load a picture from a bitmap file using the LoadPicture command. The following code shows how to load some of the pictures that were used in Exercise 3.3 into an ImageList control.

```
Dim imgCode As ListImage, sPicturePath As String
Dim sPicture As String
sPicturePath = _
"D:\Program Files\DevStudio\Vb\Graphics\Bitmaps\Tlbr_w95\"
sPicture = sPicturePath & "Copy.bmp"
Set imgCode = imlCode.ListImages.Add(, "Copy", _
LoadPicture(sPicture))
sPicture = sPicturePath & "Cut.bmp"
Set imgCode = imlCode.ListImages.Add(, "Cut", _
LoadPicture(sPicture))
sPicture = sPicturePath & "Paste.bmp"
Set imgCode = imlCode.ListImages.Add(, "Paste", _
LoadPicture(sPicture))
```

To remove one of the images, you use the Remove method of the collection and specify the index of the image to be removed.

A collection is an object that is used extensively in Visual Basic for managing groups of related objects. For controls like the ImageList where you are working with a group of items (ListImages), using a collection makes it easy to add, remove, or reference individual images. You can learn more about working with collections in Chapter 6.

Accessing Functions with Toolbars

Toolbars provide a program with a great complement to menus. The toolbars of most programs provide quick access to the most commonly used functions of the program. For a word processor, this could be formatting options or the creation of tables. For most programs, the toolbar includes functions to allow the user to create new files, open existing files, save files, and print files. Many toolbars also include the standard editing functions of Cut, Copy, and Paste. There are several advantages to using toolbars to supplement your menus in a program:

- Toolbars provide one click access to functions instead of requiring the user to navigate several menu levels.

- You can create multiple toolbars that the user can choose to display, which allows the user to customize their work area to their liking. As an example, look at the toolbars in Visual Basic. There are four separate toolbars in Visual Basic—Standard, Form Editor, Format, and Debug. The user can choose to have any, all, or none of these open at any given time. This customization is something that is not easily done with menu items.

- You can allow the user to customize the toolbars themselves, to add or remove buttons. Again, this is something that is not easily achievable with menus.

Creating a toolbar in Visual Basic requires the use of two controls. The first is the ImageList control, which contains the images that will be used for the toolbar buttons. The second control is the toolbar itself. The previous section showed you how to create an ImageList control. This section will use that control to help with the creation of the toolbar.

Microsoft
Exam
Objective

Create toolbars by using the Toolbar control.

The first step to creating the toolbar is to place the control on your form. When you do this, the toolbar will initially be placed at the top of the form and will span the width of the form, the default behavior of the toolbar. You can, of course, change this by setting the Alignment property of the toolbar. The settings of the property allow you to align the toolbar with any edge of the form, or to have no alignment, which allows the creation of a "floating" toolbar.

> **NOTE**
> If you add multiple toolbars to the form, the second one will, by default, be placed directly below the first toolbar, the third below the second, and so on.

The other key property of the toolbar is the ImageList property. This property must be set to the name of an ImageList control on the same form as the toolbar. The ImageList is the only way to provide images to be placed on the buttons of the toolbar. As is the case with setting up many of the Common Controls, the easiest way to set up the toolbar is through the use of the Property Pages. The ImageList properties is on the General page of the Property Pages, as shown in Figure 3.6.

FIGURE 3.6

The Property Pages of the Toolbar control

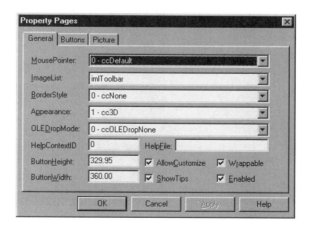

As you can see from Figure 3.6, there are several other general properties that control the appearance and behavior of the toolbar:

- **BorderStyle**   Causes the toolbar to be displayed with a single line border or no border (default).

- **Appearance**   Causes the toolbar to be shown as a 3-D (default) or flat look.

- **ButtonHeight and ButtonWidth**   Specifies the size of the buttons in the toolbar.

- **ShowTips**   Specifies whether the tool tip information entered in the ToolTips property of the Button object will be displayed.

- **Wrappable**   Specifies whether the toolbar will create a second row of buttons if there is insufficient space for all the buttons on a single row.

- **AllowCustomize**   Specifies whether the user is allowed to customize the toolbar.

Creating Buttons for the Toolbar

After you have created an instance of the toolbar control and set the general properties, you are ready to start creating the individual buttons that will be on the toolbar. Creating the buttons is most easily accomplished by moving to the Buttons page of the Property Pages, as shown in Figure 3.7.

F I G U R E   3.7

Creating buttons from the Property Pages

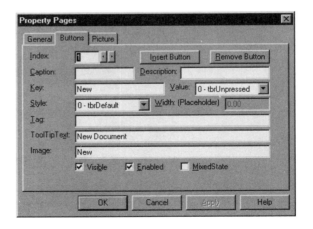

Key Properties of a Toolbar Button

To create a button in the Property Pages, click the Insert Button button in the dialog box, then set the properties of the button. The main properties that you need to set include:

Image property   The picture to be shown on the button.

Key property   The name by which the button is referenced in code.

Style property   The appearance and behavior of the button.

The Toolbar control supports five different styles of Button objects. These styles are summarized in Table 3.2.

T A B L E 3.2	Style	What it does
Button types available on the toolbar	tbrDefault	Standard button that can be clicked to launch a task.
	tbrCheck	A two-state button, such as the Bold button, that turns an option on or off and indicates the status of the option by the appearance of the button.
	tbrButtonGroup	One button of a group that allows a single option to be selected from the group. An example is the alignment buttons that allow the user to choose right-justified, left-justified, or centered.
	tbrSeparator	This button has a width of eight pixels and provides a space between other groups of buttons.
	tbrPlaceHolder	Provides a space on the toolbar for other controls such as a combo box that could be used for providing multiple options.

Optional Toolbar Properties

In addition to the Image, Key, and Style properties, there are several other properties that define the behavior of the Button object.

- **Caption**   Specifies the text that will appear on the face of the button. If only a Caption is specified (no Image property), the text will appear in the center of the button. If an Image and Caption are both specified, the text will appear below the picture in the button.

- **Description**   Provides a description of the button for the user if customization of the toolbar is allowed.

- **Value**   Sets or returns the current state of the button. The value is 0 if the button is not pressed, 1 if the button is pressed.

- **Width**   Specifies the width of the button for the Placeholder style only. For all other button types, the width is ignored.

- **Tag**   Assigns other data to the button for use in your program.

- **ToolTipText**   Specifies the text that is displayed when the user pauses the mouse over the button. This text is displayed only if the ShowTips property of the toolbar is set to True.

As you create each button, it will be added to the toolbar on your form. This way, you can see the results of setting the properties as it happens. Exercise 3.4 shows you how to create a toolbar that you would typically find in a word processing program.

EXERCISE 3.4

Creating a Toolbar

1. Open the project that you created in Exercise 3.3. This project contains the ImageList control that you will use to provide images for the toolbar.

2. Add a toolbar control to the form. Name the toolbar tlbSample. Then, open the Property Pages of the toolbar.

3. In the General section of the Property Pages, set the ImageList property to the name of the ImageList control created in Exercise 3.3 (imlToolbar).

4. Click the Buttons tab of the Property Pages, then click the Insert Button button on the page.

5. Set the following properties for the first button:

Property	Value
Key	New
Style	tbrDefault
ToolTipText	New Document
Image	New

Notice that we used the Key value of the ListImage object instead of its index number for setting the Image property of the button. Assigning key values makes it easier to remember which picture is actually contained in the ListImage object. If you assigned different Key values when you created the ImageList control, use those Key values instead of the ones presented here.

6. Create two more buttons using the tbrDefault Style setting. These buttons should be Open and Save. Be sure to use the appropriate image from the ImageList control, and be sure to assign appropriate Key values to the buttons. Both are necessary to write program code to activate the buttons.

7. Create a new button and set the Style property to tbrSeparator to provide a space between the first group of buttons and the second.

8. Create three additional buttons for Bold, Italic, and Underline. The Style property of these buttons should be set to tbrCheck.

9. Close the Property Pages and run the program to see how the toolbar looks and behaves. Notice that the ImageList control is not visible while the program is running. The completed sample toolbar is shown in Figure 3.8.

FIGURE 3.8

The toolbar created in Exercise 3.4

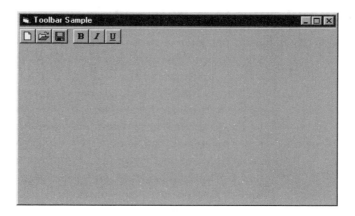

Creating Toolbar Buttons from Code

Of course, this discussion would not be complete if we did not include how to create toolbar buttons from code. As you might expect from the discussion of the ImageList control, you can manipulate the toolbar using the methods of the Buttons collection. With the collection methods, you can add buttons to the toolbar, remove buttons, or clear the entire toolbar.

The following code shows you two techniques for adding buttons to the toolbar. The first technique uses the Add method alone and specifies all the necessary information for the button. The second technigque uses the Add method to create a Button object, then sets the properties of the object. Both techniques work equally well.

```
Dim btnNew As Button
'Adding a button with the Add method alone.
tlbSample.Buttons.Add , "Paste", , tbrDefault, "Paste"
'Adding a button by creating a button object and setting
properties
Set btnNew = tlbSample.Buttons.Add
btnNew.Key = "Print"
btnNew.Style = tbrDefault
btnNew.Image = "Print"
```

Running Functions with the Toolbar

After you have created the toolbar, you need to add code to make the buttons of the toolbar perform tasks. When the toolbar button is clicked, the ButtonClick event of the toolbar is fired, passing the object reference for the button that was pressed. The object reference allows you to determine which button was pressed and to take appropriate action.

The simplest way to determine which button was pressed is to check the Key property of the button. (This is why we recommend that you always include a value for the Key property.) Because the toolbar is often closely tied to the menu of a program, you can use the same event code for both the toolbar and the menu. The following code shows how you would use a Select Case structure to identify the button, then fire the Click event of the appropriate menu item to perform the task.

```
Select Case Button.Key
    Case "New"
        filNew_Click
    Case "Print"
        filPrint_Click
    Case "Bold"
        fmtBold_Click
End Select
```

You can use the Index property of the Button object to determine which button was pressed, but this requires you to remember the index number of the button. Also, the Index property can change if you later modify the toolbar through the Property Pages or with code. Therefore, it is *strongly* recommended that you include a value for the Key property for each button and use that value in your code.

Customizing the Toolbar

These days, most applications that use toolbars (which includes almost all applications) allow the user to customize the toolbar to their own liking. The Toolbar control of Visual Basic makes it easy for you to incorporate this functionality in the toolbars you create. The only thing that you have to do is set the AllowCustomize property to True. The toolbar control takes care of the rest for you. When the user double clicks on the toolbar, the Customize Toolbar, shown in Figure 3.9, pops up. The user can then move buttons around on the toolbar or add or remove buttons. When the user clicks the Close button of the dialog box, the changes are displayed in the toolbar.

FIGURE 3.9

The Customize Toolbar dialog box lets the user modify the toolbar.

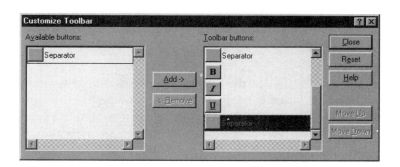

Displaying Data with the TreeView Control

The TreeView control provides you with a versatile way to look at related data. The TreeView presents data in the form of a hierarchical tree of data. The data starts with a root node that is directly related to a number of branch nodes. Each of the branch nodes is known as a Child of the root node. Each of the children can have their own children, and so on. As you look at the various nodes of data, the overall appearance is that of an inverted tree, hence the name. The most widely known example of a TreeView control is the tree used in the left hand panel of Windows Explorer, as shown in Figure 3.10.

FIGURE 3.10

Windows Explorer as an example of a TreeView control

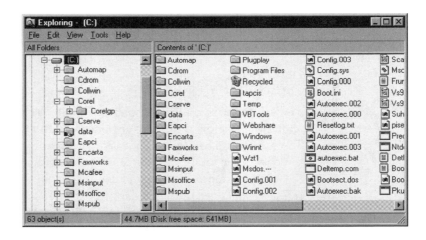

Microsoft ✓ *Exam* *Objective*

Display data by using the TreeView control.

The main attraction of the TreeView control is the capability to show direct relations between various levels of data. For example, you could use the TreeView control to display all the orders shipped to a particular customer. The root node of such an application would be the customer name.

The next level of nodes would be the individual orders shipped to the customer. The next level would be the specific details of each order.

The TreeView allows the user to view all this information at once, or to collapse or expand specific branches to change the view of the data. In addition, the TreeView control gives you the capability to modify individual nodes by assigning values to the properties of the nodes, including the capability to display pictures with the nodes and different pictures for the selected node. For the order processing example, you could indicate shipped orders with one icon and mark pending orders with another icon.

Setting Up the TreeView Control

Creating a TreeView control in your application involves two major functions, setting up the control itself by setting general properties and creating the nodes of the tree. You can set the general control properties in the design environment through the use of the Property Pages or the Properties window. You can also set most of the properties of the control with code. The creation of the nodes is something that can only be done in code. We will look at creating nodes in the next section.

After you have drawn an instance of the TreeView control on your form, there are a number of general properties that you can set to determine the appearance and behavior of the control. The more important properties include:

- **HideSelection** Specifies whether the selected node will be highlighted when the TreeView control loses focus. The default value is to not show the selection in this case.

- **ImageList** Specifies the name of the ImageList control that contains the pictures used for the nodes of the tree.

- **Indentation** Specifies the number of twips that each level of the tree hierarchy is indented from its parent node.

- **LabelEdit** Specifies how the user can edit the label of the tree node. If the property is set to automatic, the user can click on the node label and begin editing. In this case, the BeforeLabelEdit event is fired when the user clicks on the node. If the property is set to manual, the user can edit the label only after the StartLabelEdit method has been invoked. In this case, the BeforeLabelEdit event is fired after the method is run.

- **LineStyle**   Determines whether lines will be drawn between root nodes or not. The default is to not draw the lines. In either case, the control will draw lines between parent and child nodes.

- **Sorted**   Determines whether the root nodes of the tree are sorted alphabetically. There is also a Sorted property for each node of the tree, which that determines whether the child nodes of a given node are sorted.

- **Style**   Determines which combination of the following will be displayed by the TreeView control—images, text, lines, +/– signs to indicate the expansion of branches. There are eight possible settings of the Style property, as summarized in Table 3.3.

TABLE 3.3 Settings of the Style property	Setting	Description
	0	Only text is shown.
	1	Both text and images can be shown.
	2	Text and the +/– signs can be shown.
	3	Text, images, and the +/– signs can be shown.
	4	Only text is shown, but with lines between parent and child nodes.
	5	Text and images are shown, with parent/child lines.
	6	Text and +/– signs are shown, with parent/child lines.
	7	Text, images, and the +/– signs can be shown, with parent/child lines. This is the default value.

Creating the Nodes of the Tree

After you have created the control and set the general properties, it is time to start creating the nodes of the tree. As stated previously, you must create the nodes of the tree using program code. The creation of nodes is handled by the Add method of the Nodes collection of the TreeView control. The general syntax of the Add method is as follows:

```
TreeView.Nodes.Add relative, relationship, key, text, image, _
selectedimage
```

Of these parameters, only the Text parameter is required. However, if other parameters prior to Text are omitted, their places must be held by commas. Each of these parameters specifies information about the node, as summarized here:

- **Relative**   Specifies the Key value of the node to which the added node is related.

- **Relationship**   Specifies the type of relationship that exists between the new node and the node specified in the Relative parameter. The possible relationships are specified in the following list:

Setting	Description
tvwFirst	The new node is placed ahead of all other nodes at the same level of the node named in relative.
tvwLast	The new node is placed after all other nodes at the same level of the node named in relative.
tvwNext	The new node is placed immediately after the node named in relative.
tvwPrevious	The new node is placed immediately before the node named in relative.
tvwChild	The new node is created as a child node of the node named in relative.

- **Key**   Specifies a unique identifier for the new node.

- **Text**   Specifies the text to be displayed in the node.

- **Image**   Specifies the index of an image in the ImageList control that is associated with the TreeView control. This image is shown whenever the node is visible unless the node is the selected node and the SelectedImage has been specified.

- **SelectedImage**   Specifies the index of an image in the ImageList control that should be displayed when the node is selected.

The Add method of the Nodes collection can be used directly to create a node, or the method can be used to create a reference to a Node object so that other properties of the Node can be set. Both methods are shown in the following code.

```
'Create node directly
TreeView1.Nodes.Add , , "Employee", "Employees"
'Create node object and set additional properties
Set nodX = TreeView1.Nodes.Add(, , "Customer", "Customers")
nodX.Expanded = True
```

In addition to the parameters used in the Add method to create a node, there are several other properties of the Node object that you will use in writing a TreeView application:

- **Children**   Returns the number of child nodes for the current node.

- **Child, FirstSibling, Next, Previous, LastSibling**   Returns a node that is a child of the current node. You can check the help file for a complete description of the differences between the properties.

- **Parent**   Returns a reference to the node that is the parent of the current node.

- **Root**   Returns a reference to the node that is the root node for the current node.

- **Expanded**   Specifies whether the child nodes of the current node are shown or the node is shown in its collapsed form.

- **ExpandedImage**   Specifies the index of the image in an ImageList control that should be shown when the current node is expanded.

To illustrate how to create a TreeView control, Exercise 3.5 walks you through all the necessary steps to create a control that displays the players of little league teams.

EXERCISE 3.5

Creating a TreeView Control

1. Start a new project and add the reference to the Windows Common Controls.

2. Add an ImageList control to the form and add three images of your choosing to the control. You can refer back to Exercise 3.3 to refresh your memory on creating an ImageList control.

3. Add a TreeView control to the form.

4. Set the ImageList property of the TreeView control to the name of the ImageList control created in Step 2.

5. Add the root node to the tree using the following code. All the code in this example can be placed in the Load event of the form.

```
Dim nodBB As Node
'Create league
Set nodBB = tvwBaseball.Nodes.Add(, , "Shelby", _
"North Shelby")
nodBB.Expanded = True
nodBB.Sorted = True
```

6. Next, add a team to the tree as a child of the root node. Use the following code to add the first team:

```
'Create Teams
tvwBaseball.Nodes.Add "Shelby", tvwChild, "Cubs", "Cubs", _
"Diamond", "Check"
```

7. Add several more teams of your choosing to the tree. Use the same syntax as was used in Step 6. Remember to specify a Key value for each team.

8. Add a player to the first team using the following code. The player node will be a child of the team node.

```
'Add Players
tvwBaseball.Nodes.Add "Cubs", tvwChild, "Eric", "Eric", _
"Player"
```

9. Add players to the other teams using the same syntax as in Step 8.

10. Run the program. Your application should look something like the one in Figure 3.11. Try clicking and double clicking on the various node to see the effects. The code for this project is contained on the CD in BaseBall.vbp.

FIGURE 3.11

The completed
baseball tree

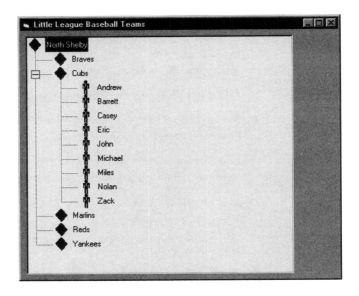

The control itself is useful for displaying data, but you will probably also want to be able to take action when the user clicks on one of the nodes. You can accomplish this with the NodeClick event. This event is triggered each time a node is clicked. The event passes an object reference to the selected node. You can use this object to determine which node was selected and take the appropriate action.

On the CD, you will find a project named TreeList.vbp. This project uses a TreeView and a ListView control to display order information for all the customers listed in the Nwind.mdb database. The TreeView control contains the names of the customers and information about each order. As an order node is selected, the ListView control is updated to display the detail information about the order. The code in the NodeClick event is used to determine which order was selected and to retrieve the appropriate detail information. Figure 3.12 shows how this program looks.

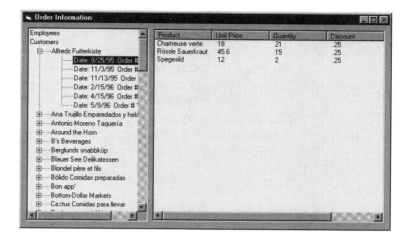

FIGURE 3.12

Displaying order information with the Tree-View and ListView controls

Displaying Data in a List

The sample project, TreeList.vbp, showed you how data can be displayed in a ListView control. This section will show you how the control is set up.

A ListView control is best exemplified either by the right side of the Windows Explorer application, or by the directory listings shown in the MyComputer application of Windows 95. Both of these applications allow you to view the files and folders on your computer as Small icons, Large icons, a simple list, or a report with detail information. You can create each of these four views with the ListView control.

Because the report view of the ListView control is the most complex view, we will examine how to create this view. The other three views really show a subset of the information displayed in the report view.

Microsoft ✓ *Exam* *Objective*   **Display data by using the ListView control.**

The report view provides you with a souped-up version of a ListBox control. Where the ListBox is limited to a single text string for each list item, the report view of the ListView control can have any number of columns displayed, making it ideal for displaying detailed information about anything. The TreeList.vbp used the ListView control to display the detail information about a given order, including the product, unit price, quantity, discount, and total cost. As another example, a membership application might use the ListView control to display information about family members, such as their name, gender, birth date, and social security number.

To create the report view, you need to perform three tasks:

1. Create an instance of the control and set the general properties of the ListView.

2. Set up the headers for each of the columns of the report.

3. Add the actual data to the report.

Setting Up the Control

The simplest way to set up the general properties of a ListView control is, of course, through the use of the Property Pages. As shown in Figure 3.13, the Property Pages for the ListView control consist of seven tabs of information. Of these, the first three contain information that is unique to the ListView control. The fourth page is column header information, which we will get to in a moment. The other pages cover information about fonts and colors, information that is familiar from working with other controls. Let's take a look at the properties on the first three pages and explain what they do (we won't cover every property).

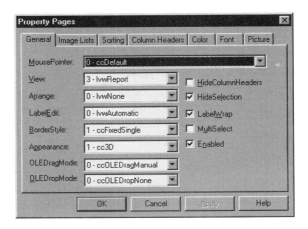

The first page has the general information for the ListView control, what style to use, how to edit labels, whether to show column headers, etc. In particular, these properties are as follows:

- **Arrange**   Specifies whether items are aligned along the left edge of the control, the top edge of the control, or not aligned.

- **HideColumnHeaders**   Specifies whether column headers are shown. This property only affects the report view of the ListView control.

- **HideSelection**   Specifies whether the selected item will be highlighted when the ListView control loses focus. The default value is to not show the selection in this case.

- **LabelEdit**   Similar to the LabelEdit property of the TreeView control described earlier.

- **LabelWrap**   Determines whether the label of an item is wrapped to additional lines if the length of the line is greater than the icon spacing defined by the operating system. This option only affects the icon views of the ListView control.

- **MultiSelect**   Specifies whether the user can select multiple ListItems in the ListView control, similar to the MultiSelect property of the ListBox control.

- **View**   Specifies how the ListItems are shown in the control. The four options are to display items as standard icons with text, small icons with text, arranged as a single column list, or arranged as a report with detail information presented for each item.

After setting the general information for the ListView control, you will need to specify the names of the ImageList controls that are used to provide the icons for the ListView control. Because the ListView is capable of showing items as either standard or small icons, the control requires two ImageList controls. The names of the ImageList controls are stored in the Icons and SmallIcons properties of the ListView. You can set these names either through the ImageLists page of the Property Pages or through code, using a standard assignment statement.

The final general characteristic of the ListView control is the sort order for the list. You probably know that you can sort a ListBox control by setting the Sorted property, which sorts the list in ascending alphabetical order. The ListView control has the same capability, but with enhancements. The ListView control is capable of sorting the list based on the contents of any of the columns defined for the list and can sort in either ascending or descending order. You have seen this capability if you have changed the sort order of files in the Windows Explorer. The sorting of items in the ListView control is dependent upon three properties. Each of these properties needs to be set before the sort will work:

- **Sorted**   Specifies whether items will be sorted in accordance with the information in the SortKey and SortOrder properties.

- **SortKey**   Specifies which column of information will be used to sort the list. If SortKey is 0, the Text property of the ListItem object will be used for the sort. If SortKey is 1 or greater, the sub-item (detail column) whose index is equal to the SortKey value will be used as the sorted field. For example, if you have sub-item information specifying the type of file, size of a file, and date of modification (in that order), specifying a SortKey value of 2 will cause the information to be sorted on the file size.

- **SortOrder**   Specifies whether the information is sorted in ascending (SortOrder=0) or descending (SortOrder=1) order.

When you have a report view showing in the ListView control, you can allow the user to change the sort order of the items by clicking the column header. This is accomplished by placing the following line of code in the ColumnClick event of the control.

```
LvwGrades.SortKey = ColumnHeader.Index  1
```

Now, let's put all this information to use by creating a sample program. The program will use the ListView control to display class grades in a report view. This will allow the user to sort information based on any of several test results. Exercise 3.6 starts the project. Exercises 3.7 and 3.8 will show you how to complete the program.

EXERCISE 3.6

Creating a ListView Control

1. Start a new project and add the reference to the Windows Common Controls.

2. Add two ImageList controls to the form and set up images in the controls as described in Exercise 3.3.

3. Add a ListView control to the form and activate the Property Pages of the control.

4. On the General page of the Property Pages, set the View property to report view.

5. On the ImageLists page of the Property Pages, set the Icons and Small-Icons property to the names of the ImageList controls created in Step 2.

6. On the Sorted page of the Property Pages, set the Sorted property to True. We will use code to handle changing the sort order and field.

7. Add the following code to the ColumnClick event of the ListView control. The code checks the SortKey property. If this does not match the index of the column that was clicked, the order is set to the new field and defaults to ascending order. If the SortKey property matches the index, the sort order is reversed, allowing the user to not only change the field that is the basis of the sort, but to also change the order of the sort.

```
If lvwGrades.SortKey = ColumnHeader.Index - 1 Then
    If lvwGrades.SortOrder = lvwAscending Then
        lvwGrades.SortOrder = lvwDescending
    Else
        lvwGrades.SortOrder = lvwAscending
    End If
Else
    lvwGrades.SortKey = ColumnHeader.Index - 1
    lvwGrades.SortOrder = lvwAscending
End If
```

8. Save the project as Grades.vbp. This project is also included on the CD.

Setting Up the Headings for Columns

The next task in setting up the report view of the ListView control is to create the column headers for the list, either from the design mode or from code. In the design mode, you simply go to the Column Headers page of the

Property Pages (shown in Figure 3.14) and click the Insert Column button for each column you want to create. As you create the column, you will need to set the following properties:

- **Text** Specifies the information that will be shown in the column header.

- **Alignment** Specifies whether the text will be left or right justified, or centered in the column header.

- **Width** Specifies the width of the column.

- **Key** Specifies a string that uniquely identifies the column.

F I G U R E 3.14

Column Headers
Property Page

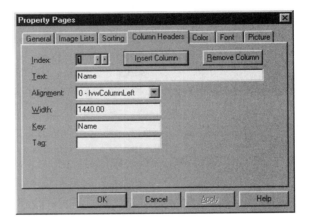

The first column header that you create (index value of 1) is the one that will correspond to the text of the ListItem object and is the main information that you will want to display for each item. The value of the text property is also the only information shown when you are using a view other than the report view. Exercise 3.7 walks you through creating the column headers for the Grades list.

EXERCISE 3.7

Adding the Column Headers

1. Starting from the previous project (Exercise 3.6), open the Property Pages of the ListView control and select the Column Headers page.

2. Click the Insert Column to create the first header.

3. Set the Text property of the first header to Name and set the Key property to Name as well.

4. Repeating steps 2 and 3, create additional headers as described in the following list:

Text	Key
First Test	Test1
Second Test	Test2
Final Exam	Final
Average Score	Average

5. Save the project.

Adding Column Headers with Code

In addition to using the Property Pages, you can also create column headers with code. The column headers are objects that are handled by the Column-Headers collection. To add a column header from code, you use the Add method of the ColumnHeaders collection. The following code shows how to create the headers for the Grades list.

```
Dim clmHead As ColumnHeader
lvwGrades.ColumnHeaders.Add , "Name", "Name", _
lvwGrades.Width / 5
Set clmHead = lvwGrades.ColumnHeaders.Add(,"Test1", _
"First Test")
ClmHead.Width = lvwGrades.Width / 5
Set clmHead = lvwGrades.ColumnHeaders.Add(,"Test2", _
"First Test")
Set clmHead = lvwGrades.ColumnHeaders.Add(,"Test3", _
"Second Test")
Set clmHead = lvwGrades.ColumnHeaders.Add(,"Final", _
"Final Exam")
Set clmHead = lvwGrades.ColumnHeaders.Add(,"Average", _
"Average Score")
```

Adding Data to the ListView Control

The final step to creating the ListView control is to add the actual data to the list. The data is added in two steps. First, you add the ListItem object to the ListItems collection. Then you set the values of the SubItem properties of the ListItem. SubItems is an array of values that correspond to the columns of information that are displayed in the report view. The following code shows how the ListItem object is created, then how the SubItem values are set. Exercise 3.8 takes you through the process.

```
Dim liStudent As ListItem
Set liStudent = lvwGrades.ListItems.Add(, , "Jackson")
With liStudent
    .SubItems(1) = 75
    .SubItems(2) = 90
    .SubItems(3) = 95
    .SubItems(4) = (Val(.SubItems(1)) + Val(.SubItems(2)) +
(.SubItems(3))) / 3
End With
```

EXERCISE 3.8

Adding the Student Information

1. Continuing with the project from Exercise 3.7, open the code window for the Load event of the form.

2. Place the code shown above in the Load event to create the data for the first student.

3. Repeat the last seven lines of the previous code to add more students. You can repeat this process for as many students as you would like.

4. Run the program. You can now click on the column headers to see how the sort order changes due to the code created in Exercise 3.6. A sample grade list is shown in Figure 3.15.

The completed grade
list project

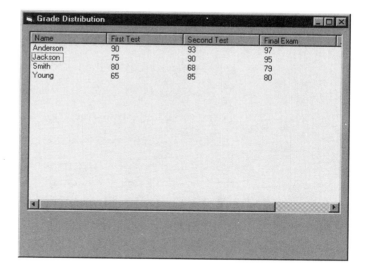

Summary

This chapter has covered a lot of material. You have seen how to use most of the controls in the Microsoft Windows Common Controls group. The chapter has shown you how to create toolbars to allow quick access to functions, and how to use the StatusBar and ProgressBar controls to provide information to the user. You have also seen how to display information using the TreeView and ListView controls.

While we have covered a lot of ground, we have really only scratched the surface of the capabilities of several of the controls. The TreeView and List-View controls in particular are very powerful and take a lot of time to master. Also, for these controls, the real power lies in being able to display data from sources such as databases or directory information, not merely the simple examples shown in the exercises. The TreeList.vbp project on the CD shows you a little of this capability. As with many other things, the best way to learn is to acquire a good understanding of the basics (from the information in this chapter), then experiment.

This chapter covered the material that you need to know in order to achieve the following exam objectives:

- Display data by using the TreeView control.

- Display items by using the ListView control.

- Provide controls with images by using the ImageList control.

- Create toolbars by using the Toolbar control.

- Display status information by using the StatusBar control.

The inner workings of several of these controls, particularly the TreeView and ListView controls can be very complex. Make sure that you have a complete understanding of the steps shown in all the exercises before you take the exam.

Review Questions

1. Which control lets you display information in a hierarchical structure?

    A. TreeView

    B. ListView

    C. ListBox

    D. StatusBar

2. Which style of StatusBar panel can be modified by your program? Check all that apply.

    A. sbrText

    B. sbrCaps

    C. sbrNum

    D. sbrIns

3. How do you update the status of a sbrCaps style panel?

   A. It is handled for you automatically by the control.

   B. You need to place code in the KeyPress event of the form.

   C. You must place code in the KeyPress event of the StatusBar.

   D. Use a Windows API call to find out when the key is pressed.

4. Name the two techniques for identifying a Panel object in the Panels collection.

   A. Refer to it by the Index property.

   B. Refer to it by the Text property.

   C. Refer to it by the Style property.

   D. Refer to it by the Key property.

5. What property of the ProgressBar determines how much of the bar is filled?

   A. Min

   B. Max

   C. Value

   D. All of the above

6. What is the purpose of the ImageList control?

   A. Display bitmaps for the user to view.

   B. Provide a repository for images used by other controls.

   C. Allow easy editing of icons.

   D. Both A and B.

7. What are valid methods of adding a picture to the ImageList control? Check all that apply.

   A. Select a picture using a dialog box in the Property Pages.

   B. Set the Picture property of the ImageList control to the name of a PictureBox control.

   C. Set the Picture property of the ListImage object to the Picture property of another control.

   D. Set the Picture property of the ListImage object using the Load-Picture command.

8. What does a button of a button group on a toolbar do?

   A. Shows you the current status of an option.

   B. Allows you to select one option from several.

   C. Simply starts a function of the application.

   D. Provides a space in the toolbar.

9. All of the following statements are true about toolbars except:

   A. You can only have one toolbar on a form.

   B. Toolbars can be positioned anywhere on the form.

   C. Toolbars can be customized by the user.

   D. Toolbar buttons can display both text and images.

10. What do you have to do to allow the user to customize the toolbar?

   A. Write code to add buttons or remove buttons based on the user selection.

   B. Set the AllowCustomize property to true and the control takes care of the rest.

   C. You cannot do this with Visual Basic toolbars.

11. How many root nodes can a TreeView control have?

   A. 1

   B. Up to 5

   C. Maximum of 2

   D. No limit

12. What must you specify to make a new node the child of another node? Check all that apply.

   A. The Key value of the node to which it is related

   B. The text of the related node

   C. The Relationship must be specified as tvwChild

   D. The image to be associated with the new node

13. What property determines whether lines are drawn between parent and child nodes? Check all that apply.

   A. Appearance

   B. Style

   C. Indentation

   D. LineStyle

14. What advantages does the ListView control have over the standard ListBox? Check all that apply.

   A. ListView can display multiple columns of data.

   B. ListBox is limited in the number of items that are allowed.

   C. Only the ListView can be sorted.

   D. ListView allows you to sort on different fields and specify the sort order.

   E. ListView can display headers over columns of information.

15. Which of the following views displays the Text property of the List-Item objects? Check all that apply.

   A. Icon view

   B. Small icon view

   C. List view

   D. Report view

16. Which views display the detail information of a ListItem that is contained in the SubItem array? Check all that apply.

   A. Icon view

   B. Small icon view

   C. List view

   D. Report view

17. Which property of the ListView control determines which field a sort is based on?

   A. Sorted

   B. SortOrder

   C. SortField

   D. SortKey

CHAPTER

4

Creating Menus for Your Programs

Microsoft Exam Objectives Covered in This Chapter:

- Add a menu interface to an application.
- Add a pop-up menu to an application.
- Dynamically modify the appearance of a menu.
- Create an application that adds and deletes menus at run-time.

Forms and the controls in the Visual Basic toolbox will make up the bulk of the visual interface of your program. However, there are two other key elements that are used in most of the programs that you will create, menus and dialog boxes. If you look at almost any commercial program today, you will find that the functions of the program are conveniently organized in a menu system. This system consists of the menu bar at the top of the screen, and a series of drop-down choices that provide single-click access to the program's functions. You will find menus in programs from simple games to the most sophisticated word-processing or database programs. Visual Basic, of course, provides you with the tools to create your own menus. Using menus gives your programs a professional appearance and helps the user work with your program.

Creating a Menu System

There are several types of menus you can create for your programs. Most people are familiar with the main menu that is shown at the top of the main screen for a program. However, most programs also include a variety of pop-up menus that present context driven options. For example, if you right-click the mouse on a paragraph in a word processor, you are typically presented with a format menu that allows you to modify the characteristics of the paragraph, as shown in Figure 4.1. These pop-up menus are displayed right next to the mouse cursor.

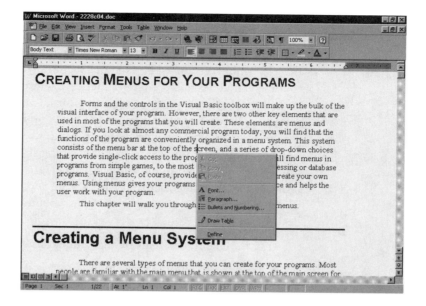

FIGURE 4.1

Pop-up menus provide context sensitive options.

Visual Basic provides you with the tools to create the main menu of an application as well as pop-up menus. In fact, you are not limited to a single menu in your programs. While it is customary to have the menu on the main form of the program, Visual Basic allows you to place a menu on any form in your program, so you can have multiple menus based on the tasks that need to be performed.

Designing the Menu

Although designing a menu is not specifically covered in the exam, you do need to know how to plan and layout your menu before you begin creating it. Also, understanding Microsoft's expectations about menu design will help you if you want to have programs certified as "Windows 95 compatible."

The first step to creating a good menu is to design the layout of the menu—not how wide the drop down menu will be, or where it will be located on the screen, but what functions will need to appear on the menu and how the functions will be grouped. Grouping of menu items is important for several reasons. First of all, unless you only have a few items, it is impractical to place them all on the main menu bar. Therefore, you will have to create sub menus. The main consideration for grouping items is determining where a user could logically expect to find the item. For example, most users would not look for the Cut and Paste functions on a Tools menu; they would look for them on an Edit menu because the functions relate to editing.

This expectation brings out a key point in menu design. There are interface guidelines that were established by Microsoft and are in common use that determine certain aspects of your menu. If your menu design conforms to these guidelines and common practices, your users will have a head start on being able to use your program. If your menu does not conform, your users may become confused and frustrated, and may not use your program.

Therefore, the best way to design a menu is to first determine what functions of your program fit into one of the typical menu groups, such as File, Edit, View, Tools, Window, and Help. Then group the rest of the functions into a few other categories that will be your top-level menus. When you finally get to actually creating your menu, you need to remember some other design guidelines:

- Group menu list items by their functions.

- Keep the function groups limited to five items or less.

- Separate function groups in a menu list with separator bars.

- Limit the number of sub-menu levels to two, if possible. Too many levels make your menu hard to navigate.

As you are designing your menu groupings, you may want to lay them out on paper to make sure the menu meets your needs. Then, with this listing in hand, it will be easy to create the actual menu in the menu editor.

Creating the Menu with the Menu Editor

The Menu Editor is the only means in Visual Basic to create or modify a menu in the design mode. And, while you can make some changes to the menu at run-time, the vast majority of the menu creation will be done in the Menu Editor. To begin creating a menu for your program, you must have a form design window active in Visual Basic, as shown in Figure 4.2. You can then access the Menu Editor by clicking the Menu Editor button on the toolbar, choosing the Menu Editor item from the Tools menu, or by pressing Ctrl+E.

After you have opened the Menu Editor, you can begin creating the items of your menu. For each item, you are required to specify a Caption and a Name property. The Caption identifies the menu item to the user and the Name identifies the menu to your program. The first item you will create is a main menu bar item. After you accept the values for the Name and Caption properties, by pressing Enter or clicking the Next button, the menu item will be shown in the selection area at the bottom of the dialog box, as shown in Figure 4.3.

F I G U R E   4.2

A form must be active in order to create a menu on it.

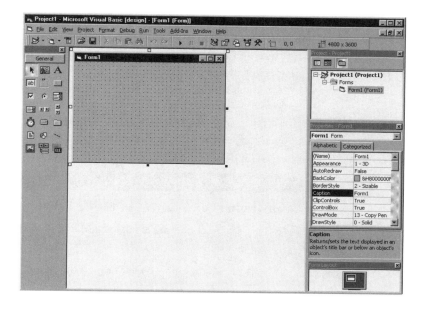

Microsoft ✓ **Exam Objective**

Add a menu interface to an application.

F I G U R E   4.3

Creating menus in the Menu Editor

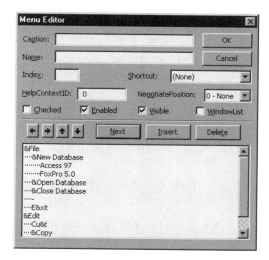

Notice that the item is positioned against the left edge of the dialog box, indicating that it is a top-level menu item. As you create other items, you will want to make them sub-menus of one of the top-level items. You can do this by clicking the Right arrow button or pressing Alt+R before you accept the properties of the menu item. Figure 4.3 also displays several levels of indentation. Each indentation indicates another menu level, similar to the organization of an outline.

Of course, the best way to learn to create a menu is to do it. Exercise 4.1 shows you how to create a basic File and Edit menu system.

EXERCISE 4.1

Creating a Menu with the Menu Editor

1. Start a project and make sure that the main form is active in the design environment.

2. Start the Menu Editor by clicking on the Menu Editor button.

3. Enter the Caption and Name properties for the first item. Use File and mnuFile respectively.

4. Press Enter to accept the properties and clear the input area for another item.

5. Press Alt+R to indent the next item in the menu. Enter **New** for the Caption and **filNew** for the Name property. Press Enter. You will notice that the next item is automatically indented to the same level as the one you just created.

6. Enter two more items with the following Caption and Name properties: **Open** and **filOpen** for the first item, **Save** and **filSave** for the second item.

7. Next create a separator bar by entering a hyphen (-) in the Caption property and **filSep1** for the Name. Even though this item cannot be accessed by the user, you must still specify a Name for the item.

8. Create the Exit item by entering **Exit** in the Caption property and **filExit** in the Name property. Then press Enter to accept the values.

9. Press Alt+L to promote the next item back to a top level menu.

10. Enter **Edit** in the Caption property and **mnuEdit** in the Name property. Then press Enter.

11. Press Alt+R to indent the Edit menu items.

12. Add the following items to the Edit menu, using the Caption and Name property listed here: **Cut**, **edtCut**; **Copy**, **edtCopy**; **Paste**, **edtPaste**.

13. Accept the entire menu by clicking the OK button. Figure 4.4 shows the completed menu in the menu editor, and Figure 4.5 shows the menu as it appears on the form.

F I G U R E 4.4

A completed menu in the Menu Editor

If you forget to enter a Name property for any menu item, the Menu editor will notify you of the problem and will not let you exit.

After you have completed the creation of the menu in the Menu Editor, you will need to add code to make the menu items perform a task. You will write code for the Click event of each menu item, similar to writing code for the Click event of a Command button. The easiest way to access the code window for a menu item is to select the item on the form. You will be placed in the Click event procedure of the menu item. You can then write any code you want to take an action.

FIGURE 4.5

The menu as seen by
the user

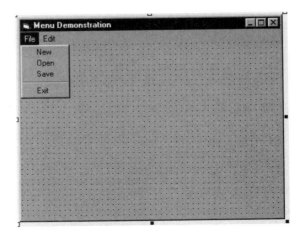

The Click event is the only event supported by the menu items.

As an example, you can write code to terminate the application in the Exit menu item by following two simple steps:

1. Click the Exit item to access the code window.

2. Insert the code Unload Me in the event procedure.

Adding Shortcut and Access Keys to Menu Items

Menus are designed primarily for navigation with the mouse; however, most users have come to expect menu access from the keyboard as well. The ability to select items without using the mouse is particularly important to data entry users. These users do not want to move their hands from the keyboard to the mouse and back. Visual Basic provides two ways to enable keyboard access to menu items:

▪ Access keys

▪ Shortcut keys

Accessing menu items from the access keys or shortcut keys has the same effect as clicking on a menu item with the mouse, the Click event for the item is triggered and the corresponding code is run.

Creating Access Keys

An access key allows the user to press Alt plus a key to cause the drop-down list of a top-level menu to appear. The user can then press a single key to access an item on the list. In Visual Basic, you can see this type of access in the menu. For example, you can press Alt+F to access the File menu, then press the N key to start a new project. With access keys, you should have a unique key combination for each of the top-level menus, then a unique key for each item within a top-level menu. It is permissible to assign the same key to different items in different menus. For example, the Paste item in the Edit menu and the Print item in the File menu both use the same access key, P.

You can have multiple top-level items with the same access key. The user can then repeatedly press Alt+ the key to loop through all the menus with the same access key. However, the user will then have to use the cursor keys to have the menu drop down, instead of this happening automatically as is the case if there is only one item for the access key.

To create an access key for a menu item, you simply place an ampersand (&) in front of the character to be used as an access key in the Caption property of the menu item. For example, to make F the access key for the File menu, you would place an ampersand in front of the F in the Caption. This makes the Caption property &File. Your users will not see the & in the menu. Instead, they will see the access key underlined. When you use access keys, you will typically make the key the first letter of the caption. This is the most intuitive letter for the user to hit. You should, however follow some simple conventions:

- The file menu should always use F as the access key. Within the file menu, you should use the following keys: N for new, O for open, C for close, P for print, S for save, A for save as, and x for exit.

- The edit menu should always use E as the access key. Within the edit menu, the following keys should be used: t for Cut, C for copy, P for paste, F for find, D for delete, and e for replace.

- Other top level menus should use the following keys: V for view, T for tools, W for window, and H for help.

The reason for using these conventions is that the user is probably familiar with them from other programs and will be confused by your interface if you deviate from the conventions. Exercise 4.2 shows you how to add access keys to the menu created in Exercise 4.1. Figure 4.6 shows how the menu appears after the access keys are added.

EXERCISE 4.2

Adding Access Keys to Your Menu

1. Open the project containing the menu sample program.

2. Open the Menu Editor for the main form.

3. Place an & in front of the following letters in the specified items:

Item	Access Key
File	F
New	N
Open	O
Save	S
Exit	x
Edit	E
Cut	t
Copy	C
Paste	P

4. Click the OK button to accept the menu changes.

FIGURE 4.6

Menu with Access keys added

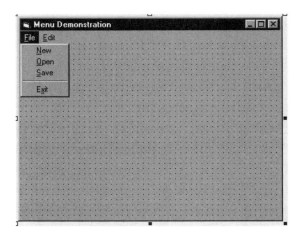

Creating Shortcut Keys

Shortcut keys allow the user to access a menu function using a single key or key combination. Typical examples of shortcut keys are Ctrl+X for Cut, Ctrl+C for Copy, and the Delete key. Visual Basic allows you to create shortcut keys for your menu items. A given shortcut key can only be used for a single item, limiting you to about 75 shortcut keys you can use in your program.

As with access keys, there are a number of shortcut keys with which users are already familiar. Some of the more common shortcut keys are identified in the following list:

Function	Shortcut Key
New	Ctrl+N
Open	Ctrl+O
Print	Ctrl+P
Save	Ctrl+S
Cut	Ctrl+X
Copy	Ctrl+C
Paste	Ctrl+V
Find	Ctrl+F
Replace	Ctrl+H
Undo	Ctrl+Z
Redo	Ctrl+Y
Help	F1

To create shortcut keys in your program, open the Menu Editor, select the item to which you want to assign a shortcut key, then select the specific key combination from the Shortcut Key list in the Menu Editor. As you select a key, the shortcut is automatically shown in the caption of the menu (though it is not part of the Caption property.) Exercise 4.3 shows you how to add shortcut keys to the menu created in the previous exercises. Figure 4.7 shows the completed menu.

EXERCISE 4.3

Creating Shortcut Keys

1. Open the Menu Editor.

2. Select the New item, then select the Ctrl+N key combination from the Shortcut drop-down list.

3. Repeat this process for the Open, Save, Cut, Copy, and Paste items, using the key combinations identified in the list above.

4. Click OK to save the menu changes.

FIGURE 4.7

The menu with Shortcut keys added

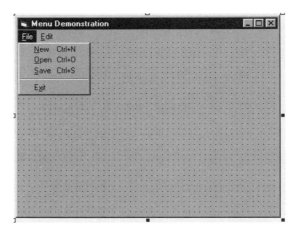

 If you assign the same shortcut key to more than one menu item, the Menu Editor will report an error and will not let you exit.

Other Menu Item Properties

The preceding sections discussed how to create a menu. In the creation of the menu, you used the Caption, Name, and Shortcut properties of the menu item object. Several other properties control the appearance or behavior of menu items.

- **Checked**   Indicates whether a check mark appears in front of the item in the menu list. This is typically used to indicate that an option of your program is turned on or off.

- **Enabled**   Determines whether the user can access the functions of the menu. If the Enabled property is set to False, the user can see the menu, but cannot click on it or access any of the sub-level menus.

- **Visible**   Determines whether the menu can be seen by the user. If the Visible property of a menu is set to false, the item and any sub-level menus are not shown in the menu.

- **WindowList**   Determines whether this menu item will be used to keep up with MDI child windows in an MDI application. This property is usually only set for a top-level menu item. Only one item in a menu may have this property set to true.

- **Index**   The index of a menu item within a control array. The items of the menu control array all have the same Name property, but different indexes. The use of indexes allows you to create additional items at run time. Indexes are discussed more in a later section.

- **HelpContextID**   Identifies the help topic that will be accessed if F1 is pressed while the menu item is selected.

Pop-Up Menus

Pop-up menus are becoming more and more commonplace in today's generation of applications. The pop-up menu is designed to provide you with the menu options you need for dealing with a particular object. Therefore, many applications support a variety of pop-up menus. For example, in Visual Basic, if you right-click the mouse on the menu bar, you will see a pop-up menu that allows you to show or hide toolbars. Right-click on the form, and you will see a menu that provides quick access to the Menu Editor, code window, and properties of the form. Right-click on a control, and you will get a menu that contains editing functions and access to the control's properties. As you can see, there is help where you need it, when you need it, and exactly what you need (or at least what the developers think you need).

Microsoft
Exam
Objective

Add a pop-up menu to an application.

Because users have come to expect to be able to use pop-up menus, you will probably want to include them in your programs. Fortunately, Visual Basic makes this easy to do. Implementing a pop-up menu requires only two steps, creating the actual menu in the Menu Editor and activating the menu using the PopupMenu method of a form.

Creating the Menu for the Pop-Up

Creating the actual menu of a pop-up menu is the same as creating a top-level menu for the main menu bar. You use the Menu Editor to define the Caption and Name properties for each item you want to appear in the pop-up menu. You can even include separator bars and access keys if you want. Exercise 4.4 shows you how to create a Format pop-up menu that you might use to change the properties of text in a text box.

EXERCISE 4.4

Creating a Pop-Up Menu

1. Open the Menu Editor on the form where you will want the pop-up menu to appear.

2. Move to a new item at the bottom of the menu list, and make sure that the item is not indented.

3. Create the top-level item for the Format menu using Format as the Caption property and popFormat as the Name property. This name is the one that will be used later to display the popup menu.

4. Set the Visible property of the menu item to False, then accept the item by pressing Enter.

5. Create the several font items in the menu using the following Name and Caption properties.

Caption	Name
&Bold	fmtBold
&Italic	fmtItalic
&Underline	fmtUnder

6. Create a separator bar by placing a hyphen in the Caption property and typing **popSep1** in the Name property.

EXERCISE 4.4 (CONTINUED)

7. Add several items for controlling the color of text using the following Name and Caption properties.

Caption	Name
Blac&k	fmtBlack
B&lue	fmtBlue
&Red	fmtRed
&Green	fmtGreen

8. Close the Menu Editor.

9. Open the code window of the form to add code to each of the menu items. Because the items are not visible on the form's menu, you will have to select each item by name in the object list of the code window to edit the code for the item. Place the code shown in Figure 4.8 in the menu items for the pop-up menu. The ActiveControl object is used to identify the control being operated on by the code, because these menu items could be called from a number of locations.

FIGURE 4.8

Code for handling the pop-up menu items

```
fmtGreen                          Click

    Option Explicit

    Private Sub fmtBlack_Click()
    Me.ActiveControl.ForeColor = vbBlack
    End Sub

    Private Sub fmtBlue_Click()
    Me.ActiveControl.ForeColor = vbBlue
    End Sub

    Private Sub fmtBold_Click()
    With Me.ActiveControl
        .Font.Bold = Not .Font.Bold
    End With
    End Sub

    Private Sub fmtGreen_Click()
    Me.ActiveControl.ForeColor = vbGreen
    End Sub

    Private Sub fmtItalic_Click()
    With Me.ActiveControl
        .Font.Italic = Not .Font.Italic
    End With
    End Sub

    Private Sub fmtRed_Click()
    Me.ActiveControl.ForeColor = vbRed
    End Sub
```

The pop-up menu can be derived from one of the items on the main menu or from a sub-level menu. However, it is typical not to show the pop-up menu as part of the main menu. Also, a pop-up menu can have sub-level menus, but this too is atypical.

Exercise 4.4 showed how to create the menu. To activate the menu, you will need to place code in an event of the form or another control. This is discussed in the following section.

Activating the Pop-Up Menu

After the menu is created, it is a simple matter to activate the pop-up menu. The PopupMenu method of the form object handles all the work for you. You simply specify the method and the name of the menu item that is the top level item of popup. For example, to activate the pop-up menu created in Exercise 4.4, you would use the following code:

```
Me.PopupMenu popFormat
```

The real key to activating a pop-up menu is choosing the event that will be used to show the menu. Typically, users expect to see the pop-up menu in response to the click of the right mouse button. You can handle this by placing the code for the PopupMenu method in the MouseDown or MouseUp event of the form or a control. These events tell you which button was clicked, whether a shift key was pressed, and the location of the mouse pointer when the button was pressed. Knowing the location allows you to activate separate menus for different areas of the form. The following code would be used to display the Format menu when the user clicks the right mouse button on any open area of the form. Figure 4.9 shows you how the menu would appear.

```
Private Sub Form_MouseDown(Button As Integer, Shift As _
Integer, X As Single, Y As Single)
If Button = vbRightButton Then
    Me.PopupMenu popFormat
End If
End Sub
```

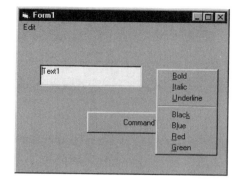

FIGURE 4.9

A pop-up menu
activated by a right
mouse button

Modifying Menus at Run-Time

Creating a menu in the Menu Editor is not the end of the menu management process. You will often need to modify the appearance of your menu while your program is running. There are several types of modifications that you may need to make in your program, such as:

- Changing the Caption of a menu item

- Changing the Checked property to indicate that an option has been turned on or off

- Showing or hiding a particular menu based on the state of the program

Microsoft ✓ ***Exam*** ***Objective***   **Dynamically modify the appearance of a menu.**

All these modifications involve changing one of the properties of the menu items. The properties that you will typically change in modifying a menu are:

- Caption

- Checked

- Enabled

- Visible

Several of the other properties of the menu items cannot be changed at run-time: Name, WindowList, Index, Shortcut, and NegotiatePosition properties.

While the HelpContextID property can be changed at run-time, this is not typically done.

Changing Menu Item Properties

Changing any of the available menu item properties is simply a matter of assigning the property a new value using an assignment statement. The following program line illustrates this for the Checked property of a menu item:

```
frmMain.toolOption1.Checked = True
```

Let's take a look first at the properties which affect the appearance of the menu item. The Caption property contains the text that is displayed in the menu. This text identifies to the user what the menu item is supposed to do. By changing the Caption property, you can change the text that the user sees. Also, because access keys are defined by placing an & in front of a letter in the Caption property, you can change the access key for a menu item by changing the Caption.

Most of the time you will not want to change the Caption property of a menu item as this will lead to confusion on the part of the user. However, one very beneficial use of this capability is in handling menu setup for programs that may be used by people with different languages. In such a case, you may wish to read the Caption properties for the menu items from a resource file and load the caption appropriate to the user's language. The following code shows how you would set the captions for the main menu of an international program.

```
mnuDatabase.Caption = TextLoad(209)
datExport.Caption = TextLoad(210)
datImport.Caption = TextLoad(211)
datUtility.Caption = TextLoad(212)
utlRepair.Caption = TextLoad(213)
utlCompact.Caption = TextLoad(214)
mnuSecurity.Caption = TextLoad(215)
```

```
secUser.Caption = TextLoad(216)
secConfig.Caption = TextLoad(217)
secChange.Caption = TextLoad(218)
secLogon.Caption = TextLoad(219)
```

TextLoad is a function that determines the selected language and pulls the appropriate resource string from the Resource file.

The other visual property of the menu item is the Checked property. This property determines whether a check mark appears next to the menu item. Figure 4.10 shows how the play level options of a game are indicated using the Checked property. The Click event of each of the option menu items contains code to turn on its own Checked property and turn off the Checked property of all the other options.

FIGURE 4.10

Game options are indicated with a check mark.

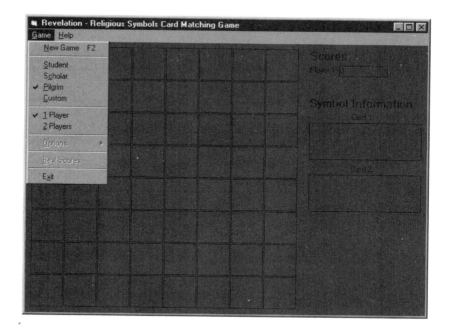

```
gamStudent.Checked = False
gamScholar.Checked = False
gamPilgrim.Checked = False
gamCustom.Checked = True
```

Enabling Menu Items in Response to Program State

The other common modification of a menu at run-time is to show and hide or enable and disable menu items as the status of the program changes. Consider a word processor. When you first start most word processors, only the File and Help menus are visible, because all the other menus are related to working with a document. If there are no documents open, you do not want the user to have access to them. As soon as you open a document, however, all the other menus appear. You can set up this type of behavior by setting the Visible property of one or more top-level menus.

Word processors also provide a good example of dynamically changing the Enabled property of menu items. If you examine the Edit menu, you will find that the Cut and Copy options are disabled (indicated by the grayed appearance) unless text is selected in the document. Likewise, the Paste option is disabled if there is no text in the Clipboard. The Cut and Copy options are enabled when the user highlights text, that is, changes the status of the program.

Like changing the Caption or Checked properties, a simple assignment statement changes the Enabled and Visible properties. Exercise 4.5 shows you how to create an MDI application that shows and hides the Edit and Window menus depending on whether documents are open. Figures 4.11 and 4.12 show the different views of the menus.

EXERCISE 4.5

Displaying Menu Items in Response to Program Changes

1. Start a new project.

2. Add an MDI form to the project by selecting the Add MDI Form item from the Project menu. Name the form mdiMain.

3. Select the Properties item from the Project menu to bring up the Properties dialog box. Change the StartupForm property to mdiMain. Then close the dialog box.

4. Open the Menu Editor for the MDI form. Create a File menu with the name mnuFile for the top-level item. The menu should contain items for New, Open, Save, and Exit. (Refer back to Exercise 4.1 for a refresher on creating a menu.)

5. Create an Edit menu with the name mnuEdit for the top-level item. Set the Visible property of the mnuEdit item to False. Add the following sub-level items to the menu: Cut, Copy, Paste.

6. Create a Window menu with the name mnuWindow. As with the Edit menu, set the Visible property to False. Add the following sub-level items to the menu: Arrange, Tile.

7. Create a Help menu with the name mnuHelp. Make sure its Visible property is set to True. Add sub-level items for Topics and About.

8. Switch to the standard form in the project. Change the Name of the form to frmNotepad and set the MDIChild property to True.

9. Add a text box to the form. Set the Name property to txtNotepad and set the MultiLine property to True.

10. In the Resize event of the frmNotepad form, add the following code to make the text box fill the form:

```
txtNotepad.Top = 0
txtNotepad.Left = 0
txtNotepad.Height = Me.ScaleHeight
txtNotepad.Width = Me.ScaleWidth
```

11. Switch back to the code window of the mdiMain form. This is where we start adding the code to display menus. In the filNew menu item (you may have named yours slightly differently), add the following code. This code creates a new instance of the frmNotepad form, changes the Caption of the form, and displays the Edit and Window menus, ensuring that the menus are displayed whenever a document is open.

```
Dim frmVar As frmNotepad
Set frmVar = New frmNotepad
frmVar.Caption = "Document" & Trim(Str(iNumNewForms))
iNumNewForms = iNumNewForms + 1
frmVar.Show
mdiMain.mnuEdit.Visible = True
mdiMain.mnuWindow.Visible = True
```

12. The final step is to add code to hide the menus when the last document is closed. To handle this, place code in the Unload event of frmNotepad. The following code checks the number of open forms using the Count property of the Forms collection. If the count is two, implying that only the MDI form and the current document are open, the code sets the Visible property of the mnuEdit and mnuWindow menu items to False in order to hide them.

```
If Forms.Count = 2 Then
    mdiMain.mnuEdit.Visible = False
    mdiMain.mnuWindow.Visible = False
End If
```

13. You can now run the program and watch how the menus are displayed and hidden as documents are opened or closed. The complete source for this project is included on the CD as ModMenu.vbp.

FIGURE 4.11

Only two menus are visible when no documents are open.

FIGURE   4.12

Other menus are shown
when the documents
are open.

Adding Menu Items at Run-Time

Microsoft ✓ *Exam Objective*	**Create an application that adds and deletes menus at run-time.**

Changing the properties of menu items is not the only way you can modify your menus at run-time. You can also dynamically add menu items to the menu. There are actually two ways to add menu items at run-time:

- You can have the program automatically add the names of MDI child forms to the menu to allow the user to quickly switch back and forth between documents.

- You can use a menu item control array to add your own menu items to the menu.

Adding Items for MDI Child Forms

Adding the MDI child forms to a menu is very simple. You basically have to do three things:

1. Create an MDI application.

2. Create a menu on the MDI form.

3. Set the WindowList property of one of your menu items to True.

In Exercise 4.6, we modify the program created in Exercise 4.5 to add the capability of keeping up with the child documents in the form.

EXERCISE 4.6

Keeping a List of MDI Child Forms

1. Open the project you created in Exercise 4.5. You can also use the Mod-Menu.vbp code included on the MCSD VB5 companion CD-ROM.

2. Move to the MDI form and open the Menu Editor.

3. Find the mnuWindow item and set the WindowList property to True.

4. Run your program and observe the effect of the WindowList property. Figure 4.13 shows the menu with several child windows added. Notice that the WindowList automatically adds a separator bar and adds the new items at the bottom of the menu.

FIGURE 4.13

MDI child windows listed in a menu

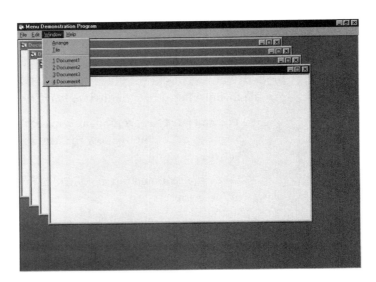

Using Menu Item Arrays

The other method of adding menu items at run-time is to use a menu control array. An array is a group of menu items with the same Name property and different values of the Index property. One of the most common uses of a menu control array is to keep a list of the most recently used files for a program. You can see this in programs like Word or Excel where the File menu contains the names of the last three or four files that you accessed.

While creating menu items on the fly is not difficult, there are several steps that you must follow:

- You must create at least one element of the array in the Menu Editor. Visual Basic does not allow you to create a control array completely in code. It only allows you to add or remove items from the array.

- You must use the Load command to add items to the array. To use the Load command, you must specify the name of the control array and the index of the element to be added. This index value must be unique. To ensure that the index value is unique, you can use the Ubound property of an array to determine the index of the last element and add 1 to that value.

- You must use the Unload command to remove elements from the array. To use the Unload command, you must again specify the name of the control array and the index to be removed.

- You can only write code in a single procedure to handle all the elements of the array. The Click event is tied to the Name of the array; however, the index information is passed to the procedure, and you can use a Select statement to handle separate tasks for individual array elements.

To give you an understanding of adding and removing menu array items, Exercise 4.7 adds some files to a most-recently-used list in the File menu. The menu also has an option to clear the list. This exercise shows the process of removing array items. The code in the exercise uses made-up names for the files. To use this in an actual program, you would want to read the names of the files from the Registry or an INI file.

EXERCISE 4.7

Adding and Removing Menu Items

1. Open the project created in Exercises 4.5 and 4.6.

2. Open the Menu Editor for the MDI form.

3. Insert a menu item ahead of the Exit item. Set the Caption property of the item to Clear MRU List, set the Name property to filMRUFile, and set the Index property to 0, creating the first element of the menu item array. Also, set the Visible property to False. You don't want the Clear List item to be visible if there are no items in the MRU list.

4. Insert a separator bar between the filMRUFile and filExit items. Set its Visible property to False.

5. Close the Menu Editor.

6. In the Load event of the MDI form, place the following code. This code creates the additional items of the MRU list and assigns the Caption property of the menu item. When an item is loaded from code, it is not visible to the user. Therefore, you need to set the Visible property to True. The code also displays the first element of the list and the separator bar.

```
Dim I As Integer, J As Integer
iNumNewForms = 1
For I = 1 To 4
    J = filMRUFile.UBound + 1
    Load filMRUFile(J)
    filMRUFile(J).Caption = Trim(Str(I)) & " - File" & _
Trim(Str(I))
    filMRUFile(J).Visible = True
Next I
filMRUFile(0).Visible = True
filSep2.Visible = True
```

7. In the Click event of the filMRUFile item, place the following code. This code unloads all the menu items except the first one and hides the first element of the array and the separator bar. This code is only activated if the user selects the Clear List item which has the index value of 0.

```
Dim I As Integer
If Index = 0 Then
    If filMRUFile.UBound > 0 Then
        For I = filMRUFile.UBound To 1 Step -1
            Unload filMRUFile(I)
```

```
        Next I
      End If
    End If
    filMRUFile(0).Visible = False
    filSep2.Visible = False
```

8. Run the program. Figure 4.14 shows the menu after the items are added to the File menu. Figure 4.15 shows the menu after the list is cleared.

FIGURE 4.14

Items added to a menu item array

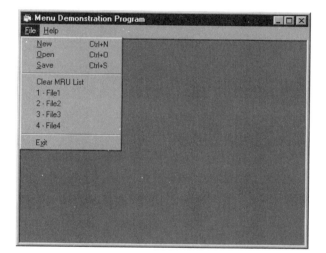

WARNING

In step 7 of Exercise 4.7, make sure you do not try to remove the original element of the menu array. Any elements of a control array that are created at design time cannot be removed with the Unload command. Attempting to do so will generate an error.

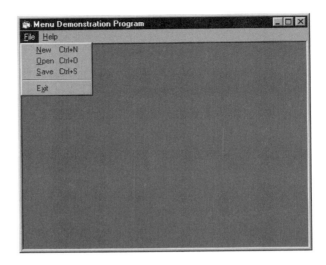

Summary

This chapter has provided you with a refresher in the creation of menus in your Visual Basic programs. You have seen how to create a main program menu and how to create and activate a pop-up menu. You have also seen how to change the appearance of the menu on the fly. Finally, you saw how you can use control arrays and the WindowList property to add and remove menu items while your program is running.

The Microsoft exam will test you on your ability to create menus, both main menus and pop-up menus. If you go through all the exercises presented in this chapter and understand the concepts behind them, you should have no problem with the following objectives:

- Add a menu interface to an application.

- Dynamically modify the appearance of a menu.

- Add a pop-up menu to an application.

- Create an application that adds and deletes menus at run time.

Review Questions

1. What properties are required to be specified for a menu item? Check all that apply.

   A. Checked

   B. Index

   C. Name

   D. Caption

2. How can you enable the user to access a menu item from the keyboard? Check all that apply.

   A. Define an access key by designating a letter in the Caption property.

   B. Define a shortcut key by setting the Shortcut property in the menu editor.

   C. The user can press F10 and use the cursor keys.

   D. Define a shortcut key by setting the Shortcut property in code.

3. All of the following statements about access keys are true except:

   A. You can have items on different menus with the same access key.

   B. The user must hold the Alt key while pressing the access key to open a top level menu.

   C. All top level menus must have a unique access key.

   D. Access keys are indicated to the user by an underlined letter in the caption.

4. Which of the following statements about pop-up menus are true? Check all that apply.

   A. A pop-up menu can be used as a main menu.

   B. A pop-up menu can be created from a sub-level menu.

   C. A pop-up menu can have multiple levels.

   D. A pop-up menu can be activated by any event the developer chooses.

5. Which form event would you use to activate a pop-up menu when the user clicks the right mouse button? Check all that apply.

    A. MouseDown

    B. Click

    C. MouseUp

    D. MouseMove

6. What is the proper syntax for activating the pop-up menu fmtFormat?

    A. Popup = fmtFormat

    B. Set PopupMenu = fmtFormat

    C. Me.PopupMenu fmtFormat

    D. Me.PopupMenu = fmtFormat

7. Which menu item properties can you change at run-time?

    A. WindowList, Caption, Index, Checked

    B. Name, Caption, Index

    C. Caption, Checked, Enabled, Visible

    D. Caption, Checked, Visible, Shortcut

8. What does the WindowList property do?

    A. Maintains a list of all forms in your program

    B. Allows you to add menu items to any menu at run-time

    C. Keeps a list of MDI child windows

    D. Works with any application

9. What is the proper syntax for adding an item to a menu array?

    A. filMRUFile.AddItem 1

    B. filMRUFile.Load 1

    C. Load filMRUFile(1)

    D. Load New filMRUFile

10. Which command is used to remove an item from a menu array?

A. Delete

B. RemoveItem

C. Drop

D. Unload

11. When removing items from the menu array, which of the following statements is true?

A. You can remove all elements of the array.

B. You must keep at least one element of the array.

C. You cannot remove any elements that were created at design time.

CHAPTER

5

Advanced Design Features

Microsoft Exam Objectives Covered in This Chapter:

- Implement drag-and-drop operations within the Microsoft Windows Shell.

- Create an application that adds and deletes controls at run-time.

In Chapter 1, you saw how forms and controls are used to make up the visual interface of the programs that you create. In that chapter, all the controls were placed on the form while you were in the design environment, and remained in the same position unless your program explicitly moved the controls through the use of program code. While this is how most of your programs will be developed, there are two advanced techniques that you can add to your programs to make them even more powerful. These two techniques are drag-and-drop features, and adding or deleting controls on-the-fly.

The first technique, implementing drag-and-drop operations, allows you to provide your users with several capabilities:

- Users can edit information on the form by using drag-and-drop to move information between the controls on a form.

- Users can move information between your program and other applications through the use of drag-and-drop.

- Users can be allowed to customize the appearance of a form to suit their needs.

Your programs can provide any or all of these capabilities, depending on the code you write.

The second technique, adding and deleting controls, allows you to create more powerful forms that change in response to the conditions of the program or to handle different tasks with the same form. Several examples of this flexibility include:

- Creating an enhanced message box that allows more command button options and user input.

- Creating a data entry form that works with any data source.

- Adding menu options (remember that menu items are a simple control) such as a list of recently used files.

This chapter will discuss both of these techniques in detail and will, of course, tell you how learning these techniques fits in with the objectives of the Visual Basic Certification exam.

Creating Drag-and-Drop Applications

Microsoft ✓ *Exam* *Objective*	**Implement drag-and-drop operations within the Microsoft Windows Shell.**

Drag-and-drop operations are one of the key features of a Graphical User Interface (GUI). With drag-and-drop, GUI applications allow the user to move text or other information with simple mouse clicks and movements instead of requiring a series of keystrokes. Additionally, many applications allow you to handle file processing tasks the same way; that is, you can drag a file to an application to open it, or drag it to the Recycle bin to delete the file.

In fact, there are two different varieties of drag-and-drop operations:

- Operations where the source of information and the target of the operation are in the same application.

- Operations where the source of information is outside the target application.

You can create both these types of applications with Visual Basic. The first type of drag-and-drop has been a part of Visual Basic for several versions. The second type of drag-and-drop is known as OLE drag-and-drop and is new to Visual Basic version 5. Fortunately, the two types of drag-and-drop operations are closely related and share a number of the same basic concepts. This section will cover first drag-and-drop within an application, then OLE drag-and-drop.

Drag-and-Drop within the Application

You are probably quite familiar with drag-and-drop operations within an application. This is the process by which you move text in a word processor, or move cells in a spreadsheet as shown in Figure 5.1. For most applications, drag-and-drop performs two basic sets of operations:

- **Cut and Paste**   You highlight information, then drag it to a new location.

- **Copy and Paste**   You highlight the information, then hold the Ctrl key while clicking and dragging the mouse. This, of course, places a copy of the original information at the location where you release the mouse button.

FIGURE 5.1

Typical drag-and-drop operations in a spreadsheet

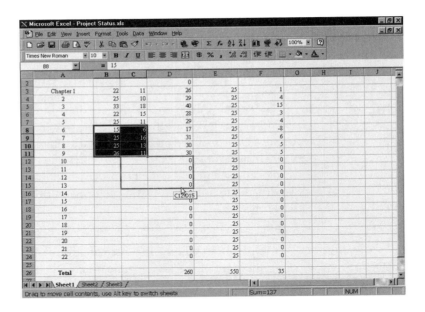

These are the typical behaviors of drag-and-drop; however, you are not limited to implementing only these features in your applications because Visual Basic does not handle the full implementation of drag-and-drop. It merely provides a framework of properties, methods, and events that enable you to create the drag-and-drop operations in your programs.

There are two required steps to enabling drag-and-drop operations in your programs. You must:

- Specify the control that is to be the source for the operation.

- Write program code for the control that is to be the target of the operation.

In all drag-and-drop operations, you will place code in the DragDrop event of the control that is the destination of the drop. This code can be as simple as copying the text from the source control, or you can perform other, more complex operations such as moving a control on the form. The DragDrop event is triggered when the user releases the mouse button after dragging a control.

Forms also have a DragDrop event that enables you to make the form the target of the drag-and-drop operation.

In setting up the source control of the drag-and-drop operation, you can choose to have drag-and-drop initiated automatically or manually. Both of these techniques will be illustrated below.

Using the Automatic Drag-and-Drop Features

Automatic mode is the easiest way to enable drag-and-drop operations in your program. In automatic mode, you do not have to write any code to start the operation; drag-and-drop is started as soon as the user clicks the mouse button on the source control. Of course, the operation only progresses if the user holds the button down and drags the control; however, the user will see the drag icon appear whenever the mouse button is clicked. The only coding that you have to do for automatic drag-and-drop is the code in the DragDrop event of the target control that takes the desired action for the operation.

Setting Up the Source Control   To set up a source control for automatic drag-and-drop operations, you simply have to set the DragMode property to automatic. You can set the property in either the design mode or at runtime. Setting the property at runtime is accomplished using a statement like the following:

```
TxtDragSource.DragMode = vbAutomatic
```

While the DragMode property is the only one that you need to set for automatic drag-and-drop operations, you will probably also want to set the DragIcon property of the source control. This property determines the icon that is displayed while the control is being dragged. If you do not set a value for this property, the outline of the control is used to indicate that a drag-and-drop operation is in progress, as shown in Figure 5.2.

F I G U R E   5.2

The outline of the control is the default indication of a drag-and-drop operation.

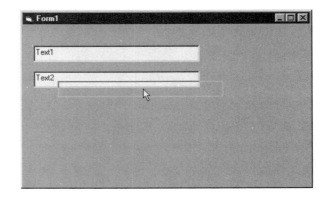

You can set the DragIcon property in design mode by choosing an icon from a selection dialog box. If you choose to set the DragIcon property at run-time, you will need to set the property to the picture property of another control, or use the LoadPicture method to retrieve an icon from a file. Both of these methods are shown in the following code:

```
txtSource.DragIcon = imgDragDrop.Picture
sPicture = \DevStudio\Icons\Drag1pg.ico
txtSource.DragIcon = LoadPicture(sPicture)
```

Enabling the Target Control   To enable the target control, you need to place code in the DragDrop event of the control or the form that will be receiving the source control. This code can be anything you want. The DragDrop event of a form or control passes three parameters to the event procedure:

- **Source**   A reference to the control that is the source of the drag-and-drop operation. The Source variable is used to access the properties and methods of the source control.

- **X**   The horizontal position of the mouse pointer within the target control or form at the time that the control was dropped.

- **Y**   The vertical position of the mouse pointer within the target control or form at the time that the control was dropped.

Exercise 5.1 illustrates how to enable drag-and-drop operations to allow the user to move a control around on a form.

EXERCISE 5.1

Creating an Automatic Drag-and-Drop Program

1. Start a new project.

2. Add a text box to the form and name it **txtSource**.

3. Set the DragMode property of the text box to Automatic.

4. Set the DragIcon property of the text box to the icon of your choice.

5. Place the following code in the DragDrop method of the form:

```
Source.Top = Y
Source.Left = X
```

6. Now run the program and try moving the text box on the form. Figure 5.3 shows the drag-and-drop operation in progress.

FIGURE 5.3

Dragging a text box around on the form

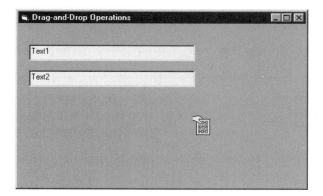

 The control remains in its original position until the drop portion of the operation is completed.

Manually Controlling the Drag-and-Drop Features

Using the automatic feature is the easiest way to handle drag-and-drop operations, but automatic drag-and-drop is not desirable for many applications. For example, you may want to create an application that allows the user to select multiple items from a list before dragging the selections to another control. Or you may want to allow the user to drag only a portion of the text in a text control. Either of these options is easier to implement using the manual setting of the DragMode property.

Creating the Source Control The key to handling manual drag-and-drop operations is to invoke the Drag method of the designated source control at the appropriate time. The Drag method uses an action parameter to determine what action to take when the method is called. This parameter has three possible values, represented by internal Visual Basic constants. These values are:

- **vbCancel** Cancels the drag operation.

- **vbBeginDrag** Starts the drag-and-drop operation.

- **vbEndDrag** Ends the drag operation and fires the DragDrop event of the target control.

The general syntax of the Drag method specifies the source control, the method itself, and the action to be taken, as shown in the following code:

```
txtSource.Drag vbBeginDrag
```

The only action that you are required to specify is the vbBeginDrag. This action is required to start the drag-and-drop operation. If you do not use the vbEndDrag in your program, the drag-and-drop operation is automatically ended when the user releases the mouse button.

Exercise 5.2 shows you how to set up the source control for an application that allows the user to drag selected text from a text box to another control.

EXERCISE 5.2

Creating the Source Control for Manual Drag-and-Drop Operations

1. Start a new project.

2. Add a text box to the form, and name the control **txtSource**.

3. Set the DragMode property of the text box to Manual (the default value) and set the DragIcon property to the icon of your choice.

4. In the MouseDown event of the text box, place the following code:

```
If Shift = vbShiftMask Then
    txtSource.Drag vbBeginDrag
End If
```

The code in Exercise 5.2 only invokes the Drag method if the user is holding down the Shift key as the mouse button is clicked, to allow the user to use normal mouse movements to highlight selected text. Without the use of the Shift key, the drag-and-drop operation would be started as soon as the user clicked the text box, which would interfere with other mouse operations. Another technique for handling this problem is through the use of a timer to impose a slight delay before the drag operation is started.

Creating the Target Control   The setup of the target control in a manual drag-and-drop operation is the same as in an automatic operation. You write the code to handle the dropped control in the DragDrop event of the control that you want to be the target of the operation. Exercise 5.3 shows how to create the target control for moving the text from the source control created in Exercise 5.2.

Accepting the Source Control in a Manual Operation

1. Open the project created in Exercise 5.2.

2. Add a second text box to the form, and name the control **txtTarget**.

3. Place the following code in the DragDrop event of the txtTarget control. This code replaces the contents of the target text box with the contents of the source text box.

```
txtTarget.Text = Source.Text
Source.Text = ""
```

4. Run the program and test out the drag-and-drop operations. Remember to hold down the Shift key when you click the source control.

Showing Where the Drop Can Occur   As you have probably seen in many applications, drag-and-drop operations usually indicate where the drop can occur by changing the icon when the cursor is passed over a valid target control. In your programs, you can accomplish this by setting the DragIcon property of the source control to different images. To handle this operation for different locations and controls on your form you will need to make use of the DragOver event.

Like the DragDrop event, the DragOver event passes a reference to the source control, and the horizontal and vertical position of the mouse cursor. The DragOver event also passes a parameter called State that lets you know whether the mouse is being dragged into, over, or out of the current control. These states are specified by Visual Basic constants as follows:

- **vbEnter**   The source control is being dragged into the area defined by the target control.

- **vbOver**   The source control is being dragged over the area defined by the target control.

- **vbLeave**   The source control is being dragged out of the area defined by the target control.

By making use of these values, you can change the DragIcon of a control to indicate that a drop is allowed when the source is first dragged over the target control. You can also change the DragIcon back to its original state when the source control is dragged out of the target area. Exercise 5.4 illustrates how to accomplish this.

EXERCISE 5.4

Indicating Where a Drop Is Allowed on the Form

1. Start with the project created in Exercises 5.2 and 5.3.

2. Add an image control to the form and name it **imgDrag**. This control will be used to store the icon prior to the drag entering the target control. Set the Visible property of this image control to False.

3. Place the following code in the DragOver event of the txtTarget control:

```
Select Case State
    Case vbEnter
        imgDrag.Picture = Source.DragIcon
        Source.DragIcon = LoadPicture( _
"D:\DevStudio\DragDrop\Drop1Pg.ico")
    Case vbLeave
        Source.DragIcon = imgDrag.Picture
End Select
```

4. Run the program and watch how the cursor changes as the dragged control is moved into and out of the target control. Figure 5.4 shows the appearance of the dragged control over the target.

FIGURE 5.4

Indicating the drop zone

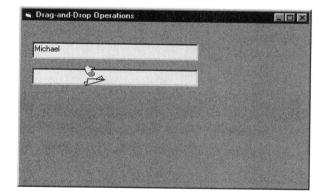

Instead of having to load pictures from a file, you may want to use several image controls on the form to store the icons used for the different values of the DragIcon that your program will need.

These exercises have shown you how to create a simple drag-and-drop program. The DragDrop.vbp project on the CD shows you a little more sophisticated version of this program. The DragDrop project handles copying the entire contents of the source control or only the selected text. The project also distinguishes between the use of the Shift key and the Ctrl key to determine whether to perform cut-and-paste or copy-and-paste operations.

Drag-and-Drop between Applications

Microsoft *Exam* *Objective*	**Implement drag-and-drop operations within the Microsoft Windows shell.**

Until version 5 came out, the capability to provide drag-and-drop between your Visual Basic program and other Windows programs was limited to using the OLE container control or writing a lot of code and using API functions. With version 5 of Visual Basic, however, implementing drag-and-drop between applications is as easy as implementing it within the application. Visual Basic now provides a series of OLE drag-and-drop properties, methods, and events that make it possible to use many of Visual Basic's controls as either the source or target of a drag-and-drop operation between applications.

Understanding OLE Drag-and-Drop

OLE drag-and-drop is implemented in Visual Basic through the use of three properties, three events, and one method, as summarized below:

- **OLEDragMode**   This property determines whether the drag-and-drop operation starts automatically from a source control or has to be initiated manually using the OLEDrag method.

- **OLEDropAllowed**   This property is used with OLE container controls to determine whether the control can be the target of an OLE drag-and-drop operation.

- **OLEDropMode**   This property determines if the control can be the target of an OLE drag-and-drop operation and, if so, how the operation is handled. The OLEDropMode property has three possible settings:

    - **vbOLEDropNone**   Specifies that the control cannot be the target of an OLE drag-and-drop operation. This is the default setting.

    - **vbOLEDropManual**   Specifies that the control can be a target control. In this mode, the OLEDragDrop event is fired when the source is dropped on the target control. The program code of the OLEDragDrop event then handles the desired drop operation.

    - **vbOLEDropAutomatic**   Specifies that the control can be a drop target. In automatic mode, the control handles the drop operation if the source contains data that the control can understand. For example, a text box could automatically accept selected text dragged from a word processor.

- **OLEDragDrop**   This event is fired when a source is dropped onto a target control and the OLEDropMode property of the control is set to manual. This event allows you to handle the drop operation with your custom code.

- **OLEDragOver**   This event is fired as an OLE source is dragged over a form or control. Typically this event would be used to set the cursor image to inform the user whether a drop is allowed at the current location. This event is almost identical to the DragOver event.

- **OLEGiveFeedback**   This event follows the OLEDragOver event and allows you to provide feedback to the user about the state of the drag-and-drop operation.

- **OLEDrag**   This method is used to manually initiate an OLE drag-and-drop operation.

Using these properties, methods, and events, you can easily create applications that are the target and/or the source of OLE drag-and-drop operations.

Creating a Target Application

Creating a target for an OLE drag-and-drop operation can be accomplished in either of two ways: you can set up a control for automatic operation, or you can write the code in the OLEDragDrop event to handle the operation manually. The simplest way, and the one most commonly used, is the automatic mode. Setting up a target in this manner is explained in Exercise 5.5.

EXERCISE 5.5

Creating an OLE Drag-and-Drop Target

1. Start a new project.

2. Add a large text box to the form and name it **txtMemo**. Set the MultiLine property of the control to True, and set the ScrollBars property of the control to Vertical.

3. Set the OLEDropMode property of the text box to Automatic.

4. Run your program and try dragging selected text from Notepad or a word processor to the text box. Figure 5.5 shows this process in action.

FIGURE 5.5

Your program as an OLE drag-and-drop target

The drag-and-drop operations work the same as they do for any other applications. A simple drag performs a Cut-and-Paste operation. Holding the Ctrl key while you click and drag performs a Copy-and-Paste operation.

Creating a Source Application

Of course, for many applications, you will need to make your program the source of a drag-and-drop operation as well as a target. Fortunately, creating a source control is as easy as creating a target control. Exercise 5.6 shows you how to add the capability of dragging information out of your program to the program created in Exercise 5.5.

EXERCISE 5.6

Creating an OLE Drag-and-Drop Source

1. Start with the project you created in Exercise 5.5.

2. Using the same text box that was the target of the drag-and-drop operations, set its OLEDragMode property to automatic.

3. Run the program again and try dragging information from the text box to another program. You will have to highlight text in the text box, as the automatic OLE drag-and-drop operations work with the selected text, not the entire contents of the text box. This operation is illustrated in Figure 5.6.

F I G U R E   5.6

Using your program as an OLE drag-and-drop source

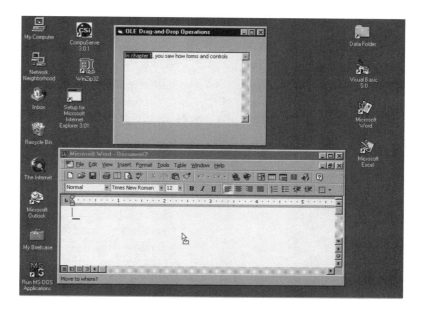

OLE Drag-and-Drop within Your Application

The OLE drag-and-drop operations are not limited to moving information between applications, they can also be used within an application. You can use these operations in place of the standard drag-and-drop operations within your program. For example, you can set up text boxes as OLE sources and targets to allow drag-and-drop operations between them. Using the OLE method allows you to create a completely automatic drag-and-drop operation instead of having to write the code for the drop as required in standard drag-and-drop operations. Also, you can make the same control a source and target of OLE drag-and-drop operations. For a text box, this allows you to implement drag-and-drop editing by simply setting two properties. Follow the steps in Exercise 5.7 to create an editor with drag-and-drop editing.

EXERCISE 5.7

Using OLE Drag-and-Drop within Your Application

1. Start a new project.

2. Add a large text box to the form and name it **txtEditor**. Set the MultiLine property of the control to True and set the ScrollBars property of the control to Vertical.

3. Set the OLEDragMode property to automatic.

4. Set the OLEDropMode property to automatic.

5. Run the program. You can enter any text in the box. Then, highlight the text and use drag-and-drop to move it around. As you move the highlighted text, you will see that the cursor indicates the position within the text box where the drop will occur. This editor is illustrated in Figure 5.7.

F I G U R E 5.7

A drag-and-drop editor implemented with just two properties

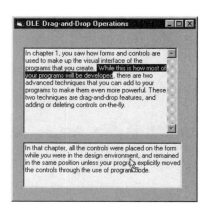

Changing Forms on the Fly

You know that you can change the appearance of your forms by changing the properties of the form at run-time, allowing you to change fonts, colors, backgrounds, and so on. You can also change the properties of controls on the forms to respond to differing needs. But how can you make the forms be really responsive to the needs of your program? For example, is there a way to create a dialog box that allows multiple inputs as well as a variable number of user-defined command buttons?

The answer is yes. One method of creating this type of dialog box is to add a whole bunch of text boxes and command buttons to the form, then display only the ones you need. This approach, however, has two main drawbacks—it wastes resources and it imposes an upper limit on the number of controls your form can display (you can only display as many controls as you create during design mode). The better approach to responsive forms is to create and delete controls as necessary.

Unlike some other languages, Visual Basic does not allow you to create a new control at run-time completely from scratch. You can, however, create a control array (or multiple control arrays) and add elements to the control array at run-time. You can also, of course, remove elements from the control array. Two great uses of this technique are enhanced message boxes (as shown in Figure 5.8) and generic data entry forms (as shown in Figure 5.9). These types of forms allow you to use a single form to perform multiple tasks throughout your program and are discussed later in the chapter. First, however, the basics of control arrays.

FIGURE 5.8

An enhanced message box lets the program specify the number and captions of the command buttons.

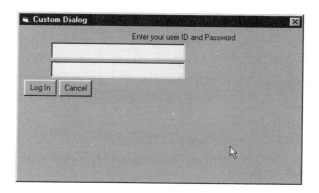

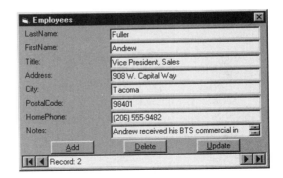

Microsoft ✓ Exam Objective

Create an Application That Adds and Deletes Controls at Run-Time.

Control Array Basics

At the simplest level, a control array is a group of controls of the same type that all have the same name. For example, you can have a series of text boxes on your form, all having the name txtMember. Because all the controls have the same name you must have another means of identifying the individual control, the Index property of the control. As you add members to the control array, you must specify a unique value for the Index property of the control. No two controls in an array may have the same value of the Index property.

WARNING

It is possible to specify non-consecutive numbers for the Index property of controls; however, this can lead to a variety of errors in your programs and is not recommended.

Using control arrays has several important programming benefits:

- You can easily set the property values of all the controls in the array using a For loop.

- You can write code in a single event to handle a number of controls.

- You can add controls to the array and remove them from the array at run-time. (This is the most important benefit for this discussion.)

Creating Control Arrays

The first step in using control arrays is to create the array. Whether you create the entire control array in the design mode or add and remove controls while your program is running, you must create at least one element of the control array at design time. It is not possible to change a single control into an element of a control array while the program is running.

After the initial element of the array is created, you can add more controls to the array by placing them on the form in design mode or by using the Load statement to add the controls at run time. We will look at both methods in this section.

Each control in a control array can have its own set of properties. The only property that the members of an array are required to have in common is the Name property.

Setting up the First Element of an Array   Two methods are available for starting a control array in the design environment. You can create the first element of the array specifically by assigning a value to the Index property of the control, or you can let Visual Basic create the array for you by copying a second instance of the control onto the form

Both methods of starting a control array begin by drawing a control on your form. After drawing the control, you give it a name and set other various properties of the control. To have Visual Basic start the control array for you, you select the control on the form, copy it to the clipboard, then paste the copy back onto the form. At this point, you are presented with a dialog box (shown in Figure 5.10) that asks you if you want to create a control array. If you answer yes, the second copy of the control will be added to the form using the same name as your base control. In addition, the Index properties of both controls will be set to 0 and 1 respectively. You now have a control array on your form with two elements.

F I G U R E   5.10

Visual Basic asks if you want to create a control array.

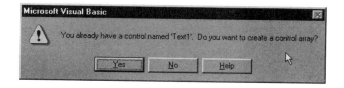

With the second method, you can only create the first element of the control array. After setting up the control, choose the Index property and set its value to 0. You now have a control array with a single element. You typically use this method if you intend to create additional controls at run-time.

Control arrays should be zero-based, meaning that the first element of the array should have an Index property value of 0. Additional elements of the array should be numbered consecutively. While Visual Basic does not enforce this, failing to follow this convention can result in problems in your programs.

Adding Controls to the Array at Design Time   After you have created the initial element(s) of the array, you can add more controls to the array while you are in the design mode. You can do this in either of two methods:

- Copy an existing element of the control array and paste it to a new location on the form.

- Create a new control of the same type as the control array and set the Name property to the name of the control array.

With either of these methods, each new control will automatically have the Index property set to the next sequential number in the array. Which method you use is a matter of personal choice.

Adding Controls to the Array at Run-Time   One of the great benefits of control arrays is that you can add more elements to the array while your program is running, allowing you to modify your forms to handle different situations on the fly. You add controls to the array using the Load statement. This statement specifies the name of the array and the element number that you wish to add. The Load statement is illustrated in the following code:

```
iUpper = txtMember.UBound + 1
Load txtMember(iUpper)
```

The code makes use of one of the properties of the array to determine the last element number of the array. The four properties of a control array are:

- **Count**   Specifies the total number of elements in the array.

- **Item**   Returns a reference to a specific element of the array.

- **LBound**   Specifies the lowest index value of the array.

- **UBound**   Specifies the highest index value of the array.

When adding new elements to a control array at run-time, you must meet two specific criteria or an error will occur. These criteria are:

- The control array must already exist. You cannot create the initial element of the array at run-time.

- The Index value specified in the Load statement must be unique.

After you have created the control using the Load statement, you can set its properties like any other control on your form. One important property to set is the Visible property. Like the Load statement used with a form, the Load statement for a control array only creates the array element in memory. It does not display the control on the form. Therefore, you must set the Visible property to True to have the control seen by the user.

The properties of the newly added control are based on the properties of the first element of the array. Therefore, you will also need to adjust the position of the new element, or it will be displayed in the same location as another control.

Removing Controls from the Array   Removing controls from the array is very similar to adding the controls. Removing controls makes use of the Unload statement. With this statement, you specify the name of the array and the element to be removed. For an element to be removed from a control array without error, it must meet two criteria:

- The Index value must be valid.

- The element must be one that was added at run-time. You cannot remove a control array element that was added in the design environment.

The Unload statement is illustrated in the following code:

```
iUpper = txtMember.UBound
Unload txtMember(iUpper)
```

Writing Code for Control Arrays

Controls that are part of a control array respond to all the same events and use the same methods as individual controls of the same type. One difference between how the events of a control array element are triggered and how you work with the methods and properties of a control array element is that the element must be identified by the Index property.

For invoking the methods or modifying the properties of a control array element, you simply place the Index value in parentheses immediately following the name of the control, telling your program that you are working with the individual control, not the array itself. The following code shows how to move a control and make it visible:

```
txtMember(iUpper).Visible = True
txtMember(iUpper).Top = txtMember(iUpper - 1).Top + 500
```

WARNING　You cannot set the property values of multiple controls by using just the control name, without the Index value. Each control is a separate entity and its properties must be set individually.

For the events of a control, the event procedure declaration is modified to pass the Index value of the particular control in which the event occurred. This modification is handled automatically by Visual Basic. The modified declaration is shown in the following code:

```
Private Sub txtMember_Change(Index As Integer)

End Sub
```

What this means is that you have only one procedure for a particular event for all the elements of a control array. Using this procedure, you can take the same actions for each control in the array, or use a Select statement or If statements to check the Index value and take appropriate actions for specific elements of the array.

Creating an Enhanced Message Box

If you are familiar with Visual Basic's MsgBox and InputBox dialog boxes, you know that while they are very useful, they are limited in what they can do. For example, you cannot specify your own captions for the command buttons, nor can you use command button sets other than the defaults. Also, the InputBox is limited to only a single input value. However, you can create your own enhanced message/input box dialog box using control arrays. With this custom dialog box, you can determine how many command buttons to use, what the captions of the buttons are, and how many input values you want to handle. Exercise 5.8 shows you how to create the skeleton of an enhanced message dialog box. The complete project is included on the CD as Custom.vbp. Feel free to use and customize this dialog box to suit your needs.

EXERCISE 5.8

Creating a Custom Dialog Box with Control Arrays

1. Start a new project.

2. Add a second form to the project and name the new form **frmCustom**.

3. Set the BorderStyle property of frmCustom to Fixed Dialog.

4. (The next several steps deal with the frmCustom form.) Add a label control to the form and name it **lblMessage**. Set the Alignment property of the label to Center.

5. Add a text box to the form and name it **txtInput**. Set the Index property of the control to 0 to create the first element of the text box array used for inputs. Set the Visible property of the control to False.

6. Add a command button to the form and name it **cmdSelection**. Set the Index property of the command button to 0 to create the command button control array.

This completes the initial set up of the visual portion of the custom dialog box. The rest of the work of the dialog box is in the code for adding and displaying additional elements of the control arrays.

7. Add a Property Let Procedure to the form and name it **Buttons**. This procedure will handle the creation of the command buttons and setting their captions. You can start the Property Let procedure by choosing the Add Procedure item from the Tools menu.

8. The code for the procedure is too long to include all of it here. The idea of the procedure is to parse a string of button names, and create the buttons for the dialog box. The names are passed to the procedure as a single string, with the individual names separated by a vertical bar (|). The key part of the procedure that loads the additional command buttons is shown below:

```
iMaxWidth = 0
For I = 0 To iBtnCount - 1
    iTextWidth = Me.TextWidth(sCommandText(I))
    If iTextWidth > iMaxWidth Then iMaxWidth = iTextWidth
    If I > 0 Then Load cmdSelection(I)
    cmdSelection(I).Caption = sCommandText(I)
Next I
```

9. Create another Property Let procedure named **Input**. This procedure will be used to tell the dialog box the number of input text boxes to be displayed on the form. The code for the procedure loads additional text box controls if needed. The code for the Input procedure is:

```
Dim I As Integer
If iNumInputs > 0 Then
    txtInput(0).Visible = True
    If iNumInputs > 1 Then
        For I = 1 To iNumInputs - 1
            Load txtInput(I)
        Next I
    End If
End If
```

10. Create one final Property Let procedure to handle passing the message information to the dialog box. This procedure should be named **Message** and contains the following code:

```
lblMessage.Caption = sMessageText
```

11. The final programming for the dialog box consists of code in the Activate event of the form. This code sets the Visible property of all the appropriate controls and sets the positions of the controls on the form. The code for the Activate event is:

```
Dim I As Integer, iBtnWidth As Integer, iBtnCount As _
Integer
Dim iInputCount As Integer
iBtnCount = cmdSelection.Count
iBtnWidth = cmdSelection(0).Width
Me.Width = iBtnCount * (iBtnWidth + 60) + 240
If Me.Width < 6450 Then Me.Width = 6450

lblMessage.Width = Me.Width - 480
lblMessage.WordWrap = True
lblMessage.AutoSize = True
```

```
If txtInput(0).Visible = True Then
    iInputCount = txtInput.UBound
    For I = 0 To iInputCount
        txtInput(I).Top = Message.Top + _
lblMessage.Height + I * (txtInput(0) _
.Height + 60) + 60
        txtInput(I).Left = lblMessage.Left
        txtInput(I).Visible = True
    Next I
Else
    iInputCount = 0
End If


For I = 0 To iBtnCount - 1
    cmdSelection(I).Left = I * (iBtnWidth + 60) + 120
    If iInputCount = 0 Then
        cmdSelection(I).Top = lblMessage.Top + _
lblMessage.Height + 60
    Else
        cmdSelection(I).Top = txtInput(iInputCount).Top +
txtInput(iInputCount).Height + 60
    End If
    cmdSelection(I).Visible = True
Next I
```

12. After setting up the dialog box, you need to call the dialog box from another form. Return to the original form of your project and add a command button to the form. In the click event of the command button, you need to place code to set the properties of the enhanced message dialog box and show the form. An example of this code is shown below. The results of the code can be seen in Figure 5.11.

```
frmCustom.Message = "Enter your user ID and Password"
frmCustom.Inputs = 2
frmCustom.Buttons = "Log In|Cancel"
frmCustom.Show
```

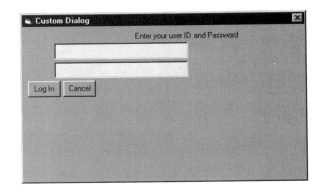

FIGURE 5.11

A sample of the dialog box you can create with the enhanced message dialog box.

Summary

This chapter has shown you how to implement two advanced design features—drag-and-drop operations and adding and deleting controls during run-time. A knowledge of these two features will help you meet two of the Microsoft certification exam objectives:

- Implement drag-and-drop operations within the Microsoft Windows shell.

- Create an application that adds and deletes controls at run time.

If you are still not comfortable with the concepts covered in this chapter, review each of the exercises to help solidify those ideas. Then it is time to put your knowledge to the test. The following questions are typical of those you might find on the Visual Basic Certification exam.

Review Questions

1. Which of the following properties determines how a control initiates a drag-and-drop operation?

A. DragMode

B. DragIcon

C. DropMode

D. Drag

2. What event can be used to indicate where a control in a standard drag-and-drop operation can be dropped?

   A. DragDrop

   B. DragOver

   C. OLEDragDrop

   D. Drag

3. A single control can be used as which of the following? Check all that apply.

   A. The source of a standard drag-and-drop operation

   B. The target of a drag-and-drop operation

   C. The source of an OLE drag-and-drop operation

   D. The target of an OLE drag-and-drop operation.

4. OLE drag-and-drop can be used for which of the following purposes?

   A. Transferring information between applications.

   B. Transferring information within an application.

   C. Both A and B.

   D. OLE drag-and-drop can only be used with OLE container controls.

5. Which of the following are advantages of OLE drag-and-drop over standard drag-and-drop operations? Check all that apply.

   A. Allows you to move information between applications

   B. Allows you to drag multiple controls simultaneously

   C. Allows automatic handling of the drop operation

   D. Allows you to use the same control as the source and target of an operation

6. How do you create the first element of a control array?

   A. Set the Index property of a control while in the design mode.

   B. Use the Load statement to load a control with an index value of 0.

   C. Use the CreateObject statement to create an instance of the control.

   D. Change the Index property of a single control at run time.

7. Which of the following restrictions apply to adding a control to a control array at run-time? Check all that apply.

   A. The form must be visible when the control is added.

   B. The control array must already exist.

   C. The Index value must be the next sequential number after the upper bound of the array.

   D. The Index of the new control must be unique.

8. Which of the following are properties of a control array?

   A. Count, Type, and Name

   B. Count, Item, LBound, and UBound

   C. Count, Name, and Index

   D. Index, LBound, and UBound

9. Which of the following statements can be used to change the value of a property in an element of a control array?

   A. txtMember.Top = 120

   B. txtMember(0).Top = 120

   C. txtMember.0.Top = 120

   D. txtMember0.Top = 120

10. What are the restrictions on removing controls from a control array? Check all that apply.

A. The control must have been created in design mode.

B. The control must have been added at run time.

C. The control element must exist.

D. All data must have been unloaded from the control.

11. Which of the following statements removes a control from an array?

A. Delete txtMember(5)

B. Remove txtMember(5)

C. Unload txtMember(5)

D. Load txtMember(5) vbRemove

CHAPTER

6

Working with Collections

Have you ever had a collection of something, like coins, dolls, baseball cards, or even bottle caps? If you have had collections, and probably even if you haven't, you know that a collection is a group of similar objects that are organized in some fashion. If you are a serious collector, you probably change the contents of your collection through buying, selling, and trading items. You also probably have a method of uniquely identifying each individual item in your collection.

Well, if you have even a basic understanding of the concept of collections, you are well on your way to understanding collections in Visual Basic. Visual Basic uses collections to provide an organizing structure for groups of related objects. In this chapter, we will look first at collections in general, then at a few of the specific collections that are used in Visual Basic. There are two collections that we will pay particular attention to—the Forms collection and the Controls collection. These two collections are of particular interest in the book because they are the subject of two of the certification exam objectives.

Understanding Collections

Collections in Visual Basic are similar to the collections that you find in real life. Visual Basic collections provide a means of organizing a group of related objects. Some examples of collections used in Visual Basic are:

- Forms
- Controls
- Database Fields
- TreeView Nodes
- ListView Items
- Toolbar Buttons

In addition to these built-in collections, Visual Basic enables you to create your own collections through the use of the Collection object. A Collection object can be used to create and manage a group of class objects, or a collection can be used as a way to store data instead of using an array.

While a collection will typically be used to handle a group of related items, Visual Basic does not require that all the members of a collection be the same. For example, you can have collection members that are different data types.

All collections in Visual Basic have the following attributes in common:

- You can add items to the collection.

- You can remove items from the collection.

- There is a method to refer to specific members of the collection.

- The Collection object keeps a count of the number of members in the collection.

While the mechanics of handling these attributes may differ (for example, forms are added to the Forms collection using the Load statement instead of the Add method), all collections in Visual Basic support these attributes.

Using the Methods of a Collection

The Collection object in Visual Basic has three methods that you can use to manage the collection of objects: Add, Item, and Remove. These methods are responsible for adding and removing elements from the collection and retrieving individual items from the collection. If you need additional methods, you can create a wrapper class around the Collection object and create new methods by using sub procedures. While this particular task is beyond the scope of this book, you can learn more about creating classes and their methods in Chapter 7, "Creating Classes in a Program." In this section, we will focus on the built-in methods of the Collection object.

Using the Add Method

Most of the collections in Visual Basic, whether they are built-in collections or ones you create with the Collection object, use the Add method to allow you to add members to the collection. The syntax of the Add method specifies the name of the collection, the method itself, and the item to be added to the collection. In addition, several optional parameters are often included:

- **Key**   Defines a unique character string used to identify the item.

- **Before**   Specifies that the new item should be placed in the collection in front of the item identified in the Before parameter.

- **After**   Specifies that the new item should be placed in the collection behind the item identified in the After parameter.

The use of the Before or After parameters allows you to handle the sorting of items in a collection as they are added, which can be a powerful method of storing information in a sorted order. The Before and After parameters can be specified as either the numeric index of an item or as the Key value of the item. The following code shows how the Add method is used to place a new item in a collection.

```
Dim colUsers As New Collection
Dim oUser As New cUser
oUser.UserID = 101
colUsers.Add oUser, "mmckelvy"
```

Using the Remove Method

Of course, if you can add items to a collection, you need to be able to remove items from the collection as well. With the Collection object, this is handled by the Remove method. To use the Remove method you simply specify the name of the collection, the method name, and the index of the item to be removed. The index used by the Remove method must be a numeric index, it cannot be the value of the Key property of the item in the collection. The following code shows the use of the Remove method.

```
colUsers.Remove 1
```

WARNING   An error will occur if the item specified in the Remove method does not exist in the collection.

Using the Item Method

The final method of a collection is the Item method. This method is used to access a specific item from the collection. The Item method is used in all collections, including the Forms and Controls collections, making it the only method that is truly common to all collections. The Item method is also the default method of any collection, meaning that if you do not specify the name of a method, the Item method is assumed. The Item method can be used in one of two manners—using the Index of an item or using the Key value of an item.

Referencing an object by its index   One use of the Item method is to retrieve a specific item of a collection using its Index value. When used in this manner, the index is enclosed in parentheses following the method name, as show in the following code:

```
Debug.Print colUsers.Item(1).UserID
```

Also, because the Item method is the default method of a collection, the following code could be used to achieve the same results:

```
Debug.Print colUsers(1).UserID
```

Because it is difficult to keep track of the index location of a number of items, the Index value is typically used with the Item method to process all the members of a collection. This can be accomplished through the use of a For loop as illustrated below:

```
Dim I As Integer
For I = 1 To colUsers.Count
    Debug.Print colUsers.Item(I).UserID
Next I
```

Using the Key property of an Object   The other way to use the Item method is with the Key value of the items in the collection. The use of the Key value makes it easier to retrieve a specific item in the collection because these string identifiers are not dependent on the location of the item in the collection. When the Key value is used, your program must pass a string (either in the form of a literal string or a string variable) to the Item method. The following code shows the use of both a variable and a literal string:

```
colUsers.Item("mmckelvy").UserID = 101
Dim sItemKey As String
sItemKey = "mmckelvy"
colUsers.Item(sItemKey).UserID = 101
```

Also, as with specifying the Index value, you can leave out the Item method name in referencing an item with the Key value, as shown below:

```
colUsers("mmckelvy").UserID = 101
Dim sItemKey As String
sItemKey = "mmckelvy"
colUsers(sItemKey).UserID = 101
```

Working with the Properties of a Collection

As stated earlier, the Collection object only has a single property, the Count property. The purpose of the Count property is to tell you how many items are in the collection. This property is read-only, meaning that you can retrieve the value of the property, but you cannot set a new value. The value of the Count property changes as items are added or removed from the collection using the Add and Remove methods. The following code shows the use of the Count property to run a loop which populates a list box with the names of all current users in a program.

```
Dim I As Integer
lstUsers.Clear
For I = 1 To colUsers.Count
    lstUsers.AddItem colUsers(I).Name
Next I
```

Working with the Forms Collection

<table>
<tr><td>*Microsoft* ✔ *Exam* *Objective*</td><td>**Use the Forms Collection.**</td></tr>
</table>

The Forms collection is a specialized collection created by Visual Basic. The collection contains a reference to each form in a program that is loaded in memory, including all MDI child forms, an MDI parent form, and any standard forms that may be loaded at a given time. It is important to note that the Forms collection contains only a list of loaded forms, not a list of all forms that you may have defined in your program. For example, Figure 6.1 shows the Project window indicating all the forms defined for a program. However, the Forms collection would only list the loaded forms, as shown in Figure 6.2.

There are several primary uses of the Forms collection in a program. The most common uses are:

- Changing the common properties (such as Font) of all loaded forms.

- Determining if a specific form is loaded.

- Ensuring that all forms are explicitly closed prior to exiting a program.

FIGURE 6.1

Many forms can be defined for a program.

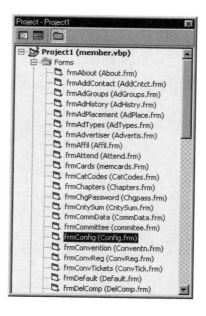

FIGURE 6.2

Only loaded forms are part of the collection.

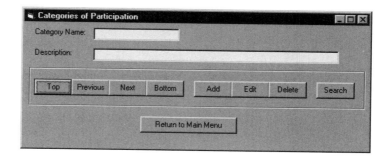

Working with the Collection Methods

In the general discussion of collections, we stated that a Collection object used the Add and Remove methods to change the membership of the collection. The Forms collection does not support the Add or Remove method, but instead uses the Load and Unload statements to control the membership of the Forms collection. To illustrate this, Exercise 6.1 walks you through the creation of a simple program for checking the names of loaded forms.

EXERCISE 6.1

Determining Which Forms Are Loaded

1. Start a new project.

2. Add a second form to the project.

3. On the second form place a single command button that unloads the form. Place the command "Unload Me" in the Click event of the command button.

4. On the first form of the project place two command buttons named cmdForm2 and cmdListForms.

5. In the Click event of the cmdForm2 button, place the code "Form2.Show." This code will load and display the second form.

6. The cmdListForms button will be used to display the names of the currently loaded forms in the program. In the Click event of the cmdListForms button, place the following code:

```
Dim I As Integer
For I = 0 To Forms.Count - 1
    Debug.Print Forms(I).Name
Next I
```

7. Run the program and check the list of forms as you start the program, after you show Form2, and after you unload Form2. Figure 6.3 shows the output in the Debug window when both forms are loaded.

FIGURE 6.3

Displaying a list of loaded forms

The Forms collection is zero-based, meaning that the first index value of the forms collection is 0 instead of 1, as is the case for many other collections.

WARNING   When using collections, whether built-in or user-created, be sure to test the operation of the collection for the item with an index value of 0. Performing this check is the only way to avoid program errors because some collections are zero-based, and others are one-based.

Using the For...Each Loop

As you saw in Exercise 6.1, you can reference the properties of a form by specifying the item in the Forms collection and specifying the property of interest. You can retrieve or set property values for any item in the Forms collection. As shown in the exercise, you can use the index value to access a specific item, or you can use the Key value as explained in the general discussion of collections. The Key value for a form is simply its Name property.

Exercise 6.1 showed the use of a For loop to display the names of all the forms. This form of the loop used *I* as an index variable and used the Count property of the Forms collection to determine how many times to run through the loop. While this is one way to write the code, there is another preferred method. There is a special case of the For loop that is used for handling collections, the For...Each loop. This type of loop performs the enclosed code once for every item in a collection. The following code shows how the loop to display the form names would appear if a For...Each loop were used:

```
Dim tstForm As Form
For Each tstForm In Forms
    Debug.Print tstForm.Name
Next tstForm
```

Exercise 6.2 shows you how to use a For...Each loop to change the background color of all loaded forms.

EXERCISE 6.2

Using a For...Each Loop with the Forms Collection

1. Starting with the project created in Exercise 6.1, add another command button to Form1 of the project. Name the command button **cmdColor** and set the Caption to Change Colors.

2. Add the following code to the Click event of the cmdColor button.

```
Dim tstForm As Form
For Each tstForm In Forms
tstForm.BackColor = vbGreen
Next tstForm
```

3. Run the code, load the second form, and click the Change Colors button.

This method can be used to set a specific property of all the loaded forms in a program. You can also use the For…Each loop in an exit routine to ensure that all loaded forms are closed before you ultimately exit the program. The following code shows how this is handled:

```
Dim frmLoaded As Form
On Error Resume Next
'Unload forms
For Each frmLoaded In Forms
    If frmLoaded.Name <> "frmMain" Then
        Unload frmLoaded
    End If
Next I
Unload frmMain
'Exit the program
End
```

If you only want to work with some of the forms in the Forms collection, do not use the For…Each loop.

Working with the Controls Collection

Microsoft ✓ *Exam* *Objective*

Use the Controls Collection.

The Controls collection is very similar to the Forms collection. The Controls collection provides you with access to each of the controls that are on a particular form. As you might guess, this implies that there is a Controls collection for each form in your program. Like the Forms collection, the Controls collection does not support the Add and Remove methods. Instead, controls are added to or removed from the collection using the Load and Unload statements.

Like all collections, the Controls collection implements the Item method (the default method) to allow you to access a specific control, and the Count property, which tells you how many controls are in the collection and, therefore, are on the given form. Some typical uses of the Controls collection are:

- Modifying a specific property of every control, such as Font or ForeColor.

- Working with database routines to create a generic data access form or data display routine.

- Showing or hiding specific types or groups of controls.

Understanding the Difference between Control Arrays and the Controls Collection

Because both control arrays and the Controls collection work with groups of controls and because both use an Index value to reference a specific control, you might think that there are similarities between the Controls collection and a control array. However, these are two different entities with two very different purposes. The following lists of characteristics should help you understand the differences between these two entities.

Control Arrays

A control array has the following characteristics:

- All elements of a control array are the same type of control.

- All elements of a control array have the same name.

- The Index properties of the control are set when the control is created and cannot be changed.

- The elements of a control array share the same set of event procedures.

- In code, an element of the control array is referenced by its name and Index property as shown in the following example:

```
cmdNavigation(1).Caption = "First Record"
```

Controls Collection

By contrast, the Controls collection has the following characteristics:

- The Controls collection contains all controls on a form regardless of type.

- The Index value of an element in the collection is determined by when the control was added to the form.

- The elements of the Controls collection can have different names.

- There are no events associated with the Controls collection.

- In code, a member of the Controls collection is referenced by its index within the collection as shown in the following example:

```
Debug.Print Controls(0).Name
```

You do not have to specify a form name when using the Controls collection. If you do not specify a name, the form containing the code is assumed to be the active form.

Making Global Changes to Controls

Like the Forms collection (and other collections), the elements of the Controls collection can be manipulated with a For loop or a For…Each loop, making it easy to change the controls on a form, for example, selecting a font to be used for all the controls. Once the user selects the font, a loop can be used to implement the requested change. This technique is illustrated in Exercise 6.3.

EXERCISE 6.3

Making Changes to All the Controls on a Form

1. Start a new project.

2. Add a series of labels, text boxes, and command buttons to the form to create a data entry form like the one shown in Figure 6.4.

3. Add another command button to the form and name it **cmdChangeText**. Set the Caption of the control to Change Text.

EXERCISE 6.3 (CONTINUED)

4. Add the following code to the Click event of the cmdChangeText button:

```
Dim chgControl As Control
For Each chgControl In Controls
    chgControl.Font.Name = "Times New Roman"
    chgControl.Font.Bold = True
Next chgControl
```

5. Run the program and see what happens when you click the Change Text button. The new appearance is shown in Figure 6.5.

F I G U R E 6.4

Initial appearance of the data entry form

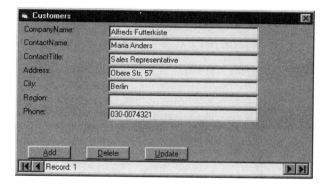

F I G U R E 6.5

The data entry form after the font change

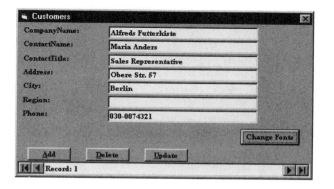

Typically, you would want to use a common dialog to allow the user to select any font, then use the selected font as the new value for the Font properties of the controls.

Working with Specific Controls in the Collection

One thing you might have noticed about Exercise 6.3 is that you only used labels, text boxes, and command buttons, controls that all have a Font property. You probably know that not all controls have a Font property. If you had such a control on your form, the code in Exercise 6.3 would still try to set a value for the property, but would, of course, cause an error. Obviously, we need a way to determine what type of control is being accessed and process or skip the control accordingly.

Determining the Type of a Control

The first step in handling multiple types of controls within the Controls collection is determining the type of control that is being accessed. You determine the type of control using the TypeOf clause. This statement is used as part of a conditional statement as illustrated in the following code:

```
If TypeOf chgControl Is CommandButton Then
    chgControl.Font.Name = "Times New Roman"
    chgControl.Font.Bold = True
End If
```

Each control in Visual Basic has a type constant that can be used with the TypeOf keyword to determine if the current control is of a particular type. You can access a list of these constants in the VB library using the Object Browser, as shown in Figure 6.6.

FIGURE 6.6

Control types displayed
in the Object Browser

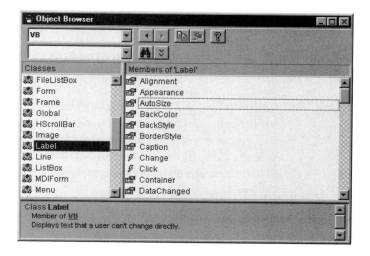

Setting the Properties of Specific Control Groups

Using the TypeOf clause and a series of If statements, you can handle processing for any type of controls. The following code modifies the code presented in Exercise 6.3 to change the Font of text boxes and labels, but leaves other controls alone.

```
Dim chgControl As Control
For Each chgControl In Controls
    If TypeOf chgControl Is TextBox Then
        chgControl.Font.Name = "Times New Roman"
        chgControl.Font.Bold = True
    ElseIf TypeOf chgControl Is Label Then
        chgControl.Font.Name = "Times New Roman"
    End If
Next chgControl
```

Using code such as this will eliminate possible errors from trying to set properties for controls that do not support them, such as setting a Font property for a Line control.

Summary

This chapter has taught you about how collections work. You have learned about the three methods common to most collections—Add, Item, and Remove methods. You also learned that all collections have a Count property that tells you how many elements are in the collection. In addition to the general information about collections, you learned how to use the Forms collection to manipulate the loaded forms in a program and how to use the Controls collection to work with all the controls on a specific form. This information will help you meet two of the Microsoft Certification exam objectives:

- Use the Forms collection
- Use the Controls collection

Review Questions

1. What three methods does the Collection object support?

   A. Load, Unload, Count

   B. Add, Remove, Item

   C. Add, Delete, Index

   D. Add, Remove, Sort

2. What method is common to all collections?

   A. Add

   B. Delete

   C. Remove

   D. Item

3. What is the only property supported by a collection?

   A. Name

   B. Index

   C. Count

   D. Type

4. What does the Forms collection contain?

A. A list of all forms in a project

B. A list of all currently loaded forms

C. A list of all visible forms

D. All the child forms of an MDI application

5. How are forms added to the Forms collection?

A. By adding a form to a project

B. Using the Add method of the Forms collection

C. Using the Load statement

D. Activating a form

6. What does the Controls collection contain?

A. A list of all controls on a form

B. A list of all the controls used by your program

C. A list of visible controls

D. The names of all control arrays on the form

7. What are key differences between the Controls collection and a control array? Check all that apply.

A. A control array contains controls of a single type, the Controls collection contains controls of many types.

B. The elements of a control array all have the same name, the elements of the Controls collection can have different names.

C. The elements of a control array do not share any events, the elements of the Controls collection do.

D. A control array is simply a subset of the Controls collection.

8. How do you determine what the type of a control is?

    A. Use the IsType function.

    B. Use the TypeOf clause.

    C. Check the Type property of the control.

    D. Use the prefix of the control name.

9. Why is it important to determine the type of a control?

    A. Process only controls that support a given property.

    B. Some control types are not included in the Controls collection.

    C. For programmer information only.

10. What are the two methods of referencing an element of a collection?

    A. Using the name value or the index value

    B. Using the index value and the Key value

    C. Using the name and type

    D. Using name and Key

11. Which of the following code segments can be used to process all the controls on a form? Check all that apply.

    A.
```
For I = 0 To Controls.Count
    Debug.Print Controls(I).Name
Next I
```

    B.
```
For All Controls
    Debug.Print Control.Name
Next Control
```

    C.
```
For Each chgControl In Controls
    Debug.Print chgControl.Name
Next chgControl
```

    D.
```
For I = 0 To Controls.UBound
    Debug.Print Controls.Item(I).Name
Next I
```

CHAPTER

7

Creating Classes in a Program

The ability to create classes in Visual Basic is probably one of the most significant capabilities that has been added to the language. While the first implementation of classes was introduced in version 4, enhancements have been made in version 5 of Visual Basic that make classes easier to create and use, and more flexible. Being able to create classes in Visual Basic laid the groundwork for creating reusable components, creating ActiveX servers, and creating ActiveX controls. A good understanding of classes is essential to most Visual Basic projects. This importance is also reflected in the Microsoft Certification exam objectives which list five specific criteria directly related to classes:

- Create and use a class module.

- Add properties to a class.

- Add methods to a class.

- Identify whether a class should be public or private.

- Declare properties and methods as Friend.

- Set the value of the Instancing property.

In this chapter, we will cover the basics of what a class is, then proceed to the creation of classes. You will see how to create the properties, methods, and events of a class. You will also learn how and when to use the Friend declaration and the purpose of the different settings of the Instancing Property. In addition, you will see how the Class Builder Add-in can be used to make creating and managing classes in your Visual Basic project easier. Finally, you will see how to actually create an instance of a class and use it in your program.

Understanding Classes in Visual Basic

Visual Basic has always been based on the principals of Object-Oriented Programming (OOP). When Visual Basic was originally developed, it allowed the programmer to create programs using pre-defined objects, forms and controls. These objects implemented the OOP principals of encapsulation and polymorphism, but not the principal of inheritance. When classes were introduced to Visual Basic, programmers could create their own objects for use in a program. Like the controls built into Visual Basic, the objects created with a class allow the encapsulation of data and procedures, and allow polymorphism, but do not allow inheritance. Also, the classes created in Visual Basic are code-only objects; they do not have a visual component.

ActiveX controls extend the class model by providing a visual interface to a class so you can use it as a control. ActiveX controls will be discussed in detail in Chapter 15, "Integrating Visual Basic with the Internet." However, the techniques you learn here about creating classes will be quite valuable in the creation of ActiveX controls.

Having the capability to create classes makes it easier for a programmer to create reusable objects that can be used within the current project, in other projects by the same programmer, and by other programmers in a multi-programmer work environment. The use of classes allows a program segment, whether it is a business rule or an interface to programming tasks, to be created once, then easily reused through the properties and methods of the class.

As stated earlier, Visual Basic does not support inheritance between objects. For each class you create, you have to code all the methods and properties that will be a part of the class. This lack of true inheritance causes a great debate over whether Visual Basic is object-oriented or simply object-based. You are left to form your own opinions about this. However, even without true inheritance, classes in Visual Basic provide a powerful tool for creating applications.

Understanding Object Oriented Programming

Three major principals you will hear quite often in the discussion of Object Oriented Programming are:

- **Encapsulation** The data about an object and the code used to manipulate the data are contained within the object itself. The data is stored as the properties of the object and the code as the methods of the object. Encapsulation allows the object data and code to stand alone, independent of outside routines.

- **Polymorphism** Relates to the use of the same method name in various objects, for example, a Print method for the printer, a form, or a picture box. While the name of the method is the same, the actual code for the method in each object can be different. However, because the code for the method is encapsulated in the object, each object knows how to perform the correct task when the method is called.

- **Inheritance** Allows one object to be created based on the properties and methods of another object. With inheritance, it is not necessary to code the properties and methods that are derived from the parent object. You only have to code new or modified properties and methods.

Uses of Classes

You can use classes in your Visual Basic applications in a number of ways. These uses can typically be categorized as one of three general types—creation of business objects, encapsulation of programming functions, and Visual Basic add-ins. No matter how you use the classes, you create reusable components that make your programs easier to create and easier to maintain.

Creating business objects is probably the most common use of classes in a program. A typical example of a business object is an employee object. When you create an employee object, you create properties that describe the employee, such as name, social security number, department, job level, pay grade, home address, and so on. You also create methods to handle tasks associated with the employee, such as retrieving the employee data from a database, saving changed data to the database, and calculating payroll for the employee. By placing all this information in a class, you make it easier to use the information in your program. More importantly, you can compile the class as an ActiveX exe or dll server to allow other programmers to use the same properties and methods. Using classes to create business objects allows you to set up business rules and information in one location, instead of having each program repeat the code. This is the basis of multi-tier, client/server programming.

We will look at creating ActiveX servers in detail in Chapter 12, "Creating ActiveX Client Applications."

Classes can also be used to encapsulate program functions for easy use. For example, you might want to encapsulate the code that opens a recordset in a class module. This class can handle the actual operations and include all the necessary error handling functions. You can then use the class each time you need to create a recordset. Using this approach eliminates the need to repeat the code and the error handling routines in multiple locations throughout your program. Another advantage of this approach is that if you change databases, requiring a change in the access methods, you only need to change the code in a single location, making code maintenance much easier.

Finally, you can use classes to create add-ins, which extend the functionality of Visual Basic itself. Add-ins can be used to build program wizards or to provide functions such as automatic comments at the beginning of a form or module.

Creating a Class

Microsoft ✓ *Exam* *Objective*	**Create and use a class module.**

Part of how you create a class depends on its intended use. You may do a few things differently if the class is used only within stand-alone programs as opposed to compiling the class in an ActiveX server. However, there are five basic steps to creating any class in Visual Basic:

- Create the class module and set its properties.

- Create the properties of the class.

- Create the methods of the class.

- Create any events needed for the class and include the code to raise the events at the appropriate time.

- Create any constants needed by the class using the Enum structure.

We will look at each of these steps in detail in the following sections.

Setting Up the Class Module

Class modules are files that contain program code. This code sets up the properties, methods, and events that define the class. Each class is created in a special file with the .CLS extension. This extension tells Visual Basic that the code is a class module, not a standard program module containing general functions and procedures.

To create a class in your program, the first thing you must do is add a class module to your project. To do this, choose the Add Class Module item from the Projects menu, or press the Add button on the toolbar and select the Class Module item. You will be presented with a dialog box that asks you the type of module you want to create. This dialog box is shown in Figure 7.1. The choices are to create a Class Module, create a Visual Basic Add-in, or open the Class Builder utility. Choose the Class Module option and click the Open button. (We will look at the Class Builder a little later.)

After you select the Class Module option, you will be placed in the code window for the class and you will notice that a new class has been added to the project window as shown in Figure 7.2. At this point, you will need to set the properties of the class module. For all classes, you will need to set the Name property. By convention, class names start with a *c* and contain a descriptive name, such as cUser for a user information class.

If you are creating a class in a standard program, the Name property is the only property available. If you are creating an ActiveX server, the class will also contain the Instancing property, which determines how the class can be used in programs that access the server. We will look at the settings of the Instancing property in a later section.

FIGURE 7.1

Add Class Module
dialog box

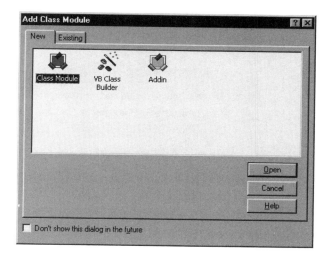

FIGURE 7.2

The initial appearance
of a new class module

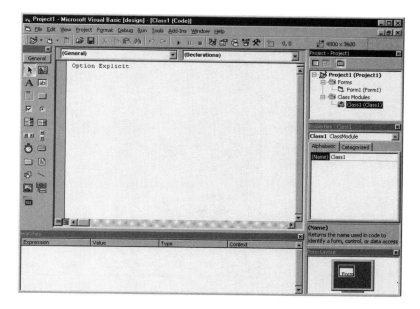

As an exercise in this chapter, we will create a user information class that handles several aspects of logging users into a system and verifying security settings. Exercise 7.1 details the steps needed to start the creation of this class.

EXERCISE 7.1

Creating the Basic Class Module for the User Information Class

1. Start a new project.

2. Add a Class Module to the program by choosing the Add Class Module item from the Project menu. Choose the Class Module item from the Add Class dialog box.

3. Name the class **cUserInfo**.

4. Place comments in the code window that identify the name of the class, the creator of the class, and the purpose of the class. While this information is optional, it is good practice in order to enhance the reusability of the class. The next picture shows an example of a class header.

5. Save the project.

F I G U R E 7.3

Class headers provide information about the creation of the class.

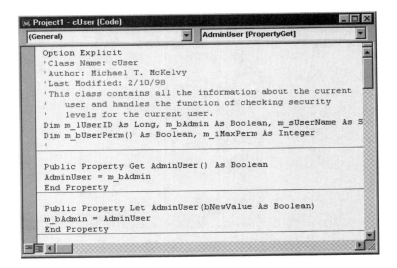

Creating the Properties of a Class

Add properties to a class.

When you are working with classes, you have to have a way to get data into the class where it can be processed. You pass data between your program and a class (actually an object created from the class) through the properties of the class. These properties provide the public interface of the class, allowing your program to set and retrieve data in the class.

There are two ways that you can create properties in a class module:

- Create a Public variable

- Create a Property procedure

You can create a Public variable by using the Public keyword in the variable declaration statement in the Declarations section of the class module. The following line shows an example of this:

```
Public lUserID As Long
```

While this is the simplest way to create a property of a class, it is not the recommended method. Using a Public variable provides open access to the information in the class without providing any means of verifying the data, or processing the data for returning a value. This means that invalid information can be passed to a class as easily as good information. Also, using a Public variable does not allow you to create read-only properties that are often needed in a class.

Therefore, the recommended method of creating a property involves three steps:

- Creating an internal variable to hold the information for use within the class.

- Creating a Property Let or Property Set procedure to allow the data to be set in the class. These procedures often provide additional processing of the information and validate the data being input.

- Creating a Property Get procedure to allow the data from the class to be retrieved. Like the Let and Set procedures, a Get procedure often provides additional processing of data prior to returning a value.

Using Internal Variables

The first step to creating a property is to create a variable to hold the information internally in the class. These variables are declared as private so that only the class can perform operations on them. Once the variables are created, you will typically assign default values to them to ensure that there is always valid information in the variable, even if no property assignment has been made.

Setting the initial values of the internal variables is usually handled in the Initialize event of the class. Exercise 7.2 shows the setup of the internal variables for the User Information class.

EXERCISE 7.2

Creating Internal Variables for a Class

1. Start with the Project created in Exercise 7.1.

2. Add Private declaration statements to the Declarations section of the class module to create the internal variables. You will need variables to hold the user name, the user ID, and whether the user has administrative rights. For this class, there is also a variable to hold the number of user permissions defined for the application. The code for these declarations is shown below:

```
Private m_lUserID As Long
Private m_bAdmin As Boolean
Private m_sUserName As String
Private m_iMaxPerm As Integer
```

3. In the code window of the class module, open the Initialize event procedure for the class. You do this by selecting Class from the object list and Initialize from the event list. (Initialize is the default event for the Class object.)

4. Place the following code in the event procedure to set the initial values of the internal variables:

```
m_bAdmin = True
m_lUserID = 0
m_sUserName = "System"
m_iMaxPerm = 0
```

5. Save the project.

The internal variables defined above are preceded by m_. This is a notation to indicate that the variables are module level variables defined for the class, but cannot be used outside the class. You may choose to use a different convention in your programming, but be sure you are consistent in your naming conventions.

Creating Property Procedures for the Public Interface

As stated above, using property procedures is the best method for creating the public interface of a class module. There are actually three different types of property procedures:

- **Property Let**   Allows you to set the value of an internal variable (property) that contains a standard data type, such as integer, single, string, and so on.

- **Property Set**   Allows you to set the value of an internal variable that contains an object reference. For example, you would need to use a Property Set procedure to pass a database to the class.

- **Property Get**   Allows you to retrieve the value of information from the class. This procedure is used whether the information is of a standard data type or an object.

Typically, for each property you will create a procedure pair containing either a Let or Set procedure and a Get procedure. If you want to create a read-only property, you create a Get procedure but omit the Let or Set procedure. If you want to create a write-only property, you omit the Get procedure.

You can create property procedures either by typing code directly into the code window of the class module or by using the Add Procedure dialog box. Using the dialog box creates a framework for a Property Let and Property Get procedure in your code. To open the Add Procedure dialog box (shown in Figure 7.4), select the Add Procedure item from the Tools menu.

F I G U R E   7.4

Add Procedure
dialog box

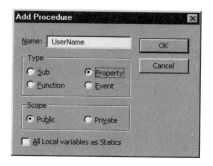

In the dialog box, enter the name of the procedure, select the Property option button in the Type selection, and select the Public option in the Scope selection. After setting the options, click the OK button to create the procedure framework, as shown in Figure 7.5.

FIGURE 7.5

Property procedure
framework

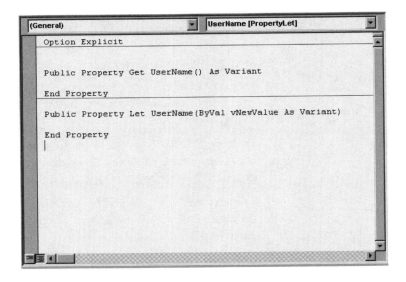

FIGURE 7.5

Property procedure
framework

Using a Property Let Procedure   In the Property Let procedure, you will need to specify an argument that contains the value being passed to the property. If you used the Procedure dialog box, you will notice that a variable was created for you with a variant type. You will also notice that the argument is passed by value, preventing the Property procedure of your class from changing the value of the variable passed to the procedure.

Unless you have a real good reason to do otherwise, pass all arguments to a Property procedure by value (ByVal).

In the declaration of the Property procedure, you will need to change the variable type from variant to whatever data type your property will contain. Also, you will probably want to change the name of the variable in the argument. (Note: If you are creating your procedure by typing in the declaration, you can set up the correct name and type initially.) After completing the declaration of the procedure, you will need to place code in the procedure that assigns the value passed by the procedure's argument to an internal variable. This is how the data is made available to the class. The following code shows an example of a completed Property Let procedure:

```
Public Property Let FileName(sInptFile As String)
'Set name of INI file
```

```
'If the input value is null or a zero length string,
'use current file
If IsNull(sInptFile) Or Len(sInptFile) = 0 Then Exit Property
m_iniFileName = sInptFile
End Property
```

Using a Property Set Procedure   The Property Set procedure is the only property procedure you cannot create automatically with the Procedure dialog box. You can, of course, type the entire declaration in (not a hard task), or create a Property Let procedure and change the Let keyword to Set. When you are creating the Set procedure, you will need to specify the argument for the procedure and specify the type of object that is being passed to the procedure. Then, in the code for the procedure, you will use the Set statement to assign the argument to the internal object that is used in the class. The following code shows an example of a property set procedure:

```
Public Property Set CurWorkSpace(newWS As Workspace)
'Allow user to set a workspace other than the default.
Set m_WS = newWS
End Property
```

Using a Property Get Procedure   The Property Get procedure is used to return a value (either a variable or an object) from the class. As such, this procedure works very much like a function procedure in a standard program module. In the declaration of the Property Get procedure, you specify the data type of the procedure. This is the type of the information that is being returned from the class.

Make sure that the program statements or variables in the calling program are of the same or compatible type as the Get procedure.

When you create a Get procedure with the Procedure dialog box, you will need to change the data type to the one that you need. After properly setting up the declaration for the Get procedure, you will need to place code in the procedure that sets the value being passed back to the calling program. For standard data types, you will use a simple assignment statement. If you are passing an object, you will have to use a Set statement. Examples of both types of Property Get procedures are shown in the following code:

```
Public Property Get DBOpen() As Boolean
DBOpen = m_bDBOpen
End Property

Public Property Get CurDataBase() As Database
'If the database is open, return the database object
If m_bDBOpen Then
    Set CurDataBase = m_DB
Else
    Set CurDataBase = Nothing
End If
End Property
```

Creating the Properties of the User Information class   The user information class that you are creating in the exercises has four main properties. These properties contain the name of the user, the ID of the user, whether the user has administrative rights, and a read-only procedure that determines whether the user has access to a specific function of a program. Exercise 7.3 takes you through the steps of creating the properties of the class.

EXERCISE 7.3

Creating Class Properties

1. Start with the project you created in Exercises 1 and 2.

2. Add a Property procedure and assign it the name **AdminUser**. This property will have both a property Let and Get component. If you create the properties using the Procedure dialog box, you will need to change the data type of the argument of the Let procedure and the Get procedure to Boolean.

3. Add code to the Property procedures to set and retrieve the value from the internal variable. The complete code for these Property procedures is shown below:

```
Public Property Get AdminUser() As Boolean
AdminUser = m_bAdmin
End Property

Public Property Let AdminUser(bNewValue As Boolean)
m_bAdmin = AdminUser
End Property
```

4. Add a second property and name it **UserName**. The data type for this procedure will be String. As before, add code to the procedures to handle transferring data to and from the internal variable. The complete code for the Let and Get procedures is:

```
Public Property Get UserName() As String
UserName = m_sUserName
End Property

Public Property Let UserName(sNewValue As String)
m_sUserName = UserName
End Property
```

5. Add a third property to the class and name it **UserID**. Set the data type for this property to Long. Add the code to the procedures as shown below:

```
Public Property Get UserID() As Long
UserID = m_lUserID
End Property

Public Property Let UserID(lNewValue As Long)
m_lUserID = UserID
End Property
```

6. Finally, add a property named **SecurityOK** to the class. This property is used to determine whether the user has access to a particular function in a program. If you are creating the property by typing in the declarations, you only need to create the Property Get procedure, as this property will be read-only. If you are using the Procedure dialog box, you will need to erase the Property Let procedure that is created by the dialog box. The Get procedure needs to have an argument passed to it to determine which program function is being checked. This argument will be passed ByVal and is an Integer data type. The property itself is a Boolean data type. The complete code for the procedure is:

```
Public Property Get SecurityOK(iPermID As Integer) As _
Boolean
'Check whether current user has appropriate security level
SecurityOK = False
If m_bAdmin Then
    SecurityOK = True
```

```
Else
    If iPermID > m_iMaxPerm Or iPermID <= 0 Then Exit
Property
    If m_bUserPerm(iPermID) Then SecurityOK = True
End If
End Property
```

7. Save the project.

Creating Methods of the Class

Microsoft Exam Objective   **Add methods to a class.**

After you have created the properties of the class, you will need to add procedures to the class to perform tasks with the information. The procedures that you use will be of two varieties:

- Internal procedures that are used only within the class
- Public procedures that are the methods of the class

Using Private Procedures for Internal Functions

A variety of small procedures are used in many programs, such as date conversions or particular formatting functions. Typically, you will have a library of such functions that you have created over time. These procedures may be stored in a module to allow you to reuse them in many programs. However, for a class to be truly reusable, it should be completely independent of other modules. Any special functions you need must be included in the class as internal procedures.

There are exceptions to having classes entirely self-contained. For example, if your class works with any API functions, you need to have a standard module that handles the declarations of the functions, as these are not allowed in a class module.

To create an internal procedure, you can use the Procedure dialog box or declare the procedure by typing in the declaration statement. In either case, you should specify the procedure as Private. Code within the class can use the code, but the procedure is unavailable to any parts of a program outside the class. As an example, the following code might be used to un-encrypt strings that were passed from an encrypted database. This routine is used inside the class but should not be available for the rest of the program.

```
Private Function StringDecrypt(ByVal sInptString As String) _
As String
Dim iChrVal As Integer, I As Integer, sPassStr As String
'Decrypt string
sPassStr = ""
For I = 1 To Len(Trim(sInptString))
    iChrVal = 255 - Asc(Mid(sInptString, I, 1))
    sPassStr = sPassStr & Chr(iChrVal)
Next I
StringDecrypt = UCase(sPassStr)
End Function
```

Using Public Procedures for the External Methods of the Class

Creating methods for a class is the same as creating internal procedures, except that the Public keyword is used in the declaration statement of the procedure to allow any program using an object created from the class to access the procedure. These procedures are the same as the Sub and Function procedures that you create for other parts of your program. (See Chapter 2, "Coding Basics," for a description of creating procedures.) The procedures can have arguments passed to them and can return a value. Exercise 7.4 shows you how to create the method necessary to set up the permissions array for the user information class.

EXERCISE 7.4

Creating Methods in a Class

1. Start with the project created in previous exercises.

2. Using the Procedure dialog box, add a procedure named **SetPermissions** to class. This is a Sub procedure and must be made Public to make it a method of the class. The appropriate settings of the dialog box are shown in the following graphic.

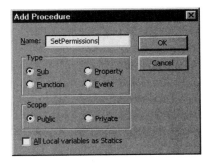

3. Add an argument to the procedure declaration. This argument will be a database object that is passed to the procedure to allow the procedure to retrieve permission information from a security database. The complete declaration of the method is shown below:

```
Public Sub SetPermissions(ByVal m_DB As Database)
```

4. Add the code to the procedure to accomplish the task of setting up the permissions array. This code is relatively long and therefore is not shown here. The complete code can be found in the cUser.cls file on the CD.

5. Save the project.

Creating Events for the Class

If you are familiar with forms and controls, you know that these objects have properties, methods, and events that control their behavior. The classes that you create in Visual Basic can also have events. These events allow your class to notify the calling application of occurrences in the class. Creating an event in a class requires two steps:

- Declaration of the event

- Writing code to raise the event

When you create the event, you can use the event to pass information to the calling program in the form of parameters. These parameters will show up in the event procedure of an object created from your class. The events that you create behave like the events that are built into Visual Basic's forms and controls. The events are triggered whenever a certain condition occurs, but the calling program only responds to the events if code is written in the Event procedure.

One of the key uses of an event in a class is to provide the calling program with information about the status of a long operation. For example, if a class is being used to perform a spell check of a long document, you might want to use an event to indicate when the task has reached certain completion points. Exercise 7.5 shows you how to create such an event in a class.

EXERCISE 7.5

Creating an Event in a Class

1. Start a new project.

2. Add a class module to the project.

3. Using the Procedure dialog box, create a public Sub procedure named **SpellCheck**.

4. Open the Procedure dialog box a second time to create an event procedure. To do this, check the Event button in the Type selection and specify the name of the procedure as CheckStatus. Click the OK button to create the procedure in the code window.

5. Add a parameter to the Event procedure declaration to allow the event to pass information to the calling program. Name the variable **Status** and set it to be passed by value. The final appearance of the declaration is shown in the next graphic.

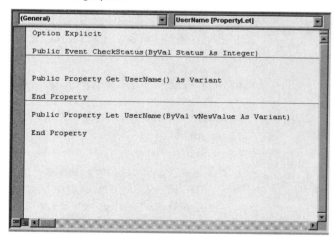

6. Add the following code to the SpellCheck procedure to raise the event.

```
iStatus = Int(100 * iCurrentPage / iTotalPages)
RaiseEvent CheckStatus(iStatus)
```

Using the Friend Declaration

Microsoft Exam Objective

Declare properties and methods as Friend.

One very useful option in the declaration of properties and methods in a class is the Friend declaration. This option is particularly useful in the creation of ActiveX servers. The Friend declaration allows you to make a property or method available to other modules in the current project (the one in which the class is defined), without making the routine truly public. You can create necessary routines for data conversion or other functions and declare them as Friend. Your ActiveX server can then use these routines internally, but programs that call the classes of the server are not permitted to use the methods or view the properties, increasing the functionality of classes in your programs.

To make a property or method a Friend function, simply replace the Public or Private (typically Private) keyword in the procedure declaration with the Friend keyword. The following code shows an example of the Friend declaration.

```
Friend Function StringDecrypt(ByVal sInptString As String) _
As String
Dim iChrVal As Integer, I As Integer, sPassStr As String
'Decrypt string
sPassStr = ""
For I = 1 To Len(Trim(sInptString))
    iChrVal = 255 - Asc(Mid(sInptString, I, 1))
    sPassStr = sPassStr & Chr(iChrVal)
Next I
StringDecrypt = UCase(sPassStr)
End Function
```

Creating Classes with the Class Builder

Adding class modules to your project is one way to build classes in your programs. Visual Basic provides you with an additional way to create and manage classes in your programs, the Class Builder utility. The Class Builder allows you to implement a sort of inheritance in Visual Basic classes by handling all the work of copying properties and methods from a base class to child classes. In addition, the Class Builder makes it easy for you to create collections of classes.

The Class Builder is one of the Add-ins that ships with Visual Basic. In order to use the Class Builder, you have to first add it to the Add-ins menu by choosing the Add-in Manager item from the Add-ins menu. This will present you with a dialog box, as shown in Figure 7.6, that allows you to choose the Add-ins you want loaded for Visual Basic. Choose the Class Builder add-in and click the OK button.

F I G U R E   7.6

Add-in Manager

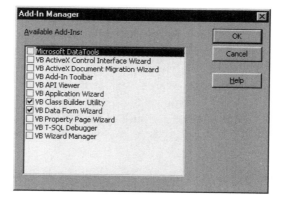

After you have made the Class Builder add-in available, you need to start it in order to start building classes. Start the Class Builder by choosing the Class Builder item from the Add-ins menu. This will bring up the Class Builder form, shown in Figure 7.7.

Creating the Base Class

Once the Class Builder is open, you are ready to start creating classes. This discussion will cover how to create a class from scratch, assuming that the class is not based on one that already exists.

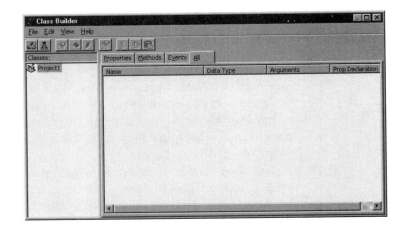

To start a new class, you can click the New Class button at the upper left of the Class Builder. You can also select the New item from the File menu, then select the Class item. In either case, you will be shown the Class Module builder seen in Figure 7.8. From this dialog box, you can set the Name of the class and, if applicable, set the Instancing property on the Properties tab of the dialog box. The Properties tab also includes a drop-down list that allows you to specify the name of a class on which the new class should be based. The names in the list are classes that are defined in the current project. The Attributes tab of the dialog box lets you include a description of the class and provide a help context ID for use in creating on-line help. After filling out the information in the dialog box, click the OK button to create the class module.

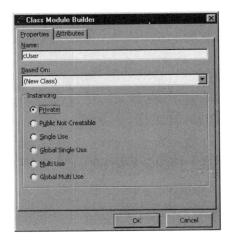

Adding Properties to the Class

After the class is created, you will want to begin adding properties, methods, and events to the class. Let's start with properties. To add a new property to the class, click the New Property button on the toolbar, which brings up the Property Builder dialog box shown in Figure 7.9.

FIGURE 7.9

Creating properties with Property Builder

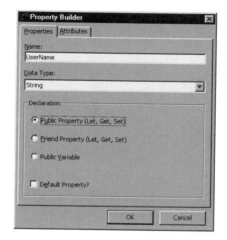

You can immediately see one advantage of using the Property Builder over using the Procedure dialog box described earlier. The advantage is that you can specify the data type of the property as well as declare the property to be a Friend function, which cannot be done from the Procedures dialog box. On the Properties tab of the Property Builder, you specify the name, data type, and declaration type of the property. If you need to use arguments in the Property procedure, you will need to add these by hand after the Class Builder creates the class in your project. As with the Class Module Builder, the Attributes tab of the Property Builder allows you to create a description of the property and to provide a help context ID. After filling out the information, you can click the OK button. The new property will then appear on the Properties tab of the Class Builder.

Adding Methods and Events to the Class

After creating the properties, you can continue creating your class by adding methods and events to the class. To add a method to the class, click the New Method button to bring up the Method Builder dialog box shown in Figure 7.10.

FIGURE 7.10

Method Builder dialog box for creating methods in the class

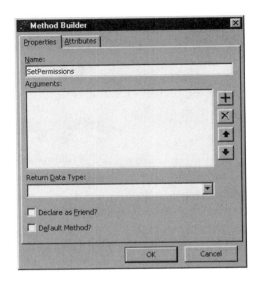

The first thing you need to do to complete the information in the dialog box is to specify a name for the method. Next, you can specify the type of data to return from the method. Specifying the return data type determines the type of procedure that is created. If you specify a data type, the Method Builder will create a function procedure. Otherwise, a Sub procedure will be created. Next, you need to choose whether the method will be declared as a Friend method. If you choose not to declare the method as Friend, the method will be declared as a Public procedure. Finally, you can choose whether to make this method the default method of the class.

After setting the basic properties of the method, you can specify the arguments that will be used to pass data to the method. Using this process makes it easier to create the declaration of the method than typing in the declaration by hand. You add a new Argument by clicking the "plus" button on the Method Builder. This will bring up the Add Argument dialog box shown in Figure 7.11. In this dialog box, you set the name and data type of the argument and indicate whether the argument should be passed by value or by reference. After adding an argument, it will appear in the argument list of the Method Builder.

The Method Builder also lets you remove arguments and change the order in which they are called in the declaration. You manage the arguments through the buttons to the right of the argument list in the Builder.

Adding events to the class is similar to adding methods. You click the New Event button to bring up the Event Builder shown in Figure 7.12. You then fill in the name of the event and create any needed arguments for the event.

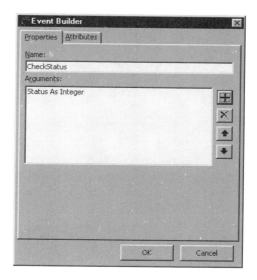

Creating the Child Classes

Once you have created at least one class in the Class Builder, you can create
additional classes that are based on another class in the project. When you add
a new class, you simply select the "parent" class from the drop-down list in the
Class Module Builder. As the class is created, the properties, methods, and
events of the parent class are copied to the new child class. This process helps
in creating hierarchies of classes, but does not provide true inheritance.

Creating the Classes for the Project

After you have defined all the necessary classes for a project, you actually create the classes by choosing the Update Project item from the File menu to create the declarations of all properties, methods, and events for all classes that you defined. At this point, you can enter the code that is required to implement all the functions that you want your classes to perform. For all the Properties you defined for a class, the Class Builder will create a local variable to hold the value of the property and will set up the assignment statements to set and retrieve the value of the property. The Builder will always create a Property Let/Get or Property Set/Get pair of procedures. If you want to create a read-only or write-only property, you will need to delete the appropriate procedure. The output of the Class Builder for a defined class is shown in Figure 7.13.

FIGURE 7.13

Procedure built by the
Class Builder

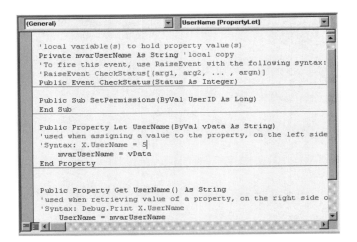

```
(General)                              ▼  UserName [PropertyLet]              ▼

'local variable(s) to hold property value(s)
Private mvarUserName As String 'local copy
'To fire this event, use RaiseEvent with the following syntax:
'RaiseEvent CheckStatus[(arg1, arg2, ... , argn)]
Public Event CheckStatus(Status As Integer)

Public Sub SetPermissions(ByVal UserID As Long)
End Sub

Public Property Let UserName(ByVal vData As String)
'used when assigning a value to the property, on the left side
'Syntax: X.UserName = 5
    mvarUserName = vData
End Property


Public Property Get UserName() As String
'used when retrieving value of a property, on the right side o
'Syntax: Debug.Print X.UserName
    UserName = mvarUserName
```

Defining the Scope of the Class

Like variables and standard procedures, classes have a specifically defined scope. That is, the use of a class can be confined to a certain application or can be made available to numerous applications. The scope of a class is determined by two things, where the class is defined and the setting of the Instancing property.

You can include a class module in almost any project. Making the class available to multiple applications refers to its availability after it is compiled into a program or ActiveX Server.

Public and Private Classes

Microsoft *Exam* *Objective*

Identify whether a class should be public or private.

A class can have one of two scopes, Private or Public. By design, any class defined in a standard executable program is a Private class. It can be used from anywhere in the program but cannot be called by other applications running at the same time.

Therefore, the only time that there is need to define the scope of a class is when you are creating an ActiveX server. In a server application, you can still create a Private class. A Private class can be used by the program routines within the server, but it is not exposed to other applications as an object available for use. However, an ActiveX server can have Public classes as well as Private classes. These public classes are used to make business objects and business rules available to multiple programs in a multi-tier client/server environment. You can create several types of Public classes. Whether a class is Public or Private and what type of Public class is created are determined by the setting of the Instancing property of the class.

Setting the Instancing Property

Microsoft *Exam* *Objective*

Set the value of the Instancing property.

The Instancing property lets you determine how your class will be used by other programs. Again, this property is only available for classes that are created in an ActiveX server (either Exe of DLL) or in an ActiveX control. The Instancing property has seven possible settings:

- **Private**   The class cannot be used outside the application in which it is defined. This is the default setting of the property.

- **PublicNonCreatable**   The class can be used by other applications. However, in order for the other applications to use the object, it must first be created by the server. Other applications cannot use the New keyword or the CreateObject function to create instances of the class.

- **SingleUse**   Other applications can create and use objects of the class. However, each time an object is created from the class, a new instance of the class is started.

- **GlobalSingleUse**   The same as SingleUse, but an application does not have to specifically create the object to use its methods and properties. The methods and properties are treated as global functions.

- **MultiUse**   Similar to SingleUse, but only a single instance of your class is created. All objects from the class are generated from the single instance.

- **GlobalMultiUse**   The same as MultiUse except that the methods and properties are treated as global functions. Applications do not have to specifically create an instance of the class.

To set the value of the Instancing property, you simply select the desired value from the list of available values in the Properties window. You cannot set the value of the Instancing property at run-time.

Using a Class in a Program

Up to this point, you have seen how to create a class and how to add properties, methods, and events to the class. However, a class by itself is not very useful. A defined class is like a Visual Basic control that is in the toolbox. It is available for use, but you are not using it in your program until you create an object from the class. While controls are created visually in the design mode, in order to create an object from a class, you have to write code.

Creating an Instance of the Class

Before you can use an object that is based on your class, you have to create the object. There are two methods of creating objects in Visual Basic, using the CreateObject function and using the New keyword.

For most of the objects you create, using the New keyword is the preferred method. Using this method allows you to specify the type of object that the program will be creating, and the compiler can bind the class information to the object variable during compilation. This is known as early binding of an object. Because the binding is handled during compilation, the creation of objects with the New keyword is faster than using the CreateObject function. Another benefit is that the compiler can perform program checking for correct method and function calls. In addition, using the New keyword makes it easier for you to use the objects as you are programming. Because Visual Basic knows the type of object you are creating, it can provide you with a drop-down list of properties and methods, as shown in Figure 7.14. This is just like the controls or built-in objects of Visual Basic.

FIGURE 7.14

Early-bound objects enable Visual Basic to display lists of properties and methods.

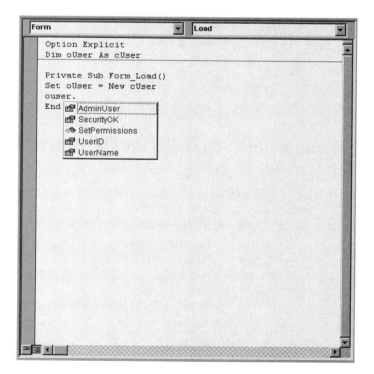

There are two ways to use the New keyword in the creation of an object from a class. First, you can specify the New keyword in the declaration of the object variable. Then, when you use any of the properties or methods of the object, the object is actually created. This is illustrated in the following code:

```
Dim oUser As New cUser
oUser.UserName = "Mike"
```

The second way to use the New keyword is in conjunction with the Set command. In this method, you declare an object variable, then use the Set command to explicitly create the object. This is illustrated in the following code:

```
Dim oUser As cUser
Set oUser = New cUser
```

The CreateObject function is typically used when you do not know in advance what type of object will by created for a specific object variable. In this case, the information about the object is not known until the program is run and the object is actually created. This is known as late binding of the object. CreateObject is also typically used with objects that are created from ActiveX servers. To use the CreateObject function, you declare a variable as an object, then use the function to create the specific instance of the object, as shown in the following code:

```
Dim oUser As Object
Set oUser = CreateObject("excel.sheet")
```

Accessing the Properties and Methods of the Class

After you have created an object from the class, you can access the properties and methods of the object like you can for forms and controls. Using dot notation, you specify the object variable, then the method or property you want to use. Depending on the setup of the property procedures (Let or Get), you can set or retrieve property values. You can also invoke methods using the dot notation. The following code shows how the properties and methods of the User Information class are used in a program.

```
oUser.UserID = LogRset!UserID
oUser.UserName = LogRset!FirstName & " " & LogRset!LastName
oUser.AdminUser = LogRset!AdminUser
oUser.SetPermissions MainDB
```

```
If Not oUser.SecurityOK(5) Then
    MsgBox "You are not authorized to access this function.", _
vbExclamation
    Exit Sub
End If
```

Destroying the Class Instance

After you have finished using an object, it is good practice to destroy the object, as it frees up any memory that was used by the object and performs housekeeping operations in your program. While objects are supposed to be destroyed automatically by Visual Basic when the object variable goes out of scope, it is best to specifically destroy the object.

To destroy an object, you set the object variable to the keyword Nothing. This action clears the object variable and releases memory assigned to it. The following code shows how to destroy the object created from the User Information class.

```
Set oUser = Nothing
```

Summary

This chapter has provided you with a detailed look at how to create classes in Visual Basic. You have seen how to create the class module and how to add properties, methods, and events to the class. You have also seen how to use the Class Builder to create and manage a hierarchy of classes in a project. You also learned about the Friend declaration and how the Instancing property affects the scope of a class. In order to successfully pass the sections of the certification exam that deal with classes, you should pay particular attention to the creation of properties and methods. You should also have a good understanding of the scope of a class and the use of the Instancing property. The specific exam objectives that were covered in this chapter were:

- Create and use a class module.

- Add properties to a class.

- Add methods to a class.

- Identify whether a class should be public or private.

- Declare properties and methods as Friend.

- Set the value of the Instancing property.

If you still don't feel comfortable with all the concepts, go over the exercises a second time before you start the review questions.

Review Questions

1. What are the three types of property procedures that can be created for a class?

   A. Add, Retrieve, Remove

   B. Item, Add, Remove

   C. Let, Set, Get

   D. Let, Get, Object

2. Which property procedure is used to retrieve the value of a property?

   A. Retrieve

   B. Get

   C. Item

   D. Value

3. How do you create a method for a class?

   A. Use a Method procedure declaration.

   B. Use a Property Set procedure.

   C. Create a Public procedure in the class module.

   D. Create a Private procedure in the class module.

4. What command triggers an event created in a class?

   A. RaiseEvent

   B. SetEvent

   C. Trigger

   D. FireEvent

5. How do you create a Public class in a standard executable?

    A. Set the Public property to True.

    B. Set the Instancing property to SingleUse.

    C. No special requirements.

    D. You cannot create a Public class in a standard executable.

6. What does the Friend declaration do?

    A. Makes a class available for use by any program

    B. Makes the methods of the class usable by other parts of the program in which the class is defined

    C. Limits your program to creating a single object from the class

    D. Keeps you from having to specify the object name to reference the methods of the class

7. What is the Instancing property for?

    A. Sets the number of objects that can be created from the class

    B. Determines whether the class inherited properties from another class

    C. Specifies how the class in an ActiveX server can be used by other programs

    D. Specifies how the class in a standard program can be used by other programs

8. How do you use a class in your program?

    A. Simply call the methods and properties like any other procedure.

    B. Create an object based on the class using the Set statement or New keyword.

    C. Use the Call statement to access the class directly.

9. Which of the following statements can be used to create an object based on a class? Check all that apply.

A. Set oUser = New cUser

B. oUser = cUser

C. Dim oUser As New cUser

D. CreateObject("cUser")

PART

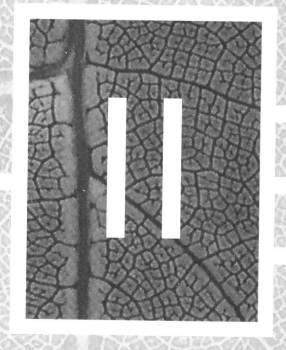

II

Creating Database
Applications

CHAPTER

8

Accessing Data
with the Data Control

Microsoft Exam Objectives Covered in This Chapter:

- Access data by using the data controls and bound controls.
- Add data to a table using the standard ListBox control.
- Add data to a table by using the DBList or DBCombo control.
- Use the Find or Seek method to search a Recordset.
- Display information by using the MSFlexGrid control.
- Display information by using the DBGrid control.

As applications move more and more from single-user programs to those that support a department, or even an entire company, the ability to access data in multiple types of databases becomes increasingly important. To meet the needs of developers writing database programs, Visual Basic has included data access capabilities since version 3. And the capabilities to access data have become more robust and easier to implement with each version of Visual Basic.

While there are numerous ways to access data from a Visual Basic program, by far the easiest is through the use of the data control and bound controls. The data control provides an easy-to-use link between your program and the data you are trying to access. This link can be created by placing a data control on a form and setting a few properties (as few as two for a default setup). When the link is established, data can be displayed on the form by using bound controls. Bound controls, in most cases, are the standard Visual Basic controls for which you set the data access properties.

Bound controls allow you to specify a data control and a field from the recordset accessed by the data control. The bound controls then handle the interface between your program and the information in the database.

In this chapter, we will take a look at how to create a data access program using the data control and bound controls. You will see how to use the data access properties of the standard controls, and take a look at some enhanced controls that were created specifically for data access programs. The next chapter will show you how to create a similar program without the use of the data control. In that chapter, you will also learn about the advantages and drawbacks of each method of creating a program.

As you are working through the material in this chapter, you should keep in mind the Microsoft exam objectives. To pass this part of the exam you will need to know how to link a data control with information in a database. You will then need to be able to link the data control to other controls to display and edit the information. Specifically, you need to know how to use some of the more advanced controls like the DBGrid, the MSFlexGrid, the DBList and DBCombo controls. You will also need to know how to find a specific record in a database.

Microsoft
✓
Exam
Objective   **Access data by using the data controls and bound controls.**

Setting Up the Data Control

The Data Control is the key element to creating data access applications with a minimum of programming. The Data Control handles two key functions for you, creating the link to the database and providing database navigation capabilities to the user. The controls that are bound to the data control then automatically handle the display and editing functions for you; there is no need to write code for displaying data. In fact, there are only a few functions for which you need to write code if you are using the data control:

- Adding new records

- Deleting a record

- Finding a specific record

- Validating the user input

- Handling database errors, such as multi-user conflicts

A typical data entry program created with the data control is shown in Figure 8.1. The figure also indicates the navigation buttons that are provided by the data control to let the user move through the records of the database.

FIGURE 8.1

A data entry program can be easily created with the data control and bound controls.

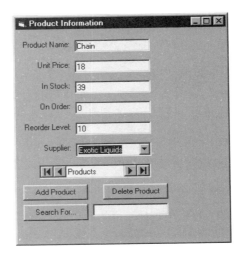

Basic Setup

Though the data control does provide you with a great deal of functionality, it is quite easy to set up. For example, to use the data control with an Access (Microsoft Jet) database, you only need to set two properties of the control, the DatabaseName and the RecordSource properties.

You will typically want to set the Name and Caption properties of the data control, like you would for any other control you use.

The DatabaseName property specifies the full path name of the database that you are trying to access. You can type the database name in or you can click the ellipsis button next to the property name in the Properties window to bring up a file open dialog box, as shown in Figure 8.2, which allows you to select the name of the database.

FIGURE 8.2

The open dialog box makes database selection simple.

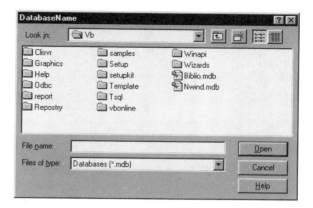

WARNING

The name specified in the DatabaseName property uses the path information for your machine. If you are distributing your application to others to use, you will need to specify the location of the database by setting the DatabaseName property in code, in the Load event of the form containing the data control. The following line of code shows how to do this for a database that resides in the same folder as the application:

```
datMember.DatabaseName = App.Path & "\Members.Mdb"
```

After the DatabaseName property has been set, you can set the Record-Source property to determine the specific information in the database that you want to access. You can set the RecordSource property to the name of a table or query in the database, or you can enter a SQL statement to access specific data. The simplest way to set the RecordSource property is to select a table or query from the drop-down list in the Properties window. When the DatabaseName property is set to a valid database, this list is populated with the names of all the available tables and queries in that database, as shown in Figure 8.3.

NOTE

If you are unfamiliar with tables, queries, or SQL statements, you may want to check out a book on database programming with Visual Basic. One book that will provide you with some of this information is *Visual Basic 5 Developer's Handbook*.

F I G U R E   8.3

A drop-down list
allows you to select
the RecordSource of
the data control.

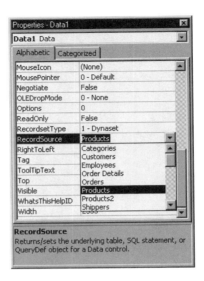

In addition to selecting a table or query from the list, you can input a SQL Select statement directly into the RecordSource property, which allows you to define specific fields and records of a table (or multiple tables) that you want to access. You are not limited to specifying the RecordSource property at design time. You can also set the RecordSource in code to a table, query, or SQL statement by using code like the following:

```
datProduct.RecordSource = "Select * From Products"&_
"Where OnHand > 0"
datProduct.Refresh
```

The second statement in the code uses the Refresh method of the data control, which forces the data control to re-create the recordset after a new value of the RecordSource property has been set.

An easy way to create SQL statements is to create your query in Access, then cut and paste the statement into the RecordSource property or your code. If you want to learn more about using Access to create SQL statements, *Mastering Access 97* from Sybex is a great reference on the subject.

WARNING If you change the RecordSource property in code, make sure that you include all the fields required by your bound controls. Otherwise, an error will occur.

To illustrate how easy it is to set up a data control, Exercise 8.1 shows you how to set up the data control as the first step of creating a data access program.

EXERCISE 8.1

Set Up a Data Control to Access a Jet (Access) Database

1. Open a new project.

2. Add a data control to your form (the data control is part of the standard tool set).

3. Set the Name and Caption properties of the data control to identify the control to the user and in the program. (Note: Typical naming conventions use the dat prefix for naming the data control.)

4. Click the ellipsis button next to the DatabaseName property to select a database. For this example, use the Northwind sample database that comes with Visual Basic, Nwind.mdb.

5. Select a RecordSource from the drop-down list in the Properties window. For the example, select the Products table.

6. Save the project to use it later in the chapter. You can save it as Ch8a.vbp.

Connecting to Non-Jet Databases

In the preceding section you saw how the data control by default works with an Access database, but the data control is capable of working with a variety of desktop database formats.

To tell the data control that you will be working with a non-Jet database, you simply have to set another property of the control, the Connect property. The Connect property tells the data control which database format to use. You can set the Connect property in the design mode by selecting the appropriate format from the drop-down list in the Properties window, as shown in Figure 8.4.

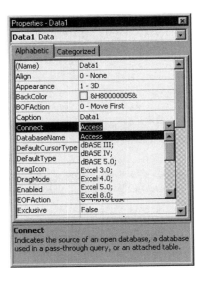

After you specify the Connect property, if you subsequently use the open dialog box to set the DatabaseName property, you will see that the dialog box automatically defaults to the correct file extensions for the data source.

As with the other properties of the data control, you can set the Connect property in code to allow changes at run-time. When you specify the property in code, you have to use specific strings to indicate the type of database you are accessing. These strings are summarized in Table 8.1 for some common desktop databases.

T A B L E 8.1

Connect strings for desktop databases.

Database Type	Connect String
dBase 5	dBASE 5.0
Excel 97	Excel 8.0
FoxPro 3	FoxPro 3.0
Lotus 1-2-3 version 4	Lotus WK4
Microsoft Jet	Access
Paradox 5	Paradox 5.x
Text files	Text

> You can also connect to data in Excel spreadsheets and text files from the Visual Basic data control.

Working with Different Recordset Types

Setting up the data control as we did in the previous sections creates a recordset of the default type. The default is a Dynaset-type recordset (also referred to as a dynaset). A dynaset returns a series of pointers to information in the tables of a database. The pointers allow your program to access the data in the table and even to modify it, but you do not have direct access to the tables themselves.

Two other recordset types can be used with the data control:

- Table-type recordset

- Snapshot-type recordset

You determine the type of recordset to use by setting the RecordsetType property of the data control. The default type is acceptable for most uses, but there are times when you will want to specify a particular type. Table 8.2 lists some of the advantages and drawbacks to each of the three recordset types.

T A B L E 8.2: Characteristics of Recordset Types

Recordset type	Advantages	Drawbacks
Table	1) Allows direct access to the information in the database. 2) Allows the use of indexes for faster searching and setting of presentation order.	1) Allows access to only a single table. 2) Searches must be based on available indexes. 3) Cannot limit the number of records returned, returns all records in a table.
Dynaset	1) Allows the selection of specific records and fields. 2) Can use SQL statements to combine information from multiple tables. 3) Searches can be based on any fields.	1) Searches are typically slower than for tables. 2) Cannot use indexes to change the order of presentation "on-the-fly".
Snapshot	1) Similar to dynaset. 2) Typically is faster in accessing records than a dynaset because it is a memory-based copy of the data.	1) Snapshots are read-only, the information cannot be updated.

Other Key Properties of the Data Control

Up to this point, we have covered the major properties of the data control. There are, however, several other properties that control the behavior of the data control. The following list summarizes these properties. For a more detailed discussion of the properties, you can look them up in Visual Basic's on-line help. The use of these properties is optional, as they are not required to connect a data control to the recordset.

- **BOFAction**   Determines what the data control does when the user moves to the beginning of the file. The options are to set the BOF flag for the recordset or move to the first record of the recordset.

- **DefaultCursorType**   Determines the type of cursor the data control will use if ODBCDirect is used to access the database.

- **DefaultType**   Determines whether the data control uses the Jet database engine to access the data or uses ODBCDirect.

- **EOFAction**   Determines what the data control does when the user moves to the end of the file. The options are to set the EOF flag for the recordset, move to the last record of the recordset, or add a new record.

- **Exclusive**   Determines whether the database specified in the Database-Name property is opened for exclusive use; that is, no other users can access it.

- **Options**   Allows you to specify other options of the recordset object.

- **ReadOnly**   Determines whether the recordset is to be accessed as read-only; that is, the user cannot edit any of the data.

Assigning Recordsets Created with DAO

You have seen some of the flexibility of the data control by reading how it can work with different databases, create different types of recordsets, and handle record navigation. You have also seen how you can set the properties of the data control at design time or set them at run time through program code. There is also another way to set up the recordset used by the data control that provides you with additional flexibility; you can create a recordset with code using the data access objects and pass the recordset to the data control.

As you will see in Chapter 9, the recordset used by the data control is an object that is part of the Data Access Objects model of the Jet database engine. The data control provides an easy way to create this object rather than go through the process of creating the recordset in code. Because there are good reasons for working directly with code for many tasks, however, the developers at Microsoft decided that there needed to be an easy way to work with both the data control and with program code. Therefore, they made it easy for you to pass recordsets to the data control and to use the recordset created by the data control in program code.

The following line of code shows how to pass a recordset created in code to the data control. Figure 8.5 shows a code segment that is used to assign the recordset from the data control to a recordset object variable, so that the recordset can be used to perform tasks.

```
Set datProducts.RecordSet = rsetAvailProducts
```

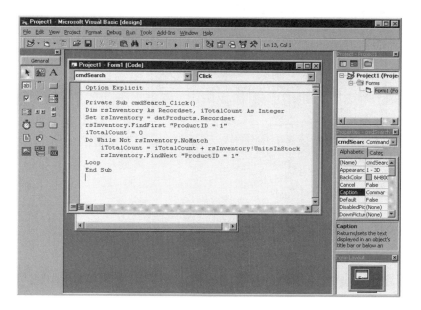

FIGURE 8.5

The recordset of the data control can be used in code to perform tasks that are not built into the data control.

Binding Controls to the Data Control

The data control can provide you with access to the information in a database, but it cannot display that information on a form. For that, you need to use the bound controls. Bound controls are directly linked to the data control and handle the tasks of retrieving values from specific fields in the database and displaying the values to the user. Also, for those controls that allow user interaction, the controls handle the editing of the information. These bound controls let you create the applications with which a user can view and modify data. The exam objectives state that you need to be able to use the data control and the bound controls to access data. The data control sets up a recordset for use, but without the use of the bound controls, you have no access to display or edit the information.

What the Controls Can Do

Visual Basic comes with a number of controls that enable you to handle data in the recordset of the data control. Eight of the controls in the standard Visual Basic toolbox are capable of being bound to the data control. Each of these controls retrieves the value of a field and assigns it to a property of the control. These eight controls and their associated properties are listed in Table 8.3.

TABLE 8.3

Standard controls can be bound to the data control.

Control Name	Property
Picture Box	Picture
Label	Caption
Text Box	Text
Check Box	Value
Combo Box	Text
List Box	List
Image	Picture
OLE Control	N/A

In addition to the standard controls, Visual Basic ships with six other controls that can be bound to the data control:

- DBGrid
- DBCombo
- DBList
- MSFlexGrid
- Masked Edit
- RichTextBox

Also, many third-party controls allow you to bind to the data control to retrieve and manipulate data.

Using Simple Data Bound Controls

The simplest data bound controls are also the ones that you will use most often in your applications—the TextBox, Label, and CheckBox controls. You bind each of these three controls to the data control by setting two properties, the DataSource and DataField properties. The steps for setting up these controls are shown in Exercise 8.2.

EXERCISE 8.2

Binding Controls to the Data Control

1. Open a project.

2. Set up a data control on the form as described in Exercise 8.1. If you saved your project from that exercise, open it and you will be ready for the next step.

3. Add a text box to the form.

4. Click the arrow button next to the DataSource property in the Properties window to bring up a list of all the data controls on the current form, as shown in the next graphic. Select the data control that contains the information you want to display.

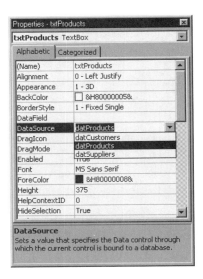

5. Click the arrow button next to the DataField property to display a list of all the fields in the recordset of the selected data control. This list is shown in the following graphic. Select the field that you want displayed in the text box.

6. Run the program and click the navigation buttons on the data control. You will see how the information for each record is displayed as it is accessed.

7. You can use this same process to set up bound label and check box controls.

Like other lists in the Properties window, you can cycle through the lists of the DataSource and DataField properties by double-clicking the mouse on the property name.

The text box enables you to display and edit text information of any kind and is useful for handling numbers and dates as well. The label control can be used to display any of the same information as the text box, but is used where you don't want the user to be able to edit the data. The check box is used to handle Yes/No choices in a program. The check box must be bound to a logical or Yes/No field in a database. These three controls can be used to create a large number of data access programs. A sample data entry program using only these controls is shown in Figure 8.6.

F I G U R E   8.6

Sample data entry program

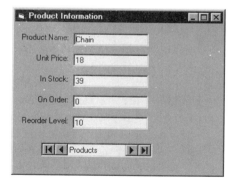

You can create a data entry program from a database using the Data Form Designer Add-in for Visual Basic. This wizard uses a data control and the text box, label, and check box controls.

Working with Lists and Combo Boxes

The text box, label, and check box controls can handle the bulk of the interface for most data access applications; however, there are many times when you want to allow the user to select items from a list, to make the data input easier for the user, and to limit the data input by the user to specified values. Visual Basic provides you with two basic types of list handling controls, the list box and the combo box. You are probably already familiar with the operation of these controls in their normal (unbound) mode. They operate in a similar fashion in bound mode but have the added capability of displaying and editing data directly in a database.

In addition to the standard list and combo boxes, Visual Basic has a DBList and DBCombo control that are specifically designed for database operations. Their purpose is similar to the standard controls, but how you set them up is quite different. Therefore, we will look at these controls separately.

Working with the Standard List and Combo Boxes

Microsoft Exam Objective	**Add data to a table using the standard ListBox control.**

The standard list box and combo box controls enable you to display the data from a field in the data control. In the case of the list box, the data field is bound to the selected item of the List property. The list that is used in the list box is input either through the Properties window or by adding items with the AddItem method in code. To modify the value of a field, the user selects an item in the list box. This item is stored in the field specified by the DataField property when the record is saved. The combo box binds the field of the data control to the Text property of the combo box, allowing the user to select items from a list or to enter new items. As with the list box, the data is stored in the field specified by the DataField property when the record is saved. Exercise 8.3 shows you how to set up a standard list box for data entry purposes.

EXERCISE 8.3

Using a List Box to Enter Data in a Database

1. Open a project containing a data control, or set up a data control as described in Exercise 8.1.

2. Add a list box to the form.

3. Add items to the List property of the list box. These items are the choices for the data field that you will link the list box to.

4. Set the DataSource property of the list box to the data control containing the data to be accessed.

5. Set the DataField property to the name of the field that contains the data represented by the items in the list.

6. Run the program. As you move from record to record, the selected item in the list will change to correspond to the data in the bound field.

WARNING If you are setting up a bound list box for use with an existing table, make sure your list includes all the values that are presently in the field in the table to avoid inadvertently changing the data or causing an error.

Working with DBList and DBCombo Controls

The standard list box and combo box allow you to handle simple list processing for your database applications. Most times, however, you will want to use the more robust capabilities of the DBList and DBCombo controls. These controls not only link the information in the list to a field in the database, but they can also derive the list choices from the database itself.

Microsoft ✓ *Exam Objective*   **Add data to a table by using the DBList or DBCombo control.**

An example will illustrate how these controls are set up and operate. In a normalized database, you would store information about suppliers in one table and information about products in another table. You then link each product to a specific supplier by storing a supplier ID in the product table. You do not store the supplier name and other information in each record of the product table, as this would lead to redundant data. Setting up data this way is a standard part of database design.

The problem with this "normalized" database occurs when the user enters a new product. You want the user to be able to enter the supplier ID by selecting an item from a list, but you want to show the supplier's name, not the ID, in the list. (This type of interface is illustrated in Figure 8.7.) Because the items in the List property of a standard list box are the ones that are bound to the database field, creating this type of interface is not possible with the standard control, and is why the DBList and DBCombo controls were created.

F I G U R E   8.7

Using a DBList to facilitate data entry

The DBList and DBCombo controls are not part of the standard toolbox for Visual Basic. These are custom controls that must be added to the toolbox using the Components dialog box. This dialog box can be accessed by choosing the Components item of the Project menu. You can also access the dialog box by pressing Ctrl+T or by using the pop-up menu available in the toolbox.

Depending on your setup, the DBList and DBCombo controls may be included as part of your standard project.

Both of these controls allow you to use one data control as the source of the items in the list, and another data control as the destination of the information. To set up the controls, you need to specify values for five properties, as described below:

- **BoundColumn**   Specifies the field from the RowSource data control that will be used as the value for the DataField information when a record is saved.

- **DataField**   Specifies the field from the DataSource data control that is the destination for information entered through the control.

- **DataSource**   Specifies the data control that provides the connection to the database that is the destination for edits or additions.

- **ListField**   Specifies the field that contains the values to be shown to the user in the list of the control.

- **RowSource**   Specifies the data control that provides the connection to the information that is the source of the list items.

Exercise 8.4 shows you how to set up a Product/Supplier data entry screen like the one shown in Figure 8.9. A DBCombo control is used as a drop-down list to provide the list of suppliers.

EXERCISE 8.4

Creating an Application with DBList or DBCombo Controls

1. Start a new project.

2. Add the DBList and DBCombo controls to the project by selecting the "Microsoft Data Bound List Controls" in the Components dialog box (if they are not already present).

3. Add a data control named **datProducts** to the form and link it to the Products table of the Nwind.mdb database. (See Exercise 8.1 for setting up a data control.)

4. Add a second data control named **datSuppliers** to the form and link it to the Suppliers table in the Nwind.mdb database.

5. Add bound text boxes to the form, linked to the datProducts data control, for the ProductName, UnitPrice, UnitsInStock, UnitsOnOrder, and ReorderLevel fields of the Products table.

6. Add a DBCombo control to the form and name it **dbcSupplier**.

7. Set the Style property of the DBCombo to dbcDropDownList to allow the user to only select items that are already in the Suppliers table.

EXERCISE 8.4 (CONTINUED)

8. Set the RowSource property of dbcSupplier to datSuppliers to specify the source of the list items.

9. Set the ListField property to CompanyName, the name of the field containing the names of each supplier.

10. Set the BoundColumn property to SupplierID, the field that is one end of the link between the tables.

11. Set the DataSource property to datProducts, the data control containing the destination table.

12. Set the DataField property to SupplierID, the other end of the link between the two tables.

13. Run the program. As you move through the Products table, you will see the supplier name for each product appear in the DBCombo list. If you change the name in the list, that new supplier ID will be assigned to the product you are currently editing.

 This sample program is supplied on the MCSD VB5 Companion CD as Lists.vbp.

Beyond Editing

So far, we have looked at displaying data in bound controls and using them to edit existing data in a database, but most database programs also need several other capabilities, specifically:

- Adding records

- Deleting records

- Finding specific records

The data control, on its own, is not capable of handling these functions. They are not among the built-in methods of the control; however, these functions are easy to add to your program using the Recordset object of the data control and three of its methods—AddNew, Delete, and Find.

Adding and Deleting Records with the Data Control

When you add a new record to the database, the data control clears the bound controls to prepare them for the addition of new information. As the user enters information in the controls, the data is stored in the properties of the controls. The new record is not actually added to the database until you move to another record or exit the form. Either of these actions tells the data control to save the information to the database.

When you delete a record using the Delete method of the data control, the record is removed from the database, but the information from the record is still displayed in the bound controls. Therefore, it is important for you to reposition the record pointer to another record. Otherwise, if the user tries to edit the information in the deleted record, an error will occur.

Exercise 8.5 continues the project created in Exercise 8.4 by adding record addition and deletion capabilities to the project. Figure 8.8 shows how the project looks after the addition of these capabilities.

EXERCISE 8.5

Setting Up for Record Addition and Deletion

1. Open the Product data entry project created in Exercise 8.4.

2. Add two command buttons to the form, one named **cmdAdd** and one named **cmdDelete**. Set the Caption properties of the buttons to Add Record and Delete Record respectively.

3. In the Click event of the cmdAdd button, place the following line of code:

```
datProducts.Recordset.AddNew
```

4. In the Click event of the cmdDelete button, place the following code segment:

```
With datProducts.Recordset
    .Delete
    If Not .EOF Then
        .MoveNext
    Else
        .MoveLast
    End If
End With
```

5. You can now run the program to see how these capabilities work.

FIGURE 8.8

Your program can now add and delete records.

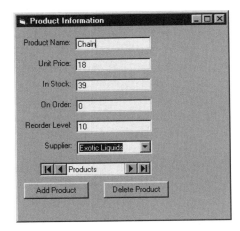

Because the data control does not verify that a user wants to delete a record, you may wish to add the following code in the cmdDelete button's Click event prior to the line that actually deletes the record:

```
Dim iReturn As Integer
iReturn = MsgBox("Do you really want to delete this record?", _
vbYesNo)
If iReturn = vbNo Then Exit Sub
```

Finding Specific Records

Microsoft *Exam* *Objective*	Use the Find or Seek method to search a Recordset.

Finding specific records in a recordset is a little more complex than adding new records or deleting existing ones. The AddNew and Delete methods work with both the dynaset- and table-type recordsets. (Neither can be used with a snapshot-type recordset because it is read-only.) The method you use to find a record depends on the type of recordset you are using. Two recordset methods are available for finding a record: the Find methods are used with dynaset- and snapshot-type recordsets; and the Seek method is used with table-type recordsets.

Four versions of the Find method are used in Visual Basic—FindFirst, FindNext, FindPrevious, and FindLast. The distinctions between these methods, as well as how to use the Seek method, will be discussed in the next chapter. For this chapter, we will keep it simple and use the FindFirst method with a dynaset-type recordset.

The basic setup of the FindFirst method consists of calling the method of the recordset and passing it the criteria for which you are searching. This criteria consists of three items:

- The field name to be searched

- The comparison operator, such as >, <, =, Like, or Between

- The value to which the field contents are compared

The field name item is the name of the field as it is listed in the recordset. The power of the find command lies in the proper use of the comparison operator and the comparison value. Simple comparisons use a single value and use an operator such as <, >, or =. You are probably familiar with these comparisons from handling logical operations in your programs. The last two comparison operators, however, require a little more discussion.

The Like operator allows you to compare a text field to a text pattern. For example, if you want to find the first record where the product name begins with S, you can use the Like operator as follows:

```
datProducts.Recordset.FindFirst "ProductName Like 'S*'"
```

The S* string is the pattern to be matched, with * being a wild card operator that indicates any string of characters. You can also use the ? wild card to match a single character. These wild cards can be used in front of or after any literal characters that you want to match. The following list shows a few sample patterns:

Search for	Sample pattern
Contains the string 'SQL'	*SQL*
Names starting with 'St'	St*
Products ending with 'board'	*board
Four letter names starting with 'M'	M???

The Between operator, unlike the other operators, takes two values for comparison. The Between operator is usually used to find records with a value in a specific numeric or date range. For example, the following line searches for shipment dates that occurred in a particular month:

```
datProducts.Recordset.FindFirst "ShipDate Between"& _
"#12/01/97# And #12/31/97#"
```

In the sample, the two comparison values follow the Between operator and are separated by the And operator. The dates are enclosed in # signs, which are required for all literal dates used in code. Several other requirements must be met when setting up the criteria for a Find method:

- The criteria for a Find method must be a literal string or string variable.

- For criterion that are literal strings, the criteria must be enclosed within double quotes.

- The comparison value must be of the same type (text, numeric, date) as the field being searched. Otherwise, an error will occur.

- Text values, including patterns, must be enclosed within quotes (single or double) in the criteria.

- Date values must be enclosed within # signs.

If you are familiar with the Where clause of a SQL statement, the criteria for the Find method is essentially a Where clause without the Where keyword.

To illustrate the Find method in action, Exercise 8.6 shows how to add the capability of finding a particular product to the sample Product data entry program created in previous exercises.

EXERCISE 8.6

Add Search Capabilities to the Program

1. Open the project containing the Product data entry screen.

2. Add a text box to the form with the name **txtProdSearch**. Also, clear the Text property of the text box.

3. Add a command button to the form with the name **cmdProdSearch**.

4. Add the following code to the Click event of the cmdProdSearch button:

```
Dim sSearchText As String
sSearchText = txtProdSearch.Text
datProducts.Recordset.FindFirst "ProductName >= '" & _
sSearchText & "'"
```

5. Run the program and try searching for different product names. The next illustration shows the addition of the search capability.

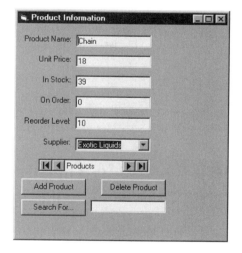

FIGURE 8.9

Search capabilities can easily be added to a program.

Notice that in the above code, single quotes were embedded in the criteria to surround the text contained in the sSearchText variable, because all text comparison values must be contained within quotes. If there is a possibility that the search string will contain an apostrophe, you would need to replace the single quotes with double quotes, as shown in the following line:

```
datProducts.Recordset.FindFirst "ProductName >= " Chr(34) & _
sSearchText & Chr(34)
```

The above search routine assumes that a record will be found. You should include code to return to the original record from which you started because a record might not be found. This enhancement will be covered in the next chapter.

Working with Grids

The examples so far have dealt with displaying or modifying a single record at a time. Most database systems, such as Microsoft Access or FoxPro, provide a way for users to look at multiple records at the same time. These views are typically in the form of spreadsheet-like grids that display a number of records. The user can still only edit a single record at a time, but they can view a number of records.

Visual Basic has two controls that can allow the user to view multiple records in a grid. These controls are the DBGrid and the MSFlexGrid. Of the two, only the DBGrid allows the user to edit the information in the grid and, optionally, to add and delete records.

Displaying Data with MSFlexGrid

The MSFlexGrid can be used in a program to display multiple records in a grid. The advantage of using the MSFlexGrid is the formatting capabilities that are inherent in the grid which allows you to apply different format options (such as bold, italic, or color) to different rows, columns, or cells in the grid. The main drawback of using the MSFlexGrid for database operations is that it cannot be used to edit data or add and delete records.

Microsoft ✓ *Exam* *Objective*

Display information by using the MSFlexGrid control.

The setup for the MSFlexGrid, in terms of data access, is simple. You only need to set the DataSource property of the grid to the name of a data control.

Then, when you run the program, the grid will display all rows and columns of the recordset from the data control. Exercise 8.7 details how to use the MSFlexGrid in a database program.

All rows and columns of a recordset may not fit on the screen at one time. The MSFlexGrid contains scroll bars that allow you to view information that is off-screen.

EXERCISE 8.7

Using an MSFlexGrid in a Database Program

1. Start a new project.

2. Set up a data control as described in Exercise 8.1.

3. Using the Components dialog box (accessible from the Components item of the Project menu), add the MSFlexGrid to your toolbox by checking the appropriate box in the dialog box.

4. After the MSFlexGrid has been added to the toolbox, add an instance of the control to your form.

5. Set the DataSource property of the grid to the name of the data control created in step 2.

6. Run your program. An example of the MSFlexGrid in action is shown in the following picture.

FIGURE 8.10

The MSFlexGrid displays information from a database.

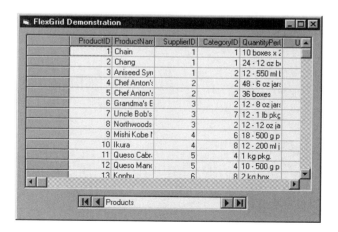

Editing Data with DBGrid

Microsoft ✓ *Exam Objective*

Display information by using the DBGrid control.

For database operations, the DBGrid is similar to the MSFlexGrid. Both will display all the rows and columns of a recordset, and both are easy to set up because both only require you to assign a data control in the DataSource property. However, the DBGrid goes beyond the MSFlexGrid in its capabilities. The DBGrid allows you to set it up so the user can modify information in existing records and add new records or delete existing ones. These capabilities are controlled through three additional properties of the DBGrid:

- **AllowAddNew**   Set to True, allows the user to add new records at the bottom of the grid. The new record input area is indicated by an asterisk in the leftmost column of the grid. When this property is set to False, users cannot add new records.

- **AllowDelete**   When set to True, allows the user to delete a record by clicking on the record selector at the left side of the grid and pressing the Delete key. When set to False, no deletions are allowed.

- **AllowUpdate**   When set to True, allows the user to edit the information in any row or column of the recordset by directly editing the grid cell. The changes are saved when the user moves to a new row, or the form is exited.

Figure 8.11 shows a DBGrid control, which is capable of editing records, adding new records, and deleting records. The setup of this DBGrid is detailed in Exercise 8.8.

EXERCISE 8.8

Displaying and Editing Database Information in a Grid

1. Start a new project.

2. Set up a data control as described in Exercise 8.1.

3. Using the Components dialog box (accessible from the Components item of the Project menu), add the DBGrid to your toolbox by checking the appropriate box in the dialog box.

4. After the DBGrid has been added to the toolbox, add an instance of the control to your form.

5. Set the DataSource property of the grid to the name of the data control created in step 2.

6. Set the AllowAddNew, AllowDelete, and AllowUpdate properties to True.

7. Run the program.

F I G U R E   8.11

DBGrid allows you to display information as well as edit it.

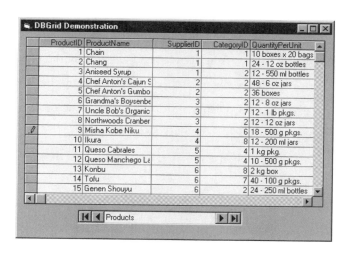

Summary

This chapter has shown you how to create data access programs using the data control and a variety of bound controls. You saw how to use the data bound capabilities of some standard controls to create the bulk of a program. You also saw how to extend the capabilities of the data control by adding a little code to the program, allowing the program to add new records, delete existing records, and to find specific records. Finally, you saw how to use the MSFlexGrid and DBGrid to display multiple rows of information from a recordset. You also saw that you can build robust data access/data entry programs using the data control and bound controls. Because the data control does so much work for you, the biggest challenge in creating a program with it is handling the Addition, Deletion, and Search capabilities. The most important thing to remember in creating these capabilities is that you will be working with the RecordSet object of the data control. In the next chapter, you will see how you can use the Data Access Objects and program code to accomplish the same tasks without the use of the data control.

Now, it is time to test your knowledge based on the following exam objectives covered in this chapter:

- Access data by using the data controls and bound controls.

- Add data to a table using the DBList or DBCombo control.

- Add data to a table by using the standard ListBox control.

- Display information by using the DBGrid control.

- Display information by using the MSFlexGrid control.

- Access data by using code.

- Use the Find and Seek methods search a Recordset.

Review Questions

1. In setting up the data control, which property do you use to specify the database that the control will link to?

   A. DatabaseName

   B. RecordSource

   C. Connect

   D. RecordsetType

2. What is a valid setting for the RecordSource property? Check all that apply.

   A. The name of a Table in the database

   B. The name of a Query in the database

   C. A valid SQL Select statement

   D. The name of another data control

3. Which RecordsetType setting would you use if you wanted to create a read-only recordset?

   A. Table

   B. Dynaset

   C. Snapshot

   D. Read-only

4. In setting up a text box as a bound control, which property specifies the field of the recordset to be displayed?

   A. Name

   B. DataSource

   C. DataField

   D. Text

5. Which list controls let you create the selection list from a table in a database? Check all that apply.

   A. Standard ListBox

   B. DBList

   C. Standard Combo Box

   D. DBCombo

6. Which of the following grid controls allow you to display data by linking to a data control? Check all that apply.

   A. Microsoft Grid control

   B. MSFlexGrid

   C. DBGrid

   D. None of the above

7. Which of the following grid controls allow you to edit data by linking to a data control? Check all that apply.

   A. Microsoft Grid control

   B. MSFlexGrid

   C. DBGrid

   D. None of the above

8. Which property of the DBList specifies the display field for the list?

   A. RowSource

   B. ListField

   C. DataSource

   D. DataField

9. Which property of the DBList control specifies where the list information comes from?

    A. RowSource

    B. ListField

    C. DataSource

    D. DataField

10. How do you handle adding and deleting records in a database program using the data control?

    A. Set the appropriate properties of the data control (AllowAddNew, AllowDelete).

    B. Write program code to invoke recordset methods (AddNew, Delete).

    C. Either A or B can be used.

    D. Neither A nor B is correct.

11. How do you handle record addition and deletion when using the DBGrid control?

    A. Set the appropriate properties of the data control (AllowAddNew, AllowDelete).

    B. Set the appropriate properties of the DBGrid control (AllowAddNew, AllowDelete).

    C. Write program code to invoke recordset methods (AddNew, Delete).

    D. All of the above will work.

12. What items must be specified as part of the criteria for the Find methods?

    A. Field name, comparison operator, comparison value

    B. Field name, database name, comparison value

    C. Data control, bound control name, comparison value

    D. Field name, comparison operator, bound control name

13. Which methods can be used to locate a specific record in a dynaset-type recordset? Check all that apply.

A. Seek

B. FindFirst

C. FindLast

D. Search

14. What must you do with literal dates in a search criteria for the Find methods?

A. Enclose the date in single quotes.

B. Enclose the date in double quotes.

C. Enclose the date in # symbols.

D. No special treatment is required.

CHAPTER

9

Creating Programs with
the Data Access Objects

Microsoft Exam Objectives Covered in This Chapter:

- Access data by using code.

- Navigate through and manipulate records in a Recordset.

- Add, modify, and delete records in a Recordset.

- Find a record in a Recordset.

- Use the Find or Seek method to search a Recordset.

The data control that you looked at in the last chapter is one way to create a database program in Visual Basic. Another way to create database applications is through programming the Data Access Objects (DAO). Actually, these two ways of developing database applications are intimately related. The data control is really a kind of wrapper around the functions of the DAO. For example, when you press a navigation key on the data control, you are invoking one of the Move methods of DAO. Also, when you set the DatabaseName and RecordSource properties of the data control, you are creating a Recordset object, one of the key objects in DAO. You saw this when you wrote code to add new records or find specific records.

So, if the data control is based on the DAO, and it handles all these functions automatically for you, why should you ever need to work directly with DAO? Good question! The key reason is that working directly with DAO gives you finer control over how and when information is saved to the database. This gives you several advantages in your programs:

- You can more easily validate all the information entered by the user before it is saved to the database.

- You reduce the possibility of locking conflicts in multi-user systems because your program controls when the record is locked.

Access database and many others actually use page locking where an entire page of data on which the record is located is locked.

- You can handle locking conflicts and other database errors more easily using standard error trapping techniques.

- You can use SQL statements to make changes to multiple records at a time.

- You can use transaction processing to speed up data storage and to help preserve data integrity.

- You can create database applications that do not require a visual interface. The data control is only good for handling programs that have a visual component.

This chapter will show you how to create the various data access objects, how to retrieve information using the objects, and how to store new or changed information to the database.

Understanding the Data Access Objects

Microsoft✓*Exam* *Objective*	**Access data by using code.**

The Data Access Object model provides Visual Basic with a robust environment for creating database applications. Each of these objects contains methods and properties that control their behavior and allows them to perform certain data manipulation tasks. While the objects of DAO are tuned to work best with the Microsoft Jet database engine, they are also capable of accessing a variety of PC databases as well as ODBC-compatible databases such as SQL Server.

There are a number of objects contained within the Data Access Objects, as shown in the simplified view of the DAO model in Figure 9.1. However, we will be looking closely at five of them in this chapter. These objects are:

- **DBEngine**   The main function of the DBEngine object, for our purposes, is to create workspaces and manage the workspace collection.

- **Workspace**   This object, as its name suggests, provides an area for a single user to work with databases. The Workspace object handles user level security and handles transaction processing for your programs, if required. The fact that DAO supports multiple workspaces allows your program to handle multiple transaction sets independently of one another. Each workspace can handle connections to multiple databases. Each database opened in a workspace is part of the Databases collection that is managed by the workspace object.

DAO can handle accessing ODBC database, but Visual Basic also makes use of Remote Data Objects, which are better suited to working with database servers. The Remote Data Objects will be covered in the next chapter.

F I G U R E   9.1

A simplified view of the DAO model

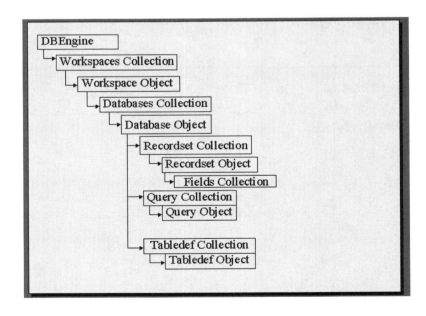

- **Database** This object provides the connection between your program and a single database. When you create the database object, you are performing the same function as the data control does when you set the DatabaseName property. Each database object can support multiple lower level objects, such as recordsets or queries. The database object manages the collections of Recordsets, Queries, and other objects.

You may notice that collections play an important role in the DAO model. You can learn more about manipulating collections in Chapter 6, "Working with Collections."

- **Recordset** This object is the link with the actual data in the database. The recordset will typically be of one of the three types described in the last chapter—Table, Dynaset, or Snapshot. It is through the recordset object that you navigate through database records, retrieve values from fields, and update information in the database.

- **Query** A query is a stored SQL command that can be run from your program. The query object can contain a SQL command that was created within your program, or it can refer to a stored procedure in the database.

These five objects are the main ones used to access data in an existing database. There are a number of other objects, especially "child" objects of the Database, that are used when you create new databases or modify the structure of an existing database.

Creating a Recordset with Code

Before you can begin to display, edit, or otherwise manipulate data in a database, you will need to create the connection to the information through the data access objects. This involves two main steps—opening the database itself and creating a recordset for the desired information. Each of these steps requires you to create an object reference for use in your program.

Before you can even create the DAO objects, however, you have to tell Visual Basic that your program will be using DAO by setting a reference to the DAO library in the References dialog box. This dialog box, shown in Figure 9.2, is accessible by choosing the References item from the Project menu.

FIGURE 9.2

The References dialog box lets you tell Visual Basic the object libraries that your program will require.

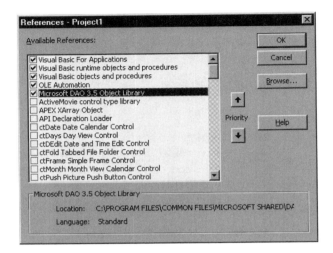

When you create an application with the data control, the reference to the DAO library is handled automatically for you.

Opening a Database

The first step to gaining access to the information in a database is to create a database object and establish the connection to the database. In code, this is done using the OpenDatabase method of the Workspace object. In the simplest case, connecting to a Jet database, the only argument that needs to be specified for the OpenDatabase method is the name of the database. The name can be specified as a literal string or as a string variable. Exercise 9.1 shows you how to get started with a database program and how to use the OpenDatabase method.

EXERCISE 9.1

Opening a Database in Code

1. Open a new project in Visual Basic.

2. Open the References dialog box by choosing the References item from the Project menu.

3. Add the reference to the Microsoft DAO 3.5 Object Library by checking the box next to the item in the References dialog box.

4. Open the code window for the form.

5. In the Declarations section of the code window, declare a Database and a Workspace object variable as shown in the following code:

```
Dim MainWS As Workspace, MainDB As Database
```

6. In the Load event for the form, create an instance of the Workspace object using the code shown below:

```
Set MainWS = DBEngine.Workspaces(0)
```

7. After the Workspace object is created, use the OpenDatabase method to open the desired database as indicated in the following line of code. This code can immediately follow the creation of the Workspace object in the Load event of the form.

```
Set MainDB = _
MainWS.OpenDatabase("C:\Data\VBCertBk\Nwind.mdb")
```

If you are connecting to an Access database version prior to Access 97, you will need to reference the Microsoft DAO 2.5 Object Library or the Microsoft DAO 2.5/3.5 Compatibility Library instead of the DAO 3.5 library. The version of the library you use will depend on the version of Access used to create the database.

Notice in the above statements that the Set command is used to assign the values to the variables. This is the standard syntax for assigning information to object variables. In the exercise, we created a Workspace variable, which is typically done if you will be using the workspace to handle transaction processing. If you are only using the workspace to open the database, you can use the following alternate code to invoke the OpenDatabase method:

```
Set MainDB = DBEngine.Workspaces(0).OpenDatabase _
("C:\Data\VBCertBk\Nwind.mdb")
```

This alternate code avoids having to create an object variable for the workspace and saves system resources. In both code segments, you make use of the Workspaces collection of the DBEngine object. When you work with DAO, Visual Basic creates a default workspace for you. This workspace is the first one in the collection, with the index value of 0. Typically, you will only need the single, default workspace for your programs. However, if you need to create additional workspaces, you can do so by using the CreateWorkspace method of the DBEngine object. For more information on creating workspaces, you should refer to Visual Basic's on-line help.

The OpenDatabase method examples above used a literal string to specify the path and database name. If you are distributing your program, you will need to have a method to retrieve the user's path for the database. You can do this by using Registry settings or by using the App.Path information if the database is in the same folder as the application.

Handling Optional Parameters

The database name is the only required parameter of the OpenDatabase method. However, there are three optional parameters that you may need to use in various situations:

- **Options**   For Jet databases, this Boolean parameter specifies whether the database is open in shared mode (the default) where others can access the database at the same time, or in exclusive mode where your program is the only one that can access the database and all others are locked out.

- **Read-only**   This Boolean parameter specifies whether the database is to be opened in read-only mode, where the users of your program cannot make changes to the information.

- **Connect** This parameter is a string that specifies additional connection information for the database such as the password for the database or the database type, if the database is something other than a Jet (Access) database.

If you use any of the optional parameters, they must appear in the proper order in the OpenDatabase method: Database Name, Options, Read-only, and finally Connect. If you omit any of the parameters, you will need to use placeholders (commas) to indicate the missing information. For example, if you want to enter information in the Connect parameter, you will need to place three commas between the database name and the connect string to indicate that two parameters have been omitted. The best practice is to specify values for each of the parameters, so you are sure what values are being used. As an example, Figure 9.3 shows the use of the Connect parameter of the OpenDatabase method for handling a database with a password.

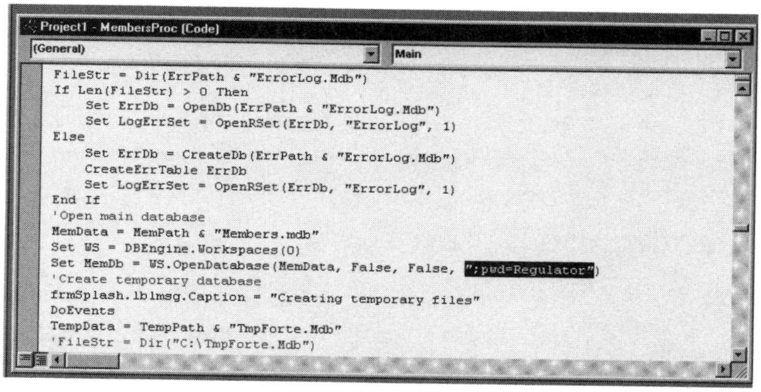

FIGURE 9.3

A password is part of the connection information needed for some databases.

```
Project1 - MembersProc (Code)
(General)                                    Main
    FileStr = Dir(ErrPath & "ErrorLog.Mdb")
    If Len(FileStr) > 0 Then
        Set ErrDb = OpenDb(ErrPath & "ErrorLog.Mdb")
        Set LogErrSet = OpenRSet(ErrDb, "ErrorLog", 1)
    Else
        Set ErrDb = CreateDb(ErrPath & "ErrorLog.Mdb")
        CreateErrTable ErrDb
        Set LogErrSet = OpenRSet(ErrDb, "ErrorLog", 1)
    End If
    'Open main database
    MemData = MemPath & "Members.mdb"
    Set WS = DBEngine.Workspaces(0)
    Set MemDb = WS.OpenDatabase(MemData, False, False, ";pwd=Regulator")
    'Create temporary database
    frmSplash.lblmsg.Caption = "Creating temporary files"
    DoEvents
    TempData = TempPath & "TmpForte.Mdb"
    'FileStr = Dir("C:\TmpForte.Mdb")
```

Connecting to Non-Jet Databases

One of the most common uses of the connect parameter of the OpenDatabase method is to specify the type of database that is being used. You will need to specify this parameter if you are going to work with a FoxPro database, Excel spreadsheet, or Text file as your data source. In addition to needing to specify the Connect parameter, many of these database types require different handling of the database name than is necessary for an Access database. For example, if you are using a FoxPro 2.5 database, the database name parameter specifies the path to the database files, not a particular file name, as shown in the code below:

```
Dim sFilePath As String, FoxDB As Database
sFilePath = "C:\Data\VBCertBk"
Set FoxDB = DBEngine.WorkSpaces(0).OpenDatabase(sFilePath, _
False, False, "FoxPro 2.5;")
```

The connect string and the appropriate setting of the database name parameter are summarized in Table 9.1 for several common data sources.

T A B L E 9.1:   Database name and Connect parameters for PC data sources

Database type	Connect string	Database Name Contains	Example
dBase 5	dBase 5.0;	Path to database files	C:\Data\dBaseV
FoxPro 2.5	FoxPro 2.5;	Path to database files	C:\Data\FoxPro
Excel 5.0	Excel 5.0;	File name including path	C:\Data\Excel\Inventry.xls
Text	Text;	Path to the text files	C:\Data\Text

Opening the Recordset

After you have opened a database, the next step is to create a recordset containing the information that you want out of the database. The recordset can contain the entire contents of a table, a few fields and records from a table, combined information from several tables, or even a single item of summary data. What is contained in the recordset depends on how you create it.

To create any recordset using the DAO, you will use the OpenRecordset method of the database object. This method only requires you to specify the information you want to retrieve, the data source. All other parameters are optional. A typical statement for creating a recordset is shown below:

```
Set RSProduct = MainDB.OpenRecordset("Products")
```

Specifying the data source is similar to setting the RecordSource property of the data control. The data source you specify can be the name of a table, the name of a stored query, or a SQL statement. The specification of the data source determines what information is contained in the recordset.

The second parameter of the OpenRecordset method specifies the type of recordset to be created. While this is an optional parameter, it is good practice to specify the recordset type. If you omit this parameter, Visual Basic will create a recordset that it determines is most compatible with the data source you specified, typically a dynaset-type recordset. The three types of recordsets are table-type, dynaset-type, and snapshot-type. Each of these recordset types is indicated in the OpenRecordset method by a Visual Basic constant. Figure 9.4 shows the code for creating several different recordsets of different types.

F I G U R E   9.4

Creating different types
of recordsets

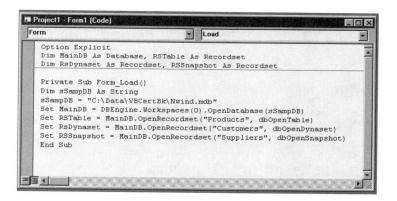

```
Option Explicit
Dim MainDB As Database, RSTable As Recordset
Dim RsDynaset As Recordset, RSSnapshot As Recordset

Private Sub Form_Load()
Dim sSampDB As String
sSampDB = "C:\Data\VBCertBk\Nwind.mdb"
Set MainDB = DBEngine.Workspaces(0).OpenDatabase(sSampDB)
Set RSTable = MainDB.OpenRecordset("Products", dbOpenTable)
Set RsDynaset = MainDB.OpenRecordset("Customers", dbOpenDynaset)
Set RSSnapshot = MainDB.OpenRecordset("Suppliers", dbOpenSnapshot)
End Sub
```

When you specify the recordset type, you must ensure that it is compatible with the data source. If you are using a table-type recordset, you must specify a data source that is the name of a table; you cannot use a query or SQL statement. If you are creating a dynaset-type or snapshot-type recordset, you can use any of the data sources specified above.

Displaying the Data from a Recordset

After you have created the recordset, you are ready to display the information from the recordset on your form, or to perform calculations with the data. To do this, you will first need to access the fields of the recordset. Then, if you are displaying the data, you will need to assign the contents of the field to the appropriate control on your form. Figure 9.5 shows a typical data entry form created with DAO. As you can see, it is quite similar to a form that you would create with the data control.

FIGURE 9.5

A typical data entry form

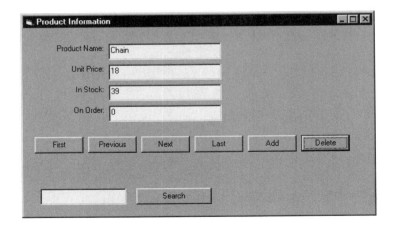

The simplest, and most efficient, way to retrieve the information from a field is to use what is known as the bang operator (!). This operator works in the same manner as dot notation; you specify the name of the recordset object, insert the bang operator, and specify the name of the field to be retrieved. The following code shows how this is used to assign the contents of the ProductName field to a variable.

```
sProdName = RSProducts!ProductName
```

There are two alternate methods that you can use to specify the field from which values should be retrieved. Both of these methods make use of the Fields collection of the recordset object. The first method allows you to specify the field using the field name, which is similar to using the bang operator. The advantage of this method is that you can use a variable to specify the name of the field, which is useful if you develop a generic routine for handling multiple fields. The second method uses the index of the field in the fields collection. This method requires that you know in which order the fields appear in the collection in order to select a specific field. Both of these methods are shown in the code below.

```
sProdName = RSProducts("ProductName")
sProdName = RSProducts.Fields(1)
```

Both of these statements will produce the same results as the original statement using the bang operator.

WARNING If you use the field index in the fields collection, you will need to make sure that your statement for creating the recordset always places the same number of fields in the same order. Otherwise an error or unpredictable results will occur.

Figure 9.5 showed a sample data entry form for handling product information using DAO. Exercise 9.2 shows you how to create the display portion of this form. Figure 9.6 shows the code window for the form with all the necessary code to display the information from the first record.

EXERCISE 9.2

Displaying Data from a Recordset

1. Start a project and open the code window for the main form.

2. Declare a database object and recordset object in the Declarations section of the form. The statement is shown below. Be sure to set the proper reference to the DAO library before creating these objects.

   ```
   Dim MainDB As Database, RSProducts As Recordset
   ```

3. Open the database and the recordset, using the following statements placed in the Load event of the form.

   ```
   Set MainDB = DBEngine.Workspaces(0).OpenDatabase _
   ("C:\Data\VBCertBk\NWind.mdb")
   Set RSProducts = MainDB.OpenRecordset("Products", _
   dbOpenDynaset)
   ```

4. Place several text controls on the form to hold the product name, unit price, quantity in stock, and quantity on order items. Name the text boxes **txtProdName**, **txtUnitPrice**, **txtInStock**, and **txtOnOrder** respectively. Place several label controls next to the text boxes to identify the information.

5. Create a Sub Procedure named ShowData. You can create a procedure using the Procedures dialog box accessible by choosing the Add Procedure item from the Tools menu.

EXERCISE 9.2 (CONTINUED)

6. Place the following code in the ShowData procedure. This code retrieves the contents of the database fields and places the information in the appropriate text box.

```
txtProdName.Text = RSProducts!ProductName
txtUnitPrice.Text = RSProducts!UnitPrice
txtInStock.Text = RSProducts!UnitsInStock
txtOnOrder.Text = RSProducts!UnitsOnOrder
```

7. Call the ShowData procedure from the Activate event of the form by placing the following statement in the event procedure.

ShowData

8. Run the program. You should see the information for the first record in the Products table of the database.

F I G U R E 9.6

The complete code for opening a recordset and showing the first record

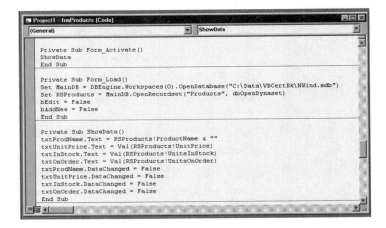

 You will probably need to specify a different directory as the location of your database file.

Exercise 9.2 showed you the basics of displaying information from a database using DAO. However, there are several things you really need to do in addition to the basic retrieval shown above. When you create a database application using the data control, the bound controls automatically handle things like type conversions and null values for you. When you use DAO, you have to handle these things yourself. One of the most common errors that you will encounter is when a null value exists in one of the database fields and you try to assign it to a text box. Because the text box does not know how to handle this, an error will occur. Therefore, you should ensure that the values passed to the text box will be handled correctly. How you do this depends on the type of information that is in the data field. For a text field, you can simply append a zero-length string to the end of the field value. If the field contains a text string, this has no effect, but if the field contains a null value, a zero-length string is passed to the text box instead of a null value. For a numeric field, you can use the Val function to ensure that an actual numeric value is passed to the text box. Implementing these changes would yield the following code for the ShowData procedure.

```
txtProdName.Text = RSProducts!ProductName & ""
txtUnitPrice.Text = Val(RSProducts!UnitPrice)
txtInStock.Text = Val(RSProducts!UnitsInStock)
txtOnOrder.Text = Val(RSProducts!UnitsOnOrder)
```

Record Navigation and Manipulation

At this point, you can display the information from the first record of the recordset. Obviously, we need to add more capabilities to the program to make it really useful. First, we will need a way to move to other records in the database. Then we need to be able to edit existing records, add new records, and delete records. You will see how to add these capabilities in this section.

Moving through the Recordset

Microsoft ✓ *Exam* *Objective*	**Navigate through and manipulate records in a Recordset.**

The way that you move from one record to another is by using one of the Move methods of the Recordset object. When you used the data control, these commands were issued automatically when you pressed one of the navigation buttons on the data control. In your program, you have to handles these functions yourself. There are five Move methods that you can use in your program:

- **MoveFirst**   Positions the record pointer at the first record of the recordset.

- **MovePrevious**   Positions the record pointer at the record prior to the current one.

- **MoveNext**   Positions the record pointer at the record after the current one.

- **MoveLast**   Positions the record pointer at the last record of the recordset.

- **Move**   Allows you to specify a number of records forward or backward of the current position that you want to move.

In addition to actually invoking the Move methods, your program also needs to be able to detect whether the record pointer has been moved to the beginning or the end of the recordset. If you are beyond the first or last record of the recordset and try to display data, you will encounter an error. Fortunately, the recordset object has a BOF and EOF property to let you know whether you are at one of the ends of the recordset. Exercise 9.3 continues the example started in Exercise 9.2 by adding the capability of moving from one record to another.

EXERCISE 9.3

Navigating Through the Recordset

1. Add a command button to the form and name it **cmdFirst**. Set the Caption property of the button to First.

2. Add the following code to the Click event of the cmdFirst button.

```
RSProducts.MoveFirst
ShowData
```

3. Add a command button to the form and name it **cmdPrevious**. Set the Caption property of the button to Previous.

4. Add the following code to the Click event of the cmdPrevious button.

```
With RSProducts
    .MovePrevious
    If .BOF Then .MoveFirst
End With
ShowData
```

5. Add a command button to the form and name it **cmdNext**. Set the Caption property of the button to Next.

6. Add the following code to the Click event of the cmdNext button.

```
With RSProducts
    .MoveNext
    If .EOF Then .MoveLast
End With
ShowData
```

7. Add a command button to the form and name it **cmdLast**. Set the Caption property of the button to Last.

8. Add the following code to the Click event of the cmdLast button.

```
RSProducts.MoveLast
ShowData
```

9. Run the program. You can now move through the recordset and see the various products.

You can also use a control array of command buttons to place all the code for recordset navigation in a single event procedure.

You will notice that we included a call to the ShowData procedure in each of the event procedures for the command buttons. By placing the code to display the data in a procedure, we avoided having to repeat this code in each of the event procedures. Figure 9.7 shows the data entry form as it exists after the addition of the navigation buttons.

FIGURE 9.7

The data entry form with navigation buttons

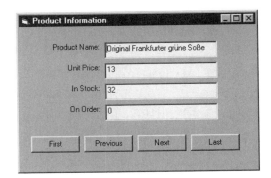

The exercise made use of four of the Move methods. These are the ones that are most typically used in a data entry program. If you need to use the other Move method to handle moving the record pointer more than one record at a time, you simply list the name of the recordset, the Move method, and the number of records you want to move. Because you can potentially move the pointer past either the beginning or the end of the file, the routine you use to invoke the Move method should also include checks for these conditions and take the appropriate action. A sample move routine is shown below:

```
lNumRecords = Val(txtMove.Text)
With RSProducts
    .Move lNumRecords
    If .BOF Then .MoveFirst
    If .EOF Then .MoveLast
End With
ShowData
```

By including the checks for the ends of the file, you assure that a record is available for display.

Adding and Editing Records

Microsoft ✓ *Exam* *Objective*   **Add, modify, and delete records in a Recordset.**

Editing Records

As with everything else in creating a data entry program with code, you have to handle the editing of data within your code; it is not handled automatically for you. After displaying the information from a record on the form, the user has the capability of changing the information in the display (assuming that the controls allow changes). Your job in setting up the edit function consists of three tasks:

- Determining that a change in the data has occurred

- Preparing the actual record for editing

- Committing the changes to the database

The first task is determining that the data has been changed. There are several ways of doing this:

- You can set a form-level flag to indicate that the data has been changed. To implement this, you need to write code in the Change or Click event of each control to set the flag, then you need to reset the flag after the data is changed. While this sounds like a lot of work, using control arrays makes it quite manageable. The advantage of using this method is that you can visually indicate that changes have been made by changing the color of the controls or displaying a Save button as soon as any changes are made.

- If your program is only using controls that can be bound to a data control (even though they are operating in unbound mode), you can make use of the DataChanged property of the controls to determine if the data was changed. In this case, you need to set the DataChanged property of each control to False after the information is displayed for the current record. Then, before you allow the user to move to another record, you check the DataChanged property of each record to determine if a change has occurred. If so, save the changes to the database.

- Finally, you can write code to compare the current contents of the controls to the fields from which the data was retrieved. Again, you would perform the check prior to allowing the user to move to another record. This is probably the slowest method of determining that a change has been made. However, it does have the advantage of not requiring you to save data if the user made a change, then reversed it.

After you have used one of the above methods to determine that the user made a change, you have to handle the task of preparing the record to accept the changes, then saving the changes to the database. The task requires the use of two recordset methods. First, you use the Edit method to tell the recordset to prepare to accept changes to the data. Next, you assign the values of the controls to the appropriate fields in the recordset. Finally, you use the Update method to tell the recordset to commit the changes to the database. An example of the code for this task is shown below:

```
With RSProducts
    .Edit
    !ProductName = txtProdName.Text
    !UnitPrice = Val(txtUnitPrice.Text)
    !UnitsInStock = Val(txtInStock.Text)
    !UnitsOnOrder = Val(txtOnOrder.Text)
    .Update
End With
```

Adding Records

The process for adding records is quite similar to one for editing records. To add a record to the database, you need to:

- Clear the controls to allow the user to enter new information.

- Tell the recordset to add a new record.

- Assign the values to the fields.

- Commit the information to the database.

The first step of this process involves simply setting the text property of a text box to a blank or default value and performing a similar function with any other controls used for data input. Next, you use the AddNew method of the recordset object to tell the recordset to prepare to receive the information for a new record. Then, assigning the values and committing the changes is handled the same way as it was for editing a record. In fact, because adding a record and editing a record are so closely related, you can put both functions in the same routine.

Adding Modification Capabilities to a Program

Now that we have looked at the concepts involved in editing or adding a record, it is time to put them into practice. Exercise 9.4 shows you how to add the Edit and Add capabilities to the sample project. The techniques shown in the exercise are relatively simple, but there are other ways to modify records, and you should feel free to experiment.

EXERCISE 9.4

Modifying Records

1. To the existing project, add three command buttons. One of these buttons should be named **cmdSave**, with the Caption property set to Save. The second button should be named **cmdCancel**, with the Caption property set to Cancel. Both of these command buttons should have their Visible property set to False. The third command button should be named **cmdAdd**, with the Caption property set to Add.

2. Declare two logical variables in the Declarations section of the form. The variables should be named **bEdit** and **bAddNew**.

3. In the Load event of the form, set the value of the bEdit and bAddNew variables to False.

4. Create a procedure called SetEditMode. In this procedure, add code to hide the visible command buttons and display the cmdSave and cmdCancel buttons. This code is shown in the following graphic.

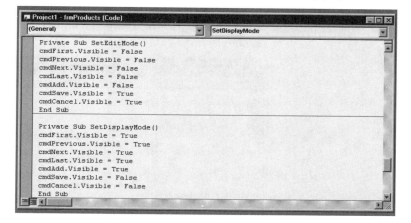

5. Create a second procedure called SetDisplayMode that resets the command buttons back to their original configuration.

6. In the Change event of each text box, place the following code. This code sets the value of the edit flag and displays the appropriate buttons.

```
bEdit = True
SetEditMode
```

7. In the Click event of the cmdAdd button, add code to clear all the text boxes and set the edit flag (bEdit) and add record flag (bAddNew) to True.

8. In the Click event of the cmdCancel button, you need to place code to redisplay the original record information, reset the edit and add record flags to False, and reset the command buttons using the following code:

```
ShowData
bEdit = False
bAddNew = False
SetDisplayMode
```

9. In the Click event of the cmdSave button, place the code to handle the editing or adding of records. This code consists of the Edit or AddNew method followed by the assignment of the values of the fields of the database. After the field values have been assigned, the Update method is used to commit the changes to the database. Finally, the edit and add record flags are set to False and the command buttons are reset to their original configuration. The code for this event is shown in the next graphic.

```
Project1 - frmProducts (Code)

cmdAdd                                    Click

    Private Sub EditRecord()
    With RSProducts
        .Edit
        !ProductName = txtProdName.Text
        !UnitPrice = Val(txtUnitPrice.Text)
        !UnitsInStock = Val(txtInStock.Text)
        !UnitsOnOrder = Val(txtOnOrder.Text)
        .Update
    End With
    End Sub

    Private Sub cmdAdd_Click()
    bEdit = True
    bAddNew = True
    SetEditMode
    txtProdName.Text = ""
    txtUnitPrice.Text = ""
    txtInStock.Text = ""
```

10. You can now run the program to test the new changes. The next two illustrations show how the form looks with the Add record button, and the form in the editing mode with the Save and Cancel buttons displayed.

FIGURE 9.8

Records can now be added to the recordset.

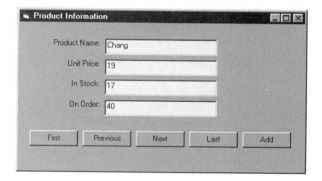

FIGURE 9.9

The Save and Cancel buttons allow the user to commit the changes or discard them.

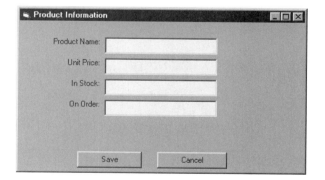

Deleting Records

The last data modification capability to be added is to allow the user to delete the current record. This capability requires the use of the Delete method of the Recordset object. In most programs you will want to verify that the user really wants to delete the record. If so, you invoke the Delete method, then move the record pointer to another record to display its data. You do not want to leave the information from a deleted record displayed, as the user might try to edit it, and an error may occur. Exercise 9.5 shows you how to add deletion capabilities to your program.

EXERCISE 9.5

Deleting Records

1. Add a command button to the form with the name **cmdDelete** and set the Caption property to Delete.

2. In the Click event of the cmdDelete button, add the following code to determine whether the user really wants to delete the record:

```
Dim iDelConfirm As Integer
iDelConfirm = MsgBox _
("Are you sure you want to delete this record?", vbYesNo)
If iDelConfirm = vbNo Then Exit Sub
```

3. After the confirmation routine, add the following line to delete the record:

```
RSProducts.Delete
```

4. Finally, add the code to move to another record and display its data. This code is shown below:

```
With RSProducts
    .MoveNext
    If .EOF Then .MoveLast
End With
    ShowData
```

Finding Specific Records

Microsoft
✓ *Exam*
Objective

Find a record in a Recordset.

The data entry program that we have create so far is very similar to the ones you can create with the data control. However, most data entry programs, and many other programs that work with database information, are not used to step through records one at a time from the beginning of the recordset to the end. Most programs need to have the capability to find a specific record or specific groups of records.

To find a record in a recordset, your program will use one of the Find methods if you are working with a dynaset- or snapshot-type recordset, and the Seek method if you are working with a table-type recordset. There are advantages and drawbacks to each of these methods which will be detailed in this section.

Using the Find Method

There are two key tasks you can perform using the Find methods. The first and most common use is to find a particular record in order to display or modify its data. This task is typically handled with the FindFirst method. The second task is to process a group of records that meet a specific criteria. This task involves a processing loop and a combination of the FindFirst and FindNext methods or the FindLast and FindPrevious methods.

As you saw in Chapter 8, the FindFirst method lets you specify the field to be searched, the comparison operator, and the value to be searched for. The specifics of several comparison operators were detailed there and will not be repeated here. We will, however, look at how the FindFirst method can be used to add search capabilities to the sample program created in the previous exercises. Exercise 9.6 details this process.

EXERCISE 9.6

Finding a Record in a Recordset

1. Start Visual Basic with the sample project open.

2. Add a text box to the form named **txtSearch** and delete the contents of the text property.

3. Add a command button to the form named **cmdSearch** and set the Caption property to Search.

EXERCISE 9.6 (CONTINUED)

4. Add the following code to the Click event to enable the program to perform search operations:

```
Dim sBookMark As String, sSearchStr As String
sBookMark = RSProducts.Bookmark
sSearchStr = txtSearch.Text
With RSProducts
    .FindFirst "ProductName >= '" & sSearchStr & "'"
    If .NoMatch Then .Bookmark = sBookMark
End With
ShowData
```

5. Run the program and try searching for specific items. The completed program is shown in Figure 9.5.

You will notice in the program listing above that a couple of new properties of the recordset object were used. First, the Bookmark property. This property contains a unique string that identifies the current record and can be used to save the position of the record pointer to return the pointer to the record after a failed search. The second property is the NoMatch property. A property value of False indicates that the search was successful, while a property value of True indicates that the search failed. When used as shown in the code above, the Bookmark is saved to a string variable; then, after the search is performed, a check is made on the success of the search. If the search failed, the record pointer is returned to its original position by setting the Bookmark property to the saved value.

WARNING Some databases do not support bookmarks. You should check the BookMarkable property of the recordset to determine if bookmarks are supported.

Finding Multiple Records

Microsoft *Exam* *Objective*	**Use the Find or Seek Method to Search a Recordset.**

The other use of the Find methods is to handle the processing of a number of related records, for example, determining the inventory value of all products of a particular group, such as perishable foods. When working with multiple records, you can move forward through the group using the FindFirst method to locate the first record meeting your criteria, then using the FindNext method repeatedly to locate the rest of the records. You can also work backward through the group, using the FindLast to locate the record nearest the end of the recordset that matches your criteria, then repeatedly using the FindPrevious method to locate the rest of the records. The following code shows how the FindFirst and FindNext methods could be used to process inventory information for a particular category.

```
Dim sngTotal As Single
sngTotal = 0
With RSProducts
    .FindFirst "CategoryID = 1"
    Do Until .NoMatch
        sngTotal = sngTotal + !UnitsInStock * !UnitPrice
        .FindNext "CategoryID = 1"
    Loop
End With
```

You can also use the FindNext to modify the search function in the data entry program. Using this method, you could have successive presses of the Search button move to the next record matching the criteria. This technique is included in the sample program for this chapter that is contained on the CD.

Advantages of the Find methods

The Find methods have several advantages over the Seek method, including:

- The ability to search on non-indexed fields
- The ability to use patterns to locate records (using the Like comparison operator)
- The ability to search for records whose value lies in a range of values
- The ability to combine multiple criteria

Using the Seek Method

The Seek method is the only method you can use to find a particular record if you are working with a table-type recordset. The Seek method basically works like the FindFirst method. It will locate the first record that matches the specified criteria. One of the limitations of the Seek command is that you must have an index for the field you are searching. For example, if you are searching a membership database for a person with a particular last name, you must have an index in the database that uses the last name as a key field. In addition, the index must be the one that is current for the recordset. While this does limit the Seek method somewhat, the advantage of using the Seek method is speed. The Seek method requires you to specify the comparison operator (<, <=, >, >=, or =) and the value to be found. The field to be searched is determined by the index currently in use. Exercise 9.7 shows you how to modify the Product data entry screen to use the Seek method to locate a record instead of the Find methods.

EXERCISE 9.7

Using the Seek Method

1. In the Load event of the Form, change the OpenRecordset call to open a table-type recordset instead of a dynaset-type recordset as shown in the following code.

   ```
   Set RSProducts = MainDB.OpenRecordset("Products", _
   dbOpenTable)
   ```

2. After the recordset is opened, set the index of the recordset using the following command.

   ```
   RSProducts.Index = "ProductName"
   ```

3. In the Click event of the cmdSearch button, replace the FindFirst method with the following line, which uses the Seek method.

```
RSProducts.Seek ">=", sSearchStr
```

Finding Multiple Records

When you were searching for multiple records with the Find methods, you could use the FindNext method to locate additional records that matched the criteria. The Seek method has no corresponding capability. The Seek method will only find the first occurrence of the record that matches the criteria. However, the nature of indexes is to order all records in ascending or descending order by the key fields. Therefore, all records with the same CategoryID (or other key field) will be grouped together, allowing you to process multiple records in a manner similar to that used with the Find methods. The following code shows how you can create the inventory total using the Seek method.

```
Dim sngTotal As Single
sngTotal = 0
With RSProducts
    .Index = "CategoryID"
    .Seek "=", 1
    Do While !CategoryID = 1
        sngTotal = sngTotal + !UnitsInStock * !UnitPrice
    Loop
End With
```

Alternatives to the Find and Seek Methods

The Find and Seek methods allow you to use loops to process multiple records. However, there are alternatives to these methods that are often more efficient in the processing of the information.

The first alternative is to create the recordset to contain only the records that match a certain criteria by specifying a SQL statement with the appropriate Where clause as the data source of the recordset. The following lines of code show you how this can be done to create a recordset containing only products of a certain category.

```
Dim sSQLCategory As String
sSQLCategory = "Select * From Products Where CategoryID = 1"
Set RSProducts = MainDB.OpenRecordset(sSQLCategory, _
dbOpenDynaset)
```

You can also use a SQL statement to create summary information directly.

The second alternative is to create a second recordset based on the original recordset, but filtered for the specific records. This operation can only be done using dynaset- and snapshot-type recordsets. The following code would accomplish this task.

```
Dim RSProd2 As Recordset
RSProducts.Filter = "CategoryID = 1"
Set RSProd2 = RSProducts.OpenRecordset(dbOpenDynaset)
```

Either of these techniques will produce a limited recordset that contains only the records of interest. These recordsets can then be manipulated using a simple loop. The advantage of using these techniques is speed. In many cases (especially for large recordsets), it is faster to create the limited recordset than to repeatedly use the FindNext method.

Summary

This chapter covered how to create a database program using the methods and properties of the Data Access Objects. You have seen how to display data, navigate through a recordset, add, edit, and delete records, and to find specific records. You have also seen how the Find and Seek methods can be used to search through a recordset to find all the records that match a specific criteria, and an alternative for working with groups of records. The specific exam objectives covered were:

- Access data by using code.

- Navigate through and manipulate records in a Recordset.

- Add, modify, and delete records in a Recordset.
- Find a record in a Recordset.
- Use the Find or Seek method to search a Recordset.

The review questions are similar to the questions you might expect to find on the MCSD Visual Basic 5 exam. If the questions do not seem familiar to you, refresh your memory by going over the exercises in this chapter again.

Review Questions

1. Which object handles the connection to a specific database?

A. DBEngine

B. Workspace

C. Database

D. Recordset

2. Which object provides the link to specific data?

A. DBEngine

B. Workspace

C. Database

D. Recordset

3. Which object is responsible for handling transaction processing?

A. DBEngine

B. Workspace

C. Database

D. Recordset

4. Which of the following is a valid data source for the OpenRecordset method? Check all that apply.

A. The name of a table

B. The name of a stored query

C. A SQL statement

D. The name of a data control

5. What type of recordset must you use if you want to use a SQL statement as the data source?

A. Table

B. Dynaset

C. Snapshot

D. Both the Dynaset and Snapshot can be used.

6. What is the proper method of referring to a field in a recordset in order to retrieve the value of the field? Check all that apply.

A. RSProd!ProductName

B. RSProd(ProductName)

C. RSProd("ProductName")

D. RSProd.Fields(3)

7. Which statement is valid for setting the ProductName field to a new value?

A. Set ProductName = "Syrup"

B. RSProducts!ProductName = "Syrup"

C. SetFieldValue "ProductName", "Syrup"

D. RSProducts.Fields(3).Set "Syrup"

8. In order to modify the value of a field, what is the proper sequence of commands?

   A. Assign the value of the field, then invoke the Edit and Update methods.

   B. Invoke the Edit method, then assign the value of the fields. The Update method is not needed.

   C. Invoke the Edit method, assign the values of the fields, then invoke the Update method.

   D. Invoke the Edit method, assign the values of the fields, then invoke the Commit method.

9. What is the proper method to use to add a record to the recordset?

   A. Edit

   B. NewRecord

   C. Add

   D. AddNew

10. Which method would you use to locate the first record in a dynaset-type recordset?

   A. FindNext

   B. Seek

   C. Search

   D. FindFirst

11. Which method would you use to locate the first record in a table-type recordset?

   A. FindNext

   B. Seek

   C. Search

   D. FindFirst

12. Which of the following are advantages of using the Find method instead of the Seek method? Check all that apply.

    A. Find is always faster than Seek.

    B. Find allows you to specify multiple criteria.

    C. Find lets you search for a range of values.

    D. Find works with all recordset types, Seek doesn't.

13. Which of the following are criteria for using the Seek command? Check all that apply.

    A. You must have an active index that contains the field to be searched.

    B. You must be working with a dynaset-type recordset.

    C. You must be working with a table-type recordset.

    D. You must specify the name of the field to be searched in the method call.

CHAPTER

10

Working with Remote Data

Chapters 8 and 9 introduced you to the concept of working with databases. You learned that it was easy to connect to a PC database such as a Jet database (the native database format that Visual Basic shares with Microsoft Access) or a FoxPro database. With the data control and bound controls, you could quickly build a program to allow the user to display and edit data. With a little more work, and the Data Access Objects (DAO), you could handle adding new records, deleting records, and several other tasks.

In today's programming environment, however, there is a need to be able to write programs that go beyond accessing local databases. You also need to be able to access large network databases, often in a client/server environment. These databases can reside on database servers running Microsoft SQL Server, Oracle, or even mainframe databases such as DB2. These databases are capable of handling multiple clients and hundreds of megabytes, even gigabytes, of data.

Fortunately, many of the techniques that you use to access local databases can also be used in accessing remote databases. In fact, if you have a solid understanding of the DAO object model, you are well on your way to being able to write the programs that access remote databases.

In this chapter, we will examine the fundamentals of remote databases, then discuss how to use the Remote Data Objects (RDO) and the Remote Data Control (RDC) to access these databases. The certification exam objectives that we will cover are some of the same ones that were covered with the Data Control and DAO:

- Access data by using the data controls and bound controls.
- Access data by using code.
- Navigate through and manipulate records in a Recordset.
- Add, modify, and delete records in a Recordset.

Remote Data Fundamentals

Typically, when referring to remote data, we are referring to the information stored in database servers such as SQL Server. Given the right setup, however, the remote data objects and the remote data control can be used to connect to almost any database, whether it is a database server or a local database. The key to using the remote data objects is having an ODBC connection to the database.

What Is ODBC?

ODBC stands for Open Database Connectivity. ODBC is a specification that database vendors use to write drivers that allow programs to link to their databases. If you have an ODBC driver for a database, you can create a connection to the database, then use RDO to access and manipulate the database information. Each ODBC driver contains a set of core functions that enable you to perform tasks with the associated database. These functions are known as the core-level capabilities and include:

- Providing a database connection
- Preparing and executing SQL statements
- Returning result sets
- Processing transactions
- Notifying the calling application of errors

Because each ODBC driver must provide these core capabilities, you can write a single application that can access data from a number of data sources. To change the database that your application works with, you simply reset the ODBC link. There is no need to recompile your code. (Assuming, of course, that table and field names are the same in both the original and the new data source.)

Using ODBC greatly simplifies the process of creating a program to access remote data. However, do not fall into the trap of thinking that you don't need to know anything about the workings of the database to which you are linked. Because there are differences between database servers, you need to understand how each server that you access works. Otherwise, you will not be able to get the best performance out of the database, nor take advantage of all of its capabilities.

Linking to an ODBC Data Source

The first step in working with ODBC data sources and the RDO is to create the link to the data source. The tool for creating these links is the ODBC Manager. This tool is installed with Visual Basic and is available in some versions of Windows. You can find the ODBC Manager in the Control Panel of Windows 95 or Windows NT. When you start the ODBC Manager, you will see a dialog box like the one shown in Figure 10.1.

FIGURE 10.1

ODBC Data Source
Administrator

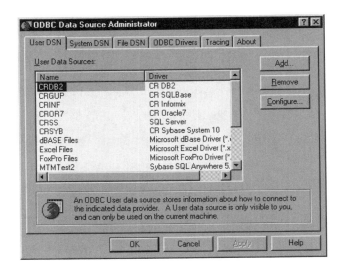

When you set up a connection to a database, the first thing you need to do is verify that the driver for your database exists on your system. The ODBC Drivers tab of the Data Source Administrator shows you a list of all available drivers. Many of these drivers, such as the ones for local databases and SQL Server, are installed with Visual Basic if you chose to have them installed. Other drivers may have come with your system or other programs. If the driver you need is not shown in the list, you will have to install it. To install a new driver, you will need the driver and the installation program from the database vendor.

After verifying that the driver exists, you can begin setting up the data source for your program. First, you need to move to the User DSN (data source name) tab of the Administrator. Then, click the Add button to bring up the

Create New Data Source wizard, shown in Figure 10.2. The first page of the wizard allows you to select the ODBC driver that will be used to access the database.

F I G U R E   10.2

Selecting an ODBC driver

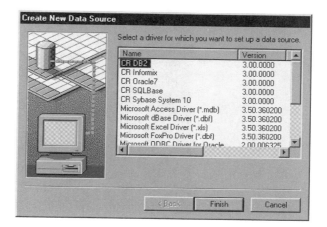

After making the selection and clicking the Finish button, you will be shown a dialog box where you set the parameters for the specific database you are accessing. The specifics of the dialog box may vary from one database to another, but there is basic information that you will supply for any database, specifically:

- **Data Source Name**   The name by which the database will be identified to your programs.

- The location of the database.

In addition to the basic parameters, you may need to supply additional information, such as a user ID and password. As an example of the data source setup dialog boxes, Figures 10.3 and 10.4 show you the dialog boxes for an Access and a SQL Server database respectively. Then Exercise 10.1 takes you through the process of creating a data source for use in programs later in this chapter.

F I G U R E   10.3

Setting up a Microsoft
Access data source

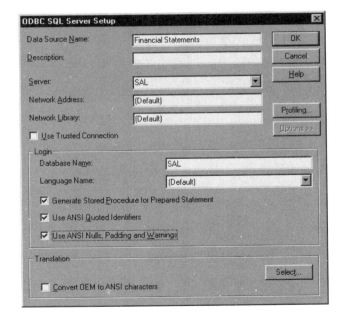

F I G U R E   10.4

Setting up a Microsoft
SQL Server data source

EXERCISE 10.1

Setting Up a Data Source

1. Open the 32bit ODBC Data Source Administrator from the Windows control panel.

2. Click the Add button on the User DSN tab of the Administrator.

3. From the selection list, choose the Microsoft Access Driver and click the Finish button.

4. The next steps are performed with the Microsoft Access Setup dialog box shown in Figure 10.3. Enter the Data Source Name as **Trading Company**.

5. Click the Select button and choose the Nwind.mdb database from the open dialog box. You will find the database in the VB folder on your machine.

6. Click the OK button to create the data source. You will be returned to the main Administrator screen and see that the Trading Company data source has been added to the list. You can now close the Administrator.

The reason we use the Access database for demonstration purposes is that it is available on the machines of almost all Visual Basic developers. In fact, the Access drivers are part of the default installation for Professional and Enterprise versions of Visual Basic.

Working with the Remote Data Control

The Remote Data Control (RDC) does for remote data access what the data control does for local data access. Specifically, it makes it easy to connect to the information in a remote database by setting a few properties, and it provides a tool for navigating the records of the resultset. If you are familiar with the data control, working with the RDC will be quite easy. The following table lists some of the key properties of the data control and their corresponding properties in the RDC.

T A B L E 10.1: Data Control Properties

Data Control Property	RDC Property	Description
DatabaseName	DataSourceName	Identifies the database to which the control is to be connected.
RecordSource	SQL	Identifies the specific data to be retrieved from the database. You must use SQL statements with the RDC.
RecordsetType	ResultsetType	Determines how the data returned by the control will be accessed. (RecordsetType will be defined further in the next section.)
BOFAction	BOFAction	Determines what action to take when the beginning of the file is reached.
EOFAction	EOFAction	Determines what action to take when the end of the file is reached.

Creating a basic data display / data entry program with the RDC is quite easy. To create a program, you follow 3 simple steps:

1. Add the RDC to your toolbox.

2. Place a copy of the RDC on your form and set its properties to make the connection to the data.

3. Add bound controls to your form and link them to specific fields in the resultset created by the RDC.

Setting Up the Remote Data Control

The first step to working with the Remote Data Control is to add it to your toolbox. You will need to access the Components dialog box and choose the RDC from the list of available controls. Upon closing the dialog box, the RDC will appear in your toolbox.

You must be using the Professional or Enterprise edition of Visual Basic in order to be able to use the RDC. The Remote Data Control is not available with the Learning Edition of Visual Basic.

After adding the control to your toolbox, place a copy of the control on your form, then set the properties of the control. These property settings create the connection between the RDC and your remote data source.

Setting the DataSourceName Property

The first property that you will need to set is the DataSourceName. This property identifies the ODBC data source that will be connected to the RDC. You can choose the data source from the drop down list in the Properties window. The list, shown in Figure 10.5, inventories every ODBC data source that is defined on your machine. Simply select the name from the list and the property is set.

F I G U R E 10.5

Selecting the data source

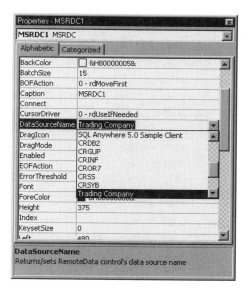

Setting the SQL Property

The next step in the process is to identify the specific data that you want to access. If you remember from Chapter 8, "Accessing Data with the Data Control," the data control provided you with a list of the tables and queries that were available in the selected database. You could either use one of these data objects or write a SQL statement to pick the data for the control.

Selecting the specific data is one of the key differences between the data control and the RDC. The RDC does not give you the luxury of selecting a table or predefined query; you must enter a SQL statement in the SQL property to determine the data to be retrieved. For most data access needs, the SQL statement can be quite simple. For example, the following statement would retrieve all the information in the Customers table of the database:

```
Select * From Customers
```

If you want to limit the fields or records that are returned, you can add conditions to the SQL statement. The explanation of SQL (Structured Query Language) is beyond the scope of this book. However, most database formats (Access or SQL Server, for example) that you connect to will have information about the SQL commands that they support in their help files.

Selecting a Type of Resultset

After you have defined the DataSourceName and the SQL property, you have entered all the **required** information for making a database connection. In many cases, however, you will want to also set the type of resultset that will be used in the retrieval of the information. The type of resultset defines what tasks can be performed on the data that is retrieved and affects the performance of the application.

You set the type of resultset for the RDC using the ResultsetType property. There are two possible settings of the ResultsetType property that are selectable from the drop-down list in the property:

- **rdOpenKeyset**   A Keyset-type resultset is the RDO equivalent of a dynaset-type recordset in DAO. A Keyset has rows that can be updated, and your movement within the resultset is unrestricted, which means you can move forward or backward through the resultset. Other types of resultsets (not available with the RDC but with RDO directly) restrict your movement within the resultset. A Keyset also allows you to add or delete rows in the resultset and, therefore, in the underlying table(s) of the database.

- **rdOpenStatic**   A Static resultset is the equivalent of the Snapshot-type recordset for the data control. The Static resultset retrieves the information that is available at the time the connection is made. Additions and deletions in the underlying tables that may be made by other users are not reflected in the Static resultset. The Static resultset is also not updateable.

Setting Up the RDC Example

Exercise 10.2 illustrates the steps necessary to set up the RDC for a sample application. This exercise uses the Data Source created in Exercise 10.1. If you have not created the data source, you need to do so now.

EXERCISE 10.2

Setting Up a Remote Data Control

1. Start a new Visual Basic project. Name the form **frmRemoteData** and set the Caption to Remote Data Control Demonstration.

2. Use the Components dialog box to add the RDC to your toolbox.

3. Add an instance of the RDC to your form. Name the control **rdcDemo** and set the Caption property to Employees. The contents of the Caption property will appear in the RDC to identify the data to the user. At this point, your form should look like the one in the following graphic:

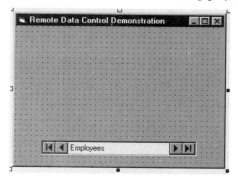

4. Click on the arrow next to the DataSourceName property to select the data source from a list. Select the Trading Company data source that was created in Exercise 10.1.

5. Enter the following statement in the SQL property of the RDC. This statement retrieves the information in the Employees table of the database.

```
Select * From Employees
```

6. Select the rdOpenKeyset option in the ResultsetType property. It should be the default setting.

7. Save the project.

Binding the RDC to Controls

After you have set up the RDC, the next step in creating a data entry application is setting up the controls that will display the data and allow the user to modify the information. The Remote Data Control will work with all the same bound controls as the Data Control. In fact, setting up the bound controls is exactly the same whether you are using the Data Control or the Remote Data Control as your data source.

For all data-bound controls, the first property you have to set is the Data-Source. This property defines which RDC (or data control) will be the source of your information. After setting the DataSource property, most controls also require you to set the DataField property. This property identifies the specific field in the resultset that should be displayed in the control. To set the DataField property, you select the field from the drop-down list in the Properties window. If your RDC is set up correctly, this list will contain all the available fields for the data source. Exercise 10.3 walks you through setting up some bound controls to work with the RDC created in Exercise 10.2. The resulting application will display information from the Employees table of the Nwind.mdb database.

EXERCISE 10.3

Displaying Information from the RDC Data Source

1. Open the project created in Exercise 10.2.

2. Add seven label controls to the form with the following captions: First Name:, Last Name:, Address:, City:, State:, Zip:, Home Phone:.

3. Add seven text box controls to the form with the following names: txtFirst, txtLast, txtAddress, txtCity, txtState, txtZip, txtPhone. Clear the text property of each of the text boxes.

4. For each text box, set the DataSource property to rdcDemo. Double-clicking on the property will pick this Remote Data Control.

5. For each text box, set the DataField property in accordance with the following list:

Control Name	DataField Setting
txtFirst	FirstName
txtLast	LastName

Control Name	DataField Setting
txtAddress	Address
txtCity	City
txtState	Region
txtZip	PostalCode
txtPhone	HomePhone

6. Save the project.

7. Run the program. Your form should look like the one in the following graphic.

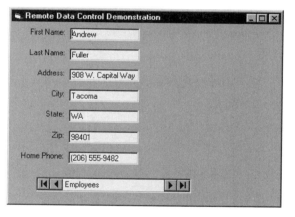

Using Remote Data Objects

Like the relationship between the data control and the Data Access Objects, the Remote Data Control is intimately related to the Remote Data Objects of Visual Basic. In fact, the RDC is a wrapper around some of the most commonly used methods of the RDO. When you set the DataSource-Name and SQL properties of the RDC, you are creating rdoConnection and rdoResultset objects. And, when you press the navigation keys of the RDC, you are using the Move methods of the rdoResultset object. In this section, we will explore how to use some of the objects of the RDO model to create a data access program without the use of the RDC and bound controls. As we progress, you will see how the RDO model is very similar to the DAO model that was described in Chapter 9, "Creating Programs with Data Access Objects."

Key Objects of the RDO Model

Because of the similarities between the DAO and the RDO object models, one of the best ways to explain the RDO model is by comparison to the DAO model. Most of the RDO objects have a DAO counterpart as described in the following table:

T A B L E 10.2 RDO and DAO Objects	**RDO Object**	**DAO Object**
	rdoEngine	DBEngine
	rdoEnvironment	Workspace
	rdoConnection	Database
	rdoResultset	Recordset
	rdoColumn	Field
	rdoQuery	QueryDef

As you might guess from the table, the key object of the RDO model is the rdoResultset. This object retrieves a specific set of information from a remote database, just as the Recordset object is used to retrieve a set of data from a local database. Once the rdoResultset has been created, you will use the methods of the object to move between records of the set and to add, modify, and delete records. The methods that you will use are the same ones that were used with the Recordset object, specifically:

Command	**Action**
AddNew	Insert a new record.
Delete	Remove the current record.
Edit	Prepare the current record to receive data changes.

Command	Action
MoveFirst	Move to the beginning of the resultset.
MoveLast	Move to the end of the resultset.
MoveNext	Skip to the next record in the set.
MovePrevious	Skip to the previous record in the set.
Update	Save changes to the record.

In fact, the only key methods of the Recordset object that are not supported by the rdoResultset object are the Find and Seek methods.

Creating a Resultset

The first step to displaying and editing data with the Remote Data Objects is to create a resultset. The resultset is created using a method of the Connection object. In turn, the Connection object is created using a method of the Environment object. For most of your applications, you will be able to create the Connection object by simply identifying the name of the data source. This data source must be one of the Data Sources managed by the ODBC Manager. The following statement creates a Connection to a remote database:

```
Set rdConn = rdoEngine.rdoEnvironments(0). _
OpenConnection("Trading Company")
```

Once the connection to the data source is created, you can use the connection object to open a resultset. When using the RDO, you have more resultset options than were available with the RDC. The types of resultsets, their Visual Basic constants, and a description of their capabilities are given in the following table.

T A B L E 10.3: Resultsets and Visual Basic Constants

Resultset Type	Constant	Description
Dynamic	rdoOpenDynamic	A set of records that is updateable. The records can be retrieved from one or more tables. Movement within the resultset is unrestricted.
Forward-Only	rdoOpen-ForwardOnly	An updateable set of records that can only be navigated from beginning to end. Only the MoveNext method is supported with this resultset.

T A B L E 10.3: Resultsets and Visual Basic Constants *(continued)*

Resultset Type	Constant	Description
Keyset	rdoOpenKeyset	Similar to the Dynamic type; this is the default resultset type.
Static	rdoOpenStatic	A snapshot of the records. You can move freely through the resultset, but the records are not updateable.

To create a resultset, you use the OpenResultset method of the connection object and use one of the above constants to define the type of resultset to create. This method is illustrated in the following code:

```
sResultSQL = "Select * From Employees"
Set rdResult = rdConn.OpenResultset(sResultSQL, _
rdOpenKeyset)
```

Displaying Data with RDO

Once you have created the resultset, you are ready to display and edit data. To display data, you simply assign the contents of a field from the resultset to a property of a control, for example, the Text property of a text box. To move between records, you use the Move methods as described above. If you need to edit data, you first invoke the Edit method, then change the values of the fields of the record, and use the Update method to commit the changes to the database. If all this sounds familiar, it is because this is the same process that you used when you were working with the DAO objects in Chapter 9. To further illustrate the use of the RDO objects, Exercise 10.4 recreates the Employee data entry form that was created earlier in the chapter; this time, however, the program is created with RDO. The program that we create is only capable of displaying data. It is left as an exercise for the reader to add the editing capabilities. (Hint: Look at the way it was done in Chapter 9.)

EXERCISE 10.4

Creating a Data Entry Form with RDO

1. Start a new project.

2. Using the References dialog box, add a reference to Remote Data Objects 2.0 to your project.

3. Set the Name property of the form to frmRDO and the Caption property to Remote Data Objects Demonstration.

4. Add seven label controls to the form with the following captions: First Name:, Last Name:, Address:, City:, State:, Zip:, Home Phone:.

5. Add seven text box controls to the form with the following names: txtFirst, txtLast, txtAddress, txtCity, txtState, txtZip, txtPhone. Clear the text property of each of the text boxes.

6. Add four command buttons to the form. Name the buttons cmdTop, cmdPrevious, cmdNext, and cmdBottom. Set the Caption properties to Top, Previous, Next, and Bottom respectively.

7. Add the following code to the Declarations section of the form. This code sets up the variables that will hold the RDO objects.

```
Dim rdConn As rdoConnection, rdResult As rdoResultset
```

8. Create a Sub procedure called ShowData and add the following code to the procedure. This code displays the contents of the fields in the resultset.

```
txtFirst.Text = rdResult!FirstName & ""
txtLast.Text = rdResult!LastName & ""
txtAddress.Text = rdResult!Address & ""
txtCity.Text = rdResult!City & ""
txtState.Text = rdResult!Region & ""
txtZip.Text = rdResult!PostalCode & ""
txtPhone.Text = rdResult!HomePhone & ""
```

9. Add the following code to the Load event of the form to open the resultset and display the first record of the resultset:

```
Dim sResultSQL As String
Set rdConn = rdoEngine.rdoEnvironments(0). _
OpenConnection("Trading Company")
sResultSQL = "Select * From Employees"
Set rdResult = rdConn.OpenResultset _
(sResultSQL, rdOpenKeyset)
With rdResult
    If Not .RowCount = 0 Then
        .MoveFirst
        ShowData
    End If
End With
```

10. Add the following code to the command buttons to move to other records and display the data of the current row. The specific buttons are identified in the procedure headers.

```
Private Sub cmdBottom_Click()
rdResult.MoveLast
ShowData
End Sub

Private Sub cmdNext_Click()
With rdResult
    If Not .EOF Then
        .MoveNext
        If .EOF Then .MoveLast
    Else
        .MoveLast
    End If
End With
ShowData
End Sub

Private Sub cmdPrevious_Click()
With rdResult
    If Not .BOF Then
        .MovePrevious
        If .BOF Then .MoveFirst
    Else
        .MoveFirst
    End If
End With
ShowData
End Sub

Private Sub cmdTop_Click()
rdResult.MoveFirst
ShowData
End Sub
```

EXERCISE 10.4 (CONTINUED)

11. Save the project, then run the program. You should be able to move back and forth through the resultset. The graphic below shows the program displaying a record.

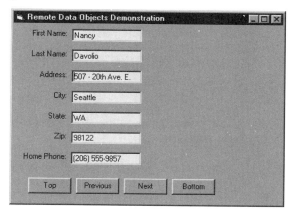

Summary

This chapter has given you an overview of the Remote Data Objects and the Remote Data Control. As you have seen, using these objects you can create data entry programs in a manner similar to the Data Control and the Data Access Objects. In fact, the similarities are so great that you can use almost the same code to access local data and remote data. The key concepts that you needed to get out of this chapter were:

- How to set up the Remote Data Control

- How to bind controls to the RDC

- How to create a resultset in code

- How to use the Move methods and assignment statements to display data from code

If you understand these concepts, you should have no problem with the certification exam objectives stated at the beginning of the chapter.

Review Questions

1. What property of the Remote Data Control determines the database accessed by the control?

   A. SQL

   B. ResultsetType

   C. DataSourceName

   D. Connect

2. What property of a bound control must be set to work with a Remote Data Control?

   A. UseRemoteData

   B. DataSource

   C. DataField

   D. You cannot bind controls to the RDC.

3. What tool do you use to set up a data source for remote data access?

   A. Remote Data Control

   B. Remote Data Objects

   C. ODBC Data Source Administrator

   D. Visual Basic's Data Form Wizard

4. Which object of the RDO model provides the link to the database being accessed?

   A. rdoEngine

   B. rdoEnvironment

   C. rdoConnection

   D. rdoResultset

5. Which of the following methods is **not** supported by RDO?

A. FindFirst

B. MoveLast

C. AddNew

D. Update

6. Which object of the RDO is used to retrieve specific data from a database?

A. rdoEngine

B. rdoEnvironment

C. rdoConnection

D. rdoResultset

PART

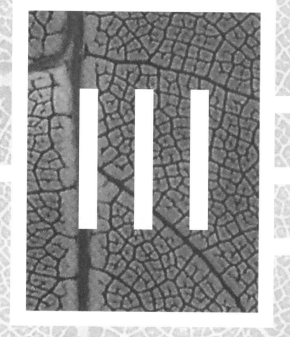

III

Communicating with Other Programs

CHAPTER

11

Using ActiveX Servers

Microsoft Objectives Covered in This Chapter:

- Create an Automation server that exposes objects, properties, methods, and events.

- Define properties for objects by using property procedures.

- Create, use, and respond to events.

- Create a method that displays a form.

- Create a multithreaded component.

- Call an object server asynchronously.

In Chapter 7, "Creating Classes in a Program," you learned that you can create a class to encapsulate data and code for a particular function. This capability to place all the information for an object made it easier to reuse code than was possible with procedures alone. ActiveX servers take the use of classes a step further. By compiling the classes and placing them in an ActiveX server, either DLL or EXE, you make the objects (and their associated properties, methods, and events) available to multiple projects. You can use the objects without adding the class itself to the project on which you are working. In addition, other programs can make use of the classes that you have written.

The certification exam objectives state that you need to know the following information about creating and using ActiveX servers:

- Create an Automation server that exposes objects, properties, methods, and events.

- Define properties for objects by using property procedures.

- Create a method that displays a form.

- Create a multithreaded component.

- Use App object properties to control server behavior.

- Call an object server asynchronously.

- Create, use, and respond to events.

Why Use ActiveX Servers?

ActiveX servers let you take functions and objects that you create in classes and make them available to other programs. By compiling these functions and objects into a server, the other applications can make use of the server objects without being able to modify them. In a client/server environment, this means that many applications can use the same server objects for database access, information validation, and other tasks. When the tasks need to be modified, only the server has to be changed, the client applications can be left alone, and the new or modified functionality is automatically available.

What Is an ActiveX Server?

An ActiveX server is a collection of objects that can be used by your program. For example, Excel is an ActiveX server that exposes spreadsheet objects that you can use in your programs. You can create instances of these objects, then load and manipulate spreadsheets from within your Visual Basic program.

When you create an ActiveX server, you are creating objects that can be used in other programs. These objects can be used to handle complex math functions, retrieve data from a local or remote database, provide messaging capabilities within a company, or perform any number of other tasks.

In Visual Basic, you have the capability of creating two types of servers:

- In-Process Servers
- Out-of-Process Servers

In-Process Servers

In-Process servers are created as DLL files. When your program accesses one of the objects of the DLL, the object is linked to your program and runs in the same process space (area of memory) as your program. When your program is finished with the object, the link is closed and the DLL is no longer active for your program. A DLL cannot be run by itself.

The key advantage of using an In-Process server is speed. Because the component object and your program are in the same process space, the transfer of information between them is much faster than is possible with an Out-of-Process server. The key disadvantage of the In-Process server is that it cannot be run on a machine separate from the client application (your program), which means that you cannot take advantage of the speed of a server to run parts of your application, such as data retrieval, where the data typically resides on a server.

Out-of-Process Servers

Out-of-Process servers are stand-alone programs that expose objects to other programs. The Out-of-Process server can be started on its own or can be started by a client application. When your application finishes with an object from an Out-of-Process server, the server can continue running, able to provide objects to other client programs or to perform tasks of its own.

The key advantage of Out-of-Process servers is that the objects run in a separate process space than the client applications, which makes Out-of-Process servers useful for client/server applications where processes such as data retrieval and storage can be run on the server machine, close to the data. The disadvantage of Out-of-Process servers is that communication between your application and the server objects is slower because the information has to cross process boundaries.

What Is the Benefit of Using a Server?

The key benefit of using ActiveX servers is to make objects and their properties and methods available to multiple programs. For example, because Excel is an ActiveX server, you do not need to write functions such as regression analysis for your applications; you can simply create an instance of a spreadsheet object and use the regression analysis capabilities built into Excel.

There are two typical uses for the ActiveX servers that you may write:

- Supplying business objects to an application
- Supplying custom functions to an application

Using Business Objects

Database applications are a major part of the computing needs of many companies. Companies use databases to handle payroll, customer support, billing, and business analysis. Typically, the data for a company is stored in central databases that are available for access by a number of applications. However, companies have rules about who can access the data and how they can access it. In addition, there are typically business rules that must be met before any data can be posted to the database. These rules might include:

- Hours worked by an employee cannot exceed 45.

- A pay raise cannot be greater than 15% of the current salary.

- If the posting of an invoice fails, all invoice line items should be removed from the database. (This is transaction processing.)

- Managers may view payroll data only for employees in their own department.

As programmers write applications that access the corporate databases, these rules must be enforced. To try to make sure all these rules make it into every application would be almost impossible. Business objects provide an alternate means of handling all the necessary tasks for enforcing the business rules. By placing the rules in business objects and placing the objects in a server, programmers only need to know how to access the object. They don't even have to know what the rules are.

This centralized containment of the business rules and objects provides another major benefit—when the rules change, only one program, the ActiveX server needs to be changed. All programs that access the server remain unaffected, reducing the cost of program maintenance.

Making Functions Available to Multiple Programs

The other major use of ActiveX servers is to make libraries of custom functions available to multiple programs. For example, if you work for an engineering firm, there are many complex math functions that are required for engineering calculations. By placing these functions in a single ActiveX server, any programmer that needs the function merely needs to call it from the server. It does not have to be rewritten in every program.

As with business objects, a key benefit is program maintenance. If a function needs to be modified, it only has to be modified in a single place.

Creating an ActiveX Server

Whether you are creating an In-Process or an Out-of-Process server, the key steps to building the server are the same:

- Start the appropriate type of project.
- Build the classes that define the objects of the server.
- Create any supporting routines needed by the server.
- Test the server.
- Compile the server and make it available for use.

Microsoft ✓ *Exam* *Objective*

Create an Automation Server that Exposes Objects, Properties, Methods, and Events.

In this section, we will examine each one of these steps in detail. Where appropriate, we will point out the differences between working with an In-Process and an Out-of-Process server. Otherwise, you can assume that the steps we show are indifferent to the type of server you are creating. To illustrate the concepts of creating an ActiveX server, the exercises in this section will create and test a server that handles payroll calculations. Information about employees is stored in a database and is accessed through the server. You can find the sample database on the CD as Payroll.mdb.

Starting a Server Project

When you begin to create an ActiveX server, the first choice that you have to make is what type of server to create. Earlier in this chapter, in the section entitled "What is an ActiveX Server," we discussed the two types of servers, In-Process and Out-of-Process. An In-Process server runs in the same process space as the client application. You create In-Process servers by creating an ActiveX DLL project. An Out-of-Process server is a stand-alone program that runs in a separate process space from the client application. To create an Out-of-Process server, you choose the ActiveX EXE project.

To start a new project, you can start Visual Basic, or select the New Project item from the File menu. You will be presented with the Project dialog box shown in Figure 11.1. From this dialog box, you can choose the type of project to create. After you have chosen the project type, a project and a class will be created for you and you will be placed in the code window of the class. You will probably want to rename both the project and the class to names that indicate what the server and objects will be doing.

FIGURE 11.1

Project selection
dialog box

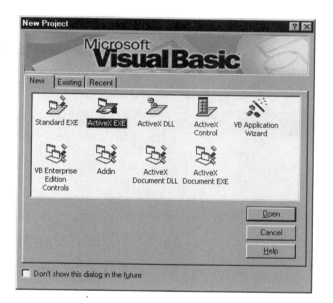

Once you are in the project, you can add more classes, BAS modules, and forms to the project to handle all the tasks the server needs to accomplish. If you are working with an ActiveX EXE project, you may want to add a module and create a Sub Main procedure to initially set up the server when it loads. Exercise 11.1 shows you how to set up the basic project for the Payroll server.

EXERCISE 11.1

Creating the Payroll Server

1. Start a new project and select ActiveX EXE as the project type.

2. Select the project in the Project window and change the name of the project to **Payroll** to identify the server to other applications. For now, we will skip the Class module. It will be covered in the next section.

3. Because the Payroll project will be working with a database, you will need to provide a reference to the database library. Open the References dialog box from the Project menu and select the Microsoft DAO 3.5 Object library as shown in the next illustration.

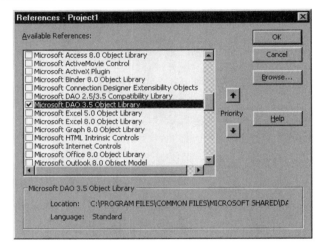

4. Add a BAS module to the Project to handle the initialization of the server. You can add a module by choosing the Add Module item from the Project menu. Name the module **DataAccess**.

5. Place the following code in the Declarations section of the DataAccess module. This code creates two database objects and makes them available to other routines in the server.

```
Public EmpRset As Recordset, EmpData As Database
```

6. Create a procedure entitled Sub Main. This procedure will handle the startup of the server and make a connection to the database. You can use the Add Procedure dialog box available from the tools menu to create the procedure or type Sub Main in the code window of the BAS module.

7. Add the following code to the Sub Main procedure. This code connects to the database.

```
Dim sMainData As String
sMainData = App.Path & "\Payroll.mdb"
Set EmpData =
DBEngine.Workspaces(0).OpenDatabase(sMainData)
```

8. Set Sub Main as the Startup Object for the Payroll project. You do this by selecting the Properties item from the Project menu, then selecting the Sub Main procedure from the list of Startup Objects as shown in the following illustration.

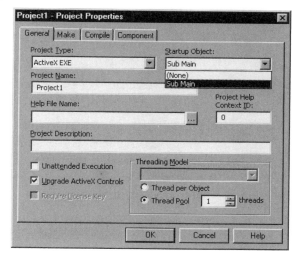

9. Select the Class module in the Project window and delete it from the project. Don't worry, we will add another one later.

10. Save the project.

Controlling the Operation of the Server

| Microsoft Exam Objective | Use App Object Properties to Control Server Behavior. |

As you are creating an ActiveX server, you will set properties of the project and properties of the classes in the server while you are in the design environment. However, there are several properties that control the behavior of the server that can only be set at runtime. These properties are part of the App object. The App object is an internal Visual Basic object that is used by an application to refer to itself. For standard programs, the properties of the App object are used to determine the name of the program, the path of the executable file, and whether another copy of the program is running.

With server applications, there are several properties which determine the response of the server when applications request objects while the server is busy with other requests. These properties are defined as follows:

- **OLEServerBusyTimeout**   specifies the number of milliseconds that an application can retry a request before the "Component Busy" dialog box is shown.

- **OLEServerBusyMsgText**   specifies the text to be displayed in the "Component Busy" dialog box when a request times out.

- **OLEServerBusyMsgTitle**   specifies the text to be shown in the title bar of the "Component Busy" dialog box when a request times out.

- **OLEServerBusyRaiseError**   determines whether an error is raised when the component request times out. If the property is set to True, an error is raised. If the property is set to False, the default "Component Busy" dialog box, or a dialog box with the custom message is displayed on a time out.

If you use any of these properties in your application, the values of the property are typically set in the Sub Main procedure which starts the server.

Creating the Classes of the Server

After you have created the ActiveX server project and set the necessary project properties, you are ready to start creating the objects that will be provided by the server. Each object that you want to provide from the server is defined as a Class in the server. We covered the creation of classes in detail in Chapter 7, but we will review some of the key points here, then create the class for the Payroll server.

To start the creation of a class, select the Add Class Module item from the Projects menu, which adds a new class to your project. You can then set the two properties of the Class, Name and Instancing. The Name property should reflect what is represented by the class and should be preceded with the letter *c*. For example, a class that represents an invoice could be named cInvoice, while the class that represents the detail items of the invoice could be named cInvoiceDetail.

Choosing the Instancing Property Setting

The setting of the Instancing property is the key to how a server provides objects to client applications. There are six possible settings of the Instancing property, as defined below for an ActiveX server:

- **Private**   The class can only be used within the server. It is not available to client applications.

- **PublicNonCreatable**   Defines a class that can be used by client applications, but only if it has already been created by the server. Client applications cannot create an instance of the class using the New keyword or the CreateObject function.

- **SingleUse**   Other applications can create and use objects of the class; however, each time a client application creates an object from the class, a new instance of the class is started by the server.

- **GlobalSingleUse**   The same as single use, but an application does not have to specifically create the object to use its methods and properties. The methods and properties are treated as global functions.

- **MultiUse**   Similar to single use, but the server creates only a single instance of your class, no matter how many clients create objects from the class. All objects from the class are generated from the single instance.

- **GlobalMultiUse**   The same as MultiUse except that the methods and properties are treated as global functions, which means that applications do not have to specifically create an instance of the class.

Depending on the type of server you are creating, all these options may not be available to you. An ActiveX EXE server can use any of the settings of the Instancing property; however, the ActiveX DLL server cannot use the SingleUse or the GlobalSingleUse settings. Fortunately, you don't have to remember this because Visual Basic will only provide you with the choices that are available for your type of project.

Creating Elements of the Class

After setting the basic properties of the class, you are ready to start creating the elements of the class. These elements are the properties, methods, and events that are exposed by the class to client applications. Again, the following sections provide a quick review of creating these elements. For more detailed information, you should review Chapter 7, "Creating Classes in a Program."

Microsoft ✓ *Exam* *Objective*

Define Properties for Objects by Using Property Procedures.

Creating Properties Properties are the elements of a class that store information. This information can be things like an invoice ID, the number of hours worked by an employee, or the dimensions of a room in a building. Properties are defined for a class by Property procedures. As you recall, there are three types of Property procedures that you can create:

- **Property Let** Sets the value of a property of a standard data type.

- **Property Get** Retrieves the value of a property.

- **Property Set** Sets the value of a property containing an object.

You create the shell of the property using the Add Procedure dialog box. In the dialog box, you select the procedure type, set the name of the procedure, and specify the scope of the procedure. Figure 11.2 shows this dialog box for a property procedure.

F I G U R E 11.2

Creating a Property procedure from the dialog box

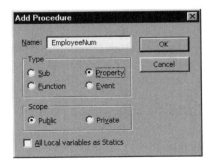

NOTE You can also create a property by typing in the declaration statement in the code window of the class.

After you create the shell of the Property procedure using the dialog box, you enter code to actually handle the setting or retrieving of values from the class. The actual data of the class is stored in variables that are private to the class and are accessible through the Property procedures. The Property procedures can simply set or retrieve the values of these private variables, or they can provide additional functionality, such as data verification.

Creating Methods   Methods are the element of a class that performs a task, anything from retrieving data to printing a report or performing a complex calculation. Methods are simply Sub or Function procedures that have been declared Public to make them available outside the class. When you are creating methods, you typically create a Function procedure whenever you need to return a value to the client program. If you do not need to return a value, you usually create a Sub procedure.

Like a Property procedure, you can create a Sub or Function procedure using the Procedure dialog box or by typing in the Declaration statement for the procedure. In addition to the Public procedures that are used as methods of the class, you can create Private procedures that can only be used in the class itself. You can also create Friend procedures that are available within the project that defines the class, but are not available to client applications.

Microsoft
Exam
Objective

Create, Use, and Respond to Events.

Creating Events   The final element of the class is an Event. An event is used to provide a client application with notification of something happening in the class. You can use an event to let a client know that a database record has been retrieved or that a statement has finished printing.

There are two parts to creating an event in a class. First, you must declare the event procedure using a Declaration statement that specified the name of the event and any arguments that are passed by the event to the client program. The following code shows an example of a declaration statement:

```
Public Event PrintFinished(ByVal Pages As Integer)
```

The second part of creating an event is to trigger the event from code in your class. You handle this with the RaiseEvent statement. This statement specifies the name of the event and the values of the parameters to be passed to the client application. An example of the RaiseEvent statement is shown in the following code:

```
RaiseEvent PrintFinished(iNumPages)
```

Creating the Employee Class for the Payroll Server

For the Payroll server, we need to create a class that handles the employee data and pay calculations for the employee. This class will be accessed by client applications that are processing payroll information. Exercise 11.2 takes you through the steps of creating the class.

EXERCISE 11.2

Creating the Employee Class

1. Add a new class to the project by choosing the Add Class Module item from the Project menu. Name the class **cEmployee**.

2. Set the Instancing property of the class to MultiUse.

3. You will be creating three public properties of the class and several internal variables to hold information such as gross pay, tax withheld, Social Security taxes, Medicare taxes, net pay, and hours worked. The first step to setting up the properties is to create the Private variables that will hold the actual data. To do this, place the following code in the Declarations section of the class module:

```
Dim m_lEmpID As Long, m_iMaxHours As Integer, _
m_iHours As Integer
Dim m_sLastName As String, m_sFirstName As String
Dim m_sngPayScale As Single, m_sngOvertime As Single
Dim m_sngTaxRate As Single
Dim m_sngPay As Single, m_sngSocial As Single, _
m_sngNetPay As Single
Dim m_sngTax As Single, m_sngMedicare As Single
```

4. You will need to provide initial values for several of these variables. You handle this in the Initialize event of the class with the following code:

```
m_iMaxHours = 0
m_iHours = 0
m_sLastName = " "
m_sFirstName = " "
```

5. The first Property is the EmployeeNum property, a write-only property that allows the user to enter the employee ID to be processed by the class. To create a write-only property, use the Property Let procedure as shown in the following code:

```
Public Property Let EmployeeNum(ByVal lNewID As Long)
m_lEmpID = lNewID
End Property
```

6. The second property is the HoursWorked property, also a write-only property that allows the user to input the number of hours worked for the week. You will notice, in the following code, that the property procedure checks the input hours against the maximum allowable for the employee.

```
Public Property Let HoursWorked(ByVal iWklyHours As _
Integer)
If iWklyHours > m_iMaxHours Then
    m_iHours = m_iMaxHours
Else
    m_iHours = iWklyHours
End If
End Property
```

7. The final property is the EmpName property, a read-only property that allows the user to see the name of the employee that was retrieved using the EmployeeNum property. This property lets the user make sure that the right employee is being processed. To create a read-only procedure, you use only a Property Get procedure, as shown below:

```
Public Property Get EmpName() As String
EmpName = m_sLastName & ", " & m_sFirstName
End Property
```

8. After creating the properties of the class, you can create the methods of the class. The Employee class has two methods, GetEmployee and CalcTax. The GetEmployee method takes the information in the EmployeeNum property and attempts to retrieve the employee information. If the procedure is successful, it returns True to the client application. Otherwise, it returns False. Because it returns a value, the GetEmployee method is implemented as a function. The code for the GetEmployee method is:

```
Public Function GetEmployee() As Boolean
Dim sSQLSearch As String
If m_lEmpID <= 0 Then
    GetEmployee = False
    Exit Function
End If
On Error Resume Next
Set EmpRset = Nothing
sSQLSearch = "Select * From Employee Where EmpID = " & _
m_lEmpID
Set EmpRset = EmpData.OpenRecordset(sSQLSearch, _
dbOpenDynaset)
If EmpRset.RecordCount = 0 Then
    GetEmployee = False
    Exit Function
End If
With EmpRset
    m_sLastName = !LastName & ""
    m_sFirstName = !FirstName & ""
    If IsNull(!Payscale) Then
        m_sngPayScale = 0
    Else
        m_sngPayScale = !Payscale
    End If
    If IsNull(!MaxHours) Then
        m_iMaxHours = 40
    Else
        m_iMaxHours = !MaxHours
    End If
```

```
            If IsNull(!OvertimeRate) Then
                m_sngOvertime = 1
            Else
                m_sngOvertime = !OvertimeRate
            End If
            If IsNull(!TaxRate) Then
                m_sngTaxRate = 0
            Else
                m_sngTaxRate = !TaxRate
            End If
        End With
        GetEmployee = True
        End Function
```

9. The final method is the CalcTax method, a Sub procedure that calculates gross pay, Social Security, Medicare, and Federal tax withholding and net pay. The code for the CalcTax method is:

```
Public Sub CalcTax()
Dim iNormHours As Integer, iOverHours As Integer
If m_iHours > 40 Then
    iNormHours = 40
    iOverHours = m_iHours - 40
Else
    iNormHours = m_iHours
    iOverHours = 0
End If
m_sngPay = Int(100 * (iNormHours * m_sngPayScale + _
iOverHours * m_sngPayScale * m_sngOvertime)) / 100
m_sngSocial = Int(100 * m_sngPay * 0.062) / 100
m_sngMedicare = Int(100 * m_sngPay * 0.0145) / 100
m_sngTax = Int(100 * m_sngPay * m_sngTaxRate / 100) / 100
m_sngNetPay = m_sngPay - m_sngSocial - m_sngMedicare - _
m_sngTax
End Sub
```

10. After creating the properties and methods of the class, you need to save the Project. The default name for the .cls file will be cEmployee, the class name.

Displaying a Form from a Class

Objects created from classes are not the only thing that can be exposed by the server. An ActiveX server can have a visual interface for some of its tasks. This visual interface is created using forms, like you would use in a standard executable file. There is, however, a difference in the way that these forms are exposed to the client applications. From a client, you cannot reference a form in a server directly. Instead, the server uses a class method to create an instance of the form and display it.

The technique for creating an instance of a form is basically the same as creating an instance of a class. You use a Dim statement to create a form object. You can then manipulate the properties of the form and use its methods like a regular form, which is very similar to creating multiple forms in a Multiple Document Interface (MDI) program. The Dim statement to create a form object is shown below:

```
Dim frmCheck As New frmPaycheck
```

Microsoft ✓ ***Exam*** ***Objective***   **Create a Method that Displays a Form.**

Of course, the form that you are creating must exist as a form within the ActiveX server project. To create the form in the project, you add a form to the project and use the same visual design tools that you would use for a form in a standard program. Exercise 11.3 shows you how to create a form for previewing a paycheck before it is printed.

EXERCISE 11.3

Creating and Displaying a Form from an ActiveX Server

1. Open the Payroll project.

2. Choose the Add Form item from the Project menu to add a new blank form to the project. Name the form **frmPaycheck**.

3. Set the Caption property of the form to Paycheck Preview.

4. Add seven label controls to the form with the following Captions: **Name:**, **Hours Worked:**, **Gross Pay:**, **Social Security:**, **Medicare:**, **Federal Tax:**, and **Net Pay:**.

5. Add a label control array to the form. Name the labels **lblPayroll** and set the BorderStyle property to Fixed Single. These labels will be used to display the payroll information. (If you do not remember how to create a control array, refer to Chapter 5, "Advanced Design Features." You will need to have seven elements of the control array, numbered 0 to 6.

6. Add two command buttons to the form named **cmdPrint** and **cmdCancel**. Set the Caption properties to &Print Check and &Cancel respectively. When you have added the command buttons, the form will look like the following illustration.

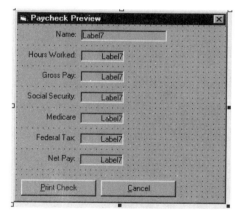

7. To the Click event of each command button, add the statement Unload Me to close the form. If you desire to actually print a check, that is left as an exercise for you.

8. Now that the form has been designed, we need a way to display it. Select the cEmployee class in the Project window and bring up its code window.

9. Add another method named **PreviewCheck** to the class. This method will create an instance of the form, populate the label controls with the current data, and show the form.

10. Create an instance of the form in the method using the following declaration statement:

```
Dim frmCheck As New frmPaycheck
```

11. Set the values of the label controls using the following code. Notice the use of the With statement to avoid having to type the object name for each label setting.

```
With frmCheck
    .lblPayroll(0) = m_sLastName & ", " & m_sFirstName
    .lblPayroll(1) = m_iHours
    .lblPayroll(2) = m_sngPay
    .lblPayroll(3) = m_sngSocial
    .lblPayroll(4) = m_sngMedicare
    .lblPayroll(5) = m_sngTax
    .lblPayroll(6) = m_sngNetPay
End With
```

12. Finally, show the form using the following statement. The form is shown modal because we want the user to examine the information before the check is printed.

```
frmCheck.Show vbModal
```

13. Save the project.

Testing the Server Components

After you have designed all the components (classes) of the server you need to test each component very carefully. The design of Visual Basic allows you to use all the debugging tools of the development environment in the testing of your server, which enables you to watch the values of variables, set breakpoints, and step through the code to determine the path of code execution. This type of debugging capability makes it much easier to find and fix errors in a server than was previously possible.

To test the components of the server, you need to do three things:

- Start the server.

- Start a second instance of Visual Basic.

- Create and run a test application in the second instance of Visual Basic.

Starting the Server

To start the server, you need to click the Run button on the toolbar. Visual Basic then compiles the initialization part of the application, and the server will be running. Another, better approach is to press the Ctrl+F5 key combination, which causes Visual Basic to compile the entire application before running it, allowing you to find any compiler errors that may exist in the application before you start the test process.

Creating a Test Application

Once the server is compiled and running, you can start the creation of the test application. To create a test application, start a new copy of Visual Basic to test the application as a true client of the server. When you start the new copy of Visual Basic, you will need to create a standard EXE project as the client application.

After starting the project, you need to open the References dialog box from the Project menu to set a reference to the server that you created. The server will be listed in the References dialog box by the project description you provided, or by the project name if no description was entered. The References dialog box showing the Payroll server is shown in Figure 11.3.

F I G U R E   11.3

References for the test application

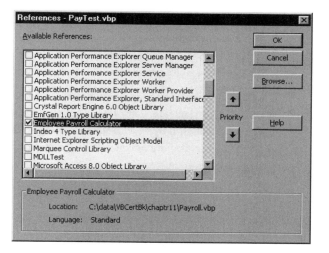

If you have not started the server, you will not be able to set a reference to it.

At this point, you can design the forms, modules, and classes of the test application like any other program that you create. In order to effectively test a server, you will need to create an instance of each public class in the server and access each property, method, and event of each class. Exercise 11.4 shows you how to create a test application for the Payroll server.

EXERCISE 11.4

Creating a Payroll Test Application

1. Start the Payroll server by pressing Ctrl+F5.

2. Start a second copy of Visual Basic and select the Standard EXE project type.

3. Open the References dialog box and set a reference to the Payroll server.

4. Set the name of the Project to PayTest.

5. Select the main form of the project and name it **frmPayInput**. Set the Caption property of the form to Payroll Input Form.

6. Add three labels to the form and set the Caption properties to Employee ID:, Name:, and Hours Worked:.

7. Add two text boxes to the form and name them **txtEmpID** and **txtHours**. Clear the Text properties of both text boxes.

8. Add another label to the form and name it **lblName**. Set the BorderStyle of the label to Fixed Single. This label will be used to display the name of the employee retrieved from the server.

9. Add four command buttons to the form and name them **cmdGetEmployee**, **cmdCalculate**, **cmdShowPay**, and **cmdExit**. Set the Caption properties to &Get Employee, &Calculate Pay, &Show Paycheck, and &Exit respectively. When you are finished, the form should look like the one in the following illustration.

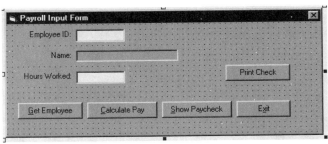

10. You will first need to create an instance of the cEmployee class that is accessible by all the procedures of the form. You do this by placing the following statement in the Declarations section of the Form:

```
Dim oEmployee As New cEmployee
```

11. The first task of the test application is to retrieve employee information, which uses the GetEmployee method of the cEmployee class. To execute this method, place the following code in the Click event of the cmdGetEmployee button. The code passes the input employee ID to the property of the class and invokes the appropriate method. If the method was successful, the name of the employee is returned.

```
With oEmployee
    .EmployeeNum = txtEmpID.Text
    If .GetEmployee Then
        lblName.Caption = .EmpName
    Else
        MsgBox "Employee not found"
    End If
End With
```

12. The next step is to calculate the employee's pay based on the number of hours worked. Place the following code in the Click event of the cmdCalculate button. The code passes the hours worked as entered by the user to the class, then invokes the CalcTax method to handle the payroll calculations.

```
oEmployee.HoursWorked = Val(txtHours.Text)
oEmployee.CalcTax
```

13. After the calculation is made, you will want to verify the calculations. Use the following code in the Click event of the cmdShowPay button to display the Paycheck Preview form that exists in the ActiveX server.

```
oEmployee.PreviewCheck
```

14. Place the following code in the Click event of the cmdExit button. The code destroys the instance of the class and unloads the test application.

```
Set oEmployee = Nothing
Unload Me
```

EXERCISE 11.4 (CONTINUED)

15. Save the test project.

16. Run the test project and enter **2** as the employee ID and **45** as the number of hours worked. Then click the Get Employee button. The test application will return the name of the employee as shown in the next illustration.

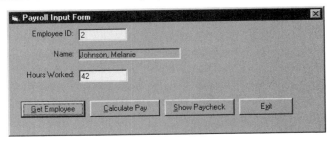

17. Continue testing the application by clicking the Calculate Pay button. Then click the Show Paycheck button to calculate all the payroll information, and display the paycheck preview as shown in the following illustration.

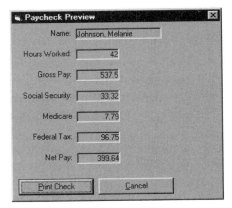

18. You can repeat the process for other employee ID values. If you are using the sample database provided on the CD (Payroll.Mdb), there are four employees, numbered 1 to 4. If you enter a number above 4, the server will not find the employee, and a message to this effect will be displayed.

Compiling the Server

After testing is complete, it is time to compile the server so it can be used by others. The process of compiling the server is basically the same as compiling standard programs, except that there are a few more options for the process.

Multithreading Objects in the Server

Microsoft ✓ ***Exam*** ***Objective***	**Create a Multithreaded Component.**

The key option involved in creating a server is the Multithreading option. Multithreading allows several processes to run simultaneously on the server, which means that one client application does not have to wait for a process of another client application to complete before its process is started. Multithreading allows a program to make good use of multiple processors on a server computer.

Prior to version 5, you could not use multithreading in a Visual Basic application. Even in this version, the type of multithreading that you create is more limited than what can be accomplished with programs developed in Visual C++. Visual Basic supports a multithreading model known as the Apartment model. In this model, each thread contains its own copy of the Global data of the object, and each thread is unaware of any objects that are parts of other threads. This model provides a "safe" multithreading environment that is less likely to cause problems than other more sophisticated models.

To set up a server to use multithreading, you specify options in the properties of the Project. ActiveX DLL servers and ActiveX EXE servers have different multithreading options as described below.

Multithreading with In-Process Servers   For ActiveX DLL servers there are two multithreading options available:

- One thread of execution

- Apartment Threading

These options can be selected from the General page of the Project Properties, as shown in Figure 11.4.

F I G U R E   11.4

Multithreading options
for ActiveX DLL servers

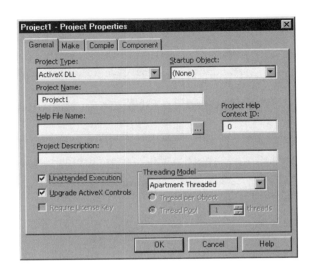

One thread of execution means that all objects created by the server will run on a single thread, resulting in no multithreading of the objects. You can choose this option by selecting Single Threaded from the drop down list in the Threading Model options.

Apartment threading allows the clients of the ActiveX DLL to make use of multithreading. The use of multiple threads is controlled by the client. Also, in order to use multithreading, the Unattended Execution option must be checked, which means that the server cannot have forms or message boxes displayed that require user interaction. To use this multithreading model, select Apartment Threaded from the drop down list in the Threading Model options.

Multithreading with Out-of-Process Servers   For ActiveX EXE servers, there are three multithreading models that you can use:

- One thread of execution

- Thread pool with thread sharing

- One thread per object

You can select the multithreading option from the General page of the Project Properties, as shown in Figure 11.5.

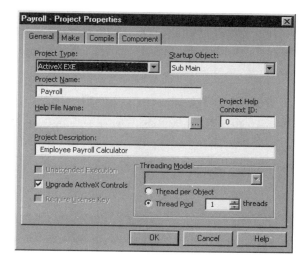

FIGURE 11.5

Multithreading
options for an
ActiveX EXE server

The one thread of execution model means that all the objects handled by
your server will execute in a single thread. In essence, there is no multithreading with this model of execution. To select one thread of execution,
choose the Thread Pool option in the Threading Model options of the Project
properties and set the number of threads to one.

The thread pool model allows you to specify the number of threads that
are available on the server for handling objects. As you create new objects,
each object is assigned to a thread. When you have reached the last thread in
the pool, the next object will be created on the first thread and the process
will be repeated. This is similar to teller lines in the bank. If a bank has three
tellers, the first three customers can each go to a different line and be handled
simultaneously. The next customer in line will line up behind one of the original three customers and wait their turn to handle their transactions. To
implement thread pooling, choose the Thread Pool option and specify the
number of threads you want to have in the pool. You can specify any number
of threads for the process, but a general rule of thumb is to have one thread
for each processor on the computer.

The final model is one thread per object. This model creates a new thread
for each object that is created by the server. The advantage of this model is
that each object operates in an independent thread and is not waiting on
other objects to finish. A major drawback to this model is that you cannot

control the number of threads that will be created. If you have an application that uses a large number of objects, many threads will be created and will eventually slow down the system performance. If you do want to choose the thread per object model, select the option button in the Threading Model options.

Setting Other Compiler Options

Because an ActiveX server provides components to other applications, there is another set of compiler options you can set that were not available for standard programs. These options are contained on the Component page of the Project Properties as shown in Figure 11.6. The options are described below.

FIGURE 11.6

Component options for the project

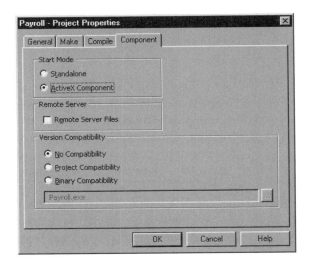

- **Start Mode**   Determines whether the server can be started in standalone mode or only as a component server. This option is not available for ActiveX DLL servers.

- **Remote Server files**   Determines whether Visual Basic creates a .vbr file that is required for the server to be run on a remote computer. This option is available for both ActiveX EXE and ActiveX DLL servers, but is only available with the Enterprise Edition of Visual Basic.

- **Version compatibility** Determines whether new versions of the project will be forced to be compatible with previous versions. There are three settings for this option:

  - **No compatibility** Version compatibility is not enforced.

  - **Project compatibility** The current version will be compatible with the project specified in the file location box.

  - **Binary compatibility** The current version will be compatible with compiled programs that used a previous version of the server.

Finishing the Compilation

Once you have set the Multithreading options and the component options for the server, you can complete the compilation by choosing the Make item from the File menu. The Make Project dialog box allows you to specify the name and location of the EXE or DLL file that you are creating. Also, the Options button provides you access to the Project Properties dialog box in case you want to make any last minute changes to the properties before compilation is finished.

When you select the OK button on the Make dialog box, Visual Basic compiles the project, checking for any compiler errors, and writes the EXE or DLL file to the specified location.

Running Asynchronous Processes

Microsoft ✓ *Exam* *Objective*	**Call an Object Server Asynchronously by Using a Call Back Mechanism.**

In the normal course of operations, a call to a procedure on the server must complete before the next step in the client application can be executed, known as synchronous operation. This process works well for short operations, a long operation on the server could tie up the client application, preventing the user from performing other tasks within the application. A better method is to use Asynchronous operation, which allows the client to spawn a process, then have the server notify the client when the operation is finished.

Asynchronous operations can be set up between a client and a server using either events created by the server object or by using callback functions.

The easiest way to set up Asynchronous operations is through the use of an event. You create an event on the server object using an event declaration and the RaiseEvents statement. Then the client uses a procedure to respond to the event. Exercises 11.5 and 11.6 show you the steps involved in setting up Asynchronous operations.

Setting Up the Server for Asynchronous Operation

The server side of the Asynchronous operation only requires the creation and triggering of an event, as illustrated in Exercise 11.5.

EXERCISE 11.5

Setting Up an Event for Asynchronous Operation

1. Open the Payroll project created earlier in this chapter.

2. Add an event declaration to the cEmployee class using the following code:

   ```
   Public Event PrintFinished(ByVal iNumPages As Integer)
   ```

3. Add a new method to the cEmployee class to raise the event. Call the method PrintCheck and place the following code in the method. In a real setting, you would actually perform a Print operation and report the actual number of pages printed.

   ```
   Public Sub PrintCheck()
   RaiseEvent PrintFinished(15)
   End Sub
   ```

4. Save the project. Then run the server to make it available to the client application.

Setting Up the Client for Asynchronous Operation

Setting up the client requires that you specify a variable using the WithEvents keyword, to let your program know that you will be expecting events from an object on the server. Because you cannot use the New keyword with the WithEvents keyword, we will have to declare the variable, then set it to an instance of the cEmployee class. After creating the variable, you will need to write an event procedure to respond to the event triggered by the server. Exercise 11.6 shows you how to accomplish this.

EXERCISE 11.6

Allowing the Client to Respond to Server Object Events

1. Start a second copy of Visual Basic and open the PayTest project created earlier.

2. Change the declaration statement for the oEmployee object to the following to allow the object to capture and respond to events.

   ```
   Dim WithEvents oEmployee As cEmployee
   ```

3. Add the following code to the Load event of the Form to create an instance of the cEmployee object:

   ```
   Set oEmployee = New cEmployee
   ```

4. In the code window, select the oEmployee object and place the following code in the PrintFinished event of the object:

   ```
   MsgBox "Printer has printed " & Str(iNumPages) & " pages."
   ```

5. Add a command button to the form and name it **cmdPrint**. Set the Caption to Print. Place the following code in the Click event of the button to start the PrintCheck method of the oEmployee object:

   ```
   oEmployee.PrintCheck
   ```

6. Save the project and run the program. When you click the Print button, the PrintCheck method is called. When the method finishes, the PrintFinished event is triggered. The client application then responds to the event by displaying a message box with the number of pages printed.

Summary

This chapter has covered a lot of information about the creation of ActiveX servers, but is by no means an in-depth study of the topic. We could write another book about creating and using ActiveX servers. However, working through the material of this chapter should allow you to meet the following Microsoft exam objectives.

- Create an Automation server that exposes objects, properties, methods, and events.

- Define properties for objects by using property procedures.
- Create a method that displays a form.
- Create a multithreaded component.
- Use App object properties to control server behavior.
- Call an object server asynchronously.
- Create, use, and respond to events.

Review Questions

1. Which of the following is **not** true of In-Process servers?

   A. An ActiveX DLL is an In-Process server.

   B. They are faster than Out-of-Process servers.

   C. They can run as a stand-alone application.

   D. They run in the same process space as the client.

2. Which of the following is an advantage of an Out-of-Process server? Check all that apply.

   A. It can run as a stand-alone application.

   B. There are more multithreading options than for an In-Process server.

   C. It can handle more objects in a single project than an In-Process server.

   D. It is faster than an In-Process server.

3. Which of the following settings of the Instancing property apply only to Out-of-Process servers? Check all that apply.

   A. Private

   B. Public Not Creatable

   C. MultiUse

   D. SingleUse

4. Why use multithreading?

    A. It allows a single object to execute on more than one processor.

    B. It significantly speeds up any server operations.

    C. Multiple objects can run in separate threads and avoid blocking each other.

    D. There is no advantage to multithreading.

5. Which of the following multithreading models uses the most resources?

    A. Apartment model

    B. Single Threaded

    C. Thread Pool

    D. Thread per Object

6. Which setting of the Instancing property creates all client objects from the same instance of the server object?

    A. Private

    B. Public Not Creatable

    C. MultiUse

    D. SingleUse

7. How do you create a property for a server object?

    A. Declare a variable as Public.

    B. Use Property Procedures.

    C. Create a Friend variable.

    D. Use a Sub Procedure.

8. What statement is used to trigger an event?

    A. LoadEvent

    B. Trigger

    C. RaiseEvent

    D. Event.Raise

9. How do you display a server form from a client application?

    A. Use the Show method and specify the form name.

    B. Call a method of the server object that creates and displays an instance of the form.

    C. Use a server event to show the form.

    D. You cannot create forms in a server project.

10. What is the advantage of asynchronous processing?

    A. There is no advantage.

    B. The server can accomplish other tasks while the requested task is running.

    C. The client can accomplish other tasks while the requested task is running.

    D. It allows the client to display a server form.

11. What keyword must be used in a declaration statement to allow an object to respond to events?

    A. Notify

    B. New

    C. WithEvents

    D. UseEvents

CHAPTER

12

Creating ActiveX Client Applications

Microsoft Objectives Covered in This Chapter:

- Use the Dim statement to reference an object.
- Use the Set statement to create an instance of an object.
- Use the CreateObject function to create an instance of an object.
- Build a Microsoft ActiveX client.

I n Chapter 11, "Creating and Running ActiveX Servers," you learned how to create an ActiveX server to provide business objects and other functions to other programs. ActiveX clients are the counterpart to the ActiveX servers. ActiveX clients are the programs that create instances of the objects and use them to perform tasks.

ActiveX clients are not limited to using objects from servers that you create. Client applications can work with objects from any program that is an ActiveX server, including Microsoft Word, Microsoft Excel, and many others. All that you need to create an ActiveX client is a connection to a server and an understanding of the objects of the server.

In this chapter, we will look first at the fundamentals of creating ActiveX clients. Then, we will create some specific applications that make use of ActiveX server objects. Along the way, we will cover the information that you need to know to pass the following certification exam objectives:

- Build a Microsoft ActiveX client.
- Use the Dim statement to reference an object.
- Use the Set statement to create an instance of an object.
- Use the CreateObject function to create an instance of an object.

ActiveX Client Fundamentals

When you create an ActiveX client, you are using the objects that are made available by the server(s) that you are accessing. Therefore, it is important to understand object models in general and in particular the object model of the particular server you are working with.

After you have an understanding of the objects of the server, there are three basic steps to creating an ActiveX client:

- Set a reference to the server you are accessing.

- Create object variables for the objects that you will be using.

- Write code to use the properties, methods, and events of the objects.

Understanding Object Models

From working with Visual Basic, you should have a basic understanding of how object models work. All the forms and controls in Visual Basic are objects, and you create your own objects by defining classes in a program. (If you are unfamiliar with the creation of classes, review Chapter 7, "Creating Classes in Your Program.") Each time you create a new form or a new control on a form, you are creating an instance of a form or control object.

Unlike the form and control objects, many of the objects that you use from ActiveX servers will not have a visual component; they will be handled only in code. If you are familiar with writing code for the forms and controls of Visual Basic, however, you are already familiar with the process of writing code with objects. Each object can have properties, methods, and events, like the forms and controls. To access these elements of the objects, you write code using dot notation as shown in the following code:

```
oEmployee.EmployeeNum = txtEmpID.Text
If oEmployee.GetEmployee Then
    lblName.Caption = oEmployee.EmpName
Else
    MsgBox "Employee not found"
End If
```

In this code example, you specify the variable that contains the instance of the object, followed by a period (or dot) and the name of the property or method. You can see that setting a property of the object (shown in the first line) uses the same type of notation and statement as setting the property of a control (shown for the label control in the third line). As this sample illustrates, your knowledge of working with Visual Basic's objects translates to any other objects that you may use from ActiveX servers.

Finding Help for Object Models

Now that you have seen how to access the properties and methods of an object, you need to find out what properties and methods are available for a given object. Fortunately, there are several sources of help available to you. For many of the commercial applications, such as Microsoft Word, there are help files available that describe the objects, and help you work with the properties and methods. Figure 12.1 shows you the object model for Microsoft Word. This information is contained in the VbaWrd8.hlp help file that comes with Word.

F I G U R E   12.1

Word's Object Model

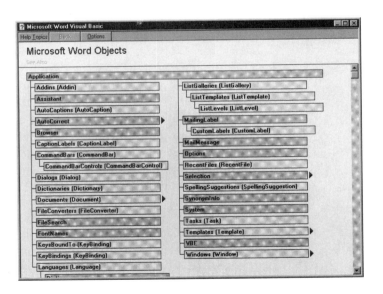

If you are working with a server created by another programmer, you will need to look for documentation of the objects of the server in either printed or help file form. By the same token, if you create an ActiveX server, make sure that you document it well so others can use it.

How Visual Basic Helps You with Object Models

Two other sources of help for working with object models are contained within Visual Basic itself. The first source of information is the Object Browser. The Object Browser allows you to look at any objects that are part of the references for the project. The Browser shows you the different objects and the properties, methods, and events of each object. This information may not necessarily tell you the purpose of each of the objects, but it will give you information about the following:

- What properties are contained in the object and which are read-only.

- The data type of each property.

- What arguments are required for a method call and which of the arguments are optional.

- The return data type of a method that is a Function procedure.

- What parameters are passed by an event of the object.

- Any constants defined for the object.

To access this information, you need to have set a reference to the ActiveX server in the References dialog box for your project. Then, you can invoke the Object Browser by clicking the toolbar button, selecting the Object Browser item from the View menu, or pressing the F2 key. The Browser contents for Microsoft Word are shown in Figure 12.2.

FIGURE 12.2

Viewing Objects in the Object Browser

The second form of help from Visual Basic comes from the Auto List Members and Auto QuickInfo tools of Visual Basic. As you are writing code, Auto List Members displays a drop-down list of properties and methods of an object when you type the dot after an object variable name. This list is shown in Figure 12.3. Auto QuickInfo shows you the syntax of a method as a tooltip when you enter the name of the method, providing you with a quick reference of the required and optional arguments of the method as well as their data types. The Auto QuickInfo tool is shown in Figure 12.4.

F I G U R E   12.3

Auto List Members Displaying Properties and Methods

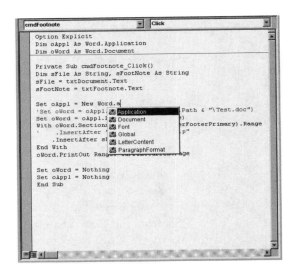

F I G U R E   12.4

Auto QuickInfo Displaying Method Syntax

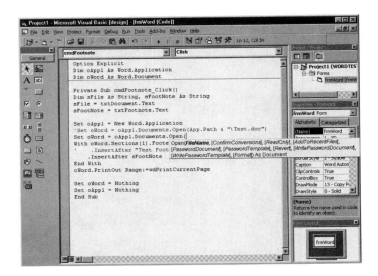

Creating Objects in a Program

When you create objects in a program, you are actually creating variables that hold an instance of the object. You create the object variables using a declaration statement like you would for a variable of any other data type. You can use Dim, Private, or Public keywords in the creation of the object variables. You can then assign an object to the variable using a Set statement or the CreateObject function.

When you create an object variable, you have two options. You can create a variable to hold a specific type of object, such as a Word Application or Excel Spreadsheet, or you can create a generic object variable that can work with any object. This situation is somewhat analogous to using a specific data type or the Variant data type for other variables. Declaring a specific object type is known as early binding of the object. Declaring a generic object variable is known as late binding of the object.

Early Binding versus Late Binding

Microsoft ✓ *Exam* *Objective*   **Use the Dim statement to reference an object.**

Whenever possible, you should use early binding of objects in your code. There are several advantages of early binding:

- Objects are created faster because a specific object type is known.

- Information about the properties and methods of the object are known at design time, which allows Visual Basic's tools (Auto List Members and Auto QuickInfo) to provide you with information about the properties and methods of the object.

Early binding occurs when you specify the object type in the declaration statement for the object variable, as shown in the following statements:

```
Dim oWord As Word.Document
Dim oAppl As Word.Application
Dim oSheet As Excel.Worksheet
```

The only real advantage to late binding is that it allows you the flexibility of defining the object type while the program is running, in contrast to early binding where the object type is specified in design mode. One example for using late binding would be in the creation of a program where you allow the user to pick the tool to be used. For example, you might write a program that uses Word or WordPerfect to open and print a document. The program that is used will depend on which is available on the user's machine. You would need to write your program to handle either program, and allow the user to pick the appropriate one. When you need to use late binding, you declare a variable as simply Object, then use the CreateObject function to assign an object to the variable. Only when the object is assigned to the variable is the type of the object known. The following code shows an example of late binding:

```
Dim oWord2 As Object
Set oWord2 = CreateObject("Word.Application")
```

Setting Up a Reference to an Object

For many of the ActiveX servers that you will work with, you can specify the server in the References of the project, which allows you to identify the specific object type in your declaration statements to enable early binding. To set up a reference to a server, choose the References item in the Project menu and select the ActiveX server in the dialog box. If the server is not listed, you can click the Browse button to look through the available DLL, TLB, and EXE files available to your computer to find the particular server. Once the server is identified, specific object information is available through the Object Browser or the Auto List Members and Auto QuickInfo tools of Visual Basic. Figure 12.5 shows the References dialog box for a typical project using the Microsoft Word Object Library.

Creating an Object Instance

When you declare an object variable, you are only specifying a placeholder for the object. An instance of the object is not actually created in the declaration statement. The creation of the object instance occurs later in code through one of the three methods discussed below.

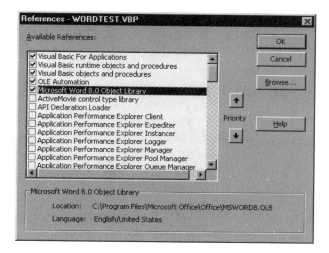

Use the Dim statement to reference an object.

Using the New Keyword   The first method of creating an instance of an object is to use the New keyword in the declaration statement of the object variable. The New keyword tells Visual Basic that a new instance of the specified object is to be created. This instance is not created when the declaration statement is executed. Rather, the instance is created when the object variable is first used, either in setting a property or calling a method. The following code illustrates the use of the New keyword:

```
'An object variable is defined here. The object
' is not created here.
Dim oAppl As New Word.Application

'The object is actually created here.
oAppl.Documents.Open "Test1.Doc"
```

Use the Set statement to create an instance of an object.

Using the Set Command   The second method of creating an instance of an object is to use the Set command. This command assigns an object to an object variable. The Set command can be used to assign an existing object to a variable. You can also use the Set command with the New keyword to create a new instance of an object. When the Set command is to be used to assign the object to the object variable, the declaration statement for the object variable cannot use the New keyword.

The Set command creates an instance of an object when the command is executed. The following code shows how the Set command is used to assign existing objects and to create new objects:

```
'Object variables are defined here
Dim oWord As Word.Document
Dim oWord2 As Word.Document

'An existing object is assigned to a variable
Set oWord = oAppl.Documents(0)

'A new object is created and assigned to a variable
Set oWord2 = New Word.Document
```

Microsoft ✓ *Exam Objective*

Use the CreateObject function to create an instance of an object.

Using the CreateObject Function   The final method of creating an instance of an object is with the CreateObject function. This function is typically used to create a specific object type with a generic object variable. That is, you will typically use this function only when the object type is unknown at design time. When using the CreateObject function, the object variable is declared as simply Object. The object is then created with the Set command and the CreateObject function. The following code shows the use of the CreateObject function to create an instance of an Excel spreadsheet:

```
'Declare an object variable
Dim oSpread As Object

'Create an Excel object
Set oSpread = CreateObject("Excel.Sheet")
```

Destroying an Instance of an Object

One final bit of information. When you create objects in your program, each object uses memory and other system resources. These resources are held until the object is destroyed, or until your program finishes. The object instance should be destroyed when the object variable goes out of scope or when the program ends, but this is not always the case. Therefore, it is a good practice to specifically destroy each object instance when you are through with it. You destroy an instance of an object by setting the object variable to the special value of Nothing. The following code illustrates how to do this:

```
Set oWord = Nothing
Set oAppl = Nothing
Set oSpread = Nothing
```

The use of the Nothing value will destroy an object instance no matter how the object was created.

Creating a Client for Microsoft Programs

One of the most common uses of ActiveX client applications is to automate tasks using the components of Microsoft Office. To create these types of clients, follow these steps:

- Set a reference to the proper object library for the task.

- Create an object of the proper type.

- Use the methods and properties of the object to accomplish the task.

- Destroy the object.

In the next two sections, we will cover exercises that illustrate how to accomplish a task in Microsoft Word and Microsoft Outlook. These two exercises will show you the basics of automating Microsoft Office tasks.

Working with Microsoft Word

Microsoft ✓ *Exam Objective*   **Build a Microsoft ActiveX client.**

With a client application created in Visual Basic, you can automate almost any task that can be performed in Word. Exercise 12.1 shows you how to open a document, add a footnote to the document, and print the first page of the modified document.

EXERCISE 12.1

Creating a Microsoft Word Client

1. Start a new project in Visual Basic.

2. Using the References dialog box, add a reference to the Microsoft Word 8.0 Object Library. (Note: If you are using an older version of Word, you will need to add the appropriate reference. Also, you may need to modify the code presented in the exercise.)

3. Add two label controls to the form and set the Caption properties to "Document to be Modified" and "Footer to be Added."

4. Add two text boxes to the form and name them **txtDocument** and **txtFootnote**. Clear the Text property of each text box.

5. Add a command button to the form and name it **cmdFootnote**. Set the Caption property of the button to Add Footnote. The completed form is shown in the following illustration.

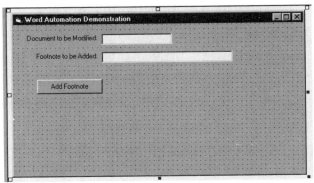

6. Add the following code to the declarations section of the form. This code declares the object variables to hold instances of the Word Application and Document objects.

```
Dim oAppl As Word.Application
Dim oWord As Word.Document
```

7. In the Click event of the cmdFootnote button add the code to open a document and set the footnote for the document. The code first retrieves the document and footnote information from the text boxes. It then creates the appropriate Word objects. The objects are then used to invoke the methods that set the footnote and print the page. Finally, the objects are destroyed by setting them to Nothing. The code for the command button is shown below:

```
Dim sFile As String, sFootNote As String
sFile = txtDocument.Text
sFootNote = txtFootnote.Text

Set oAppl = New Word.Application
Set oWord = oAppl.Documents.Open(sFile)
With _
oWord.Sections(1).Footers(wdHeaderFooterPrimary).Range
.InsertAfter sFootNote
End With

oWord.PrintOut Range:=wdPrintCurrentPage

Set oWord = Nothing
Set oAppl = Nothing
```

8. Save the project. Then, run the program. If you specify the name of a file (including the full path to the file) and a footnote, then click the command button, the first page of the modified document will print.

Linking Your Program to Microsoft Outlook

Microsoft
Exam
Objective

Build a Microsoft ActiveX client.

Microsoft Outlook is a contact manager, e-mail client, and scheduler that comes as part of Microsoft Office. Outlook has its own forms that enable you to work with contacts; create, send, and receive e-mail messages; and handle appointment scheduling. However, you may have occasion to create custom applications that access, add to, or modify the information that is handled by Outlook. By using the Outlook object model and an ActiveX client program, you can do just that. Exercise 12.2 shows you how to add a new contact to Outlook from a Visual Basic program. This example comes from an application that managed loan applications. The client desired to have the contact information placed in Outlook for follow-up calls.

EXERCISE 12.2

Creating an Application that Links to Microsoft Outlook

1. Start a new Visual Basic project.

2. In the References dialog box, set a reference to the Microsoft Outlook 8.0 Object model.

3. On your form, add six label controls with the following captions: First Name, Last Name, Address, City, State, Zip Code.

4. Add six text boxes to the form with the following names: txtFirst, txtLast, txtAddress, txtCity, txtState, and txtZip. Clear the Text property of each of the text boxes.

5. Add a command button to the form with the Caption "Add Contact." Name the command button **cmdAdd**. The completed form should look like the following illustration.

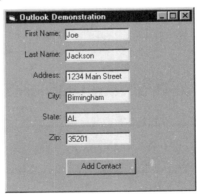

6. Add the following code to the declarations section of the form. This code sets up the variable for the Outlook application object.

```
Dim oOutlook As New Outlook.Application
```

7. Add the following code to the Click event of the command button. This code takes information from the text boxes, creates a new contact item in Outlook, and sets the contact information.

```
Dim oContact As Outlook.ContactItem
With oOutlook
    oContact = .CreateItem(olContactItem)
    With oContact
        .FirstName = txtFirst.Text & ""
        .LastName = txtLast.Text & ""
        .HomeAddressStreet = txtAddress.Text & ""
        .HomeAddressCity = txtCity.Text & ""
        .HomeAddressState = txtState.Text & ""
        .HomeAddressPostalCode = txtZip.Text & ""
        .Save
    End With
End With
Set oContact = Nothing
```

8. Place the following code in the Unload event of the form to destroy the object instance created by the program:

```
Set oOutlook = Nothing
```

9. Save the project. When you run the program, you can enter information in the form and click the command button to add the data to Outlook. The following illustration shows Outlook with the contact information added.

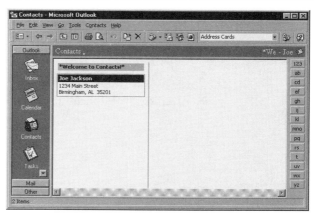

Summary

This chapter has shown you how to create ActiveX client programs that allow you to access the objects of ActiveX servers. You have seen how to declare object variables and to create the actual objects. You have seen specific examples of creating applications that use Microsoft Word or Microsoft Outlook as the ActiveX server. The information in this chapter should help you pass the following certification exam objectives:

- Build a Microsoft ActiveX client.
- Use the Dim statement to reference an object.
- Use the Set statement to create an instance of an object.
- Use the CreateObject function to create an instance of an object.

Review Questions

1. Which statement or function do you use to create an object variable?

   A. Dim oWord As Word.Application

   B. Set oWord = Word.Application

   C. Set oWord = CreateObject("Word.Application")

   D. Dim oWord As String

2. How is early binding set up in an application?

   A. Declare a variable as Object.

   B. Declare a variable as Variant.

   C. Use the CreateObject Function.

   D. Declare a variable as a specific object type.

3. How do you declare an object variable for late binding?

A. Declare a variable as Object.

B. Declare a variable as Variant.

C. Use the CreateObject Function.

D. Declare a variable as a specific object type.

4. Which of the following statements creates an instance of an object? Check all that apply.

A. Dim oWord As Object

B. Dim oWord As New Word.Document

C. Set oWord = New Word.Document

D. Set oWord = CreateObject("Word.Document")

5. What are advantages of early binding? Check all that apply.

A. Objects are created faster.

B. You can use an early bound variable with any object.

C. Information about properties and methods is available while you program.

D. There is no advantage.

6. What are advantages of late binding? Check all that apply.

A. Objects are created faster.

B. You can use a late bound variable with any object.

C. Information about properties and methods is available while you program.

D. There is no advantage.

7. Which of the following statements show the proper use of the New keyword? Check all that apply.

A. Dim oWord As New Object

B. Dim oSheet As New Excel.Sheet

C. Set New oSheet = CreateObject("Excel.Sheet")

D. Set oWord = New Word.Document

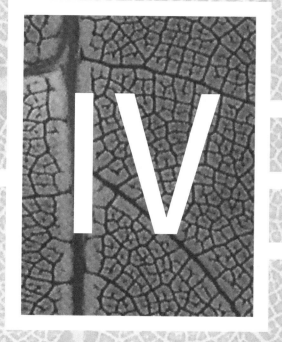

PART

IV

Extending the
Capabilities of
Visual Basic

CHAPTER

13

Declaring and Using
External Functions

Microsoft Objectives Covered in This Chapter:

- Declare and call a DLL routine.

- Identify when it is necessary to use the Alias clause.

- Pass an argument by value and by reference.

- Pass a string to a DLL.

- Pass a null pointer to a DLL routine.

- Pass a function pointer to a DLL by using a callback function.

- Create a DLL routine that modifies string arguments.

As you develop more and more complex programs in Visual Basic, you will start to find that some of the tasks you want to accomplish in your program are very difficult, or even impossible, to implement with Visual Basic code alone. For example, it is a tedious task to find the Windows directory on a machine using only Visual Basic code.

Fortunately, you are not limited to using Visual Basic alone for creating your applications. You have already seen how custom controls can help you write programs without having to write all the routines yourself. Another source of routines are DLL libraries. These libraries contain functions for getting the Windows directory, reading and writing to INI files or the registry, performing block copies of parts of the screen, and myriad other functions. One rich source of routines is the Windows API (Application Programming Interface) that is available on every Windows-based machine. These API libraries are available to everyone, and we will use these in the discussion of working with DLLs; however, Windows libraries are not the only ones you can use. There are also many specialized libraries that you can purchase from third parties to accomplish a variety of tasks. You can even create your own library of functions using Visual Basic.

Microsoft places quite a bit of importance on being able to work with DLLs. The certification exam objectives state that you need to be able to do the following:

- Incorporate dynamic-link libraries (DLLs) into an application.

- Declare and call a DLL routine.

- Identify when it is necessary to use the Alias clause.

- Create a DLL routine that modifies string arguments.

- Pass a null pointer to a DLL routine.

- Pass an argument by value and by reference.

- Pass a function pointer to a DLL by using a callback function.

- Pass a string to a DLL.

What Are DLLs?

DLL stands for Dynamic Linked Library. Windows itself is built on DLLs, and Visual Basic requires a number of DLLs to run. You even have to distribute DLLs with your programs in order for them to run on your clients' machines. The reason for using DLLs to create programs is to avoid having to try to load all of a large program into memory. Windows, for example, contains a large number of functions that are only needed occasionally (if at all) for a typical Windows session. If the executable code for all those functions were in memory all the time, either there would be no room for data or we would all have to have gigabytes of RAM. With DLLs, a function is loaded by a program only when it is needed, then it is unloaded when its function is completed.

DLLs are obviously of benefit to all users, but how are they directly beneficial to Visual Basic programmers? First, you can write DLLs yourself that can be used by many of your programs, which means that you do not have to include the code for these functions (for example, a specialized math library) in each of your programs that needs them. Second, and perhaps more importantly, you can use DLLs created for other programs in your Visual Basic programs. Specifically, this gives you access to many of the functions that are part of the Windows interface. Using these functions allows you to perform some tasks that are not possible with Visual Basic by itself.

You should be very careful when using Windows API functions from DLL libraries. Many of these functions are incompatible with the inner workings of Visual Basic. Whenever you use DLL functions, be sure to test your application thoroughly to make sure the DLL does not cause problems.

Declaring DLL Routines

Before you can use any DLL routines in your Visual Basic program, you will need to declare the function. Because these functions are external to Visual Basic, you have to tell Visual Basic the name of the function, where it can be located, what arguments must be passed to the function, and what return value can be expected from the function. In many ways, this is similar to setting up the declaration statement of an internal function that you would place in a module, form, or class module.

When you start working with DLL functions, there is one very important point to remember when declaring the function. Declare statements may only be used in the Declarations section of a BAS module. You cannot declare a function in a form, in a class module, or inside a procedure. Placing the declaration statement anywhere outside the Declarations section of a BAS module will result in a compile error when you try to run your program.

Setting Up a Declaration Statement

For any DLL function that you want to use, you have to use a declaration statement to notify Visual Basic that you will be using the function. If you are using the Windows API functions, you can enter the function declarations either of two ways:

- Type in all the required information for the declaration statement yourself.

- Use the Win API Viewer to copy the declaration statement from a list of API statements.

We will look first at how you enter all the information by hand, which is not as easy as using the Win API viewer, but you will learn the fundamentals of creating a declaration statement. Also, it may be the only way to create the declaration statement for other DLLs, either ones that you purchase or ones that you create.

Many commercial DLL libraries provide a function similar to the Win API viewer to make it easy to enter the declarations for their functions.

Entering Declarations in Code

When you create a declaration statement, you use the Declare statement and provide all the following information:

- Whether the DLL procedure is a Sub or Function type procedure. A Function declaration indicates that the procedure will return a value. A Sub declaration means that no value will be returned by the procedure.

Most DLL procedures are functions that at least return a value to indicate whether they ran successfully.

- The name of the procedure. The name that you will use in your code to access the procedure. In most cases, this is also the name that is used in the DLL itself to identify the procedure. Be careful with your declarations, as DLL entry points (names) are case-sensitive.

- Lib keyword. Indicates that the procedure is contained in a DLL library. This keyword is required for all declarations.

- The name of the library. A string that specifies the name of the library containing the DLL procedure, which is a required parameter.

- Alias keyword. Indicates that the procedure is specified by another name inside the DLL library. An Alias is typically used if the procedure has the same name as a Visual Basic keyword. Also, many of the 32-bit procedures contain both an ASCII and a Unicode version of the procedure. The two procedures have the same name but have an *A* or *W* suffix respectively. For example, the function to retrieve a user name is specified in the DLL library as GetUserNameA.

- The list of arguments to be passed to the DLL. Similar to the argument list of an internal function that you create. We will look more closely at passing arguments later in this chapter.

- The return data type for the procedure. Specifies the type of data that will be returned by the DLL procedure and is only used if the procedure is a function-type procedure.

In addition to the information that is required for the DLL, you can also specify whether the declaration is Public or Private. A procedure that is declared as private can only be used within the module in which it is declared. A public procedure can be used anywhere in your program. If you omit both the Public and Private keywords, the procedure is assumed to be Public.

Microsoft
Exam
Objective

Declare and call a DLL routine.

Of course, the best method of learning how to declare a procedure is to actually do it in code. Exercise 13.1 shows you how to declare and use a simple API function, MessageBeep. This function simply generates a sound through the PC's speaker.

EXERCISE 13.1

Declaring a DLL Procedure

1. Start a new project.

2. Add a BAS module to the project by choosing the Add Module item from the Project menu. The BAS module is needed for the procedure declaration. Remember, you cannot declare DLL procedures from inside a form, class module, or another procedure.

3. Open the code window of the BAS module.

4. Place the following statement in the Declarations section of the BAS module. The statement identifies the name of the procedure, the library where the procedure is located, the Alias name of the procedure, and the arguments that you must supply to call the procedure.

```
Declare Function MessageBeep Lib "user32" (ByVal wType As _
Long) As Long
```

5. Go to the form of the project and place a command button on the form.

6. Open the code window for the Click event of the command button and place the following code in the event procedure. This code actually calls the MessageBeep function. Notice that because the MessageBeep procedure returns a value, we needed to declare a variable of the appropriate type to hold the return value.

```
Dim lMsgRet As Long
lMsgRet = MessageBeep(1)
```

7. Run the program and click the command button. The computer will beep each time the button is clicked.

Where do you get the information about the name of the function and its required arguments? For the Windows API functions, Visual Basic provides you with the information in the form of a text file in the WinAPI folder of Visual Basic. For other libraries that you may use, you will have to obtain the information from the developer of the library.

Using the Win API Viewer

The other alternative to entering Windows API declarations by hand is to use the Win API viewer. This Visual Basic Add-in enables you to easily search for particular API functions, then copy the required declaration statement directly into your program. This speeds the declaration process and makes sure that the declaration statement is correct. Exercise 13.2 shows you how to enter a declaration statement using the Win API viewer.

Creating Win API Declarations with the Win API Viewer

1. Start a project and add a BAS module to the project. Open the code window of the BAS module.

EXERCISE 13.2 (CONTINUED)

2. Select the Add-In Manager item from the Add-ins menu to bring up the Add-ins dialog box shown in the next illustration.

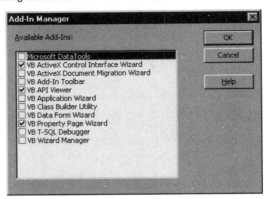

3. Select the Win API viewer and click the OK button on the dialog box.

4. Select the Win API viewer from the Add-Ins menu to bring up the API viewer as shown in the next illustration.

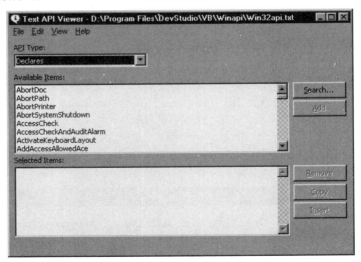

5. You will need to load the appropriate definitions for the API Viewer. To do this, select the Load Text Database item from the File menu. You will then need to select the Win32API.txt file from the WinAPI folder of Visual Basic. You may have some other text files like the MAPI32.txt file that provides declarations for other DLL libraries.

6. The API Viewer is now loaded with the declarations for all the available API functions. You can scroll down through the list to find the function you want, or use the Search button to enter part of the function name. Find the GetUserName function in the list.

7. Click the Add button on the API Viewer, which will place the declaration statement in the second list of the viewer.

8. When you have added all the declaration statements that you need to the declarations list, you can click the Copy button to place the declarations on the Clipboard.

9. Close the API Viewer and go to the code window of your BAS module. Press Ctrl+V to paste the declarations in your code. The next illustration shows the code window with several declarations added. As you can see, this method of adding a declaration is much easier and more accurate than typing the declarations in by hand.

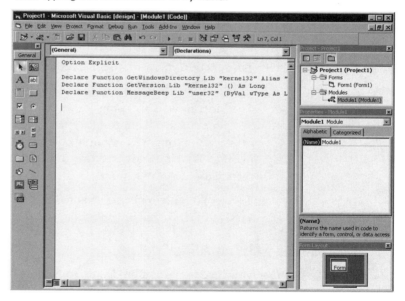

Going by Another Name

On occasion, you will find it necessary to declare a DLL procedure by a name other than the one it was given. You can do this by using an Alias name in the declaration statement. Using an alias tells Visual Basic both the name you wish to use for the procedure and the name by which the procedure is identified in the DLL library.

Why Use an Alias?

Microsoft ✓ *Exam* *Objective*	**Identify when it is necessary to use the Alias clause.**

The most common reasons for using an alias in a declaration statement are:

- You need to use two or more functions that happen to have the same name from different libraries. In this case, you would need to provide an alias for at least one of the functions.

- The function you want to use has the same name as a Visual Basic keyword, or a function that you developed.

- The function you are using comes in multiple versions, such as for ASCII and Unicode. In this case using an alias allows you to switch between the routines by simply changing the declaration statement instead of having to track down and modify each use of the procedure throughout your program.

- The actual function name is quite long and you want to use a shorter version of the name in your code.

Setting Up an Alias

When you need to name a procedure something other than its name in the DLL library, you need to use the Alias clause of the Declare statement. When you include this clause, the name that you give the function is the one that you will use throughout your code. The name that follows the Alias keyword is the name by which the procedure is identified in the DLL. The following code shows the use of the Alias keyword for using the GetUserName function of the Windows API.

```
Declare Function GetUser Lib "advapi32.dll" Alias _
"GetUserNameA" (ByVal lpBuffer As String, nSize As Long) As _
Long
```

In this example, GetUserNameA is the name of the procedure that is defined in the advapi32.dll library. The name GetUser is the one used in code to actually call the function as shown by the following line of code:

```
lMsgRet = GetUser(sUser, lNameLen)
```

Calling DLL Routines from Your Program

In most cases, calling DLL routines from your programs is the same as calling an internal procedure that you create or calling a Visual Basic built-in procedure. That is, you call a DLL routine by specifying the name of the routine and including all the required arguments for the procedure. If the DLL routine returns a value, you will typically use it in an assignment statement or other expression. If the DLL does not return a value, you can place the statement by itself.

Basic Procedure Calls

With almost all calls to DLL procedures, you will need to pass information to the procedure from your Visual Basic program. This information is in the form of the arguments that are expected by the DLL procedure. In the declaration statement for the procedure, you defined the number and type of variables that would be passed to the procedure. As you set up the procedure call, you need to ensure that you pass both the correct type and correct number of arguments. Otherwise, you will encounter errors or, at the very least, have the DLL procedure fail.

Passing Standard Data Type Arguments

For many procedures, you can pass information as a variable of the correct type or as a literal value to be used. Exercise 13.3 illustrates how to implement a simple DLL procedure by passing a literal value for the required argument.

EXERCISE 13.3

Passing an Argument to a DLL Procedure

1. Start a new project and add a BAS module to the project.

2. To the BAS module, add the declaration for the Sleep function from the Windows API. You can use the Win API viewer to add the declaration or type in the following line of code:

```
Declare Sub Sleep Lib "kernel32" (ByVal dwMilliseconds As _
Long)
```

3. On the form of the project, place a command button, then open the code window for the button.

4. Place the following code in the Click event of the command button. The code prints to the form to notify you that the program will pause, then uses the Sleep function to tell the computer to pause execution for 2 seconds. After the Sleep function is finished, the computer reports that it is back.

```
Me.Print "Going to Sleep"
Sleep (2000)
Me.Print "Re-awakened"
```

5. Run the program and check it out.

You also could have used a long variable to handle the value being passed to the Sleep procedure:

```
Dim lSleep As Long
Me.Print "Going to Sleep"
lSleep = 2000
Sleep (lSleep)
Me.Print "Re-awakened"
```

Passing by Value or Reference

Microsoft ✓ *Exam Objective*

Pass an argument by value and by reference.

Typically, you will pass information to a procedure by value, which means that a copy of the data is passed to the procedure, and any variable that you use as an argument of the procedure remains unchanged. In some cases, however, you will pass information by reference. In this case, Visual Basic is passing a pointer to a memory location. The value in the memory location is used by the procedure, then the results of the procedure are placed in the same location. After the completion of the procedure, the variable that you specified as an argument of the procedure will contain the new value, which can be used in your program.

To know whether you have to pass an argument by value or by reference, you need to look at the declaration statement for the procedure. If the argument is by value (ByVal), you can use a variable or a literal value. If the argument is by reference (ByRef), you will have to use a variable to pass the information to the procedure. One exception to this behavior is in the use of string arguments as discussed below.

A more detailed discussion of the use of ByVal and ByRef appears in Chapter 2, "Coding Basics," of this book.

Passing Strings to a DLL

Microsoft
Exam
Objective

Pass a string to a DLL.

Passing strings to a DLL procedure is a little different from passing numbers to a procedure. The reason is that many DLL procedures (written in C or C++) treat strings differently than does Visual Basic. DLL procedures use null-terminated strings, strings with an ASCII character 0 attached to the end of the string. In order to use a string in a DLL procedure, Visual Basic translates an internal string variable to a null-terminated string, then passes the pointer from this string to the DLL procedure, allowing the DLL to modify the string, even though the string is passed ByVal.

In order to handle passing information to the DLL procedure this way, you need to always use variables to pass string information. Also, you need

392 Chapter 13 · Declaring and Using External Functions

to set the length of the string that will be passed to the DLL. This size represents the maximum number of characters that the DLL can return using the specified variable. You can set the length of the string by using a fixed-length string variable declaration statement or, more commonly, by using the Space function to place the correct number of spaces in the string before it is passed to the DLL. Exercise 13.4 shows you how to pass a string to a DLL procedure to retrieve the location of the Windows directory.

EXERCISE 13.4

Passing a String to a DLL Procedure

1. Create a project and add a BAS module. In the BAS module, add the declaration for the GetWindowsDirectory API function. You can use the Win API viewer or enter the following line of code:

```
Declare Function GetWindowsDirectory Lib "kernel32" Alias _
"GetWindowsDirectoryA" (ByVal lpBuffer As String, ByVal _
nSize As Long) As Long
```

2. On the form of the project, place a text box and a command button. Open the code window for the Click event of the command button.

3. The first task is to dimension the variables that will be used for calling the DLL function. You can use the following statement to declare the variable:

```
Dim sWinDir As String, lStrLen As Long, lRetCode As Long
```

4. Next, you need to set the size of the string that will be passed to the DLL function. To set the size of the string, use the Space function of Visual Basic as shown below. You also need to set the value of the variable that specifies the size to the DLL.

```
sWinDir = Space(128)
lStrLen = 128
```

5. Next, you call the procedure to retrieve the information about the Windows directory. This call includes the variables you set as arguments. The directory information will be returned in the sWinDir variable. If the information is greater than the length of the string, the string will be truncated at its specified size and data will be lost.

```
lRetCode = GetWindowsDirectory(sWinDir, lStrLen)
```

6. Finally, include this line of code to display the directory information in a text box:

```
Text1.Text = sWinDir
```

7. Run the program and click the command button. The location of your Windows directory will appear in the text box as shown in the next illustration.

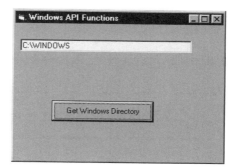

Passing Null Pointers to a DLL

Microsoft ✓ ***Exam*** ***Objective***   **Pass a null pointer to a DLL routine.**

Some functions that you use may require you to pass a null string or null pointer to the DLL procedure. A common mistake is to pass an empty string that you have created with a statement like the following:

```
sNullIHope = ""
```

When the DLL receives this string, it is really receiving a pointer to a zero-length string, not a true ASCII 0 value. In order to properly pass a null pointer to a DLL procedure, you should use the vbNullString constant. For example, the FindWindow function can be used to determine if a particular application is running on your system. This function requires a null string to be passed to the function. The following code checks to see if Microsoft Word is running and reports the information to the user:

```
Dim lRetCode As Long
lRetCode = FindWindow(vbNullString, "Microsoft Word")
If lRetCode = 0 Then
    MsgBox "Word is not running on this system."
Else
    MsgBox "Word is running on this system."
End If
```

Passing Function Pointers to a DLL

Microsoft ✓ *Exam* *Objective*   **Pass a function pointer to a DLL by using a callback function.**

Some of the DLL procedures that you use allow you to specify one of your procedures to be run by the DLL procedure. When your procedure is run by a DLL, it is known as a callback procedure. To implement callback procedures, you must pass the DLL procedure a pointer to the function that you wish to have run.

The Purpose of Callback Functions   Callback procedures enable you to process information supplied by the DLL procedure as it is being generated. For example, using the EnumFontsFamilies procedure in the Windows API, you can create a list of all the fonts that are currently installed on your system. As each font is listed by the EnumFontFamilies procedure, the procedure can call an internal procedure in your code to display the name of the font, or place the name in a list box. Each time your procedure is accessed, a callback has been made from the API procedure. Being able to use callbacks opens up many of the functions of the Windows API that were not possible in previous versions of Visual Basic.

Using the AddressOf Operator   In order to use a callback procedure, you must determine the pointer to the procedure in your code that you will be calling. This task is handled by the AddressOf operator in Visual Basic. You use the AddressOf operator to precede the name of a function in the arguments list of the DLL procedure that you are calling. The following code shows how this is done to call the AddToList procedure from the EnumFontFamilies API procedure.

```
EnumFontFamilies hDC, vbNullString, AddressOf AddToList, LB
```

When you are using the AddressOf operator, there are several restrictions that you must follow:

- The procedure that you are calling back to must be placed in a BAS module in your code. It cannot be located in a class module or a form.

- The callback procedure must be located in the same project as the DLL procedure that is calling it.

- You can only use the AddressOf operator with user-defined procedures and functions. It cannot be used with declared functions or with Visual Basic's internal functions.

Creating a DLL Routine

Microsoft Exam Objective

Create a DLL routine that modifies string arguments.

One of the objectives of the exam requires that you be able to create a DLL to modify a string. While writing DLLs is a topic that can be expanded to several chapters on its own, we will take a look at the process for writing a specific DLL. The DLL that you will create contains a function that reverses the order of characters in a string. The three major steps to creating and using the DLL are:

- Create an ActiveX DLL project and set up the functions to be included in the DLL.

- Compile the DLL to a file.

- Access the DLL from another program.

These three major steps are illustrated in Exercises 13.5 through 13.7.

Creating an ActiveX DLL Project

Creating functions in a DLL requires the following steps:

- Create an ActiveX DLL project.

- Set the Name and Instancing properties of the class in the DLL project.

- Create the necessary Sub and Function procedures for the tasks you want to accomplish.

EXERCISE 13.5

Creating Functions in a DLL Project

1. Open a new ActiveX DLL project. Name the project **DLLTest**.

2. You will notice that a Class Module has already been created for you. Name the Class Module Functions.

3. Set the Instancing property of the class module to Global MultiUse, which allows the functions you create to be called by the function name instead of having to create an instance of the class and then using its methods.

4. Create a new function in the Class by entering the following Function declaration statement:

```
Public Function ReverseStr(ByVal sInptStr As String) As _
String
```

5. Set up the routine for the function by entering the following code. The code inverts the string that is passed to it.

```
Dim sNewStr As String, I As Integer
sNewStr = " "
For I = Len(sInptStr) To 1 Step -1
    sNewStr = sNewStr & Mid(sInptStr, I, 1)
Next I
ReverseStr = sNewStr
```

6. Save the project.

Compiling an ActiveX DLL

The next step in the process of creating a DLL is to compile it. These steps are illustrated in Exercise 13.6.

EXERCISE 13.6

Compiling a DLL Project

1. Open the project created in Exercise 13.5.

2. Select the Make .dll item from the File menu of Visual Basic.

3. Click the Options button on the File dialog box to work with the options of the DLL.

4. On the Make tab of the Options dialog box, verify that the Title of the program is set to DLLTest. Also, input any version or company information that you wish.

5. On the Compile tab of the Options dialog box, select the Compile to Native Code option. You can also set other options as desired. You can find these other options described in Chapter 19, "Compiling Your Visual Basic Program."

6. Click OK to return to the File dialog box. Set the name of the DLL and its path.

7. Click OK to compile the DLL.

Using the DLL in Other Programs

Once you have created the functions of the DLL and compiled it to a file, you are ready to use the functions in other programs. To do this, you must provide access to the DLL, then call the functions from your Visual Basic program. Exercise 13.7 walks you through an example of using the ReverseStr function from the DLLTest library that you created in the previous exercises.

EXERCISE 13.7

Using the DLL That You Created

1. Start a new standard project.

2. Select the References item in the Project menu to display the References dialog box. Using this dialog box, you will provide a link to the DLL that you created. The References dialog box is shown in the next illustration.

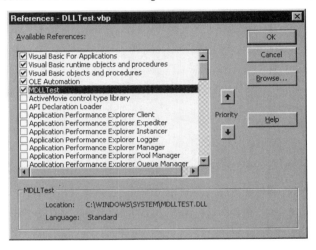

3. Click the Browse button of the dialog box and use it to find and open the DLLTest library. When you open the file, it will be added to the References dialog box and automatically selected. After opening the file, click the OK button on the References dialog box.

4. Add a text box and a command button to the form of the project.

5. In the Click event of the command button, place the following code to call the ReverseStr function.

```
Dim sMyStr As String, sMystr2 As String
sMyStr = Text1.Text
sMystr2 = ReverseStr(sMyStr)
Text1.Text = sMystr2
```

6. Run the program. Each time you click the command button, the text in the text box will reverse itself.

Summary

This chapter has shown you how you can extend the capabilities of Visual Basic through the use of DLL functions contained in the Windows API and other libraries. You have even seen, briefly, how to create your own DLLs and access them from other programs. The key criteria of the Microsoft exam objectives that were covered in this chapter are:

- Incorporate dynamic-link libraries (DLLs) into an application.

- Declare and call a DLL routine.

- Identify when it is necessary to use the Alias clause.

- Create a DLL routine that modifies string arguments.

- Pass a null pointer to a DLL routine.

- Pass an argument by value and by reference.

- Pass a function pointer to a DLL by using a callback function.

- Pass a string to a DLL.

Review Questions

1. Which statement is used to identify an external procedure to Visual Basic?

   A. Declare

   B. Dim

   C. Public

   D. DLLProc

2. Why would you use an Alias with a DLL procedure? Check all that apply.

    A. When you need to use a DLL with the same name as a Visual Basic keyword

    B. When you want to keep the real name a secret

    C. When you need to use two or more procedures with the same name in separate DLLs

    D. To shorten the name of the procedure to avoid typing

3. How do you pass a null pointer to a DLL procedure?

    A. Create an empty string with a statement like sPassStr = " ".

    B. Use the Space function to create a zero length string.

    C. Pass a numeric value of 0.

    D. Use the vbNullString constant.

4. What is a null-terminated string?

    A. An empty string

    B. A string with an ASCII 0 appended to the end of the string

    C. Any fixed length string

    D. A string with the character 0 in it

5. What value of the Instancing property should be used in creating a DLL for your own functions?

    A. Global MultiUse

    B. MultiUse

    C. Public Not Creatable

    D. Private

6. What does the AddressOf operator do?

    A. Specifies a memory location where information from the procedure can be placed

    B. Passes the pointer for a user-defined function to a DLL procedure

    C. Generates a pointer for a string

    D. Nothing

7. What is a callback procedure?

    A. A procedure in your program that is called by a DLL procedure

    B. A recursive procedure that repeatedly calls itself

    C. Part of a modem protocol

    D. A specific DLL procedure in the Windows API

CHAPTER

14

Creating ActiveX
Controls with Visual Basic

Microsoft Objectives Covered in This Chapter:

- Create and use an ActiveX control.

- Declare and raise events.

- Create and enable a property page.

- Use control events to save and load persistent control properties.

- Create and use an ActiveX control.

- Add an ActiveX control to a Web page.

Visual Basic has always had the capability to use custom controls to extend its functionality. This capability has created a thriving third-party control market and has made it easy for Visual Basic developers to find controls that they need to perform a task, instead of having to write tons of code. Until version 5 of Visual Basic came out, however, VB developers have been lacking in one capability, being able to write their own controls. You could learn C++ and write a control, but there was not an easy way to create that one perfect control for your application.

Visual Basic version 5 changed all that. You can now write controls using Visual Basic, employing the same techniques and code you are familiar with for writing standard programs. These controls, called ActiveX controls, cannot only be used in your Visual Basic applications, they can also be used in Office 97 applications, web pages, or any other environment that supports ActiveX controls. For the average developer, this means tremendous benefits in the reuse of code and custom controls. For the more ambitious, this means a large potential market for a commercial control to be developed.

This chapter will focus on the techniques for creating ActiveX controls in Visual Basic. The exam objectives that are covered are fairly broad:

- Create and use an ActiveX control.

- Declare and raise events.

- Create and enable a property page.

- Use control events to save and load persistent control properties.

- Add an ActiveX control to a web page.

In preparing you for these objectives, we will cover in detail how to create the basic interface of the control, how to add properties, methods, and events to the control, and how to test a control. When you finish the chapter, you will understand the exam objectives, have a basic knowledge of control creation, and have a couple of controls to use in your own applications.

Control Creation Basics

Creating an ActiveX control is very closely related to writing class modules in Visual Basic. Like a class, you create the Public interface of the ActiveX control by coding Property procedures to create properties, writing Sub and Function procedures to create methods, and using declarations and the Raise-Event statement to create events. If you have a good understanding of creating classes, you are well on your way to understanding the creation of ActiveX controls.

The subject of creating classes is covered in Chapter 7, "Creating Classes in a Program," of this book.

The key difference between an ActiveX control and a class is that the control has a visual interface. This interface provides a means for the developer and users to interact with the control. The creation of the user interface is similar to creating a form with which a user would interact. You either place Visual Basic controls on the user control or you draw components on the control using Line, Circle, and Print methods (the same techniques you use for creating forms).

The methods you use for creating the user interface are dependent on the type of control that you want to create. There are three basic categories of ActiveX controls that you will create with Visual Basic:

- **An extension of an existing control**   You take a standard control and add capabilities to it. For example, you might create a text box that only accepts numeric input or a list box that is capable of sorting items in descending order.

- **A new control created from constituent controls** You use several standard controls working together to create a control for a specific task. You may wish to create a command button array for recordset navigation, or a single control that handles all the tasks associated with a two-column pick list.

- **A user drawn control** You create the entire interface of the new control with drawing methods and the Print method. This is the most difficult method of creating a control. An example of this type of control would be a round command button.

No matter what type of control you are going to create, you need to approach the creation of the control the same way you approach any other programming project. You need to have a well-planned design for creating the control and a test plan for making sure the control works.

Creating an ActiveX Control

Microsoft ✓ *Exam* *Objective*   **Create and use an ActiveX control.**

The simplest way to create the user interface of an ActiveX control is to use controls that already exist. This is known as creating from constituent controls. (Even when creating an extended standard control, you are using a constituent control.) To illustrate the techniques for creating a control, we are going to create a simple Security control that allows the user to enter a user ID and password. If you handle logins for your applications, or have to pass user information to a database, you at some time have had to ask for a user ID and password. Typically, you place a couple of labels and text boxes on a form and do a little bit of text processing. This is a simple enough task, but wouldn't it be nice if all you had to do was draw a single control on the form, then access its properties to get all the needed information? This is what the Security control does.

Starting the Project

The first step in creating an ActiveX control is to start the project by choosing New Project from the File menu. This will bring up the New Project dialog box shown in Figure 14.1. This dialog box lists all the project types you can create with your version of Visual Basic. (This dialog is also typically displayed when you first start Visual Basic.)

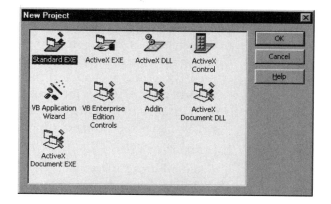

From the Project dialog box, select the ActiveX Control project to start your new control. After you have selected the project type, Visual Basic opens a new UserControl design form, as shown in Figure 14.2. Notice that this UserControl looks similar to a standard form, but without the borders. Once the project is created, you will need to set the Name property of the control, otherwise your control will go through life with the generic name User-Control1 (or 2, and so on).

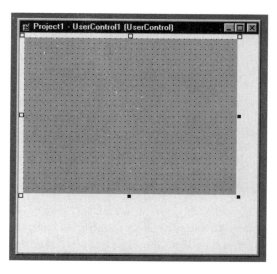

If you look closely at Figure 14.2, (if you are following along on your computer, look at the properties window) you will see that there are a number of properties associated with the UserControl object. Many of these properties are the same as properties for a form, and a couple of them deserve special mention:

- **BackStyle** Determines whether the form behind the control is visible through the blank areas of the UserControl. This is the same as the BackStyle property of a Label control. For most controls you create, you will want to set this property to Transparent (0), especially if you are creating a control from multiple constituent controls. (Note: you can also leave the setting of the control up to the developer who is using your control.)

- **ToolboxBitmap** Determines the image that is displayed for your control in the toolbox of anyone who is using the control. If you do not specify a value for this property, the control will be shown in the toolbox with the default image, meaning that there is nothing to distinguish your control from any other using the default value. The bitmaps used for this property must be 16×15 pixels, and icon files are not usable.

Adding Constituent Controls

The next step in creating your control is to add the constituent controls to the UserControl object. There are two steps involved in handling the constituent controls:

- Setting the initial appearance of the controls

- Handling the position of the controls as the UserControl object is resized

This second step is extremely important. Unless you are going to restrict the size of the control to a single value (like the timer or other invisible Visual Basic controls), you will need to change the size and/or position of the constituent controls in response to the user resizing the UserControl object.

Setting the Initial Appearance

Placing controls on a UserControl is like placing them on a standard form. You simply select the control from the toolbox and draw an instance of the control on the object. After drawing the control, you need to set the basic properties of the control, such as its name, or the Caption property for a label or command button. However, one difference between creating a standard form and a UserControl is that you typically draw the constituent controls to fill the entire UserControl. You start the controls in the upper left corner of the UserControl, then, after placing all the controls, set the size of the UserControl to just enclose all the constituents. To illustrate the actual creation of a UserControl, Exercise 14.1 walks you through the steps of creating the initial interface of the Security control. The completed control is contained on the CD as Security.ctl.

EXERCISE 14.1

Starting the Security Control

1. Start a new ActiveX Control project by selecting the appropriate project type from the New Project dialog box.

2. Change the Name property of the UserControl to Security, change the BackStyle property to Transparent, and set the ToolboxBitmap to an appropriate icon. (I used a modified version of the Key.bmp file found in the Graphics folder of Visual Basic.)

3. Add a label control to the UserControl. Place the label in the upper left corner of the UserControl. Change the Name of the label to **lblSecurity**, set the Caption property to "User Name:", set the Alignment property to Right Justified. Also, because we will be using multiple label controls, make this label the first element of a control array by setting the Index property to 0.

4. Copy the existing label and place a second copy on the UserControl below the first instance of the control. Change the Caption property to "Password:"

5. Add a text box next to the first label control. Set the Name property of the text box to txtUserName and delete the information in the Text property.

6. Add a second text box to the UserControl. Place this one below the first text box and next to the second label control. Set the Name property to txtPassword, delete the information in the Text property, and set the PasswordChar to * to keep the information typed by the user from being visible to others.

7. Resize the UserControl to just enclose all the constituent controls. When you are finished, your UserControl form should look like the one in the next illustration.

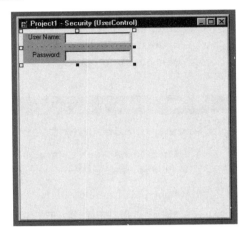

8. Save the project.

This appearance of the UserControl is the initial appearance if a developer creates a default instance of the control by double-clicking on the control in the Toolbox of a project. If the developer draws the control on a form, the size of the UserControl will be different from what you designed. Figure 14.3 shows several instances of the Security control on a form, showing the default size and two different sizes. Notice how the appearance of the control is changed by changing the size. What this means for you is that you will have to accommodate size changes for the control.

FIGURE 14.3

Several sizes of the Security control

Handling the Resizing of the Control

As a developer draws an instance of your control on a form, the Resize event of the UserControl is fired. Using this event you can make changes to the size and position of the constituent controls to allow for different sizes. You can also include code in the event, which would limit the size of the control to a particular minimum or maximum value. In Exercise 14.2, you will add the code to handle the resizing of the Security control.

EXERCISE 14.2

Accommodating the Changing Size of the Security Control

1. Start with the Security control project.

2. Open the code window for the UserControl object.

3. Place the following code in the Initialize event to set the initial position of the constituent controls:

```
lblSecurity(0).Top = 1
lblSecurity(0).Left = 1
lblSecurity(1).Top = lblSecurity(0).Top + _
lblSecurity(0).Height + 225
lblSecurity(1).Left = 1
txtUserName.Top = lblSecurity(0).Top
txtUserName.Left = lblSecurity(0).Left + _
lblSecurity(0).Width + 105
txtPassword.Top = lblSecurity(1).Top
txtPassword.Left = lblSecurity(1).Left + _
lblSecurity(1).Width + 105
```

4. Place the following code in the Resize event to make sure the control meets a minimum size requirement and to expand the text boxes to fill the width of the UserControl:

```
If UserControl.Width < txtUserName.Left + 800 Then
    UserControl.Width = txtUserName.Left + 810
Else
    txtUserName.Width = UserControl.Width - _
txtUserName.Left - 10
    txtPassword.Width = UserControl.Width - _
txtPassword.Left - 10
End If
If UserControl.Height < 810 Then UserControl.Height = 810
```

EXERCISE 14.2 (CONTINUED)

5. At this point, you are ready to try the control out in a project. Close the code and design windows of the UserControl. Be sure not to exit the project.

6. Select Add Project from the File menu to add a Standard project to the Project group. You will notice that the Toolbox of the new project contains the UserControl that you have created, as shown in the next illustration.

7. Select the Security control and add an instance of the control to the form of your standard project. You will notice that the control will only allow you to size it down to a certain minimum. This is due to the code in the Resize event.

8. Save the project.

Creating the Control's Interface

After you have created the visual interface of your control, you will need to create the programming interface of the control. The programming interface is made up of the properties, methods, and events of the control. These elements are used by a developer to set the appearance of your control in their program and to work with your control from the code in their program. As you create an ActiveX control, there are two categories of properties, methods, and events that your control may use:

- **Custom properties, methods, and events**   The controls you create through code in Property, Sub, Function, and Event procedures.

- **Properties, methods, and events of constituent controls**   Part of the controls you used to create the user interface, but they need to be assigned to elements accessible by the user of your control.

Adding Your Own Properties, Methods, and Events

As stated earlier, creating ActiveX controls is very similar to creating class modules. This is particularly true in the case of creating properties, methods, and events. In this section, we will discuss in general the process of creating these elements of your controls, then we will look at adding particular elements to the Security control that we are creating as a sample.

Adding Properties to the Control   You add properties to a control by creating Property procedures in the code of your control. There are two basic types of Property procedures:

- **Property Let**   For setting the value of a property

- **Property Get**   For retrieving the value of a property

A third type of Property procedure is the Property Set, which is basically the same as the Property Let procedure but is used with objects instead of standard data types.

The easiest way to create a property is to use the Add Procedure dialog box accessible from Visual Basic's Tools. In the procedure dialog box, shown in Figure 14.4, you identify the procedure as a Property type and set a name for the property. The dialog box then creates the shell of a Property Let and Property Get procedure. You then add the necessary code to the procedure to set or retrieve the property values or handle any other appropriate tasks.

F I G U R E   14.4

Add Procedure
dialog box

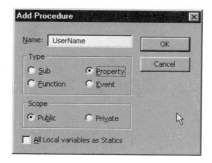

As you are writing the code for the Property procedures, there are a few things to keep in mind:

- You need to specify the data type of the Property Get function. The default type is Variant.

- You need to specify the data type of the variable passed to the Property Let procedure. This data type should match the one set for the Property Get function.

- If you want to create a read-only property, delete the Property Let procedure.

- If you are working with an object, change the Property Let procedure to a Property Set procedure.

Adding Methods to the Control   Methods, as you know, allow the control to perform a function. The methods you create for a control are Sub or Function procedures that are declared as Public. As such, you can write methods to perform any task that you want. For example, you could write a routine to sort the items in a list box in descending order. By making the procedure Public, the routine becomes a method that is accessible to a program using the control.

To create a method for the control, you can use the same Add Procedure dialog box you used to create Properties. In the case of a method, you specify the procedure type as either a Sub or a Function procedure. You use a Function if your procedure should return a value. Otherwise, use a Sub procedure. After you fill out the information in the dialog box, Visual Basic creates the procedure declaration statement and the skeleton of the procedure.

Microsoft
✓ *Exam*
Objective

Declare and raise events.

Creating Events   Creating events is only a little more difficult than creating properties or methods. You still use the Add Procedure dialog box to create the shell of the Event. However, you have to do a little more work to implement the event. The basic steps of creating an event are:

1. Use the Add Procedure dialog box to create the Event declaration.

2. Add to the declaration statement the names of the arguments that will be passed by the event to a program using the control. These arguments will show up in the header for the event procedure in code.

3. Use the RaiseEvent statement to trigger the event and pass information to the calling program.

Creating the Code Interface of the Security Control   Continuing with the creation of the sample control, Exercise 14.3 shows you how to add properties, methods, and events to the Security control. The exercise will show you how to create the following:

- **UserName property**   For setting and retrieving the user name entered in the control

- **Password property**   For setting and retrieving the password information entered in the control

- **MaxNameLength**   For limiting the size of the user name

- **MaxPassLength property**   For limiting the size of the password

- **EncryptPass method**   For applying a simple encryption to the password

- **Change event**   For notifying the calling program that either the UserName or Password property was changed

---

EXERCISE 14.3

Creating the Public Interface of the Control

1. Open the project created in Exercises 14.1 and 14.2.

2. Use the Add Procedure dialog box to create the UserName property.

3. Change the data type of the Property Get statement and the argument of the Property Let statement to String.

4. Add code to the procedures as shown below:

```
Public Property Get UserName() As String
UserName = txtUserName.Text
End Property
Public Property Let UserName(ByVal sUser As String)
txtUserName.Text = sUser
End Property
```

5. Create the Password property using the Add Procedure dialog box and the following code:

```
Public Property Get Password() As String
Password = txtPassword.Text
End Property
Public Property Let Password(ByVal sPassword As String)
txtPassword.Text = sPassword
End Property
```

6. Create the MaxPassLength and MaxNameLength properties using the following code:

```
Public Property Get MaxNameLength() As Integer
MaxNameLength = txtUserName.MaxLength
End Property
Public Property Let MaxNameLength(ByVal iMaxLen As _
Integer)
txtUserName.MaxLength = iMaxLen
End Property
Public Property Get MaxPassLength() As Integer
MaxPassLength = txtPassword.MaxLength
End Property
Public Property Let MaxPassLength(ByVal iMaxLen As Integer)
txtPassword.MaxLength = iMaxLen
End Property
```

7. Create a Sub procedure named EncryptPass and add the following code to the procedure. This code simply reverses the order of the letters in the txtPassword text box. You can create a more sophisticated routine if you desire.

```
Dim sOriginal As String, sEncrypt As String
Dim iPassLen As Integer, I As Integer
sOriginal = txtPassword.Text
iPassLen = Len(sOriginal)
sEncrypt = ""
For I = 1 To iPassLen
    sEncrypt = sEncrypt & Mid(sOriginal, I, 1)
Next I
txtPassword.Text = sEncrypt
```

8. Create an event declaration statement for the Change event using the Add Procedure dialog box. The declaration statement will look like the following line of code:

```
Public Event Change()
```

9. You will want to activate the Change event whenever a change occurs to either text box in the control. Therefore, you need to add the following statement to the Change events of the txtUserName and txtPassword text boxes:

```
RaiseEvent Change
```

10. Save the project and exit the code window. If you have another project loaded with a copy of the control on the form, the properties, methods, and events will now show up when you write code for the control.

Using the Control Interface Wizard

The custom elements you create are only part of the programming interface of your control. You may want to give your users access to several of the more standard properties, methods, and events, such as Font, ForeColor, BackColor, and so on. While you could code each of these by hand, Visual Basic has provided you with an easier method.

Selecting the Members of the Interface   Visual Basic comes with the Control Interface Wizard to facilitate the creation of the interface for your control. To use the Control Interface Wizard, you must first add it to the list of Visual Basic's Add-Ins using the Add-In manager. Then, to start the wizard, select it from the Add-Ins menu of Visual Basic. The wizard starts by displaying a start-up screen. After clicking the Next button on the start-up screen, you will start the process of creating public properties for your control. Figure 14.5 shows this second screen of the wizard.

The second page of the wizard contains two lists. The first is a list of members that you might want to include in the interface of your control. The second list shows those members that you have selected, or members that have been made public through code that you have already created. You can select members by highlighting them and using the buttons on the wizard or by double-clicking the name. After you have selected all the desired items, click the Next button to move to the next step.

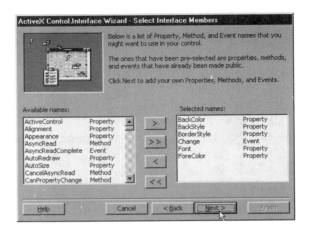

Managing Custom Properties and Methods   The next page of the wizard shows you the custom elements that you have created in code. This page, shown in Figure 14.6, also allows you to create new elements or edit or delete existing elements. Creating new elements accomplishes the same function as the Add Procedure dialog box, only the shell of the procedure is created. You still have to add the code for the procedure after the wizard has finished its work. When you are satisfied with the custom elements of the control, you can move to the next page of the wizard.

F I G U R E   14.6

Managing the custom
elements of your
control

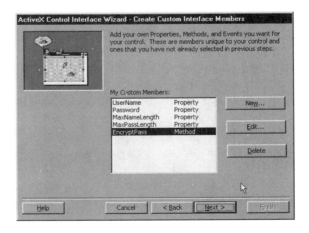

Assigning Properties to the Proper Constituent   The next step of the Control Interface Wizard is where you specify what the public properties and methods of the control will do. This part of the wizard allows you to assign a Public property or method to a property or method of one of the constituent controls. This process of assigning public interface members is called mapping. As an example of mapping, suppose you specified Back-Color as one of the public properties to create. This page lets you assign the property to the BackColor property of the UserControl. When the wizard actually creates the Public property, it will create a set of procedures like the following:

```
Public Property Get BackColor() As OLE_COLOR
Attribute BackColor.VB_Description = "Returns/sets the
background color used to display text and graphics in an
object."
    BackColor = UserControl.BackColor
End Property

Public Property Let BackColor(ByVal New_BackColor As OLE_
COLOR)
    UserControl.BackColor() = New_BackColor
    PropertyChanged "BackColor"
End Property
```

To map public members to the properties or methods of a constituent, select the member to be assigned from the list at the left of the page. (The Mapping page is shown in Figure 14.7.) Then, select the constituent control (or the User-Control) and the specific property from the combo boxes on the right of the page. Repeat this process for each public member you need to map.

FIGURE 14.7

Mapping properties to constituents

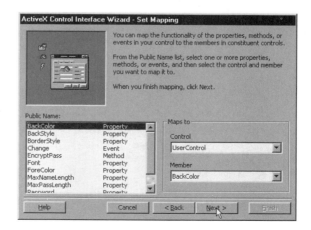

Setting Property Attributes   The final step in using the wizard is to set the attributes of the properties, methods, and events of your control. The Attributes page, shown in Figure 14.8, makes it easy for you to create Read-only properties and to specify the arguments of methods and events. The attributes that you can set are determined by the type of member you are creating. The specific attributes for each member are:

- **Properties**   You can specify the data type, default value, design time accessibility, and run time accessibility of a property. The accessibility options determine whether the property is read/write, read-only, write-only, or not available.

- **Methods**   You can specify the data type of the return value. If you specify a data type, a Function procedure is created, otherwise a Sub procedure is created. You can also specify the arguments of the procedure.

- **Events**   You can specify the arguments of the event which determine the information that will be passed to the calling program.

FIGURE 14.8

Specifying the attributes of the members

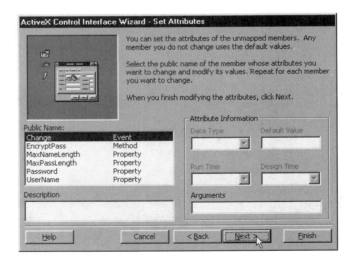

After you have specified the attributes, you can complete the creation of the public interface by pressing the Finish button in the wizard. The wizard will then create the code for all the properties, methods, and events that you have defined. Figure 14.11 shows you a sample of the code that is created. As you can see, the wizard does a lot of work for you. You can find the complete code for the Security control on the CD (in the file Security.ctl).

Creating the Members of the Security Control   As always, working through the process of a task is better than only reading about it. Exercise 14.4 continues the process of creating the Security control by using the Control Interface Wizard to create additional parts of the Public interface of the control.

EXERCISE 14.4

Creating the Public Members of the Security Control

1. Add the Control Interface Wizard to your Add-Ins menu using the Add-In Manager.

2. Start the Control Interface Wizard and proceed to the second page of the wizard.

3. Select the following properties to add to the Public interface: BackColor, BackStyle, BorderStyle, Font, ForeColor.

4. Select the following events as well: KeyDown, KeyPress, KeyUp. After selecting the properties and events, skip to the Mapping Page of the wizard.

5. Map each of the properties and events selected in steps 3 and 4 to the corresponding properties and events of the UserControl object. Do this by selecting all the properties and events listed in steps 3 and 4 in the Public Name list. Next, select the UserControl object in the Control drop-down list.

6. Click the Finish button to tell the wizard to write the code for you.

Developing a Property Page

Microsoft ✓ *Exam* *Objective*   **Create and enable a property page.**

You have probably noticed that many of the controls you find in version 5 of Visual Basic have a way for you to easily work with the properties of a control. Of course, you have the Properties window that can now be organized alphabetically by property name or by categorized groups of properties. But many controls also have a Custom property, which gives you access to Property Pages. These pages, like the one shown for the TreeView control in Figure 14.9, organize the properties of the control into functional groups and present these groups on pages of a dialog box. The properties typically display default values and allow you to choose other values through drop-down lists, option buttons, or check boxes. The property pages make it easy for you to see all the related properties of a control at the same time.

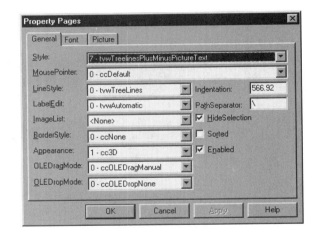

Setting Up the Property Page Wizard

We wouldn't be talking about property pages here if you didn't have the capability to create property pages for your own controls. Visual Basic version 5 makes it easy for you to create and implement property pages for your control. The Property Page Wizard does most of the work for you. To use the Property Page Wizard, you have to access Visual Basic's Add-In manager by choosing the Add-In Manager item from the Add-Ins menu. From this dialog box, you can select to use the Property Page Wizard in your project. After closing the Add-In Manager, the Property Page Wizard will be available as one of the options of the Add-Ins menu.

Running the Property Page Wizard

To begin creating the property pages for your control, start the Property Page Wizard by selecting it from the Add-Ins menu. You will first see a title page that tells you a little about the wizard. Clicking the Next button takes you to the first page where you start the actual creation process.

Defining the Pages of the Dialog Box

The first working page of the wizard, shown in Figure 14.10, lets you define the pages that you want to include in your Property Pages dialog box. The wizard inserts a couple of standard pages for you, StandardColor and StandardFont. You can keep these pages or remove them by clearing the check box next to the name of the page. If you wish to add more pages, click the Add button which brings up an input dialog where you can enter the name of a new page.

FIGURE 14.10

Creating the pages of your Property Pages dialog box

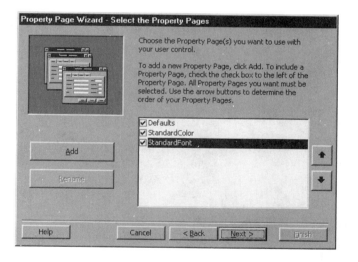

As you add pages to your dialog box, the page names appear in the list of pages for your dialog box. In addition to being able to add or remove pages, you can also control the order of the pages by changing the order of the names in the list. To move a page, select it in the list and use the arrow keys to the right of the list to change its position. When you have finished defining the pages for your dialog box, you can move to the next step of the wizard.

Assigning Properties to a Page

The next step in the process is to assign the properties that you have created to the pages of the dialog box. The Add Properties page of the wizard, shown in Figure 14.11, makes it easy for you to create these assignments. Simply select the tab that represents the page where you want the properties to go. Then, select the properties to be placed on the page and use the arrow buttons to move the properties from the selection list to the desired page. You will see that if you used the default property pages, the properties for these pages are already assigned for you.

FIGURE 14.11

Assigning properties to a page

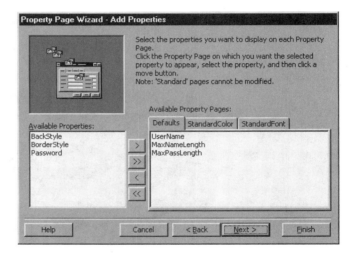

You cannot add new properties to the StandardColor or StandardFont pages, nor can you remove the properties assigned to these pages. These defaults are set by the wizard and cannot be changed. You can only assign properties to the pages you create.

After you have finished the assignment of properties, click the Finish button to create the property pages for your control.

Creating the Property Pages for the Security Control

Now that you have seen the basics of creating property pages, let's put this information into practice by creating pages for the Security control. Exercise 14.5 shows you how to do this.

Creating Property Pages

1. Start the Security control project if you do not already have it open.

2. Start the Property Page Wizard by selecting its option from the Add-Ins menu.

3. Move to the second page of the wizard to create additional pages.

4. Click the Add button and enter the text Defaults in the input dialog box. Click OK on the dialog box to add the page to the list.

5. Using the arrow buttons, move the new Defaults page to the top of the list. Then click the Next button to move to the next page of the wizard.

6. From the Available Properties list, select the UserName, MaxName-Length, and MaxPassLength properties to be included on the Defaults page. You can use the arrow buttons or drag and drop the properties onto the page.

7. Click the Finish button to complete the process.

8. If you have a test form loaded, create a new instance of the Security control and look at the properties window. You will see a Custom property located at the top of the Properties list. Clicking the ellipsis button next to this property will display the property pages for the Security control as shown in the next illustration.

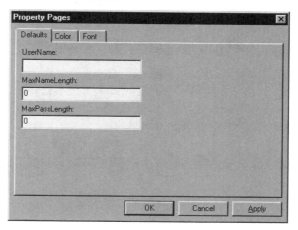

Saving Developer Information for the Control

Microsoft ✓ *Exam* *Objective*	**Use control events to save and load persistent control properties.**

As a developer works with your control, she will probably change the settings of several of the properties of the control. After the project containing your control is saved, she will expect to be able to reopen the project and have the control appear as it was left. Unfortunately, there is no automatic mechanism for saving the property information that the developer uses. With a little code, however, you can save and restore settings of the control so the developer does not have to reset the values each time.

There are two key events involved in storing developer information:

- **WriteProperties** Used to save the information
- **ReadProperties** Used to retrieve the information

Each of these events works with an object called the PropertyBag, a storage device for the design-time properties of the control.

Saving the Developer Information

There are two steps involved in saving the property information for your control. First, you must notify Visual Basic that the property value has changed. Second, you must write the property information to the PropertyBag.

To notify Visual Basic of a property change, you use the PropertyChanged function in the Property Let procedure of each property. This function specifies the name of the property and sets a flag that triggers the WriteProperties event when the instance of the control is closed. The PropertyChanged function for a typical property is shown in the following line of code:

```
PropertyChanged "BackStyle"
```

The PropertyChanged function only notifies Visual Basic that a property value needs to be saved. You must write the code in the event procedure of the WriteProperties event to actually save the information. For each property to be stored, you will need to use the WriteProperty method of the PropertyBag object. This method specifies the property name, the current value of the property and the default value of the property. The WriteProperty method is illustrated below:

```
Private Sub UserControl_WriteProperties(PropBag As _
PropertyBag)
PropBag.WriteProperty "BackColor", UserControl.BackColor, _
&H8000000F
PropBag.WriteProperty "BackStyle", UserControl.BackStyle, 0 _
PropBag.WriteProperty "BorderStyle", _
UserControl.BorderStyle, 0
PropBag.WriteProperty "ForeColor", UserControl.ForeColor, _
&H80000012
End Sub
```

Retrieving Property Settings

Of course, if you save the setting information, you will want to retrieve it as well. The ReadProperties event of the UserControl is triggered whenever the project containing your control is loaded, allowing you to retrieve the property information stored in the PropertyBag object. To retrieve the values, you use the ReadProperty method of the PropertyBag object. This method specifies the name of the property and the default value, in case a value had not been saved. The following code shows the use of the ReadProperties event and the ReadProperty method:

```
Private Sub UserControl_ReadProperties(PropBag As
PropertyBag)
UserControl.BackColor = PropBag.ReadProperty("BackColor",
&H8000000F)
UserControl.BackStyle = PropBag.ReadProperty("BackStyle", 0)
UserControl.BorderStyle =
PropBag.ReadProperty("BorderStyle", 0)
UserControl.ForeColor = PropBag.ReadProperty("ForeColor",
&H80000012)
End Sub
```

If you use the Control Interface Wizard to create the public interface of your control, most of the code for saving and retrieving properties will be written for you. You will only need to handle this task manually for properties that were not created through the Control Interface Wizard.

Exercise 14.6 shows you how to handle saving and retrieving the property information for the Security control.

EXERCISE 14.6

Saving and Retrieving Developer Settings

1. Select the Property Let procedure for the MaxNameLength property.

2. Add the following line of code to the procedure:

```
PropertyChanged "MaxNameLength"
```

3. Repeat this process for the MaxPassLength and UserName properties. Be sure to use the appropriate name in the PropertyChanged function.

4. Place the following code in the WriteProperties event of the UserControl to save the information about the properties of the control:

```
PropBag.WriteProperty "MaxNameLength", _
txtUserName.MaxLength, 0
PropBag.WriteProperty "MaxPassLength", _
txtPassword.MaxLength, 0
PropBag.WriteProperty "UserName", txtUserName.Text, ""
```

5. Place the following code in the ReadProperties event of the UserControl to retrieve the saved property information:

```
txtUserName.Text = PropBag.ReadProperty _
("UserName", "")
txtUserName.MaxLength = PropBag.ReadProperty _
("MaxNameLength", 0)
txtPassword.MaxLength = PropBag.ReadProperty _
("MaxPassLength", 0)
```

Testing the ActiveX Control

Once you have created the ActiveX control, you need to test it to make sure that all the procedures work as you think they should. You can use all the standard debugging techniques that are available in Visual Basic to debug your control. There are only a few different steps involved in setting up a test for your ActiveX control.

1. Add a standard project to your development environment to create a project group, which is the mechanism used for testing ActiveX controls and servers.

2. Close the UserControl window of your control project. If the User-Control (form) window is open, Visual Basic assumes that you are still working on the design of the control and will not allow you to create an instance of the control in another form.

3. Create an instance of the control on your test form. Then you can test the properties of the control and write code to test its methods.

You can learn more about debugging techniques in Chapter 18, "Debugging Your Application."

If you find you must make changes to the design of the ActiveX control, delete the instance of the control from your test form and recreate it after you have made the design changes. Otherwise, the changes will not appear in the test.

Using the ActiveX Control

After you have finished developing and testing your control, you can use the control in many programs. You can easily use the control in any other Visual Basic program that you write. You can also use the control in any other application that supports ActiveX controls. These applications include

Microsoft Office, other development tools such as FoxPro, and even Internet applications or web pages that support ActiveX. With this type of usage available, you can see why the capability to create ActiveX controls is such a powerful feature in Visual Basic.

Compiling the Control

The first step to being able to use your control in other applications is to compile it. When you compile a control, you are creating an OCX file that can be accessed by other programs. Compiling your control involves the following steps:

1. Select the project in your project group that contains the control.

2. Select the Make OCX item from Visual Basic's File menu.

3. From the Make Project dialog box, click the Options button to set any necessary compilation options. (You will find these options described in Chapter 19, "Compiling Your Application.")

4. In the Make Project dialog box set the name and path for the OCX file.

5. Click the OK button to start the compilation.

When the process is finished, you will have an OCX file that others can use to access your control.

Working with the Control in Visual Basic

Microsoft ✓ *Exam* *Objective*	**Create and use an ActiveX control.**

To use your ActiveX control in other Visual Basic programs, you have two options:

- You can use the OCX that contains the control.
- You can add the CTL control definition file to the project.

Using the OCX for the control is the preferred method of accessing the control unless you are going to modify the control. Even then, you are better off modifying the original control project and recompiling the control than making modifications in a new project. To add your OCX control to your Visual Basic toolbox, open the Components dialog box by pressing Ctrl+T. Then, click the Browse button in the dialog to bring up the Open dialog that allows you to specify the name and path of the control. When you select the control, it will appear in the Components dialog and will be marked to be added to your toolbox (shown in Figure 14.12 for the Security control). After closing the Components dialog, your control will appear in the Toolbox and will be accessible to the current project, like any other control.

FIGURE 14.12

Making the control available for use

Using the Control in a Web Page

Microsoft Exam Objective

Add an ActiveX control to a Web page.

Internet Explorer 3.0 and 4.0, as well as some other Internet programs, are capable of displaying and using ActiveX controls. The key to using the control is the use of the <object> tag in the HTML code for the web page. The <object> tag specifies the following information about the control:

- The control's ID
- A name for the instance of the control
- The ClassID of the control

This information identifies the control to your web browser and allows the control to be displayed if the browser supports ActiveX. The following code shows one instance of the HTML code needed to embed an ActiveX control in a page:

```
<object id="Test1" name="Test1"
classid="clsid:21F43727-A8FD-11D1-BCCD-0000C051F6F9"
border="0"
width="188" height="54"></object>
```

Web page designers make it easy to add ActiveX controls to your pages. These designers handle all the object information for you so you don't have to remember all the details about ClassIDs and the other information. Figure 14.13 shows you a web page with the Security control inserted in the page.

FIGURE 14.13

A web page using the Security control

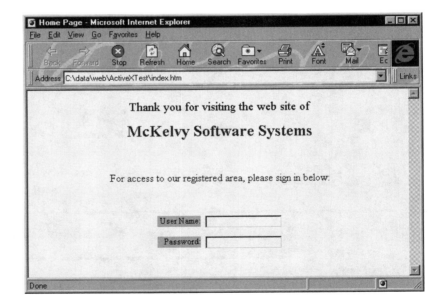

Summary

This chapter has shown you how easy it can be to create your own ActiveX controls using Visual Basic. You have seen how wizards in Visual Basic can do most of the interface work for you, leaving you to focus on the visual design and functionality of the control. Along the way you have learned how to use constituent controls to create the user interface and how to create properties, methods, and events to create the public programming interface of the controls. By now, you should also realize how powerful the capability to produce controls is. These controls allow you to reuse components not just in other Visual Basic applications, but in any application that supports ActiveX controls, including some web browsers.

After completing this chapter, you should now be ready for the following objectives of the Microsoft certification exam:

- Create and use an ActiveX control.

- Declare and raise events.

- Create and enable a property page.

- Use control events to save and load persistent control properties.

- Add an ActiveX control to a Web page.

Review Questions

1. Which of the following statements is true about creating ActiveX controls?

A. You must create the control completely from scratch.

B. You can only use a single standard control in the creation of an ActiveX control.

C. You cannot add properties to a standard control to enhance its capabilities.

D. You can use multiple standard controls as well as drawing methods to create the interface of your control.

2. What statement is used to trigger an event in your ActiveX control?

A. LoadEvent

B. RaiseEvent

C. FireEvent

D. Trigger

3. Which property statement is required for a read-only property?

A. Property Get

B. Property Let

C. Property Set

D. Property Read

4. How do you create a method of a control?

A. Use a Method declaration statement.

B. Create a Sub or Function procedure and declare it as Public.

C. Create a Sub or Function procedure and declare it as Private.

D. Creation of the method is automatic because all procedures in a control are public.

5. What does the Control Interface Wizard do for you? Check all that apply.

A. Designs the visual interface of your control.

B. Helps you create properties, methods, and events for your control.

C. Lets you assign properties of the control to properties of the constituent controls.

D. Handles the code for storing property changes.

6. What is the purpose of Property Pages?

   A. To make it easier for you to create properties of your control

   B. To provide a developer with easy access to the properties of your control

   C. To automatically test the property settings of your control

7. Which of the following programs can use ActiveX controls that you create? Check all that apply.

   A. Visual Basic

   B. Microsoft Office

   C. Microsoft Visual FoxPro

   D. Internet Explorer 3.0

8. Which event is used to store developer settings for your control?

   A. WriteSettings

   B. StoreProperties

   C. WriteProperties

   D. Save

9. What is a PropertyBag?

   A. Another name for Property Pages

   B. An object used to store developer settings for a control

   C. A term we made up

   D. A list of properties that can be included in a UserControl

10. What method is used to retrieve developer settings for your control?

   A. The Read method of the UserControl object

   B. The Retrieve method of the PropertyBag object

   C. The ReadProperty method of the PropertyBag object.

   D. The ReadProperty method of the UserControl object.

11. What type of file is created when you compile an ActiveX control?

    A. EXE

    B. CTL

    C. OCX

    D. CAB

12. Which HTML tag is needed to insert an ActiveX control in a web page?

    A. control

    B. object

    C. bold

    D. ActiveX

PART

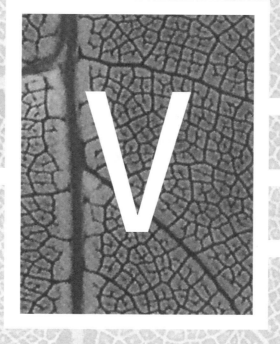

V

Integrating Visual
Basic with the
Internet

CHAPTER

15

Writing Internet
Applications with Visual Basic

So far in this book, we have been looking at applications that run on a single PC or across a network. However, most people know that a big part of the computing game is being played on the Internet. Most of you are probably familiar with the Internet and have used a browser to view web pages and to download files. But what about writing applications that work with the Internet?

In this chapter and the next, we will look at ways that Visual Basic enables you to write applications that access the Internet and that can run over the net on a web browser and maybe even better over your company intranet. In Chapter 16, "Creating ActiveX Controls," we will look at ActiveX documents, structures that make it easy for you to write applications that run over the Internet. In this chapter, we will concentrate on applications that give you access to the Internet and handle some of the more typical Internet tasks.

Specifically, we will be covering material that will help you with the following Microsoft exam objectives:

- Create applications that can access the Internet.

- Create an application that has the ability to browse HTML pages.

- Create an application that enables connections to the Internet.

Introduction to the Internet

The Internet is probably the most talked about phenomenon in computer history. Every day you read articles about the Internet in the paper and maybe see segments on the TV news. It seems like everyone has a web site, from the largest corporation down to the local gas station. But what is it and how do you tap into the Internet from Visual Basic?

The Internet is a large network of interconnected computers all over the world. The Internet was originally designed to allow scientists and university staff and students to communicate with each other from anywhere to anywhere. Within the last few years, however, the World Wide Web, which runs over the Internet, has become a way for people to:

- Find information about any topic

- Advertise new products and technologies

- Handle commerce

Every day, there are more and more things that you can do on the Internet through the World Wide Web.

The thing that made the Internet take off so rapidly was the advent of HTML and web browsers. HTML (HyperText Markup Language) is a set of codes (called Tags) that allow you to format text and embed objects such as graphics, audio, and video. With each generation of HTML, more capabilities are added. So, if what you want to do on the Web is not possible today, wait a month or so.

Web browsers are the counterpart of the HTML language. These browsers take the HTML information and render it into the web pages that you see when you "surf" the Internet. The two major browsers on the market today are Microsoft Internet Explorer and Netscape Navigator. Each of these browsers will handle standard HTML, and each has its own extensions to provide additional capabilities. The programs that you write with Visual Basic will typically work best (if not only) on Internet Explorer.

Viewing HTML Pages from a Visual Basic Program

One of the most basic tasks that you perform on the Internet is the viewing of HTML pages. These pages provide you with lots of information about any subject that you can think of. The information can be in the form of text, graphics, sound, video, and any combination of these pieces. A good browser is essential to making your Internet experience enjoyable and beneficial.

Because there are a number of good browsers on the market, why would you want to create your own with Visual Basic? Several reasons come to mind. First, you could create a browser that allows you to view multiple pages in the same form. These multiple views could reside on separate tabs of a tab control or could exist side by side on the same form. Another reason might be to create a browser that automatically navigates certain pages, then notifies you when it has found them all. You could then quickly review the pages instead of waiting for each to download. There are more reasons, but for now we'll look at how to create a browser application. Later, you can figure out what you want to do with one.

Setting Up the WebBrowser Control

Microsoft ✓ *Exam* *Objective*	**Create an application that has the ability to browse HTML pages.**

The heart of a browser application in Visual Basic is the WebBrowser control. This control is not one of the standard controls that you find when you first install Visual Basic; however, the WebBrowser control is on your system if you have Internet Explorer. If you do not have Internet Explore, you can find the WebBrowser control in the Tools\Unsupprt\Webbrwsr folder of the Visual Basic CD. Also, the WebBrowser control is not an OCX file like a standard control. Rather, it is contained in the SHDOCVW.DLL file. In order to be able to use the control, you will have to have this file installed and registered on your system.

Making the Control Available to Visual Basic

The first step to being able to use the WebBrowser control is to make it available to Visual Basic. To do this, you need to choose the References item from the Project menu to bring up the References dialog box shown in Figure 15.1. From the dialog box, you need to click the Browse button and locate the SHDOCVW.DLL file in the open dialog box.

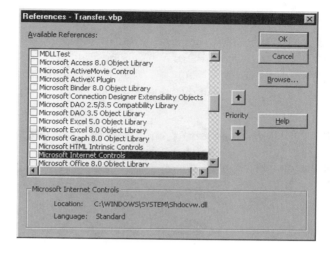

When you open the file, the reference to Microsoft Internet Controls will be added to the references for your project. At this point, you can close the References dialog box and open the Components dialog by choosing Components from the Project menu. The Components dialog box, shown in Figure 15.2 lets you add the Internet controls to your toolbox. You can add the control by checking the box next to the Microsoft Internet Controls in the Components dialog box, and you are ready to start using the control in a program.

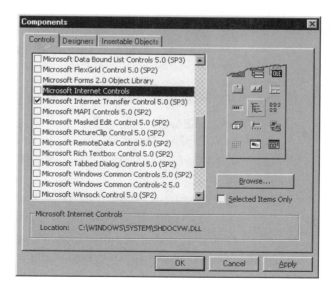

Creating an Instance of the WebBrowser

Once you have added the WebBrowser control to your toolbox, you can use it like any other control. You add a copy of the control to a form by selecting the control from the toolbox and drawing it on the form. When you draw the control, it only shows up as a borderless box on the form. This box is only visible when the control is selected as shown in Figure 15.3.

F I G U R E   15.3

WebBrowser control on a form

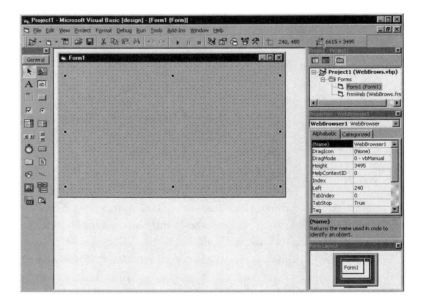

After you have placed the control on your form, you can begin setting up the properties of the control and using its methods and events in code. In addition to the standard properties that you will find with most controls, the WebBrowser control has two properties that are of particular interest:

- **LocationURL**   Identifies the URL string of the currently displayed web page. This information can be used to add the pages to a favorites list or to let the user know the identity of the current page.

- **LocationName**   Identifies the title of the currently displayed page. This information is typically used in conjunction with the LocationURL property to provide information to the user and for setting up favorites lists.

One other task that you will want to perform when setting up the Web-Browser is to resize the control in response to the user resizing the form. This operation allows the user to adjust the size of the form to see more of the web page that is currently displayed. The code to resize the control should be placed in the Resize event of the form. The following code resizes the Web-Browser while making sure that the navigation controls at the top of the form are not covered up:

```
webTest.Height = Me.ScaleHeight - webTest.Top - 60
webTest.Width = Me.ScaleWidth - webTest.Left - 60
```

Exercise 15.1 shows you how to create the initial interface of a browser application. We will extend the capabilities of this browser in other exercises in the chapter.

EXERCISE 15.1

Setting Up a Web Browser

1. Start a new standard exe project.

2. Add the WebBrowser control to your toolbox using the Components dialog box. If the Microsoft Internet Control is not in the Components dialog box, you will need to add it to the project references through the References dialog box.

3. Place a label control near the top of the form. (You will need to allow room for command buttons that we will add in the next exercise.) Set the Name property to lblAddress and the Caption to Address:.

4. Place a text box next to the label control. Set the Name property to txtAddress and clear the information in the Text property.

5. Add a WebBrowser control to the form and name it **webTest**. The control should fill most of the rest of the form. After you have added the Web-Browser control, your form should look like the next illustration.

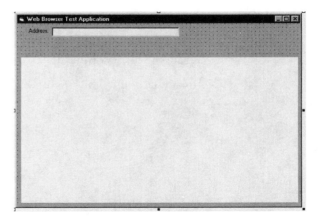

6. Add the following code to the Resize event of the form. This code prevents the form from being sized below a certain point and resizes the Web-Browser control to fit the space available in the form.

```
If Me.WindowState = 1 Then Exit Sub
If Me.Height < webTest.Top + 1500 Then Me.Height = _
webTest.Top + 1500
If Me.Width < webTest.Left + 1500 Then Me.Width = _
webTest.Left + 1500
webTest.Height = Me.ScaleHeight - webTest.Top - 60
webTest.Width = Me.ScaleWidth - webTest.Left - 60
```

7. Save the project.

Navigating between Web Pages

Of course, a browser is no good unless it has a way to move to different web pages. You have to be able to specify the URL or a web page on the Internet or the file location of a page on a company intranet. Once specified, your browser needs to be able to move to that page, download it, and display it. The WebBrowser control comes with a variety of methods that are used for navigating to the different pages.

Using the Basic Navigation Methods

There are two basic navigation tasks that you will need to be able to accomplish with a web browser application:

- You will need to be able to go to specific pages that are either specified in code or are specified by the user.

- You will need to be able to move back and forth between pages that have already been displayed.

The WebBrowser control has methods that allow you to perform both of these tasks.

Navigating Directly to Pages   The most basic form of navigation is moving to a specific page, either on the Internet or on a local network. You need to be able to specify the name of a file or the URL of a web page and have the browser find the page. The WebBrowser control uses the Navigate method to accomplish this. The Navigate method allows you to specify the page you want to find. The basic syntax of the Navigate command is:

```
WebTest.Navigate URLName
```

Working with a History List   One of the features of the WebBrowser control is that it automatically maintains a history list of the pages that have been displayed in the current navigation session, making it easy for you to move back and forth between the pages that have been viewed. The two methods that you use are the GoForward and GoBack methods of the control. The methods have no arguments associated with them, so you simply issue the method to perform the task.

The one thing that you will need to include with the method is error handling. If there is no page ahead of the current one in the history list, an error will occur if you use the GoForward method. The same is true for using the GoBack method if there is no page behind the current one in the history list. The following code shows how to handle the errors that might occur using the GoForward method.

```
On Error GoTo ForwardErr
webTest.GoForward
Exit Sub

ForwardErr:
MsgBox "You are at the last page in the History list"
```

There are also two other navigation methods that you can use in your web browser application:

- **GoHome**   Navigates directly to the home page specified in your Internet setup.

- **GoSearch**   Navigates directly to the search page specified in your Internet setup.

Exercise 15.2 shows you how to add these navigation features to the browser application that was begun in Exercise 15.1.

EXERCISE 15.2

Adding Navigation Features

1. Open the browser project created in Exercise 15.1.

2. Add 6 command buttons to the form, above the address and text box for displaying the page address. Name the command buttons **cmdGo**, **cmdForward**, **cmdBack**, **cmdHome**, **cmdSearch**, and **cmdExit**. Set the Caption properties of the buttons to &Go, &Forward, &Back, &Home, &Search, and &Exit respectively. After adding the buttons, your form should look like the next illustration.

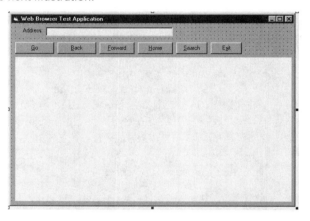

3. Add the following code to the cmdGo button. This code retrieves the name of a file or a URL from the text box and navigates to the requested page.

```
Dim sNewPage As String
sNewPage = txtAddress.Text
If sNewPage = "" Then Exit Sub
On Error GoTo NavError
webTest.Navigate sNewPage
Exit Sub
NavError:
MsgBox "Could not find requested page"
```

4. Add the following code to the cmdForward and cmdBack buttons as indicated below:

```
Private Sub cmdBack_Click()
On Error GoTo BackErr
webTest.GoBack
Exit Sub

BackErr:
MsgBox "You are at the first page in the History list"
End Sub

Private Sub cmdForward_Click()
On Error GoTo ForwardErr
webTest.GoForward
Exit Sub

ForwardErr:
MsgBox "You are at the last page in the History list"
End Sub
```

5. Add the following code to the cmdHome and cmdSearch buttons:

```
Private Sub cmdHome_Click()
On Error GoTo HomeErr
webTest.GoHome
Exit Sub
HomeErr:
MsgBox "Cannot find Home page"
End Sub

Private Sub cmdSearch_Click()
On Error GoTo SearchErr
webTest.GoSearch
Exit Sub
SearchErr:
MsgBox "Cannot find Search page"
End Sub
```

6. Place the following code in the cmdExit button's Click event to exit the program:

```
Unload Me
```

7. Finally, place the following code in the Load event of the form. This code calls the Click event of the cmdHome button to cause the browser to navigate to the home page when the application is opened.

```
cmdHome_Click
```

8. Save the project. Then run the program. If Internet Explorer has been set up on your system, your Internet connection will automatically open and you will navigate to the home page defined in your setup. The next illustration shows the web browser application with the Sybex home page displayed.

Advanced Navigation

The basic syntax of the Navigate method allows you to move to any page that you want, and have it displayed in the control. In addition to the URL-Name, the Navigate method supports several optional arguments that determine how the page is displayed:

- **TargetFrameName** Specifies which frame will contain the document to be displayed, assuming that the current HTML page has frames defined.

- **PostData** Specifies the string to be sent to the server during an HTTP POST transaction.

- **Headers** Specifies additional HTTP headers to be sent to the server.

- **Flags** Specifies how the page being retrieved will be handled. The flags argument is a value that contains the numerical sum of one or more of the following flags:

Flag	Value	Description
NavOpenInNewWindow	1	Open the document in a new window.
NavNoHistory	2	Do not add the current page to the history list.
NavNoReadFromCache	4	Read the page directly from the server, not from the disk cache.
NavNoWriteToCache	8	Do not write the retrieved page to the disk cache.

The complete syntax of the Navigate method is:

```
WebTest.Navigate UrlName, Flags, TargetFrameName, PostData, _
Headers
```

One other method that you may want to include for your browser is the Stop method. This method cancels any pending download operations and displays the currently available parts of the page.

Working with WebBrowser Events

When you are navigating between web pages, you need to keep your user informed as to what is going on in the program. Because web pages can take a significant amount of time to open, especially over some modem lines, your user may think the program is hung if you do not provide information about the current process. To keep up with the progress of your web application, you need to make use of the events of the WebBrowser control. These events can tell you the progress of the navigation and when particular steps of the process have occurred.

Determining When Pages Start and End

There are several key events of the WebBrowser control that let you know when pages are being loaded and even when elements of pages are being loaded. You can use these events to display messages to your user about the progress of accessing a web page. The key events of the WebBrowser control are:

- **BeforeNavigate** Occurs when the browser is about to move to a new page. You can use the event to handle any necessary cleanup of the current page or check on pending actions of the current page before moving on. The event includes a Cancel argument. If you set the Cancel argument to True, the navigation to another page is terminated.

- **NavigateComplete** Occurs when the navigation to the new page is completed, meaning that the page has been located and information is being transferred from the page to the browser. This event may be fired before all the elements of the page are downloaded. If you use Internet Explorer, you may have noticed the "Web Site Found" message that you get at the bottom of the window. This message can be triggered in your applications by the NavigateComplete event.

- **DownloadBegin** Occurs after the BeforeNavigate event and indicates that the application is in the process of downloading the elements of the requested web page. This event is typically used to change the cursor to an hourglass to indicate that an operation is in progress.

- **DownloadComplete** Occurs when all the elements of the page have been downloaded and displayed. Typically, you would use this event to reset the cursor to its original style.

- **TitleChange** Occurs when the title of the web page changes or becomes available. This event can be used to display the title of the web page on the form.

The following code shows the use of the DownloadBegin, DownloadComplete, and TitleChange events in a typical application:

```
Private Sub webTest_DownloadBegin()
Screen.MousePointer = vbHourglass
End Sub
```

```
Private Sub webTest_DownloadComplete()
txtAddress.Text = webTest.LocationURL
Screen.MousePointer = vbDefault
End Sub

Private Sub webTest_TitleChange(ByVal Text As String)
Me.Caption = Text
End Sub
```

Keeping Up with Progress

The other event of interest in the WebBrowser control is the ProgressChange event. This event is periodically fired during the download of information to indicate how much of the information has been downloaded. It is triggered for every resource that appears on the web page you are accessing, and is the reason Internet Explorer shows you individual element completion percentages instead of an overall page percentage. The ProgressChange event passes two arguments to you, the Progress argument (the amount of information already downloaded) and the ProgressMax argument (the total amount of information to be downloaded). The following code shows how you can update the progress of a download by writing to the txtAddress text box. For your applications, you may want to include a StatusBar or ProgressBar control for this purpose.

```
Private Sub webTest_ProgressChange(ByVal Progress As Long, _
ByVal ProgressMax As Long)
Dim sPctProg As String
If ProgressMax = 0 Then Exit Sub
sPctProg = Str(100 * Progress / ProgressMax)
txtAddress.Text = "Download is " & sPctProg & " Complete."
End Sub
```

WARNING If you do not check for a ProgressMax value of 0, you may encounter a division by zero error.

Creating a Connection to the Internet

Microsoft ✓ *Exam* *Objective*	**Create an application that enables connections to the Internet.**

The WebBrowser control is great for displaying web pages from the Internet or from an internal network. But what about the other tasks that you might need to accomplish over the Internet? For example, how do you create a connection to the Internet to check mail or download files? One of the other Internet controls for use with Visual Basic is the Microsoft Internet Transfer Control. This control lets you make a connection to the Internet, then transfer text and files between your computer and sites on the Internet.

The Internet Transfer Control works with both major protocols of the Internet, HTTP, and FTP, which means that the control allows you to issue commands and work with data on both web servers and FTP servers. By setting the properties of the control, you establish the parameters that allow the Internet connection to be made. Then, you invoke one of the methods of the control, such as Execute or OpenURL, to create the connection and start working with the remote data.

Setting Up the Internet Transfer Control

The first step to setting up the Internet Transfer Control is to add it to the toolbox. You do this by right-clicking on the toolbox to bring up the Components dialog box, then selecting the control in the dialog box. After you have added the control to the toolbox, you can add an instance of the control to your form. The Internet Transfer Control does not have a user interface, so, like the Timer or CommonDialog control, it appears only as an icon on your form, as shown in Figure 15.4.

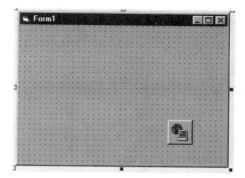

After placing the control on the form, you can set a few of the basic properties of the form:

- **RemoteHost**   Specifies the host server for the information you wish to retrieve. You can either specify the name of the host, such as `http://www.sybex.com` or an IP address such as 100.1.1.1. Either of these must be in the form of a literal string, or a string variable if you are setting them from code.

- **RemotePort**   Specifies the port to use for the connection. For connecting to the Internet this should be 80.

- **URL**   Specifies the URL location to connect to on the Internet.

- **UserName**   Specifies your user name for the site to which you are connecting. UserName is only required for a secured site. If you are connecting to a public site, you can leave this blank.

- **Password**   Specifies the password needed to connect to a specific site. Like the UserName, Password is only required if you are connecting to a secured site.

WARNING   When setting the URL, UserName, and Password in code, make sure to set the URL first. Otherwise, setting the URL will delete the settings of the User-Name and Password properties.

Retrieving Data with the Internet Transfer Control

Once you have created the basic setup for the Internet Transfer Control, you are ready to start transferring data with the control. There are two basic methods of the control that you can use to transfer data:

- **OpenURL** Goes to the specified URL and retrieves the information at that location. OpenURL can be used with either HTTP or FTP sites.

- **Execute** Specifies an action to take on a specific URL. The type of action that is allowed depends on whether you are connecting to an HTTP site or an FTP site. We will look at the details of the actions in the next section.

Working with Data from HTTP Sources

The easiest way to retrieve data from an HTTP site is to use the OpenURL method. With this method, you can specify the URL to open, or if you do not specify a URL, the URL property of the control will be used. If you specify a web page, the data that is transferred is the HTML code for the page. It will not show up as a rendered page, but as text in your program.

The OpenURL method will retrieve the entire web page. If you only wish to retrieve the header information for the page, you can use the GetHeader method. This method will query the web page and return any header information that is found. Exercise 15.3 takes you through the steps necessary to retrieve HTML information or header information from an HTTP site.

EXERCISE 15.3

Retrieving Information from an HTTP Site

1. Start a new project.

2. Add an Internet Transfer Control to the form. If you need to, add the control to your toolbox using the Components dialog box. Set the Name property of the control to itcTest. Because we will be working with public sites, there is no need to specify a UserName or Password property.

3. Set the URL property of the Internet Transfer Control to `http://www`
   `.sybex.com`.

4. Set the RemotePort property of the control to 80.

5. Add a text box to the form and name it **txtRetrieve**. Make the text box large enough to hold several lines of text. Set the Multiline property to True, and clear the Text property. You might also want to add scroll bars to the text box by setting the ScrollBars property to vertical.

6. Add three command buttons to the form below the text box. Name the buttons **cmdHTML**, **cmdHeader**, and **cmdClose**. Set the captions of the buttons to HTML, Headers, and Close respectively. When you have finished, your form should look like the next illustration.

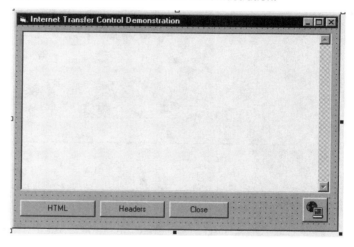

7. Add the following code to the cmdHTML button. This code retrieves the HTML text for the Sybex site.

```
txtRetrieve.Text = itcTest.OpenURL
```

8. Add the following code to the Click event of the cmdHeader button. This code will retrieve any header information from the site.

```
txtRetrieve.Text = itcTest.GetHeader
```

9. Add the following code to the Click event of the cmdClose button. This code uses the Cancel method to break the connection with the site.

```
itcTest.Cancel
```

10. Save the project.

11. Run the code and try the different buttons. The form will look like the following illustration after you click the HTML button.

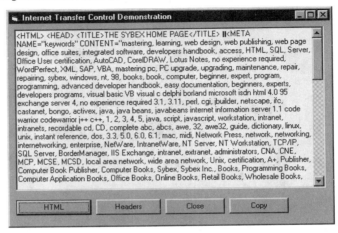

The OpenURL method is the easiest way to retrieve data from a site, but you can also use the Execute method. The Execute method uses the following four arguments:

- **URL**   Specifies the name of the URL where the data is located.

- **Operation**   Specifies the type of operation to perform. Four operations are supported:

    - **GET**   Retrieves data from the URL.

    - **HEAD**   Sends request headers to the URL.

    - **POST**   Sends data to the URL.

    - **PUT**   Replaces the contents of a page on the URL.

- **Data**   A text string that contains any data required for the operation listed above.

- **RequestHeaders**   Specifies the additional headers to be sent from the server.

Working with Data from FTP Sources

Like the HTTP data sources, you can use the OpenURL method to retrieve data from an FTP source. A command similar to the one shown in Exercise 15.3 could be used to display data from an FTP source in a text box; however, the Execute method is the one that you will typically use with FTP data sources. The Execute method supports more operations for FTP data sources than for HTTP data sources. For FTP data sources, the basic syntax of the Execute method is:

```
itcTest.Execute urlName, operation
itcTest.Execute "ftp://ftp.microsoft.com", _
"GET Disclaimer.txt C:\Disclaimer.txt"
```

Each operation specifies the operation name and either one or two "file" names, depending on the operation. Some of the operations that are available with FTP sites are:

- **CD**   Used to change directories on the remote site. The directory is specified as a file name.

- **CDUP**   Used to move to the parent directory on the site. No file name is specified with this operation.

- **DELETE**   Used to delete a file on the site. The file to be deleted is specified with the operation.

- **GET**   Retrieves a file from the remote site and places a copy on the local drive. The remote file is specified first, followed by the local file name.

- **MKDIR**   Makes a new directory on the remote site. The directory name is specified with the operation.

- **PUT**   Copies a local file to the remote site. The local file is listed first, followed by the remote file name.

- **RECV**   Works the same as GET.

- **RENAME**   Renames a file on the remote site. The original file name is listed first, followed by the new name.

- **RMDIR**   Removes a directory from the remote site.

- **SEND**   Works the same as PUT.

Exercise 15.4 shows you how to retrieve a file from a remote site and place a copy on your local disk.

EXERCISE 15.4

Copying a File from an FTP Site

1. Open the project created in Exercise 15.3

2. Add a command button to the form. Name the button **cmdCopy** and set the Caption property to Copy.

3. Place the following code in the Click event of the button. This code will retrieve a file from the Microsoft FTP site and copy it to your hard drive. In your application, you may want to add text boxes to specify the URL, the source file to be copied, and the target file on your disk:

```
itcTest.Execute "ftp://ftp.microsoft.com", _
"GET Disclaimer.txt C:\Disclaimer.txt"
```

4. Save the project.

5. Run the program. After you click the Copy button, you should have a copy of the Disclaimer.txt file on your local drive.

Summary

This chapter has covered two major topics regarding Internet programming, creating an application to view web pages and creating a connection to the Internet to upload and download information. The applications that you create use two basic controls for Internet access, the WebBrowser control and the Internet Transfer Control. With these two controls you can create all types of applications that access the Internet for special needs. The information that we covered should prepare you for the following exam objectives:

- Create applications that can access the Internet.

- Create an application that has the capability to browse HTML pages.

- Create an application that enables connections to the Internet.

Review Questions

1. Which control would you use to display a rendered web page?

   A. WebBrowser

   B. Internet Transfer Control

   C. WinSock

   D. Picture Box

2. Which control would you use to retrieve HTML text?

   A. WebBrowser

   B. Internet Transfer Control

   C. WinSock

   D. Picture Box

3. What method of the WebBrowser control lets you move to a specific web page?

   A. GoForward

   B. Navigate

   C. GoBack

   D. OpenURL

4. Which methods of the WebBrowser control work with the History list? Check all that apply.

   A. GoForward

   B. GoHome

   C. GoSearch

   D. GoBack

5. Which event of the WebBrowser control lets you know when you have successfully moved to another web page?

   A. DownloadComplete

   B. NavigateComplete

   C. BeforeNavigate

   D. ProgressChange

6. What port number should be used for the RemotePort property of the Internet Transfer Control for an Internet connection?

   A. 1

   B. 100

   C. 80

   D. 65

7. When do you use the UserName and Password property of the ITC?

   A. For all Internet access

   B. For access to secured sites

   C. For access to FTP sites only

   D. For access to HTTP sites only

8. Which method of the ITC allows you to retrieve HTML text from an HTTP site?

   A. OpenURL

   B. GetHeaders

   C. Navigate

   D. Retrieve

9. How do you copy a file from an FTP site?

   A. Use the OpenURL method.

   B. Use the Execute method with a GET operation.

   C. Use the Execute method with a PUT operation.

   D. Use the Copy method.

CHAPTER

16

Creating and Using
ActiveX Documents

Microsoft Objectives Covered in This Chapter:

- Compare ActiveX documents to embedded objects.

- Create and use ActiveX documents.

- Persist data for an ActiveX document.

- Create an ActiveX project with one or more UserDocument objects.

- Gain access to the Internet or an intranet by using the Hyperlink object.

- Automate an ActiveX document.

- Distribute an application over the Internet.

- Add an ActiveX document to a Web page.

With Visual Basic, you have long been able to create great stand-alone programs and programs that access network data. Visual Basic also gives you the capability to write multi-tier client server programs. But, wouldn't it be great if you also had an easy way to create Internet applications? After all, the Internet is the next frontier for computer programs.

A way to use Visual Basic to write Internet programs has arrived in version 5. Version 5 introduced ActiveX documents, programs that run in containers that support ActiveX, such as Internet Explorer. With ActiveX documents, you can easily write programs that run across the Internet or on your corporate intranet. These programs can have most of the capabilities of standard Visual Basic programs but with fewer hassles in distributing the programs and with a wider audience.

This chapter will take you through the process of creating ActiveX documents. You will learn how to create an ActiveX document from scratch and how to leverage your current programming efforts by converting projects to ActiveX documents. Along the way, you will learn several things about ActiveX documents that you need to know in order to meet the following certification exam objectives:

- Compare ActiveX documents to embedded objects.

- Create and use ActiveX documents.

- Persist data for an ActiveX document.
- Create an ActiveX project with one or more **UserDocument** objects.
- Distribute an application over the Internet.
- Automate an ActiveX document.
- Add an ActiveX document to a Web page.

The examples in this chapter are built with Internet Explorer 3.0. These programs will work equally well in Internet Explorer 4.0.

Understanding ActiveX Documents

ActiveX documents have a dual personality. On the one hand, they are programs that users can run to accomplish all kinds of tasks, from a simple calculator to a program that accesses database information and displays it in a grid. On the other hand, the documents have the characteristics of a Word document or Excel spreadsheet in that they cannot stand alone. ActiveX documents can only be used within a container that supports them. In fact, the term document comes from this similarity to Word and Excel "documents."

One of the key containers for using ActiveX documents is Microsoft's Internet Explorer. IE's support of ActiveX documents gives you the capability to easily create Internet applications. This ease of creation is what makes ActiveX documents so exciting.

Advantages of Using ActiveX Documents in Internet Programs

Just as Visual Basic made it easy for programmers to develop Windows applications, the introduction of ActiveX documents makes programming for the Internet easier. With ActiveX documents, you can apply all the skills you have creating Visual Basic programs to the development of Internet or intranet programs, which means that there is no steep learning curve for understanding a new language. You simply change the "container" for your program and dive right in. The only caveat is that the browser used by you and your users must be capable of supporting ActiveX components.

Microsoft
Exam
Objective

Compare ActiveX documents to embedded objects.

For the types of programs that you can create with ActiveX documents, your alternatives are to use HTML pages with embedded objects such as text boxes, lists, command buttons, and so on. Being able to use ActiveX documents provides you with a number of advantages over using these methods:

- Your knowledge of Visual Basic can be directly applied to creating the programs that you want to create for the Internet.

- Laying out forms is much easier in Visual Basic's design environment than is possible when you are coding tags and then having to run the program to verify that controls are where you want them.

- You can debug an ActiveX document using the tools of Visual Basic's development environment.

- ActiveX documents support the Hyperlink object, which makes it easy to move from one document to another or even to another web page.

- ActiveX documents can persist data between sessions.

Convinced? If you need to write programs for the Internet, ActiveX documents can make the job a whole lot easier.

Comparison of ActiveX Documents to Visual Basic Forms and ActiveX controls

ActiveX documents are designed to work with the Internet, but there are many similarities between creating ActiveX documents and creating forms for standard programs. An ActiveX document starts with a UserDocument object, shown in Figure 16.1, which is very similar to a form without a border. The border is not needed because the document will be contained within Internet Explorer or some other container.

FIGURE 16.1

UserDocument for
creating an ActiveX
document

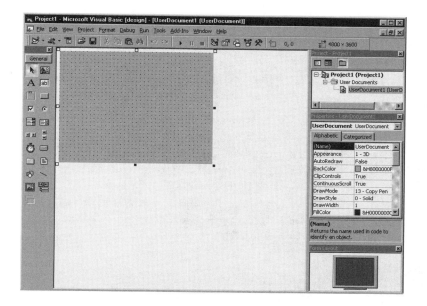

FIGURE 16.1

UserDocument for
creating an ActiveX
document

While we usually refer to the Internet Explorer as the container for ActiveX documents, there are other containers that support ActiveX documents. These containers include the Office Binder and the Visual Basic Integrated Development Environment (IDE).

When you are creating an ActiveX document, you design the interface just as you would a form's interface. You select controls from the toolbox and draw instances of the controls on the UserDocument. To write code, you open the code window and enter the necessary program lines in the event procedures of the controls. Also, like a form, you can create custom properties and methods by using Property procedures and publicly declared Sub and Function procedures.

There are, however, a few differences between a form and a UserDocument object. Some of the key differences are:

- The UserDocument does not support the Load or Unload events, which means that you cannot use these events to initialize information for the UserDocument.

- You cannot use the Load method to start a UserDocument or Unload to terminate it. Displaying a UserDocument object is handled by directly opening the file in the container or by using the Hyperlink object.

- You cannot use the OLE container control on a UserDocument, nor can you create links to other applications, such as Word or Excel.

The UserDocument may have many similarities to the Form object, but in one way it is closer to the UserControl object that you use to create ActiveX controls. Both the UserDocument and the UserControl can use an object called the PropertyBag to store data about the properties of the UserDocument or UserControl. We will look more closely at the PropertyBag as it relates to the UserDocument later in this chapter. If you want to know more about creating ActiveX controls, refer to Chapter 14, "Creating ActiveX Controls with Visual Basic."

Creating ActiveX Documents

Microsoft ✓ *Exam* *Objective*	**Create and use ActiveX documents.**

Creating an ActiveX document is very similar to creating a standard program in Visual Basic. As with a standard program, you follow a sequence of steps to create the document:

1. Start the project.

2. Create the user interface of the document.

3. Write the code to handle the tasks required of the document.

4. Test the document program.

5. Compile the document and prepare it for distribution.

We will look at each of these steps in detail in this section.

Creating the ActiveX Document Project

The first step in creating an ActiveX document is to start an ActiveX document project. You can start the project by choosing the ActiveX Document EXE option from the New Project dialog box shown in Figure 16.2. You open the dialog box by choosing the New Project item from the File menu of Visual Basic.

FIGURE 16.2

New Project dialog

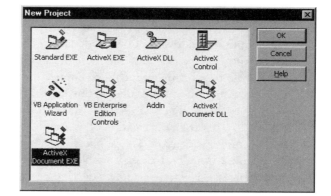

There are two types of ActiveX Document projects, EXE and DLL. The DLL type document can only be used as a subprogram of another project. To create documents that can be used in Internet Explorer, you must choose the EXE type of ActiveX document.

The new project starts with a single UserDocument object created for you. Typically, the UserDocument will automatically open to allow you to begin your design. If not, you can click on the UserDocuments folder in the project window, then double-click the UserDocument object to display it. Like a form, a UserDocument has a default name, in this case UserDocument1. The first thing that you will need to do is to set the name to something meaningful. The name you assign is also the default name of the document file that you create when you compile the document and the name that you will use to retrieve the document using Internet Explorer. After setting the Name property, you can set any of the other properties that you wish to change.

Creating the User Interface

Once you have the UserDocument object open, you can start placing controls on the document. Just as with the form of a standard program, these controls provide the user interface for the document. You can use almost any control available in Visual Basic, except the OLE container control. You can even use custom controls obtained from third parties (be sure to check licensing requirements) or ActiveX controls that you have created.

After you have added the controls to the UserDocument and set their properties, you can start writing the code for the document. To access the code window, double-click on the document or on any control, or click the code button in the Project window. You can write code to handle almost any task from the document, including connecting to databases, reading and writing information in files, and printing. The statements that you use are the same ones that you would use for a standard program.

To illustrate the creation of an ActiveX document, we will create and test a sample application. This application can be used to print trip requests for a corporate intranet. To keep it simple, the design of the sample application prints the request on paper. If you were developing this application for your company, you might want to connect directly to the e-mail system to send the request to the proper person for approval. Exercise 16.1 starts the process of creating this application.

EXERCISE 16.1

Creating an ActiveX Document

1. Start a new project in Visual Basic and select the ActiveX Document EXE option from the New Project dialog box.

2. Open the UserDocument object by double-clicking on UserDocument1 in the project window.

3. Change the name of the UserDocument object to **TravReq**.

4. Add four labels to the UserDocument to indicate what information will be entered in the document. These labels will have the captions **Name:**, **Destination:**, **Trip Dates:**, and **Purpose of Trip:**. Align all the labels, make them the same width, and set the Alignment property of all the labels to Right Justify.

5. Add four text boxes to the UserDocument. Name the text boxes **txtName**, **txtDestination**, **txtDates**, and **txtPurpose**. Clear the Text property of each of the boxes. For the txtPurpose text box, set the MultiLine property to True and set the ScrollBars property to Vertical. Also, make the box large enough to hold several lines of text.

6. Add a command button to the UserDocument. Name the command button **cmdPrint** and set the Caption property to Print Request. The final appearance of the UserDocument should be something like the following illustration.

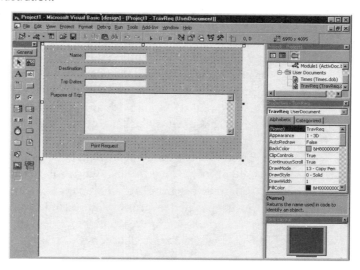

7. Open the code window for the command button by double clicking on the button. Enter the following code in the Click event of the command button. This code will print the travel request.

```
Printer.Print "Name: " & txtName.Text
Printer.Print "Destination: " & txtDestination.Text
Printer.Print "Trip Dates: " & txtDates.Text
Printer.Print "Purpose: " & txtPurpose.Text
Printer.EndDoc
```

8. Save the document by clicking the save button on Visual Basic's toolbar. You can use the default name of TravReq for the user document.

When you saved the project containing the UserDocument, you created a file with the extension dob. This file contains the information about the UserDocument in text form, like the frm file contains information about a form. If you have graphical controls on the UserDocument, information about them is contained in a dox file, similar to the frx file for forms.

Running and Testing the ActiveX Document

After you have created the user interface and the program code for the ActiveX document, you are ready to run and test the document. This is where there are some key differences between working with ActiveX documents and standard programs. In a standard program, you can simply click the run button or press the F5 key to run your program, and the results will show up instantly on the screen. This is not the case for an ActiveX document.

With an ActiveX document, clicking the run button compiles the program and creates a file containing the working version of the document. This file has the same name as your UserDocument and an extension of vdb and is placed in the same subdirectory as Visual Basic. In order to view the document, you must open it with an application that is capable of working with ActiveX documents, such as Internet Explorer.

While you are working with the document in a browser, it is still active in the Visual Basic development environment, which means that you can still use all of Visual Basic's debugging tools to check the values of variables, step through the program, and set breakpoints to pause the execution of the program at specified locations. Figure 16.3 shows the execution of the TravReq document paused in the development environment. To learn more about debugging, check out Chapter 18, "Debugging Your Application."

FIGURE 16.3

Using debugging tools with an ActiveX document

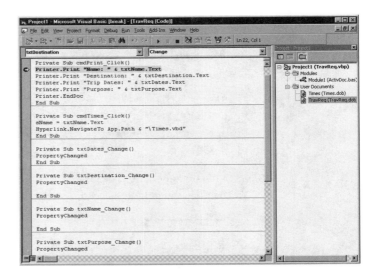

To demonstrate how to run and test an ActiveX document, Exercise 16.2 continues where Exercise 16.1 left off, with running the TravReq document.

EXERCISE 16.2

Running and Testing the TravReq Document

1. If it is not already open, open the TravReq project created in Exercise 16.1.

2. Click the Run button to start the ActiveX document. Then minimize Visual Basic.

3. Start Internet Explorer.

4. From the File menu of Internet Explorer, choose the Open item.

5. Click the Browse button in the Open dialog box to bring up the Open file dialog box shown in the next illustration. Choose the All Files option from the Files of Type dropdown list, then find the VB folder on your computer.

6. Double-click the TravReq.vdb file to open it. Then click the OK button on the Internet Explorer Open dialog box. The TravReq document will be displayed in Internet Explorer as shown in the following illustration.

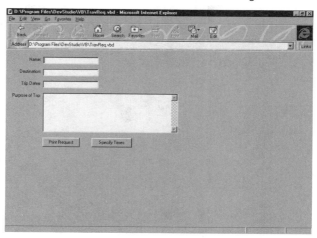

EXERCISE 16.2 (CONTINUED)

7. You can now enter information in the text boxes of the document and click the command button to print the information.

8. When you have finished, you will need to close Internet Explorer or move to another page before terminating the program in Visual Basic.

Using the Office Binder

If you do not have version 3.0 or higher of the Internet Explorer on your machine, you can use the Office Binder of Office 95 or Office 97 to view ActiveX documents created in Visual Basic. To use the Office Binder, follow these steps:

1. Open the Office Binder application, typically found in the same program group as the other office applications.

2. Select the Add from File item from the Section menu in the Office Binder.

3. Use the Browse button to locate the TravReq.vdb file in the VB folder on your computer.

4. When you open the file, it will appear in the binder as shown in the next illustration. You can then work with the document like you would with Internet Explorer.

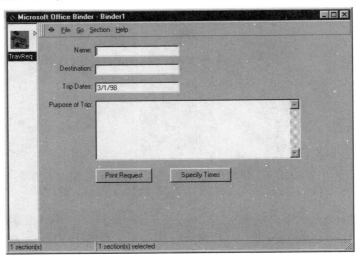

Storing Data Created in ActiveX Documents

Microsoft ✓ *Exam* *Objective*

Persist data for an ActiveX document.

If you have the users of your document entering data, you will need a way to store the information. Because you can perform almost any programming task with an ActiveX document, you can save the information in a file or save it in a database. However, you may only want to save the information between times that the user accesses the document. For example, you may want to save the name of the person so that it will appear the next time they use the document. It is also helpful to save all the information in the document in case the user closes the browser before they have had an opportunity to finish the form.

ActiveX documents support the PropertyBag object, like the ActiveX controls described in Chapter 14. The PropertyBag is a storage device that allows you to write and read property information for the document. The PropertyBag has two methods that you use for handling information, ReadProperty and WriteProperty. When you issue the ReadProperty method, you specify the property to be retrieved and a default value, in case the desired property cannot be located. With the WriteProperty method, you specify the property to be written, the value to use, and a default value. The following lines of code show examples of these two methods.

```
txtName.Text = PropBag.ReadProperty("Name", "")
PropBag.WriteProperty "Name", txtName.Text, ""
```

The PropertyBag works like the registry or INI files. You do not have to have actual properties in your document to use it. You can store any information by specifying a key and a value.

In order to use these methods, you need to know when a property has changed. You notify the UserDocument that a property value has been changed by issuing the PropertyChanged method. You do not have to specify a specific property with this method; the method is merely used to trigger the WriteProperties event of the UserDocument.

The two events of the UserDocument object that are used in storing and retrieving properties are the ReadProperties event and the WriteProperties event. The ReadProperties event is triggered when the document is first loaded from a file, which allows you to retrieve the property information from the PropertyBag and set the initial values of properties or controls. The WriteProperties event is triggered when the document is unloaded, if the PropertyChanged method has been used in the program. Exercise 16.3 shows you how to use these events and methods to create persistent data in the TravReq document.

EXERCISE 16.3

Reading and Writing Information for the Document

1. Open the project created in Exercise 16.1.

2. In the Change event of each of the text boxes, place the following code statement:

```
PropertyChanged
```

3. In the ReadProperties event of the UserDocument, place the following code to read in the information to be placed in the text boxes. Note that you must specify a default value for each of the ReadProperty calls. Also, note that the code uses the Format function to set a default date of the current date.

```
txtName.Text = PropBag.ReadProperty("Name", "")
txtDestination.Text = PropBag.ReadProperty("Destination", "")
txtDates.Text = PropBag.ReadProperty("Dates", _
Format(Date, "Short Date"))
txtPurpose.Text = PropBag.ReadProperty("Purpose", "")
```

4. In the WriteProperties event of the UserDocument, place the following code to write the new values of the information in the text boxes. Note that you should also specify a default value for the WriteProperty method.

```
PropBag.WriteProperty "Name", txtName.Text, ""
PropBag.WriteProperty "Destination", txtDestination.Text, ""
PropBag.WriteProperty "Dates", txtDates.Text, ""
PropBag.WriteProperty "Purpose", txtPurpose.Text, ""
```

5. Your document is now capable of storing and retrieving information entered by the user.

Working with Multiple Documents

Microsoft ✓ Exam Objective	Create an ActiveX project with one or more UserDocument objects.

Like a single form program, a single document program is of limited usefulness. There are only so many controls that you can place on a single form. However, you are not limited to working with just a single document. ActiveX documents are capable of navigating to other documents through the use of the HyperLink object, which enables you to use as many documents as you need to achieve your program goals.

Adding Documents to a Project

If you are creating multiple documents to work together, you can add more documents to the project. Choose the Add User Document item from the Project menu to place a second (or third, and so on.) document in the project. You can now design the interface for the second document and add code to its events as well. There is no limit to the number of documents that you can have in a single project.

In addition to adding documents, you can also add standard forms to the project. These forms can be used for any purpose that you wish. Forms in an ActiveX document project can be called using the standard Show method.

Navigating Between Documents

Microsoft ✓ Exam Objective	Gain access to the Internet or an intranet by using the Hyperlink object.

When you start working with more than one document, you need a way to move back and forth between the documents. This capability is provided by the HyperLink object. The HyperLink object has no properties, but contains three methods:

- **NavigateTo**   Tells the container to move to a specific file or URL specified as an argument of the method.

- **GoForward**   Tells the container to move to the next item in the History list.

- **GoBack**   Tells the container to move to the previous item in the History list.

Also, if you are working with multiple documents, you will need a way to pass information between them. Unfortunately, UserDocuments do not allow you to create properties that can be set from another UserDocument object. Therefore, you have to use Global variables to pass data. Global variables must be declared in a BAS module that is part of the project. Exercise 16.4 shows you how to add multiple documents and navigate between them. The exercise adds a second page to the TravReq document you created previously.

EXERCISE 16.4

Working with Multiple Documents

1. Open the TravReq project that you created in Exercise 16.1.

2. Add a second document to the project by selecting the Add User Document item from the Project menu.

3. Name the second document **Times**.

4. Add three labels and three text boxes to the document. The labels should have the captions **Name:**, **Departure:**, and **Return:**. The text boxes should be named txtName, txtDeparture, and txtReturn.

5. Add a command button to the document and name it **cmdReturn**. When you have finished, your form should look like the next illustration.

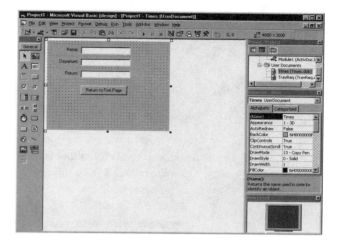

6. Place the following code in the Click event of the command button. This code uses the HyperLink object to return to the previous page of the project:

```
Hyperlink.GoBack
```

7. Add a module to the project to hold a global variable. Add the module by selecting the Add Module item from the Project menu.

8. Place the following code in the module to declare a global variable:

```
Public sName As String
```

9. Place the following code in the Show event of the Times document. This code places the name of the user in the txtName text box when the document is displayed:

```
txtName.Text = sName
```

10. Go to the TravReq document and add a command button to the document. The command button should have the name **cmdTimes** and the caption **Specify Times**.

EXERCISE 16.4 (CONTINUED)

11. Place the following code in the Click event of the cmdTimes button. This code places the name of the user in the global variable and navigates to the second page of the document:

```
sName = txtName.Text
Hyperlink.NavigateTo "D:\VB\Times.vbd"
```

The directory you specify may be different because of your directory structure.

12. Run the program and open the document in Internet Explorer. When you enter a name in the first document and click the Specify Times button, you will be taken to the second document. You will see that the name from the first document has been transmitted to the second document, as shown in the following illustration.

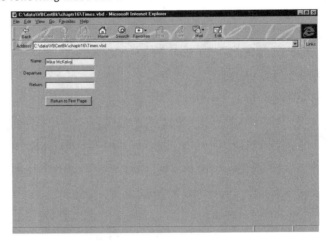

You may have noticed when you moved to the second document in Internet Explorer that the Back button of Explorer became enabled. You can use the navigation buttons of Internet Explorer to move between documents, but it is better to use the HyperLink object to specify an exact document to use.

When you compile your document, you will need to change the line that contains the specific navigation path to one that reads: HyperLink.NavigateTo App.Path & "\Times.vbd".

Compiling and Distributing ActiveX Documents

After you have finished designing and testing your ActiveX documents, you will want to compile them and distribute them to others. The process is very similar to compiling and distributing other programs; however, a few minor differences occur because the prime medium for distributing and running your documents is the Internet.

How to Compile Your Documents

To compile your ActiveX documents, you need to choose the Make item from the File menu of Visual Basic. You specify the name of an exe file and any compilation options that you want to include. The compiler will create the exe file, but it will also create a vbd file for each of the documents listed in the project. These vbd files are the ones that will be distributed to and used by others.

Creating Distribution Files for the ActiveX Documents

Microsoft
Exam
Objective

Distribute an application over the Internet.

The setup wizard that comes with Visual Basic is capable of creating the setup files that are necessary for distributing your ActiveX documents. The setup program will create cabinet (cab) files for your program and provide links to the Microsoft site to allow the user to download other files that may be necessary for the proper operation of your program. Exercise 16.5 walks you through the process of compiling your program and creating the distribution files.

EXERCISE 16.5

Distributing Your Files

1. Open the TravReq project created in previous exercises.

2. Choose the Make item from the File menu.

3. Click the OK button on the dialog box to use the default name for the executable.

4. After compilation, exit Visual Basic and start the Application Setup Wizard.

EXERCISE 16.5 (CONTINUED)

5. After skipping the opening screen of the wizard, you will be presented with the screen shown in the following illustration. Choose the option to Create Internet Download Setup. Then click the Browse button to find the project that contains your ActiveX documents. Click the Next button.

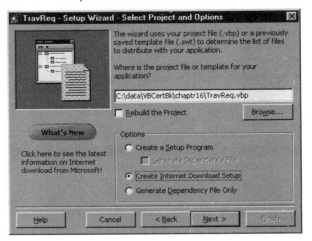

6. The next page allows you to select the location to place your Internet distribution files. For many cases, you will move these files later to a server accessible by others. Therefore, it is safe to accept the default directory and click the Next button.

7. The next page allows you to choose whether to have runtime files downloaded from the Microsoft web site or another location. Because the Microsoft site should have the latest versions, it is usually safe to choose the Microsoft site. Click the Next button.

8. The next page determines whether you have ActiveX server components in your project. The Setup Wizard will typically find these for you, but the page allows you to add other components if necessary. When you are done, click the Next button.

9. The File Summary page, shown in the next illustration, shows you all the files that Setup Wizard has determined need to be in your setup. If you wish to add other files, such as a ReadMe file, you can do so on this page. When you are finished, click the Next button.

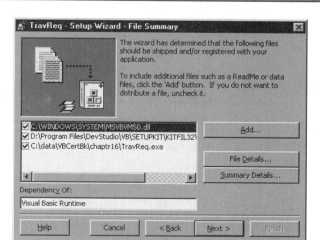

10. At this point, you have reached the final page of the wizard. To create your distribution files, click the Finish button on the page. When setup finishes creating the files, it will display a message indicating completion of the task and advising you to check your files for viruses before distribution.

Automatically Creating ActiveX Documents

You probably have a lot of work invested in programs that you have created over the years. ActiveX documents provide you with an easy way to create programs that are ready for the Internet. In addition, Microsoft included the Document Migration Wizard to help you convert your existing programs to ActiveX documents. The wizard handles a large part of the work for you, but it cannot handle all the conversion. Some of the items that you will need to do by hand are:

- Move or remove code that is in the Load or Unload events of your forms.

- Remove OLE container controls and their associated code.

- Set up code in the Initialize and Terminate events of the documents to handle the tasks that would have been performed in the Load and Unload events.

- Set up global variables to pass information between user documents.

- Remove any references to form names.

Microsoft ✓ ***Exam Objective***

Automate an ActiveX document.

As always, an example makes things easier to understand. Exercise 16.6 shows you how to convert the Calc program from the Visual Basic samples to an ActiveX document.

EXERCISE 16.6

Converting an Existing Program to an ActiveX Document

1. Open the Calc.vbp program in the Visual Basic samples directory.

2. If the Document Migration Wizard is not in the Add-Ins menu, add it using the Add-In Manager. Then open the Document Migration Wizard.

3. Skip the opening page of the wizard to move to the Form Selection page, shown in the next illustration. Select the Calculator form and click the Next button.

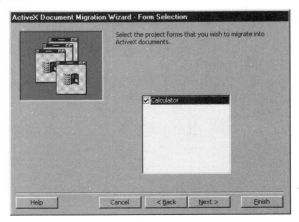

4. The next page is the Options page, shown in the following illustration. This page allows you to specify: 1) Whether to comment out invalid code, 2) Remove the original forms from the project, 3) Select the type of project to create. You should choose the Comment out invalid code option and leave the rest at their default settings.

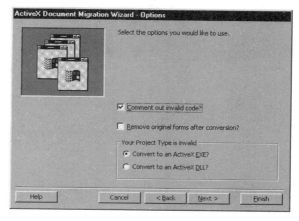

5. Click the Finish button to complete the process. The wizard will then display a report that tells you what you have to do to finish the migration.

When you are finished with the document migration, you can run your document in Internet Explorer. Figure 16.4 shows the Calculator program running inside Internet Explorer.

Using ActiveX Documents with Internet Explorer

Once the ActiveX document is programmed, tested, and compiled, you can distribute it and run it in any browser or other container that supports ActiveX documents. One such container is, of course, Internet Explorer. When you are working with the Internet Explorer, there are two ways that you can get your ActiveX document to run:

- Directly open the vbd file that contains the ActiveX document.

- Create an HTML page that points to the ActiveX document.

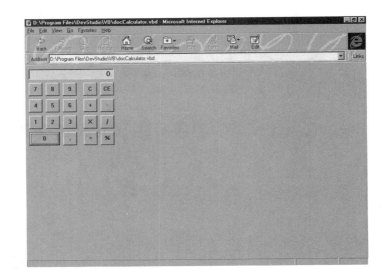

Using ActiveX Documents Directly

Using the document directly is an available option if you know the location of
the file. You will typically use this option once the document has been distributed and a copy of the document is on your local machine. You may also use
this method if you are running the document over a network internal to your
company.

To directly access an ActiveX document, you choose the Open item from
the File menu in Internet Explorer and either type in the file location or use the
Browse button to find the file. This method is the one that we have been using
all along to test ActiveX documents.

Embedding ActiveX Documents in a Web Page

The other alternative for using ActiveX documents with Internet Explorer is to
embed the document in a web page, the only method that you can use to distribute your documents over the Internet. Embedding the ActiveX document
in a web page requires two steps, downloading the document and running the
document.

To cause Internet Explorer to download the ActiveX document, you will need to specify an HTML object that specifies:

- The class ID of the document
- The name of the cab file containing the document
- Version information for the document

Fortunately, Visual Basic's Setup Wizard creates a sample HTML file for you that contains this information. The OBJECT tag information for the TravReq document is shown in the following code:

```
<OBJECT ID="TravReq"
CLASSID="CLSID:B044F674-B017-11D1-BCCD-0000C051F6F9"
CODEBASE="TravReq.CAB#version=1,0,0,0">
</OBJECT>
```

The code in the OBJECT tag will tell Internet Explorer to download the document and register it in the Windows registry.

Microsoft ✓ ***Exam*** ***Objective***   **Add an ActiveX document to a Web page.**

The second step to running the document from a web page is to set up HTML code to activate the document. You can do this with VBScript using the following code:

```
<SCRIPT LANGUAGE="VBScript">
Sub Window_OnLoad
Document.Open
Document.Write "<FRAMESET>"
Document.Write "<FRAME SRC=""TravReq.VBD"">"
Document.Write "</FRAMESET>"
Document.Close
End Sub
</SCRIPT>
```

This code is also created for you by the Setup Wizard.

Summary

As you can see, ActiveX documents open up a whole new frontier for programming. With these documents, you can easily create applications for the Internet. You can even convert some of your existing programs to ActiveX documents with the help of the Document Migration Wizard. In this chapter, we have covered a number of certification exam objectives. You have learned:

- How to create ActiveX documents that contain multiple pages.

- How to persist data between sessions.

- How to create a setup program.

- How to distribute your application over the Internet.

- How to call your application from a Web page.

Review Questions

1. What is the primary object used in creating ActiveX documents?

    A. UserControl

    B. Form

    C. UserDocument

    D. Class Module

2. How many documents are allowed in a single project?

    A. 1

    B. Maximum of 5

    C. There is no set limit.

    D. Maximum of 10

3. Which of the following is not allowed in an ActiveX document?

   A. Custom controls

   B. User created controls

   C. OLE container control

   D. Database controls

4. How do you store information from an ActiveX document so it is available when the document is reloaded?

   A. Write the information to a file.

   B. Use the methods of the PropertyBag object.

   C. It cannot be done.

   D. Specify the initial settings in the HyperLink object.

5. What does the Document Migration Wizard do for you?

   A. Helps you move documents to another folder.

   B. Helps you create an ActiveX document from an existing program.

   C. Creates a file that lets you distribute your document over the Internet.

   D. Lets you move from one document to another.

6. Which of the following can run an ActiveX document? Check all that apply.

   A. Internet Explorer

   B. Visual Basic development environment

   C. Windows Explorer

   D. Office Binder

7. Which file do you load to run an ActiveX document?

   A. dob

   B. vbd

   C. cab

   D. vbp

8. Which file is downloaded over the Internet to install and register an ActiveX document?

   A. dob

   B. vbd

   C. cab

   D. vbp

9. How are multiple documents handled when you compile your project?

   A. All documents are compiled into a single file.

   B. Each document is created in a separate file.

   C. You cannot create multiple documents in a single project.

   D. Files with links to each other are grouped together.

10. How do you display one document from another?

   A. Use the Show method of the document.

   B. Use the NavigateTo method of the HyperLink object.

   C. Use the Display method of the document.

   D. Use the Navigate method of the UserDocument object.

11. How do you pass information from one document to another?

   A. Set the value of a property in the target document.

   B. Use a global variable to contain the data.

   C. Use the PropertyBag.

   D. You cannot pass data between documents.

PART

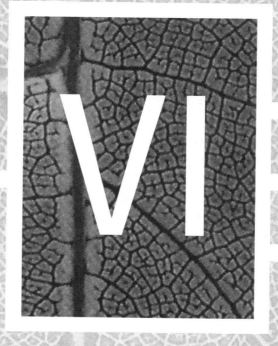

VI

Debugging and
Error Handling

CHAPTER

17

Handling Errors in Visual Basic Programs

Microsoft Exam Objectives Covered in This Chapter:

- Display an error message in a dialog box by using the Err object.

- Implement error-handling features in an application.

- Create a common error-handling routine.

- Raise errors from a server.

- Use the appropriate error-trapping options, such as Break on All Errors, Break in Class Module, and Break on Unhandled Errors.

No matter how well you create your program or how carefully you test it, there will always be runtime errors that can occur in your program. These runtime errors can occur when the user forgets to put a disk in the floppy drive and tries to read the disk. Or an error can occur when you expected that a user would know to enter a number, but they enter a string instead. In any case, a runtime error can stop your program dead in its tracks.

Visual Basic does not handle errors automatically. It simply notifies your program of the error. If your program has been set up to handle errors, you can retry an operation, allow the user to correct a value, or exit the program. If you do not have an error handler in your program, your program will terminate, with an error message like the one shown in Figure 17.1. This type of message is something that you want your user to never see.

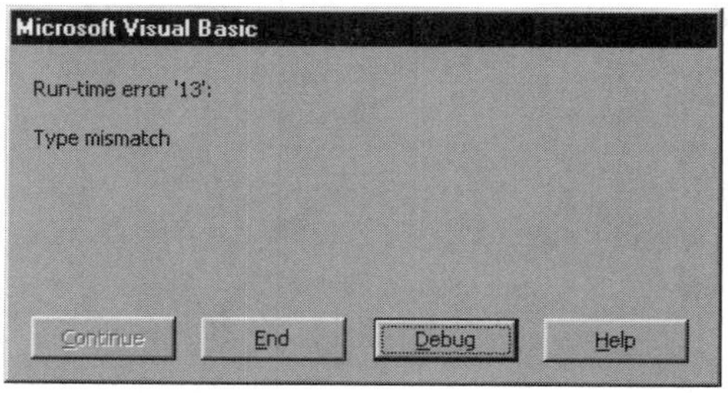

FIGURE 17.1

Error messages you get from Visual Basic

There are several processes that you need to understand in handling errors. The importance of these processes is indicated by the Microsoft exam objectives. To handle errors well in your program, and to pass the exam, you need to:

- Have a good understanding of the Err object.

- Be able to create an error handling routine using the On Error statements.

- Know how to use proper error trapping options.

If you are creating ActiveX servers, you also will need to know how to raise an error. Raising the error is the only way to communicate a problem back to the ActiveX client. Raising errors is also one of the exam objectives.

Understanding Errors

Before we get into the mechanics of handling errors, take a moment to review what program errors are. As you are developing programs, there are three classes of errors that you can encounter:

- **Syntax errors**   You have incorrectly entered a line of code.

- **Logic errors**   Your program does not produce the correct output, but runs OK.

- **Runtime errors**   A condition in your program causes a problem.

Visual Basic provides you with tools to track down syntax errors. These tools are discussed in detail in Chapter 18, "Developing Your Applications." Logic errors require meticulous testing and tracking of the code's execution to track down. Chapter 18 also discusses tools that help you with this function. The final category, runtime errors, is the focus of this chapter.

Causes of Errors

Runtime errors occur when something unexpected happens in your program, or when a statement in your program cannot be correctly resolved. Some examples of runtime errors are:

- Trying to open a file that does not exist

- Trying to assign a string to a numeric variable

- Dividing a number by zero

- Saving a database record that is locked by another user

Some of these errors can be avoided, but many times the causes of the errors are beyond your control. For example, if a user deletes a file that your program needs, an error will occur, even though it was not your fault. Likewise, two users trying to save the same database record will cause an error, because both are not allowed to write to the same record at the same time. There is no way to avoid these errors, but you must take appropriate action when the errors occur.

Avoiding Errors

Your program will need an error handler for many tasks, and there are ways to avoid certain types of errors. For example, you can trap a division by zero error, but it is easier to avoid the error in the first place. The following code illustrates how you can avoid such an error:

```
If Y = 0 Then
    MsgBox "Enter a non-zero value for Y"
    Z = 0
    Exit Sub
Else
    Z = X / Y
End If
```

Likewise, you can check for the existence of a file before you try to open it. If the file does not exist, you can give the user the option of specifying an alternate location or even an alternate file. Careful planning of your programs will allow you to avoid many errors, leaving your error handler to take care of the errors that are unavoidable.

Working with the Err Object

The Err object is the centerpiece of Visual Basic's error notification and handling capabilities. Using the Err object, you can determine what error occurred, get a description of the error, and find out where the error occurred. You can even use the Err object to raise your own errors from code. This capability is required to report errors in an ActiveX server that you create.

Like most objects in Visual Basic, the Err object provides information to the program and takes action through the properties and methods of the object. The Err object has no events. The following sections will give you a good overview of the properties and methods of the error object. We will then look at how to use the information in the Err object to display detailed error messages. Then, in the section "Trapping Errors in Your Programs," you will see how to use the Err object to write error handling routines for your programs.

Using the Properties of the Err Object

When an error occurs in Visual Basic, the program populates the properties of the Err object to provide information about the error to you and your program. These properties tell you the kind of error encountered and give you an indication of the location where the error occurred. This information enables you to determine the appropriate action to take to recover from the error and provides you with descriptions of the error that you can display to your users or can log to a file.

Determining Which Error Occurred

The most important property of the Err object is the Number property. This property tells you which of Visual Basic's hundreds of possible errors has occurred. This number is used in error handling routines to determine what action to take. For example, in the following code, if an error occurs during a save operation for a database program, the type of error is used to determine whether to retry the save operation or report the error and continue with the next line of code.

```
Select Case Err.Number
    Case 3046, 3158, 3186, 3187, 3188, 3189, 3218, 3260
        'Record is locked by another user
        iTriesCnt = iTriesCnt + 1
        If iTriesCnt > 10 Then
            iErrReturn = MsgBox( _
"Record is locked by another user. Try again?", _
vbExclamation + vbYesNo)
```

```
                    If iErrReturn = vbYes Then
                        iTriesCnt = 0
                        Resume
                    Else
                        bUpdateOK = False
                        Resume Next
                    End If
                Else
                    fPauseTime = Timer
                    Do Until Timer > fPauseTime + 0.1
                    Loop
                    Resume
                End If
        End Select
```

In looking at this code, two questions probably arise in your mind:

- How do I find out what the error codes are?

- How do I know which errors to check for?

The answer to the first question is easy. Visual Basic's help file provides a comprehensive list of error codes that can occur in your program. This list tries to group some of the errors into logical sets. For each error number, you will find a description of the error and some information about why the error occurred. Figure 17.2 shows an example of the help file for one of the database errors listed in the above code.

The answer to the second question is a little more difficult. It is obvious that if you are not working with database functions that you do not need to look out for database errors; however, the only way to determine which errors to look for is through experience and testing. Also, it helps to have your programs create an error log so that users can easily report errors that might occur after you have distributed your program.

The counterpart of the Number property is the Description property of the Err object. The Description property provides you with a brief description of the error that occurred. This information is more useful for error messages displayed to the user or messages that are written to an error log. For example, the following code will produce an error:

```
X = 5
Y = 0
Z = X / Y
```

FIGURE 17.2

Database error
descriptions

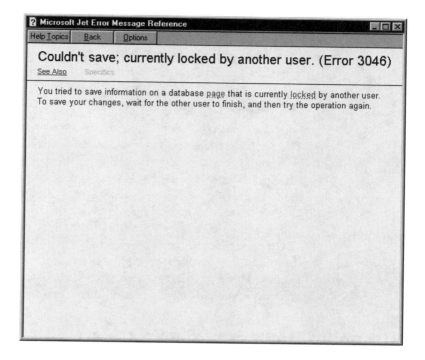

If you check the properties of the Err object after the error occurs, you will see that the Number property is 11. This is great for the error handler in your program, but doesn't really tell you much, unless you have memorized the complete error list for Visual Basic. If you check the Description property, however, you will find the text "Division by Zero," which tells you immediately what has happened and what action can be taken to avoid the error in the future or to recover from the error.

Where Did the Error Occur

Another property of the Err object is the Source property. This property gives you a general idea where the error occurred. General, because if an error occurs in a standard module or form of your program, the Source property will contain only the name of your project, which could give you a fairly large area to search for the occurrence of the error. The Source property is most useful when an error occurs in a class module or an object in an ActiveX server. When this is the case, the Source property contains the name of the class or object. For example, if you were linked to an instance of Microsoft Word and an error occurred in one of the Word commands, Source would contain the string Word.Application, telling you that one of the commands in a Word document or one of the Word commands passed by your program created the error.

Errors in DLLs

One final property to mention for the Err object is the LastDLLError property. This property is used only when DLL calls are made from your Visual Basic program. When your program makes a DLL call, the DLL typically returns a value to indicate whether the DLL ran successfully or failed. If the DLL failed, the error causing the failure is stored in the LastDLLError property. Like regular Visual Basic error messages, knowing the cause of the error lets you determine whether to retry an operation or simply log the error and continue on.

One key difference between standard Visual Basic errors and DLL errors is that a DLL error will not raise an exception that can be trapped by your error handler. Therefore, your code must check the success status of the DLL call and immediately check the LastDLLError property if the operation failed.

Using the Methods of the Err Object

In addition to its properties, the Err Object has two methods that you can use in your programs, the Clear method and the Raise method.

The Clear method of the Err object is used to reset all the property values of the object. You typically use this method after an error has occurred and been processed using deferred error handling (described later in this chapter). Once the Clear method has been called, all information about the last error is deleted. The Clear method is automatically called by Visual Basic when a Resume statement is used, when an On Error statement is used, or when your program leaves a Sub, Function, or Property Procedure.

The Raise method is used to generate an error in Visual Basic. You may ask why you would want to generate an error when your code will probably generate enough on its own. The Raise method enables you to indicate that an error has occurred in a class module or other part of your program (an error that you determine, not one of the built-in errors of Visual Basic). By using the Raise method, you cause the error to be generated so that it can be handled by an error handler elsewhere in your program, which is particularly useful for class modules, especially if you will be compiling them into a DLL or ActiveX server. We will look more closely at raising errors in the section "Raising Errors from Your Program."

Displaying Errors Using the Err Object

Microsoft ✓ **Exam Objective**

Display an error message in a dialog box by using the Err object.

Now that you have some information about the Err object, it is time to put the information to use. One of the exam objectives states that you should be able to display an error message using the Err object. Exercise 17.1 shows you how to do exactly that.

EXERCISE 17.1

Displaying an Error Message

1. Start a new Visual Basic project.

2. Place a command button on the form of the project.

3. Open the code window and place the following code in the Click event of the command button:

```
Dim X As Single, Y As Single, Z As Single
X = 5
Y = 0
Z = X / Y
```

4. Run the program and you will see that an error is generated as shown in the next illustration. You will also see that Visual Basic terminates the program when the error occurs. After checking out the message, go back to the design environment.

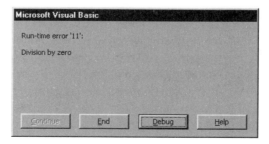

5. Place the following line of code immediately after the Dim statement. This statement tells Visual Basic to continue processing after an error has occurred.

```
On Error Resume Next
```

6. After the assignment statement for Z, place the following code to display an error message:

```
If Err.Number > 0 Then
    MsgBox "The following error has occurred: " & _
Err.Description
End If
```

7. Run the program again and notice that the new error message is displayed and Visual Basic does not terminate the program. The error message you receive should look like the one in the following illustration. The process shown in these steps is the essence of error handling, albeit a simple example.

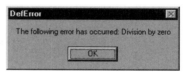

Trapping Errors in Your Program

Understanding the Err object is only part of the equation for providing effective error handling in your programs. In order to handle the errors, you must capture from Visual Basic the fact that an error has occurred, known as trapping the errors. Once you trap an error, you can take appropriate action based on the type of error that occurs, and often on a decision you allow the user to make regarding the error. For example, if the user forgets to insert a disk in the disk drive, you would want to give the user the option of retrying or aborting the operation. In other cases, you would handle the error automatically, or log the error and give the user the option of continuing or terminating the program.

In designing your error handling routines, you will need to choose between two methods of trapping and handling the errors. Each of these methods has merit and in many cases you may use both methods in the same program but not in the same routine.

The first method is immediate handling. In this case, you force your code to branch to the error handling routine immediately after the error occurs. You will typically use this method if you intend to retry an operation. The second method is known as deferred handling. In this case, you tell Visual Basic to proceed on to the next statement when an error occurs. Then, later in your procedure, you check the contents of the Err object and take any necessary action. We will cover both methods of trapping and handling errors in this chapter. But first, we will take a look at the statements that you will use to trap and handle errors. You will use these statements regardless of the method of error handling you choose.

Microsoft
Exam
Objective

Implement error-handling features in an application.

Defining the Error Handling Statements

When you are handling errors in your program, there are two basic statement types that you will use:

- **On Error statements**   To tell Visual Basic where to go when an error occurs

- **Resume statements**   To tell the program what to do after the error is handled

These two types of statements form the basis of Visual Basic's error handling capabilities. Each statement has several forms that will be described in the next sections.

Working with the On Error Statement

The On Error statement is used to tell Visual Basic what to do in the event of an error. This statement can be used in one of three ways:

- **On Error GoTo line**   Tells Visual Basic to branch to the line number or line label specified in the command whenever an error occurs. This line number or label will correspond to the beginning of the error handling routine in the procedure. This form of the On Error statement is used with immediate error processing. The following code shows an example of the use of this form of the On Error statement.

```
On Error GoTo CaptureErrE
'This procedure copies the contents of a grid cell
 or text box
If TypeOf ActiveControl Is SSDBGrid Then
    CrRow = ActiveControl.Row
    CrBkMrk = ActiveControl.RowBookmark(CrRow)
    CrCol = ActiveControl.Col
    HoldCell = ActiveControl.Columns _
(CrCol).CellText(CrBkMrk)
End If
Clipboard.SetText HoldCell

Exit Sub
CaptureErrE:
LogError "Capture", "CopyVal", Err.Number, Err.Description
Resume Next
```

- **On Error Resume Next**   Tells Visual Basic to move to the next line in the code if an error occurs. If the error is in the current procedure, the next line of code is executed. If the error occurs in a sub-procedure called from the current procedure, execution will continue on the next statement after the procedure call. This form of the On Error statement is used with deferred error processing or when you want to ignore any errors that might occur. This type of error statement was illustrated in Exercise 17.1.

- **On Error GoTo 0**   Tells Visual Basic to disable the error handlers in the current procedure. If an error occurs, the error is passed up the call stack to determine if an error handler can be found. If there are no error handlers, a Visual Basic runtime error will be generated and your program will terminate. Typically, you only use this statement to allow higher level procedures to handle the errors.

Using the Resume Statement

The second piece of the error handling function tells Visual Basic what to do after an error is encountered. The Resume statement can be used in either of three forms to allow the program to continue execution after an error has been trapped and handled:

- **Resume**   Tells Visual Basic to retry the statement that caused the error. If the statement is a sub-procedure call, the call is repeated and the sub-procedure is run from the beginning.

- **Resume Next**   Tells Visual Basic to continue execution on the line following the one where the error occurred. If the error occurred in a sub-procedure, the line following the procedure call is the next one executed.

- **Resume line**   Tells Visual Basic to continue execution at the line number or line label specified in the Resume statement. The line number or label must be in the same procedure as the Resume statement. Using the Resume line statement enables you to redirect the execution of a program if an error occurs. You use this to branch around statements that would cause additional errors after the first one has occurred.

Any of the forms of the Resume statement can only be used inside an error handling routine like the one shown in the following code. Use of the statement outside an error handling routine will cause an error.

```
EdtCopyErr:
Select Case Err.Number
    Case 524
        Resume Next
    Case Else
        LogError "Capture", "Edit Copy", Err.Number, _
Err.Description
        Resume Next
End Select
```

Placement of Error Handling Statements

Before we set about creating the actual error handling routines, you may wonder where these routines need to be placed. Some programming languages allow you to set one On Error-type statement and create a single procedure for handling any error that occurs in your code. Visual Basic does not support this type of centralized error handling directly. In order to properly handle errors in your Visual Basic programs, you will need to place error handling code in each procedure where an error may be encountered, in other words, in almost every procedure.

Now, the error handling can be simple. For some procedures, you may wish to include only the On Error Resume Next statement to cause Visual Basic to ignore any errors in the procedure. Also, the error handling can branch to a section of code that makes a call to a central error routine, which is how centralized error handling is accomplished in Visual Basic.

But, what if you don't have an error handler in a particular routine? In this case, Visual Basic will move up the call stack to the procedure that called the one containing the error. If the calling procedure contains error handling code, the error is handled there. If the calling procedure contains no error handling code, Visual Basic continues up the call stack until the top-level procedure is encountered. If no error handling code has been found to that point, Visual Basic generates a runtime error. The following code shows a modification of the "Division by Zero" example shown in Exercise 17.1. In this case, the error occurs in the DivideError procedure, but the error is handled in the Click event procedure of the command button. This modified code shows how the search for error handling would proceed up the call stack.

```
Private Sub DivideError()
Dim X As Single, Y As Single, Z As Single
On Error GoTo 0
X = 5
Y = 0
Z = X / Y 'Error occurs here
End Sub

Private Sub Command1_Click()
On Error Resume Next
DivideError
```

```
If Err.Number > 0 Then 'Error is handled here
    MsgBox "The following error has occurred: " & _
Err.Description
End If
End Sub
```

For more information on the call stack refer to Chapter 18, "Debugging Your Application."

Deferred Handling of Errors

In the beginning of this section, we talked about deferred and immediate handling of errors. In the case of deferred handling, Visual Basic is told to ignore the error when it occurs, but your code comes back and checks the error later in the procedure. This method of error handling is useful for some types of errors, such as the division by zero. The error handling code can be used to reset the value of variables, to allow processing to continue. However, there are drawbacks to using this method of deferred error handling:

- You must place error handling code in several places in your procedure; that is, wherever an error that needs to be handled might occur.

- The Err object only stores information about the last error that occurred. If the error handling is very far removed from the source of the error, additional errors may occur prior to the error handling routine, and you will lose the information about the original error.

To use deferred error handling in a procedure, you need to start the procedure with the On Error Resume Next statement, which tells Visual Basic to continue execution of the program after an error has occurred. Then you must create the error handling routine itself. For deferred error handling, the routine will always start with a statement that checks the Number property of the Err object. If the property is greater than 0, an error has occurred. Finally, the error handling routine typically ends by clearing the Err object properties using the Clear method, which sets up the Err object for the next possible error. Exercise 17.2 shows you how to use deferred error processing to handle possible errors in the addition of two variables.

Microsoft
Exam
Objective

Implement error-handling features in an application.

EXERCISE 17.2

Deferred Error Handling

1. Start a new project.

2. Add three text boxes and three labels to the form to serve as the input and output areas for the addition function. Also, add a command button to the form.

3. In the Click event of the command button, declare three variables to be used and enter the addition equation as shown in the following code. This code allows the possibility of several errors including division by zero and assigning a string to a numeric variable.

```
Dim X As Single, Y As Single, Z As Single
X = Text1.Text
Y = Text2.Text
Z = X / Y
```

4. After the Dim statement, add the On Error Resume Next statement to indicate that deferred processing will be used.

5. After the statement that assigns a value to Z, place the actual error handling code. This code, shown below, checks for the occurrence of an error, then takes action depending on the error number. For division by zero, the code sets the result to zero. For other errors, a message is displayed. The code ends with the Clear method to reset the Err object.

```
If Err.Number > 0 Then
    If Err.Number = 11 Then
        Z = 0
    Else
        MsgBox "Invalid input."
        Exit Sub
    End If
    Err.Clear
End If
```

6. After the error handling routine, enter a statement that displays the results of the calculation to the third text box:

```
Text3.Text = Z
```

EXERCISE 17.2 (CONTINUED)

7. Run the program and try several "errors" such as using zero for the second value and entering a string in the text box. Note the actions of the program. You may notice that if you enter a string in the text box, the result still displays 0 because Visual Basic encounters the second error of dividing by zero before the error handling routine is run, which means that the contents of the Err object indicates a division by zero error.

Immediate Handling of Errors

The immediate method of handling errors causes your program to branch to an error handling routine as soon as the error occurs. This method of handling errors begins with an On Error GoTo line statement that tells Visual Basic the location of the error handling routine in the procedure. The actual error handling routine starts with a line label that corresponds to the line identifier given in the On Error statement. The error handler then evaluates the error, takes the appropriate action, and returns the execution of the program to the proper point, either the line where the error occurred or the line immediately following.

One other key piece of an immediate error handling routine is that a line of code is required immediately prior to the routine to exit the procedure. This line is needed to prevent the error handler from being run if no errors exist. The code to exit a procedure is:

```
Exit Sub
```

If your procedure is a function or property procedure, you will need to use the Exit Function or Exit Property statement instead of the Exit Sub statement.

Microsoft ✓ *Exam* *Objective*   **Create a common error-handling routine.**

The advantage of using immediate error handling is that all errors are handled as soon as they occur. Also, all the error handling for a procedure can be located in a single place instead being spread out through the procedure. Exercise 17.3 shows how to implement immediate error handling for the same project as exercise 17.2.

EXERCISE 17.3

Using Immediate Error Handling

1. Create a new project with three text boxes, three labels, and a command button, as you did in Exercise 17.2.

2. Place the following code in the Click event of the command button to perform the calculation.

```
Dim X As Single, Y As Single, Z As Single
X = Text1.Text
Y = Text2.Text
Z = X / Y
Text3.Text = Z
```

3. Place the following statement immediately after the Dim statement in the procedure. This statement tells Visual Basic where to go when an error occurs.

```
On Error GoTo DivError
```

4. Place an Exit Sub statement immediately after the last statement of the procedure to prevent the error code from being run if no errors are encountered.

5. Place the following code after the Exit Sub statement. This code is the error handler for the procedure. If the error is divide by zero, a default value of Z is set. Otherwise, a message is displayed and the program exits the procedure.

```
DivError:
If Err.Number = 11 Then
    Z = 0
    Resume Next
Else
    MsgBox "Invalid input."
    Exit Sub
End If
```

6. Run the program and try different values of input, including strings. Notice that the program responds differently under this type of error handling because each error is trapped as it occurs.

Creating a Common Error Handling Procedure

Because Visual Basic requires you to place error handling code in most of the procedures of your program, you can imagine that there could be a lot of code duplication. For example, if you have a number of routines that handle saving information to a database, you could repeat the same error handling code in each of these procedures. There are several ways around this type of problem:

- Create a class that handles all the database activities and include the error handling code in the procedures of the class.

- Create a procedure that is called whenever database information needs to be saved and include the error handling code in the procedure.

- Create a central procedure for handling all database errors.

Microsoft ✓ *Exam* *Objective*

Create a common error-handling routine.

The last option still requires you to add error handling code to all of your procedures, but the code required to determine the type of error and to determine the appropriate action is located in only one place. As an example, the following function could be used to determine the type of error that occurred and indicate to the procedure whether to retry the operation, resume execution with the next statement, or exit the procedure.

```
Public Function DataError(ByVal iErNum As Integer) As _
Integer
Select Case iErNum
```

```
        Case 3046, 3158, 3186, 3187, 3188, 3189, 3218, 3260
            'Record is locked by another user
            iTriesCnt = iTriesCnt + 1
            If iTriesCnt > 10 Then
                iErrReturn = LabMessage(751, vbExclamation + _
vbYesNo, 752)
                If iErrReturn = vbYes Then
                    iTriesCnt = 0
                    DataError = 1
                Else
                    bUpdateOK = False
                    DataError = 2
                End If
            Else
                fPauseTime = Timer
                Do Until Timer > fPauseTime + 0.1
                Loop
                DataError = 1
            End If
        Case 3167
            bUpdateOK = False
            DataError = 2
        Case 3020
            DataError = 2
        Case Else
            LogError "Capture", "Change SubArchive", Err.Number,
Err.Description
            bUpdateOK = False
            DataError = 3
    End Select

End Function
```

The error handling code in your database procedure would then be reduced to the following code:

```
ErrOccur:
Select Case DataError(Err.Number)
    Case 1
        Resume
    Case 2
        Resume Next
    Case 3
        Exit Sub
End If
```

You can use this same technique to create an error log that writes the contents of the error message to a database or text file.

Raising Errors from Your Program

One final major objective of the Microsoft certification exam is for you to be able to raise errors from a server. When you create an ActiveX server, you are actually creating class modules that provide objects for other programs to use. In these modules, you may have things occur that you would want to inform a calling program about. For example, if you were unable to open a recordset in the class, you would want to inform the calling program to avoid additional operations that required access to the database. Or, if you lost the database connection in the middle of an operation, you would want to inform the calling program.

One method of informing a calling program is to set properties that indicate whether a condition exists; however, this method makes it difficult to notify the calling program when the condition changes. The way to handle changes that create problems is to raise an error in the server component. To raise an error, you use the Raise method of the Err object.

Microsoft ✓ *Exam* *Objective*   **Raise errors from a server.**

When you use the Raise method, you can include one required argument and four optional arguments. These arguments set the properties of the Err object in the calling program. The required argument of the Raise method is the Number argument. The Number argument is a long integer that identifies the error to the calling program. Visual Basic supports error numbers between 0 and 65535; however, these numbers are for Visual Basic's internal errors as well as errors you generate. In order to be sure that you do not conflict with Visual Basic's internal numbers, you should add the constant vbObjectError to any error number you wish to indicate. The following line of code shows you how to raise error number 101 from a class module.

```
Err.Raise 101 + vbObjectError
```

In addition to the required argument, there are four optional arguments that you can specify with the Raise method. These arguments provide additional information to the Err object for use by the calling program in determining the error. The optional arguments are:

- **Source**   Identifies the name of the object that generated the error. If you omit this argument, Visual Basic will use the programmatic ID of your project.

- **Description**   Provides text that describes the type of error that occurred. If this is omitted, Visual Basic will use the message "Application-defined or object-defined error" as the description.

- **Helpfile**   Specifies the help file that contains more information about the error, if such a file exists.

- **Helpcontext**   Specifies the specific context ID of the help file topic that contains more information about the error.

When using the optional arguments, you must enter the arguments in the following order: Number, Source, Description, Helpfile, and Helpcontext. You must also separate the values with commas. The following code shows how several of the arguments are used to generate an error.

```
Err.Raise 39 + vbObjectError, "Command", "Division Error"
```

You can also enter the value of arguments using named arguments as shown in the following line of code:

```
Err.Raise Number:=39 + vbObjectError, _
Description:="Division Error"
```

Displaying Errors During Testing

As you are testing your program, your error handler will trap any errors that occur in a procedure that has an error handler. Sometimes, however, you will need to avoid having errors trapped. For example, if your error handler logs errors to a file, it may be able to tell you what error occurred and in which procedure it occurred, but it cannot tell you on which line the error occurred. Often, though, this information is crucial in determining why the error occurred and how to fix it.

Microsoft ✓ *Exam* *Objective*

Use the appropriate error-trapping options, such as Break on All Errors, Break in Class Module, and Break on Unhandled Errors.

To help you with identifying errors while you are testing your program, Visual Basic provides you with several error trapping options. These options, shown in Figure 17.3, can be accessed from the Options item of the Tools menu. The error trapping options are located in the Break on Errors frame of the General tab of the Options dialog box.

You can choose any of the following three options for breaking the execution on errors in your code:

- **Break on all errors**   Causes Visual Basic to pause on any error, even if the error is handled by an error handler in your code.

- **Break on Unhandled errors**   Causes Visual Basic to pause only for errors that are not handled by an error handler in your code.

- **Break in Class Module**   Similar to Break on Unhandled Errors, except that an error in a class module will cause Visual Basic to show the actual error line in the class module. The Break on Unhandled Errors option causes Visual Basic to show the line that called the class module.

If you want to see the errors in a procedure with an error handler, you will need to select the Break on All Errors option.

FIGURE 17.3

Error trapping options
for testing

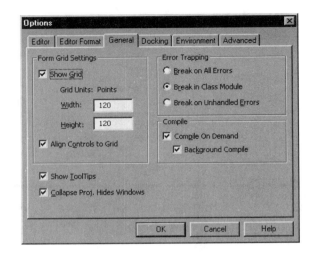

FIGURE 17.3

Error trapping options
for testing

Summary

This chapter has delved into the creation of error handling code for your program. Error handling is often overlooked but is an extremely important part of any good program. You don't want your users to see a default error message, then have your program terminate.

Knowing about error handling is also important for successfully passing the Microsoft certification exam. The exam objectives specify the following things you need to know about handling errors:

- Implement error-handling features in an application.

- Raise errors from a server.

- Create a common error-handling routine.

- Display an error message in a dialog box by using the Err object.

- Use the appropriate error-trapping options, such as Break on All Errors, Break in Class Module, and Break on Unhandled Errors.

Review Questions

1. Which of the following statements is used to turn off error handling in a procedure?

   A. On Error GoTo line

   B. On Error Resume Next

   C. On Error GoTo 0

   D. Error Off

2. Which of the following statements tells Visual Basic to retry the statement that caused the error?

   A. Resume Next

   B. Resume

   C. Retry

   D. Resume line

3. Which statement is used with deferred error handling?

   A. On Error GoTo line

   B. On Error Resume Next

   C. On Error GoTo 0

   D. On Error Defer

4. Which of the following are drawbacks of deferred error handling? Check all that apply.

   A. It runs slower than immediate error processing.

   B. Errors may occur between the original error and your error handler.

   C. Your error code is spread throughout your procedure instead of being located in a single place.

   D. If multiple errors occur, your program will crash.

5. What does the Clear method of the Err object do?

    A. Transfers error handling to the next higher procedure.

    B. Generates a runtime error.

    C. There is no Clear method.

    D. Resets the properties of the Err object.

6. Which of the following is a required argument of the Raise method?

    A. Description

    B. Number

    C. Source

    D. Helpfile

7. What is the purpose of the Raise method?

    A. Transfer error handling to the next higher procedure.

    B. Generate a runtime error.

    C. Trap errors that occur in your program.

    D. Reset the properties of the Err object.

8. What happens if you use a Resume statement outside of an error handling routine?

    A. Your program retries the statement that generated the error.

    B. Nothing happens.

    C. An error occurs as the Resume statement is not allowed to be used outside an error handler.

    D. Your error handler enters an infinite loop.

9. What are some ways that you can centralize error handling? Check all that apply.

A. Write a class to encapsulate functions and include the error handling in the class.

B. Place an On Error GoTo procedure statement as the first line of your program and write an error procedure.

C. Have the error handling code in each procedure call a function that identifies the error and indicates the appropriate action.

D. Place your function in a public procedure that includes error handling capabilities.

CHAPTER

18

Debugging Your Application

Microsoft Objectives Covered in This Chapter:

- Use the appropriate error-trapping options, such as Break on All Errors, Break in Class Module, and Break on Unhandled Errors.

- Monitor the values of expressions and variables by using the debugging windows.

- Set watch expressions during program execution.

- Monitor the values of expressions and variables by using the debugging windows.

- Explain the purpose and use of the Locals window.

- Define the scope of a watch variable.

- Use the Immediate window to check or change variables.

- Implement project groups to support the debugging and development process.

- Test and debug a control in process.

- Debug DLLs in process.

Unless you are writing very small applications, it is almost impossible to write perfect code the first time through. You will almost always find some kind of errors in your programs. These errors can be anything from a simple typographical error to a logic error that causes the code to do something that you didn't intend for it to do.

The next best thing is to have a solid understanding of debugging techniques and a good suite of debugging tools at your disposal. Visual Basic provides you with a good suite of tools for finding errors in your program, and, because the debugger is integrated with the programming environment, the tools make it easy to correct these errors on the fly. Visual Basic has the tools, and this chapter will give you some of the understanding that you need for using the tools.

As debugging relates to the requirements of the certification exam, you will learn about the following exam objectives:

- Set watch expressions during program execution.

- Monitor the values of expressions and variables by using the debugging windows.

- Use the Immediate window to check or change values.

- Explain the purpose and usage for the Locals window.

- Implement project groups to support the debugging and development process.

- Debug DLLs in process.

- Test and debug a control in process.

- Define the scope of a watch variable.

Techniques for Debugging

The certification exam will test your ability to apply the mechanics of debugging, using Visual Basic's debugging tools. But, to successfully use the tools available to you, you need to have some understanding of what is involved in tracking down and eliminating bugs in a program. There are numerous types of errors that can creep into your programs, but most of them can be grouped into one of three categories:

- **Syntax errors**   You incorrectly type a statement or use a variable that has not been defined.

- **Invalid value errors**   Such as assigning a string value to an integer variable, or trying to load a file that does not exist.

- **Logic errors**   Your program runs fine but produces incorrect results.

For the first two groups of errors, Visual Basic will notify you when the error has occurred and help you locate the actual line that caused the error. For logic errors, Visual Basic does not find the errors for you but does provide you with a means to determine what is wrong with the logic of the program.

The only hard and fast rule for creating a truly bug-free program is test, Test, TEST! Testing is the only way to find bugs. Beyond this one rule, there are a number of good practices that you can follow to make the debugging of a program easier and more successful:

- Create a test plan with sets of inputs and expected outputs from the program.

- Test the program on multiple machines, not just your development machine, to help find errors such as hard-coded file paths.

- Try to write and test your code in modules. Working with smaller program components makes it easier to find a bug.

- Place plenty of comments in your code, which enables you to come back to the program later and still know what a particular module is designed to do.

Checking Out Visual Basic's Debugging Tools

The key component of Visual Basic that enables you to easily debug programs is the integrated development environment (IDE). The IDE allows you to run your programs in the development environment instead of having to compile the program, run it, then try to determine what went wrong. By running in the IDE, you have the capability of watching the values of variables as they change, stepping through your program line by line, and even making changes to the program on the fly.

As part of the IDE, Visual Basic provides you with a number of tools to make it easier for you to find and correct errors. These tools can be grouped into three broad categories:

- Tools for avoiding errors

- Tools for watching the value of variables and watching program calls

- Tools for pausing the program and for executing one or a few lines of code at a time

Tools for Avoiding Errors

The best place to start eliminating errors is to avoid them in the first place. Visual Basic gives you four tools to help you avoid errors. The use of these tools is not specifically covered in the objectives of the certification exam, but you should know what these tools are and how to use them. The use of these four tools will help you avoid a large number of programming headaches:

- Auto Syntax Check

- Require Variable Declaration

- Auto List Members

- Auto Quick Info

These tools can be turned on or off using the Options dialog box. You can access the dialog box, shown in Figure 18.1, by choosing the Options item from the Tools menu. You turn on an option by checking the box next to the option. You turn the option off by clearing the box. Let's take a closer look at what these options do for you.

FIGURE 18.1

Setting the editor options for debugging

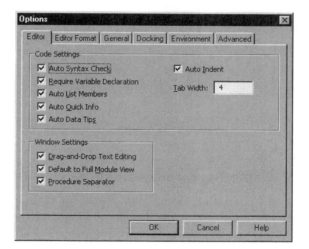

Using Automatic Syntax Checking

The Auto Syntax Check option tells Visual Basic to check the syntax of each statement as you type it. Using this option prevents you from making simple typing mistakes such as forgetting to include the *Then* keyword at the end of an If statement or forgetting to enter a value on the right side of an assignment statement. If you make this type of error, Visual Basic will notify you of the mistake as soon as you try to move to another line in your code. Figure 18.2 shows a sample of this message.

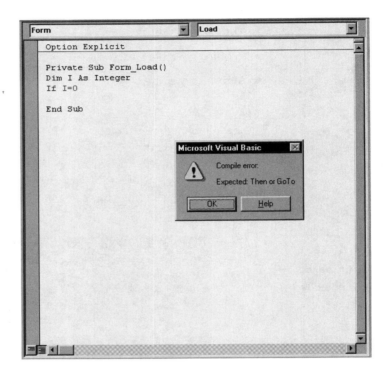

Using Required Variable Declaration

Another common typographical error is mistyping the name of a variable in your code, which is easy to do but often hard to find. For example, you might create a variable named sLastName and accidentally refer to it later as sLstName. The code looks fine on an initial read-through, but will not work correctly because the two variable names represent different values. By choosing to require variable declaration, Visual Basic places the following statement as the first line in each form or module of your program:

```
Option Explicit
```

This statement is only added to new forms and modules, not ones that have already been created. If you are working with existing forms, you can force the variable declaration by manually placing the statement at the beginning of the code in a form or module.

This statement requires that you define a variable using a declaration statement before you can use it in code. Visual Basic will not give you any messages while you are editing code, but it will give you an error if it encounters an undefined variable when you try to run the program. Figure 18.3 shows how this would work for the sLastName/sLstName example stated above.

FIGURE 18.3

Finding undeclared variables

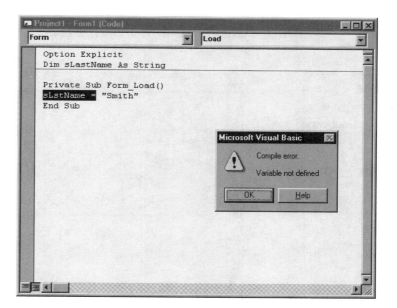

You can learn more about declaring variables in Chapter 2, "Coding Basics."

Using Auto List Members

The Auto List Members feature is one of the features that was introduced in version 5 of Visual Basic. If you have worked with Visual Basic much at all, you know that there are hundreds of properties and keywords that are used in creating programs. Often, it is very difficult to remember which properties belong with which controls, or to remember the exact spelling of a keyword. With the Auto List Members feature, Visual Basic presents you with a drop-down list of appropriate properties or keywords as you type.

For example, if you enter the name of a text box on your form, as soon as you type the dot (period) after the name of the box, a list of properties will appear. As you type a letter of the property, the selected item in the list will move to the first item that matches the letters you have typed. When the desired property is selected, you can accept it by pressing the Tab, Space, Enter, or = key. Visual Basic will then enter the entire property name in your code, saving you keystrokes and helping you avoid typographical errors. An example of this feature is shown in Figure 18.4.

FIGURE 18.4

Letting Visual Basic complete your code

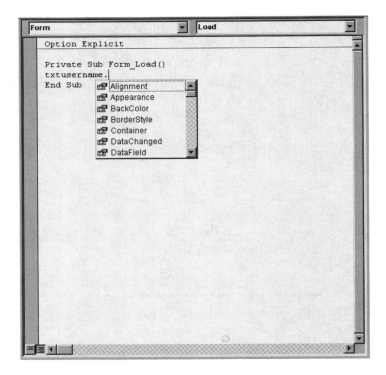

Getting Hints about Functions

The last feature mentioned, Auto Quick Info, is another new feature in version 5. This feature displays the required syntax of a function as a ToolTip. The ToolTip is enabled as soon as you type in the name of the function you are calling. The information displayed tells you the required and optional parameters of the function and what information is returned by the function. The main benefit of Auto Quick Info is that it saves you a lot of trips to the help files to look up information about a function. Figure 18.5 shows how Auto Quick Info works for the MsgBox function.

FIGURE 18.5

Getting help with command syntax

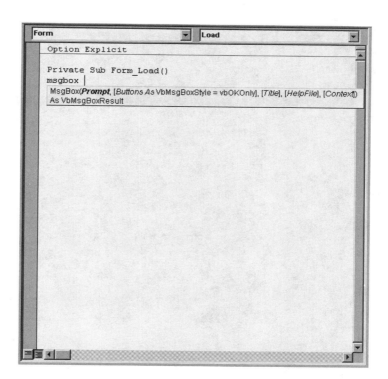

How the Environment Finds Errors for You

After you have done all you can to avoid errors, the real work of finding the remaining errors and eliminating them begins. Now the real power of Visual Basic's IDE and debugging tools comes into play. The first thing that Visual

Basic does for you in finding errors is tell you where they occur. When you are running your program from the development environment, you can have Visual Basic stop the execution of the program when an error occurs and show you the line of code where the error occurred, giving you a starting point for determining why and how the error actually occurred. When the error occurs, Visual Basic will display a message that tells you what type of error occurred. If you click the Debug button on this message dialog box, Visual Basic will place you in "Break" mode, display the code window for the current form or module, and highlight the line of code where the error occurred, as shown in Figure 18.6.

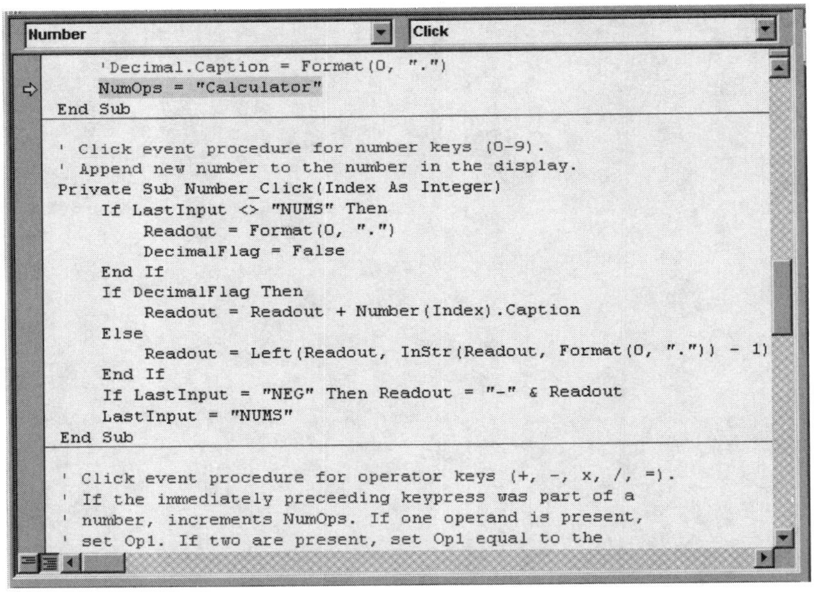

FIGURE 18.6

Visual Basic shows you where an error occurs.

```
Number                              ▼   Click                          ▼
        'Decimal.Caption = Format(0, ".")
⇨       NumOps = "Calculator"
  End Sub

  ' Click event procedure for number keys (0-9).
  ' Append new number to the number in the display.
  Private Sub Number_Click(Index As Integer)
      If LastInput <> "NUMS" Then
          Readout = Format(0, ".")
          DecimalFlag = False
      End If
      If DecimalFlag Then
          Readout = Readout + Number(Index).Caption
      Else
          Readout = Left(Readout, InStr(Readout, Format(0, ".")) - 1)
      End If
      If LastInput = "NEG" Then Readout = "-" & Readout
      LastInput = "NUMS"
  End Sub

  ' Click event procedure for operator keys (+, -, x, /, =).
  ' If the immediately preceeding keypress was part of a
  ' number, increments NumOps. If one operand is present,
  ' set Op1. If two are present, set Op1 equal to the
```

Microsoft
✓ *Exam*
Objective

Use the appropriate error-trapping options, such as Break on All Errors, Break in Class Module, and Break on Unhandled Errors.

Visual Basic also allows you to specify what types of errors will cause the program to pause. You can set the Error Trapping option from the General Tab of the Options dialog box. There are three options for trapping errors:

- **Break on all errors**   Causes Visual Basic to pause on any error, even if the error is handled by an error handler in your code.

- **Break on Unhandled errors**   Causes Visual Basic to pause only for errors that are not handled by an error handler in your code.

- **Break in Class Module**   Similar to Break on Unhandled Errors, except that an error in a class module will cause Visual Basic to show the actual error line in the class module. The Break on Unhandled Errors option causes Visual Basic to show the line that called the class module.

The second part of taking care of errors is the creation of error handling routines in your code. The creation of error handlers is the topic of Chapter 17, "Handling and Logging Errors in Visual Basic Programs."

Observing the Values of Variables

After you have determined that you have an error in your program and have found out where the error occurred, you can start looking into the cause of the error. One of the most common causes of errors is an invalid or unexpected value of a variable. With this in mind, Visual Basic includes a number of tools for observing (or "watching") the values of variables in your code. Using these tools, you can find out what the actual value of a variable is at any point in your code. You can also use some of these tools to watch how the value of the variable changes as you move from line to line in the program.

Working with the Watch Windows

Visual Basic contains four tools specifically designed to let you determine the value of a variable while your program is running:

- Watch Window
- Locals Window
- Quick Watch Dialog Box
- Auto Data Tips

Two of these tools, the Watch window and the Locals window, enable you to create a permanent view of variables while you are in the development environment. Using these tools allows you to observe the values of a variable or expression as the program executes, so that you can see the value at any point in time and determine where the value is changing.

Displaying Information in the Watch Window

Microsoft Exam Objective	Monitor the values of expressions and variables by using the debugging windows.

The most versatile of the variable observation tools is the Watch window. The Watch window lets you track the value of any variable or expression anywhere in your program. The Watch window will display the following information for each watch that you create:

- The variable or expression being observed
- The current value of the expression
- The data type of the expression
- The context of the expression, where the expression is currently being used

Figure 18.7 shows a typical Watch window in use.

FIGURE 18.7

The Watch window shows you the value of variables.

Expression	Value	Type	Context
66 LastInput	"NUMS"	Variant/String	Calculator
66 NumOps	1	Integer	Calculator
66 TempReadout	"56."	Variant/String	Calculator

Microsoft Exam Objective	Set watch expressions during program execution.

Adding a Watch in Your Program   In order to observe the value of a variable in your program, you need to add a watch to the Watch Window. You add a watch by choosing the Add Watch item from the Debug menu to bring up the Add Watch dialog box shown in Figure 18.8. In the dialog box, you specify:

- An expression or the name of a variable that you want to watch.

- The context in which the expression should be viewed. You can specify that the expression only be observed in a single procedure, within a module, throughout the program, or any scope in between.

- The type of watch. There are three types of watches that you can chose, depending on the purpose for setting the watch:

  - **Watch Expression**   Simply evaluate the expression and show its value.

  - **Break When Value Is True**   Causes the program execution to stop when the value of the expression is True. This watch can only be used for a logical expression or a Boolean variable.

  - **Break When Value Changes**   Causes the program execution to stop when the value of the expression changes.

F I G U R E   18.8

To add a watch, specify the expression, scope, and type of watch.

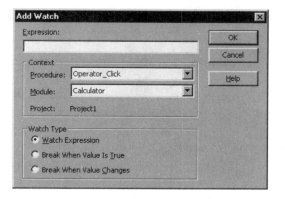

After specifying the information for the watch, you click the OK button to add the watch to the Watch window. Exercise 18.1 shows you how to add several watches to the Watch window and lets you see how this process works.

EXERCISE 18.1

Creating Watches in a Program

1. We will use one of Visual Basic's sample applications to write a program to set watches. Open the Calc.Vbp program found in the Samples\Pguide\calc folder under the VB folder on your computer.

2. Open the code window of the main form for the calculator.

3. Open the Add Watch dialog box by choosing the Add Watch item from the Debug menu.

4. For the first watch, enter **Op1** as the variable name and set the watch type to Break When Value Changes. Then click the OK button on the dialog box.

5. Using the Add Watch dialog box, set another watch for the program. This time, enter **NumOps** as the variable name and set the watch type to Watch Expression.

6. For the last watch, set the expression to NumOps = 0 and set the watch type to Break When Value Is True.

7. Run the program. You will notice that the program stops in several places as you access different parts of the program. Each time the program stops, you can look at the values of the variables. To continue the program after it stops, press F5 or click the Run button again.

Editing a Watch   After you have initially created a watch, you will often find that you need to make changes to the watch. You may need to change the expression, modify the scope, change the type of watch, or even delete the watch completely. Editing the watch is as easy as creating it. To edit a watch, highlight the watch in the Watch window, then right click the mouse to bring up the pop-up menu for the watch. From here you can delete the watch or call up the edit dialog box. This dialog box is the same as the Add Watch dialog box. After making any necessary changes, you can save the changed watch by clicking the OK button on the dialog box.

Monitor the values of expressions and variables by using the debugging windows.

Using the Quick Watch Feature   Sometimes when you are checking variables in your programs, you only need to check the current value of a single variable or expression. While the program is paused, either due to an error condition or another watch, you can use the Quick Watch feature to check the current value. To use this feature, highlight a variable or expression in the code window of a form or module and call up the Quick Watch dialog box by choosing the Quick Watch item from the Debug menu or by pressing Shift+F9. The dialog box, shown in Figure 18.9, will show you the chosen expression, its context, and its current value. After viewing the value of the expression, you can close the dialog box by clicking the Cancel button, or you may choose to add the expression to the Watch window by clicking the Add button.

FIGURE 18.9

Quick Watch gives you a way to determine the value of a single expression.

Another way to check the value of a single variable is through the use of a new feature in version 5. This feature, called Auto Data Tips, allows you to determine the value of a variable by resting the mouse cursor on the variable while the program is paused. The value of the variable will appear as a tool tip beneath the mouse cursor, as shown in Figure 18.10. Exercise 18.2 illustrates the use of the Quick Watch and Auto Data Tips.

You activate the Auto Data Tips by choosing the option on the Editor tab of the Options dialog box of Visual Basic.

FIGURE 18.10

Data tips provide quick
access to the value of
variables.

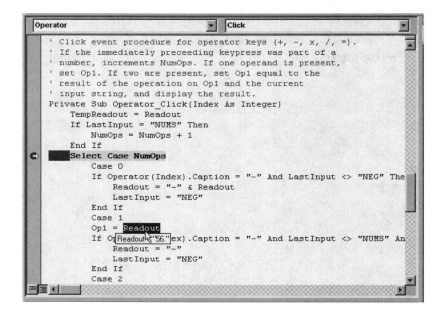

```
Operator                          ▼  Click                        ▼
' Click event procedure for operator keys (+, -, x, /, =).
' If the immediately preceeding keypress was part of a
' number, increments NumOps. If one operand is present,
' set Op1. If two are present, set Op1 equal to the
' result of the operation on Op1 and the current
' input string, and display the result.
Private Sub Operator_Click(Index As Integer)
      TempReadout = Readout
      If LastInput = "NUMS" Then
         NumOps = NumOps + 1
      End If
   ⇨  Select Case NumOps
         Case 0
         If Operator(Index).Caption = "-" And LastInput <> "NEG" The
            Readout = "-" & Readout
            LastInput = "NEG"
         End If
         Case 1
         Op1 = Readout
         If Op Readout = "56." ex).Caption = "-" And LastInput <> "NUMS" An
            Readout = "-"
            LastInput = "NEG"
         End If
         Case 2
```

EXERCISE 18.2

Using the Quick Watch and Data Tip Features

1. Using the same program from Exercise 18.1, make sure that you have the
   same watches set for the program.

2. Run the program.

3. When the program pauses, highlight an expression in the code window,
   then activate the Quick Watch dialog box from the Debug menu. Examine
   the contents of the dialog box.

4. After closing the dialog box, rest the mouse cursor on several variables in the
   code window. Notice how the value of the variable is displayed in a data tip.

5. Stop the execution of the program.

You can also access most of the debugging functions from the Debug
toolbar, which can be displayed from the Toolbars item of the View menu.

Using the Locals Window

Microsoft
Exam
Objective

Explain the purpose and use of the Locals window.

The Watch window allows you to specify the individual variables and expressions that you want to observe. However, sometimes you need to check out all the variables in a particular procedure. While you could add each variable to the Watch window, there is an easier method. Visual Basic also has a Locals window. This window will show the value of all the variables that are local to the current procedure. In addition, the window will show the properties of the current form and all its controls. The properties are presented in a hierarchical view that you can expand or collapse to show as much detail as you wish. Exercise 18.3 walks you through the use of the Locals window.

EXERCISE 18.3

Using the Locals Window

1. Open the Mouse.vbp project in the Visual Basic samples directory.

2. Open the code window of the frmMain form.

3. Move to the Click procedure for the mnuInstructions menu option.

4. Place the cursor on the line that starts CR =.

5. Press the F9 key to create a program breakpoint. (We will discuss break-points more shortly.)

6. Run the program and choose the Instructions item from the menu.

7. When the program pauses, choose the Locals window item from the View menu of Visual Basic. At this point, you can see the value of locally defined variables and the properties of the form and any of its controls. The next illustration shows you an example of the Locals window.

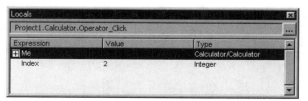

EXERCISE 18.3 (CONTINUED)

8. To see how the values of the variables change as you move through the program, press the F8 key to move through the program one line at a time.

9. When you have finished viewing variables, exit the program.

Understanding the Scope of Watch Variables

Microsoft ✓ *Exam* *Objective* — **Define the scope of a watch variable.**

As you were creating watches, you saw that you could specify the context of the watch variable, which is similar to the scope of a variable, but with a key difference. The context setting of a variable tells you only where the watch expression will be evaluated. It does not have an effect on the actual usage scope of a variable. For example, you can create a global variable in your program, but if you set a watch for the variable with a context of a single procedure, the Watch Window will only display the value of the variable while that procedure is running. All other times, the watch will be out of scope. A watch can also be out of scope if you are trying to watch a local variable and you are outside of the procedure in which the variable was defined.

Using the Immediate Window to Check or Change a Value

Up to this point, we have concentrated on viewing the values of variables. As you are debugging a program, however, you will often need to change the value of a variable during program execution. For example, when you have determined that you have an invalid value, but want to make sure that the rest of the program works correctly if a proper value is used.

Microsoft ✓ *Exam* *Objective* — **Use the Immediate window to check or change values.**

The Watch window and the Locals window only allow you to view variables and expressions. To edit variables, you will need to use the Immediate window. The Immediate window lets you enter any valid line of code and execute it, allowing you to change values as well as determine the values of variables. To determine the value of a variable, you can use a question mark followed by the variable name in the Immediate window as shown in the following line of code:

```
? Op1
```

To change the value of the variable, you use an assignment statement, like you would in your program, as shown in the following code:

```
Op1 = 5
```

Figure 18.11 shows the appearance of the Immediate window after the value of a variable has been checked, then changed.

FIGURE 18.11

Changing values in the Immediate Window

The Immediate window is typically displayed at the bottom of the screen when the program is paused. If the window is not visible, you can display it by selecting the Immediate window item from the View menu. You can also display the window by pressing Ctrl+G. Exercise 18.4 shows you how to use the Immediate window in a program.

EXERCISE 18.4

Changing the Value of a Variable

1. Open the Calc.vbp project from the Visual Basic samples.

2. Add a watch to the program using the variable Op1 as the expression, and set the watch type to Break When Value Changes, pausing the program when a value is assigned to the variable.

3. Run the program. Enter a couple of digits in the calculator and press the key to start any math function (for example, the + key).

4. With the program paused, press the Ctrl+G key combination to display the Immediate Window.

5. Enter the code ?Op1 in the Immediate Window and press enter. The value of the variable will be displayed right below the code.

6. Change the value of Op1 using an assignment statement.

7. Check the value of the variable again using the ?Op1 statement. The program should return the new value of the variable.

8. Stop the execution of the calculator program. (You can, if you wish, continue to prove that the new value is actually the one used in further operations. To do this, press the F5 key to finish running the program.)

Stepping Through the Program

What we have looked at so far is how to stop the program for either an error or in response to a specific condition occurring with a watch variable, which has allowed us to evaluate a variable at a single point in time or to change the value. This, however, is only part of the task of debugging a program. Unless the bug is a very simple one, you will need to see how the values of variables change as the program progresses. You will also need to see which statements and procedures in the program are executed. Watching the progression of the program is also crucial in determining the cause of logic errors. Often a logic error is caused when a program takes an unexpected branch.

Stopping at a Specific Line of Code

You have seen how you can pause the execution of a program based on a certain condition. You do this by setting a watch to break when an expression is true or when its value changes. You also know that the program will pause automatically when it encounters an error. What do you do if you want to pause at a particular line in your program? Fortunately, Visual Basic provides a tool for this as well.

Visual Basic allows you to set what is called a Breakpoint in your program. You set a Breakpoint in your code by placing the cursor on the line of code where you want to pause, then pressing the F9 key. You can also set the Breakpoint by clicking in the margin to the left of the program line. Either action will toggle the Breakpoint for the line; that is if a Breakpoint is not set, the action will set one; and if the Breakpoint is set, it will be cleared. When a Breakpoint is set, the line will be indicated by a special highlight color and a dot in the margin to the left of the line, as shown in Figure 18.12. If you wish to clear all the Breakpoints in a code, you can press the Shift+F9 key combination.

FIGURE 18.12

Setting Breakpoints in your code

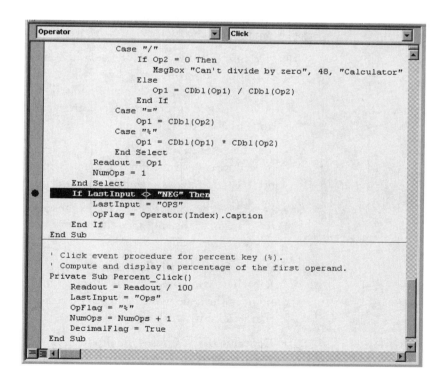

```
                        Case "/"
                            If Op2 = 0 Then
                                MsgBox "Can't divide by zero", 48, "Calculator"
                            Else
                                Op1 = CDbl(Op1) / CDbl(Op2)
                            End If
                        Case "="
                            Op1 = CDbl(Op2)
                        Case "%"
                            Op1 = CDbl(Op1) * CDbl(Op2)
                    End Select
                    Readout = Op1
                    NumOps = 1
                End Select
                If LastInput <> "NEG" Then
                    LastInput = "OPS"
                    OpFlag = Operator(Index).Caption
                End If
End Sub

' Click event procedure for percent key (%).
' Compute and display a percentage of the first operand.
Private Sub Percent_Click()
    Readout = Readout / 100
    LastInput = "Ops"
    OpFlag = "%"
    NumOps = NumOps + 1
    DecimalFlag = True
End Sub
```

WARNING   You cannot set a Breakpoint on a declaration statement for a variable or on a comment line. Most other statements can be used as a Breakpoint.

Another way to pause the execution of your program is through the use of the Stop statement. The Stop statement is placed directly in code to pause the execution of the program at the statement. The statement is used without any additional arguments or parameters. The Stop statement only has an effect on your program when you are running in the development environment. The statement is ignored when your program is compiled.

Continuing the Program

After you have paused the program, you can set watches or view and set the values of variables using the Immediate Window. At some point, though, you will want to continue the execution of the program. You can either have the program continue running until it encounters the next Breakpoint, or you can step through the program in one of several ways. The methods for stepping through the program (along with the keyboard shortcuts for the commands) are:

- **Step Into (F8)**   Executes the next line of code in the program. If the execution point (indicated by a yellow highlight on the line) is a procedure call, the Step Into command will move to the first line of the procedure and execute the procedure one line at a time as you continue to issue the command.

- **Step Over (Shift+F8)**   Works the same as Step Into, except when a procedure call is encountered, the procedure is run in its entirety, and the execution pauses again on the next line after the procedure call.

- **Step Out (Ctrl+Shift+F8)**   Causes the execution of the current procedure to run to the end, then the program pauses on the line following the procedure call.

- **Run to Cursor (Ctrl+F8)**   Allows you to place the cursor on the next line where you want to pause the program execution, then runs to that point of the code, which allows you to skip loops or sections of code that you know work correctly.

- **Continue (F5)**   Causes the program to run as normal until the next Breakpoint is encountered.

All these commands are available as key combinations. They are also available from the Debug menu and from the Debug toolbar shown in Figure 18.13. You can display the Debug toolbar by choosing it from the Toolbars item in the View menu. Exercise 18.5 takes you through the use of some of the continuation commands.

FIGURE 18.13

The Debug toolbar holds all your debugging tools in one place.

EXERCISE 18.5

Stepping Through a Program

1. Open the Calc.vbp project from the Visual Basic samples.

2. Open the code window of the form and go to the Click procedure of the Operator button.

3. Place the cursor on the first executable line after the procedure declaration.

4. Press the F9 key to set a Breakpoint on this line.

5. Run the program. Then enter a couple of digits and click a math operator button. The program will pause at the Breakpoint in the click event.

6. Open the Watch Window and set watches for the TempReadout and NumOps variables.

7. Place your cursor on the line that starts with "Select Case" and press the Ctrl+F8 key combination. You will see that execution proceeded from the original Breakpoint to where the cursor was located. You may also notice that the values of variables in the Watch Window changed.

8. Press the F8 key several times to observe the execution of the program one line at a time. Notice that this allows you to easily determine which branch of a conditional programming structure is executed.

9. When you are ready to continue execution without interruption, press the F5 key.

Working with the Call Stack

Sometimes it is necessary to know why a particular procedure was called in order to determine why an error occurred. Visual Basic also provides you with a tool for determining how you got to a particular place in the code. This tool is the Call Stack window.

When your program pauses, you can display the Call Stack by choosing the Call Stack item from the View menu. The Call Stack window, shown in Figure 18.14, displays all the procedures that lead up to the call to the current procedure. The calls are listed in order from the top of the window to the bottom, with the current procedure listed at the bottom. From the Call Stack window, you can highlight a procedure and click the Show button to display the actual line that called a subsequent procedure.

FIGURE 18.14

Determining where the Call came from

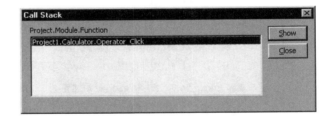

Debugging Servers and Controls

Version 4 of Visual Basic introduced the capability to create servers in Visual Basic, but these programs were difficult to debug. In order to debug a server, you had to start a second instance of Visual Basic and write a program to call the server. Even then, it was difficult to trace the execution of the program in the server.

Version 5 of Visual Basic not only allows you to create ActiveX servers (DLLs and executables), but also gives you the capability to create your own controls. Fortunately, it also provides a new tool for testing these elements, the program group. Using a program group allows you to create a control or a server, then, in the same Visual Basic session, create a program to test the component. With both programs in the same session, it is much easier to trace the progress of the program through the calls to the server or control and determine what is causing errors in the component.

Creating a Program Group

The first step to debugging a control or ActiveX server is creating the component itself. We looked at creating ActiveX servers in Chapter 11, "Creating and Running ActiveX Servers." We also looked at creating ActiveX controls in Chapter 14, "Creating ActiveX Controls with Visual Basic."

Microsoft ✓ *Exam* *Objective*   **Implement project groups to support the debugging and development process.**

After you have created the component that you want to test, the next step is to create a program group and create the project that will be used to call the component. Fortunately, this is all accomplished in one simple step. While you have your server or control project loaded, you choose the Add Project item from the File menu of Visual Basic to bring up the Add Project dialog box, which is the same as the New Project dialog box that you use to create a new project in Visual Basic. This dialog box allows you to create a new project or open an existing project for use in testing your ActiveX component. When the project is added to the development environment, you will see information about both projects shown in the Project window. You will also see that the caption of the Project window changes to indicate that you are now working with a project group. The caption will also show the name of the project group file once it has been saved. An example of a project group is shown in Figure 18.15.

FIGURE 18.15

Project groups are used to test ActiveX components.

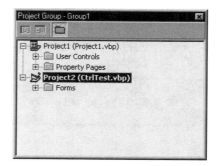

When you save the project group, each project is saved in its own .vbp file. One other file is created with a .vbg extension, the group file that contains information about which projects are included in the group. Exercise 18.6 shows you briefly how to create a project group to test an ActiveX control.

EXERCISE 18.6

Creating a Project Group

1. Create a new User Control project in Visual Basic.

2. Add a control to the "form" of the user control to give Visual Basic something to display in the test project.

3. Close the form of the User Control.

4. Choose the Add Project item from Visual Basic's File menu, then add a standard executable.

5. You will see that the Project window now contains two projects and has Project Group in the caption. You will also notice that the User Control is one of the controls in the toolbox of the new project.

6. You can now place instances of the User Control on your form.

Executing the DLL or Control

After you have created the program group, you need to create a client application as your test project. This client application is the one that you will execute in the testing. In turn, the client application will cause the program code of the DLL or control to run as needed. As the code is run, you can use the standard debugging techniques to find and eliminate errors in the program.

Microsoft
✓ **Exam**
Objective

Test and debug a control in process.

If you are working with a User Control, you can actually debug the control without ever running the test program, because the user control's program is running while you are creating instances of the control in the test project. As you edit the properties of a User Control, you are running the code associated with the Property Procedures of the control. You will, however, have to run your test program to test the methods of the user control, because methods are called by your program code, and this code will not be executed until the program is run. As you are setting properties or running your test program, you can use the standard debugging tools to check variables. Visual Basic enables you to set Breakpoints and Watches in the User Control like you would have in a standard program.

Microsoft ✓ *Exam* *Objective*	**Debug DLLs in process.**

If you are working with an ActiveX DLL, you can only test the DLL by running your test program. The test program will create objects from the classes of the DLL. As the properties and methods of these objects are used, the program code in the DLL is run. As with the User Control, you can set Breakpoints in the DLL and set Watches to observe the values of variables.

In working with either User Controls or DLLs, you should make sure that your test program checks all the properties and methods of the components. You should also be sure that all optional code is executed, which gives you the best opportunity of discovering all the errors in the code before someone else uses the component and stumbles across a problem.

Summary

After working through this chapter, you should have a good understanding of Visual Basic's debugging tools. You have seen how you can observe the values of variables and how you can change their value while the program is executing. You have also seen how you can pause the program and step through it one or a few lines at a time. Finally, you have seen how using a program group makes it relatively easy to handle the debugging process for an ActiveX control or server.

Working though the text and exercises of this chapter should prepare you for the following objectives of the Microsoft certification exam:

- Set watch expressions during program execution.
- Monitor the values of expressions and variables by using the debugging windows.
- Use the Immediate window to check or change variables.
- Explain the purpose and use of the Locals window.
- Use the appropriate error-trapping options, such as Break on All Errors, Break in Class Module, and Break on Unhandled Errors.
- Define the scope of a watch variable.
- Implement project groups to support the debugging and development process.
- Debug DLLs in process.
- Test and debug a control in process.

Review Questions

1. Which of the following tools helps you avoid errors in your programs? Check all that apply.

   A. Auto Syntax Check

   B. Require Variable Declaration

   C. Call Stack

   D. Immediate Window

2. Which of these tools will display the value of a variable? Check all that apply.

   A. Immediate Window

   B. Watch Window

   C. Call Stack

   D. Locals Window

3. Which of these tools will show you the properties of a form and its controls?

   A. Watch Window

   B. Immediate Window

   C. Auto Data Tips

   D. Locals Window

4. Which of these tools allows you to change the value of a variable?

   A. Watch Window

   B. Immediate Window

   C. Auto Data Tips

   D. Locals Window

5. How can you cause a program to pause execution? Check all that apply.

   A. Set a Breakpoint in code.

   B. Set a watch to break when the value changes.

   C. Insert the Stop command in your program.

   D. Right click the mouse on the program while it is running.

6. How are the scope of a variable and the scope of a watch related?

   A. The scope of the variable determines the scope of the watch.

   B. The scope of the watch determines the scope of the variable.

   C. The scope of the watch and scope of the variable are set independently and are, therefore, unrelated.

7. Which command do you use to skip over a procedure when you are stepping through a program?

    A. Step Into

    B. Step Out

    C. Run to Cursor

    D. Step Over

8. What Visual Basic element must you use to debug an ActiveX DLL?

    A. Call Stack

    B. Immediate Window

    C. Project Group

    D. The Compiler

9. When is the program code of a User Control running and able to be tested? Check all that apply.

    A. When the control is being built

    B. When the control is being added to another project and the properties are being set

    C. When a project containing the control is running

    D. During compilation of the control

PART

VII

Distributing
Your Application

CHAPTER

19

Compiling Your
Visual Basic Program

Microsoft Objectives Covered in This Chapter:

- Select appropriate compiler options.

- List and describe the differences between compiling to P-code and compiling to native code.

- List and describe options for optimizing when compiling to native code.

- Compile an application conditionally.

- Use the #If...#End If and #Const directives to conditionally compile statements.

- Set the appropriate conditional compiler flags.

In earlier versions of Visual Basic compiling your program was a simple task. You chose the Make Exe option of the File menu and let Visual Basic do the rest. Visual Basic created an exe file that you could distribute along with the VB run-time libraries. These libraries provided the support routines that were necessary for other people to use your program.

Things started changing a little in version 4 of Visual Basic. In version 4, you had the capability to create not only regular programs, but you could also create ActiveX servers (though they weren't called that at the time). You had two options for compiling your programs, create an exe file or create an OLE DLL file. Both options were accessible from the File menu. Programmers still weren't completely happy, however; one of the major complaints was about the speed of some programs. The other complaint was that Visual Basic lacked a native code compiler, a feature that was available with other programming languages.

In version 5, things changed again. Not only could you create a standard program or an ActiveX DLL, now you could create ActiveX server exe files, ActiveX documents, and ActiveX controls. In addition to giving you more types of programs that you could create, Visual Basic now had a multitude of compiler options available to let you optimize your code. These choices, as well as the ability to conditionally compile your project, are the subject of this chapter.

This chapter will cover the following topics that you need to know to achieve the following Microsoft exam objectives:

- Select appropriate compiler options.

- List and describe options for optimizing when compiling to native code.

- List and describe the differences between compiling to P-code and compiling to native code.

- Compile an application conditionally.

- Use the #If...#End If and #Const directives to conditionally compile statements.

- Set the appropriate conditional compiler flags.

Choosing the Correct Options

Microsoft
Exam
Objective

Select appropriate compiler options.

The first decision you have to make in compiling your program is whether to use P-code or native code compilation. The main difference between the two is the size of the executable file and the speed of some parts of the program. Contrary to what many people might think, compiling to native code does not create a stand-alone application that does not need run libraries. With either a native code or a P-code program, you will have to distribute the Visual Basic run-time libraries in order for your program to work. You will also have to distribute any custom control OCXs that your program uses.

Also, compiling to native code does not guarantee a major improvement in speed over the use of P-code. The speed improvements that you see will depend on what your program is designed to do and how it is written. If your program performs extensive number crunching, native code may give you a speed advantage. If, however, your program is designed to access a database and display information, the speed bottlenecks will most likely be the retrieval speed of the database engine, something that you cannot significantly control in your program.

To determine what compilation option is right for you, let's take a closer look at P-code and native code.

What Is P-code?

The term P-code originally derives from pseudo-code. Original versions of BASIC were interpreted. That is, an interpreter read a line of code in your program and created instructions for the computer's processor on-the-fly. By comparison, native code is the language that the processor uses, so native code instructions can be directly run by the processor in the computer. In the earlier days of PC programming, native code was typically written in Assembler, then later in C.

As Basic became more complex, and Visual Basic came on to the scene, purely interpreted code was too slow to be effective. A better way was needed to run the code in order to achieve better speed. With the use of P-code, instructions written in your programs are translated into a tokenized code that already contains instructions for performing operations and links to runtime libraries that are required for many functions. While still not directly executable by the processor, P-code is much faster than the original interpreted code. In some cases, almost as fast as native code.

Deciding between P-code and Native Code

Microsoft ✓ *Exam* *Objective*	List and describe the differences between compiling to P-code and compiling to native code.

Making a decision between P-code and native code involves considering the tradeoffs between the two. Each type of compilation has its own advantages and disadvantages.

If you compile your program to P-code, you will get the following advantages:

- Faster compile times
- Smaller exe file sizes

The key disadvantage of P-code is that your program will run slower than one compiled to native code. Compiling to native code gives you the advantage of faster program execution, at the expense of slower compile times and larger exe files.

The best way to determine which compilation is best for your program is to try compiling and running the code both ways. If native code gives your particular program a speed boost, and that boost is needed, compile to native code. If you are looking for small distribution sizes, compile to P-code.

Most people will find the use of P-code acceptable for the majority of their programs.

To tell Visual Basic which compilation method to use, you will need to specify an option in the Compile options of the project. You can get to the compile options by choosing the Properties item of the Project menu or by clicking the Options button from the Make Project dialog box. Either way, you will be presented with a dialog box with several tabs. The Compile tab of the dialog box is shown in Figure 19.1. From this dialog box, you choose whether to use P-code or native code compilation.

F I G U R E   19.1

Compile options for
your project

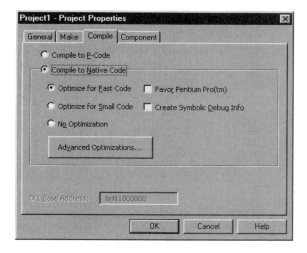

Native Code Compiler Options

If you choose to compile to native code instead of P-code, you have a variety of other options available to you for compiling the program. As you can see in Figure 19.1, these options are enabled when you select the Native Code option in the Compile dialog box. There are two sets of options that we will cover, basic options and advanced options.

Basic Options

Microsoft ✓ *Exam* *Objective* — **List and describe options for optimizing when compiling to native code.**

The basic native code compilation options are those that are shown on the main part of the Compile page of the Project Options dialog box. There are five options broken into two groups. The first group of three options determines the type of optimization that will be performed during compilation:

- **Optimize for Fast Code**   Causes the compiler to produce the fastest possible code. The compiler does this by examining all the program structures in your code and changing some of them to equivalent faster structures. For example, if you had a For loop whose function was to simply count from one to ten, the compiler could set the value of the variable to 10 and eliminate the loop. The following code illustrates the equivalence of these two structures:

```
'The ultimate result of this loop is to set J
'    equal to 10.
For I = 1 To 10
    J = I
Next I
'This statement performs the same task and is faster
J = 10
```

- **Optimize for Small Code**   Causes the compiler to create the smallest possible executable file. Sometimes, the optimizations that make a program faster increase the size of the executable file. With this option set, an optimization that increases the size of the executable would not be made.

- **No Optimization**   Causes the compiler to simply create an executable file without trying to optimize for either size or speed.

The three optimization options of the compiler are mutually exclusive. As you can see from the use of option buttons in the dialog box, only one of these options can be selected at any given time. The other two basic options can be used separately or together, and can be used with any of the three optimization options. These other two options are:

- **Favor Pentium Pro ™**   Causes the compiler to optimize the code to take advantage of features of the Pentium Pro ™ processor. This option should only be used if you know that your target machines will all have this processor. A program compiled with this option will run on other processors, but the performance will not be as good as if the program were compiled with the option turned off.

- **Create Symbolic Debug Info**   Causes the compiler to create a separate file (with the extension .pdb) that contains symbolic debugging information. This information is not needed to debug your program in Visual Basic, but several more sophisticated debuggers such as Microsoft's CodeView or BoundsChecker by NuMega use the information to handle debugging chores. These programs can help you find very difficult errors such as memory leaks.

Advanced Options

In addition to the basic options for compilation, the native code compiler allows you to specify a number of advanced options. These options are for the programmer who wants to wring every last bit of performance out of his/her program. You can access the advanced options by clicking the Advanced Optimizations button on the Compile options dialog box. The Advanced Optimizations dialog box is shown in Figure 19.2.

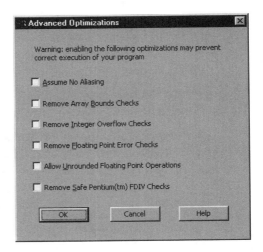

For most of your programs, you will not use any of these advanced optimizations; however, if you decide you want to try them, here is what each of the six options can do:

- **Assume No Aliasing**   Aliasing allows you to use more than one variable name to reference a specific variable location, which typically occurs when you pass arguments to a subroutine by reference. Selecting this option tells the compiler that your program does not use aliasing. Typically, this option should be left off.

- **Remove Array Bounds Checks**   Whenever Visual Basic accesses an element of an array, it checks to make sure that the index it is using is within the bounds of the array. If the index is out of bounds, an error occurs. With this option turned on, Visual Basic does not perform the bounds check and will not generate errors, which can cause your program to retrieve a value from an invalid memory location and can result in crashes or strange behavior of your program. You should use this option only if you are sure that all array indexes are within bounds or if you perform your own bounds checking.

- **Remove Integer Overflow Checks**   This option causes Visual Basic to bypass the normal checks that make sure a value will fit in the data type defined. When the checks are in place, an error occurs if the number you are storing is larger than the capacity of the variable that you created. When this option is on, the checks are removed and no overflow error occurs, but you may get incorrect results from some of your calculations.

- **Remove Floating Point Error Checks**   Similar to the checks performed for integers, Visual Basic checks floating point operations to determine whether the value will fit in the declared variable and to verify that there is no division by zero. With this option turned on, these checks are bypassed, eliminating the reporting of overflow errors and division by zero errors. If these conditions occur, however, the results of your program may be incorrect.

- **Allow Unrounded Floating Point Operations**   This option keeps the compiler from forcing floating point operations to be rounded to a particular size. The benefits of using this option are:

  - Floating point registers are used more efficiently.

  - Some memory operations associated with rounding are avoided.

  - Floating point number comparisons are performed more efficiently.

- **Remove Safe Pentium FDIV Checks**   Some time back, a floating point division error was reported in some versions of the Pentium processor chip. This error would produce floating point results that were off in one of the last decimal places, but was not a problem for most programs. By default, Visual Basic produces code that is not affected by this bug, but at the expense of size and speed of the program (minor effects). With this option set, floating point calculations will be faster and your executable may be smaller, but there is the possibility that the Pentium bug will cause an incorrect result. As more computers are using later versions of the Pentium chip and using the Pentium Pro or Pentium II chip, this option can be safely used with most programs.

It is left to you the user to determine which of these options you use for compiling your programs. The one caveat to using any of the options is to make sure that you test your program completely to ensure that the compiler options do not create problems for you. Also, testing should always be done on multiple machines, particularly if you are using options that treat one processor preferentially over others.

Compiling Only Parts of the Program

Microsoft ✓ *Exam* *Objective*

Compile an application conditionally.

Another important aspect of compiling your program is determining which parts of the program to compile. Visual Basic does not give you the option of only compiling a single module or a single form. Each time you compile the program, each file in your project will be compiled. Rather, Visual Basic provides you with a means to choose whether to compile a specific code segment in a form or module, known as conditional compilation.

What Is Conditional Compilation?

You should be familiar with the If...Then...Else...End If programming structure. This structure is used in most programs to determine whether to run a particular segment of code based on whether the condition in the If statement is True or False. The following code segment illustrates a typical If construct:

```
If Len(FileStr) > 0 Then
    Set ErrDb = OpenDb(ErrPath & "ErrorLog.Mdb")
    Set LogErrSet = OpenRSet(ErrDb, "ErrorLog", 1)
Else
    Set ErrDb = CreateDb(ErrPath & "ErrorLog.Mdb")
    CreateErrTable ErrDb
    Set LogErrSet = OpenRSet(ErrDb, "ErrorLog", 1)
End If
```

Conditional compilation uses a similar construct to determine whether the compiler should include a particular segment of code. Before we look at the specifics of how conditional compilation works, let's take a look at why you might want to use conditional compilation.

Maintaining Multiple Versions of Code

One of the primary reasons for using conditional compilation is to maintain multiple versions of a program. In version 4 of Visual Basic, you could produce an executable for 16-bit or 32-bit systems from the same code base. This capability made it easier to create and maintain programs that had to operate on different operating systems.

However, you are probably aware that several programming elements, specifically API declaration statements, must be coded differently for the 16-bit and 32-bit systems. Using conditional compilation allows you to keep both sets of code in the same module, and compile the correct code based on the value of the condition. The following code shows one such use of conditional compilation:

```
#If Win16 Then
    Public glbValid As Integer, glbWinDir As String
    Public lpReturnString As String, Size As Integer
#Else
    Public glbValid As Long, glbWinDir As String
    Public lpReturnString As String, Size As Long
#End If
```

Maintaining 16-bit and 32-bit Code in Visual Basic Version 5

You might think that because version 5 of Visual Basic is a 32-bit only system, you don't have to worry about maintaining multiple versions of a program. However, if you converted a program from version 4 and still have to support the program for 16-bit clients, it is still a concern. Visual Basic 5 does use a different format for its project file; therefore, these files are not readable by version 4. You can, however, share form, module, and class module files between VB4 and VB5. If you need to continue to work with multiple versions of a program, you will still need conditional compilation.

You should use caution in working with multiple versions of your program across multiple versions of Visual Basic, as many of the controls available in version 5 may not exist or may not work the same in version 4.

Using Conditional Compilation for Debugging

Another typical use of conditional compilation is for debugging your programs. As you are going through the debugging process, you may need to write the contents of variables to the debug window, or to keep a detailed log of the progress of the program. This information may be crucial for finding bugs, and you may want to keep the code in your program for maintenance purposes. However, you don't want the code to be running in the released version of your program. By surrounding the debug code with conditional compilation statements and setting the proper conditional values, you can compile your program with the debug code during development and without the code for the commercial release. The following code segment shows this possibility:

```
#If InDebugMode Then
    Debug.Print I, J, "Form_Load Routine"
    LogRun "Form_Load", Date
#End If
```

Other Uses of Conditional Compilation

You can probably think of a number of other uses for conditional compilation of your programs. A few possible uses are:

- Creating demonstration versions of a program. You can use conditional compilation to only include key features, such as printing, in the full version of the program.

- Creating different versions of a program for different user levels. For example, if you have several related programs for managing different non-profit organizations, these programs can use a common code base, but implement different features depending on the organization type.

- Creating single-user and network versions of a program.

Determining What to Compile

Now that we have covered what conditional compilation is and why you might want to use it, we are ready to cover how to implement conditional compilation. Implementing conditional compilation requires two steps:

- Setting up the areas of code to be compiled
- Setting the values of the conditions

Defining the Code Segments

Microsoft ✓ *Exam* *Objective*

Use the #If...#End **If** and #Const **directives to conditionally compile statements.**

The actual construct for setting up conditional compilation is very simple. It is a variation of the standard If...Then...End If construct that you probably use extensively in your programs. The only difference is that for the conditional compiler statements you precede the If, ElseIf, Else, and End If keywords in the code with a # sign. This instructs Visual Basic that this is a compiler directive instead of a program statement. The rest of the statement is like the standard If statement. You specify the name of a variable or expression to be evaluated as the condition. If the condition is True, the segment of the code following the If statement will be compiled. Otherwise, the code segment will be ignored. Exercise 19.1 shows you how to set a conditional compilation to include a print feature only in the production version of a program.

The variables that you specify with compiler directives look the same as standard variables and are named the same way. These variables have no use in the normal course of your program, however, and are evaluated only as the program is being compiled.

EXERCISE 19.1

Conditional Compilation of Code Segments

1. Start a new project.

2. Add a command button to the form and set its Caption property to Print. Set the Name of the command button to cmdPrint.

3. In the Click event of the command button, place the following code:

```
#If Production Then
    Printer.Print "General Report for Membership Program"
#Else
    MsgBox "Print functions are not available in"&_
"the demonstration version."
#End If
```

The exercise shows a simple two level condition. If you are compiling the production version, the printer functions are enabled. Otherwise, a message is displayed telling the user that the functions are not available. Like a standard If statement, you can have multiple conditions using ElseIf statements as shown in the following code:

```
#If YouthMode Then
    'Enable youth group functions
    mnuYouth.Enabled = True
#ElseIf FinancialMode Then
    'Enable contribution menus
    mnuGifts.Enabled = True
#Else
    'Enable membership menus
    mnuMember.Enabled = True
#End If
```

Setting Conditions for Conditional Compilation

Microsoft ✓ *Exam* *Objective* | **Set the appropriate conditional compiler flags.**

After you have defined the segments of code to be compiled and specified the variables or expressions to be used as conditions, you must set values for the conditions. One set of conditions is handled by Visual Basic itself. The other conditions are those that you define, and you must set the values of the variables prior to running the compilation process.

Visual Basic's Internal Constants   Visual Basic supplies two constants that you can use in conditional compilation to determine the target operating system of your program:

- **Win16**   Indicating that the target system is 16-bit Windows

- **Win32**   Indicating that the target system is 32-bit Windows

For any programs that you create with Visual Basic version 5, the Win16 constant will be set to False and the Win32 constant will be set to True. If you are using Visual Basic version 4, the value of the constants will be determined by the version of VB4 that you are using. If you are using the 16-bit version of VB4, the Win16 constant will be True and the Win32 will be False. For the 32-bit version of VB4, the value of the constants will be reversed.

Creating Your Own Variables   Win16 and Win32 are supplied by Visual Basic, but all other variables that you use in conditional compilation you must create for yourself. You are not required to declare variables that are used in conditional compilation. Therefore, the variables are defined as you use them in the conditions of the #If statements. When you compile your code, you need to provide values for these variables. If you fail to provide values, Boolean variables will default to False, numeric variables will default to 0, and string variables will default to a null string.

There are three methods that you can use to provide values for the variables that are used in the conditional compilation:

- Set the variable in code using the #Const directive.

- Using the Project Properties Box

- Using Command Line Switches

Microsoft
✓ *Exam*
Objective

Use the #If...#End **If** and #Const **directives to conditionally compile statements.**

The first method of setting the value of a variable is to use the #Const directive. To use this method, simply specify the directive, the name of the variable (now a constant), and the value that you want to assign. The following line of code illustrates this method:

```
#Const InDebugMode = True
```

Setting the value of a conditional variable using the #Const directive only sets the value for the module in which the directive is used. You have to set the value in each module that uses the variable in order. Using this method also makes it more difficult to change values, because you need to make sure that you make the appropriate change in each required location.

The best method for setting the value of conditional variables is through the use of the Project Properties box. You can open the Project Properties by choosing the Properties item from the Project menu. After opening the dialog box, click the Make tab to display the dialog box shown in Figure 19.3.

FIGURE 19.3

Setting the Conditional
Compilation Arguments

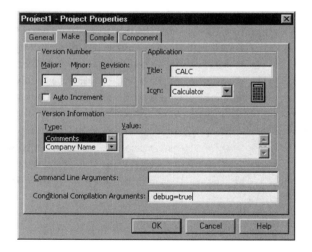

In the dialog box, you set the value of the variables by entering the name of the variable and its value in the Conditional Compilation Arguments box at the bottom of the dialog box. If you need to specify more than one variable, you will need to separate the assignment statements with a colon, as shown in the following program line:

```
InDebugMode=True:Production=True
```

Exercise 19.2 illustrates the steps for setting the compiler arguments.

EXERCISE 19.2

Setting Conditional Compilation Arguments

1. Start with the project created in Exercise 19.1.

2. Choose the Properties item from the Project menu.

3. Select the Make tab in the dialog box.

4. Place the cursor in the Conditional Compilation Arguments text box and enter the following text:

Production=True

5. Close the dialog box.

NOTE You can access this same dialog box by pressing the Options button on the Make Project dialog box shown in Figure 19.4.

F I G U R E 19.4

Make Project dialog box

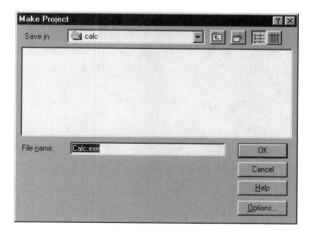

The final method of setting the conditional compilation arguments is through the use of command line switches. These switches are used when Visual Basic is started to set certain parameters of the program. The compilation arguments are set with the /d command line switch. The arguments and their values follow the /d switch. As with the arguments in the Project

Properties dialog box, multiple arguments are separated by colons. The following command line could be used to start Visual Basic and set the compilation constants:

```
vb5.exe /make DemoProject.vbp /d
InDebugMode=False:Production=False
```

Creating the Executable File

After you have set the compiler options and specified values for all the conditional compilation arguments, you are ready to compile your program to an executable file. To start the compilation process, simply choose the Make item from the File menu to display the dialog box shown in Figure 19.4. In this dialog you specify the name of the executable file that will be created. You can also select the Options button to change any options that you previously selected. When you are ready, click the OK button to start the compilation process. Visual Basic will compile each form, module, and class module in your program and notify you of any compilation errors that it encounters. After the compilation of each component is completed, Visual Basic will write the executable file. When this process is completed you will be returned to the development environment.

If you look closely at the Make tab of the Project Properties dialog box, shown in Figure 19.5, you will see that there is other information that you can set for your project prior to compilation. This information provides details about your program and about the specific version of the program that you are compiling. This information is stored in the properties of the App object and can be retrieved by your program when it is running. The following table specifies the information that is contained in the dialog box and the corresponding property of the App object.

Make Dialog Information	App Object Property
Major version number	Major
Minor version number	Minor
Revision number	Revision
Program Title	Title
Comments about the Program	Comments

Make Dialog Information	App Object Property
Your company name	CompanyName
Copyright information	LegalCopyright
Trademark information	LegalTrademarks
Description of the executable file	FileDescription
Name of the product	ProductName

One other bit of information that can be specified in the dialog box is the icon to be used to represent the program. This icon must be one that is assigned to a form in the program. A list of all forms is shown next to the property, allowing you to easily choose which form's icon you wish to use.

FIGURE 19.5

Details provided on the Make tab of the Project Properties dialog box

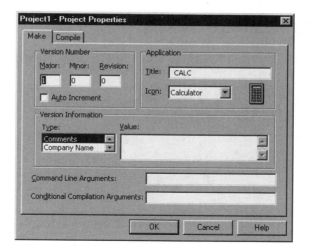

Summary

While compiling your program is one of the last steps of the development process, you can see that the options you select can have a significant impact on the performance of your code. You have also seen in this chapter how you can use the same code base to handle multiple versions of a program by using conditional compilation.

The information in this chapter should prepare you for the following Microsoft exam objectives:

- Select appropriate compiler options.

- List and describe options for optimizing when compiling to native code.

- List and describe the differences between compiling to P-code and compiling to native code.

- Compile an application conditionally.

- Use the #If...#End If and #Const directives to conditionally compile statements.

- Set the appropriate conditional compiler flags.

Review Questions

1. Which compilation option typically produces the smaller executable file?

   A. Compile to native code.

   B. Compile to P-code.

   C. Both options produce the same size file.

2. Which compilation option typically produces the faster executable?

   A. Compile to native code.

   B. Compile to P-code.

   C. Both options produce equally fast programs.

3. Which compiler options would be a benefit for a program to be run on a Pentium Pro machine? Check all that apply.

   A. Favor Pentium Pro

   B. Create Symbolic Debug Information

   C. Assume No Aliasing

   D. Remove Safe Pentium FDIV Checks

4. How can you set the value of conditional compilation arguments? Check all that apply.

    A. Use the #Const directive.

    B. Use the Const statement.

    C. Use an assignment statement in your program.

    D. Use the Project Properties dialog box.

5. What are reasons for using conditional compilation? Check all that apply.

    A. To maintain multiple versions of a code

    B. To incorporate debug information

    C. To compile a single module for testing

    D. To create demonstration programs

6. What compiler options can lead to unexpected results from your program? Check all that apply.

    A. Remove Integer Overflow Checks

    B. Remove Floating Point Error Checks

    C. Create Symbolic Debug Info

    D. Favor Pentium Pro

7. How can you access version information about your program that is input in the Make dialog box?

    A. It is unavailable while your program is running.

    B. Through the properties of the App object

    C. Through the properties of the Program object

    D. Read the header information in your code files.

CHAPTER

20

Adding Help to Your Application

Microsoft Objectives Covered in This Chapter:

- Implement Help features in an application.

- Set properties to automatically display Help information when a user presses F1.

- Use the HelpFile property to set the default path for Help files in an application.

- Use the CommonDialog control to display the contents of a Help file.

One of the most overlooked aspects of any programming project is the documentation. This neglect occurs whether the documentation is in the form of written manuals or included in help files. As the cost of producing written documentation rises, however, many firms have begun the practice of only including on-line help with their products. What this means for the programmer is that users have come to expect a help file associated with every program they run. Moreover, they expect the help to be easy to use and to be context-sensitive; they expect specific help to pop up when they need it.

Fortunately, Visual Basic provides you with tools that make it easy for you to associate a help file with your application and to reference specific topics on demand. Unfortunately, for those who hate writing documentation, they have not invented a simple way for the program to document itself; programmers still have to write the text for the help files and create the files.

The main focus of this chapter is how to incorporate an existing help file into your Visual Basic application. Specifically, we will cover information to help you with the following Microsoft exam objectives:

- Implement Help features in an application.

- Set properties to automatically display Help information when a user presses F1.

- Use the HelpFile property to set the default path for Help files in an application.

- Use the CommonDialog control to display the contents of a Help file.

In addition, we will look briefly at how you actually create the help files for your application, and we will examine some of the alternatives to help files for providing information to your users.

Help Basics

If you have worked with Windows for any length of time, you are probably familiar with the Help system that is used in most Windows applications. For most programs, the simple press of the F1 key brings up a dialog box that contains either general information about the program, or information specific to the task you are trying to perform. A typical help window is shown in Figure 20.1.

FIGURE 20.1

Typical Help dialog box

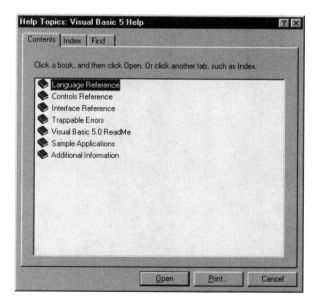

As you can see in the figure, the help dialog box typically includes three tabs—Contents, Index, and Find. The Contents page works like the table of contents in a book, showing you the overall structure of the information in the help file. The great advantage of the online contents is that it allows you to move directly to the topic of interest with the click of the mouse, which is much easier than turning pages in a book. The contents that are shown on this page are determined by the contents information that you build into your help file. If you do not include contents information, this page will not be displayed when the user invokes the help dialog.

The Index page of the help dialog is similar to the index in the back of a book. It contains a list of every topic included in the help file, listed in alphabetical order. You can access individual topics by scrolling through the list or by entering the topic of interest in the text box at the top of the page. As you type the topic name, the list of topics scrolls to the first topic that matches the letters you have typed. A typical index page of a help dialog box is shown in Figure 20.2. The topics that are shown in this index are the names of the individual topics that you create in the help file.

F I G U R E 20.2

Help Index topics

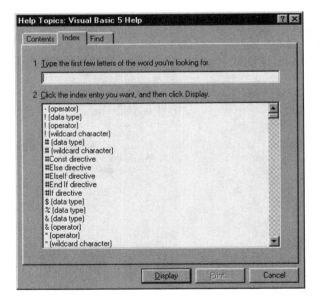

The final tab of the help dialog is the Find page. When first accessed for a help file, this page invokes a wizard that helps you create a database of information in the help file. This database contains almost every word that occurs anywhere in your help file. This feature makes it easier for a user to find specific information in the event that they do not remember the topic name. The find page of Visual Basic's help dialog is shown in Figure 20.3.

F I G U R E   20.3

Find help with the
Find page.

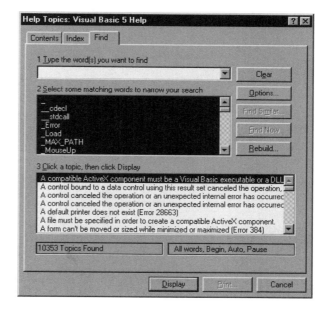

 The organization of information in a help file is not a topic specifically covered in the Microsoft certification exam, but it is important that you understand the concepts in order for you to successfully create and implement a good help system.

Help Components

The Contents, Index, and Find pages of the help dialog are only the initial part of the interface to the information in the help file. Like a book, the real information is contained in the pages of the help file. The pages of a help file contain text and graphics that describe a particular topic or function of your program, very much like the pages of any reference book that you read. A typical page from a help file is shown in Figure 20.4.

FIGURE 20.4

Help pages contain the real information for the user.

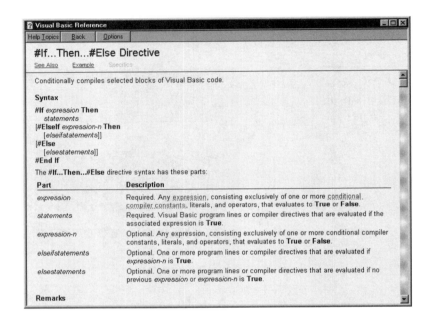

In addition to the text information that you find, help pages have a few special elements that can make them far more useful than their printed counterparts:

- **Jump**   A direct link to another page in the help file. A jump is indicated on the help page by green text underlined with a single solid line.

- **Pop-up**   A small window containing additional information about a specific key word or phrase. A pop-up is indicated by green text underlined with a single dashed line.

- **See Also**   A collection of related topics that might be of interest to the user. The topics are accessible through the See Also list at the upper left corner of the help page.

Each of these features can be included in your help system by creating the proper structures in your help files.

Characteristics of Good Help Files

You know that you will find help files with almost every program that you encounter. You have probably also seen that some of the help files in programs are not very helpful. Help file design is a major topic unto itself, but the following tips will help you create help files that are easy for your users to use and provide helpful information in a concise manner.

- **Use short pages**   The text for a single help topic should be contained on one or two screens if possible to avoid making the user scroll through pages of information to find what they want. If a topic is too long, consider breaking it into multiple topics or place some of the information in a pop-up.

- **Make it well organized**   You should use a contents page with sufficient detail to cover the major topics of the program. Also, make judicious use of jumps and See Also lists to allow the user to quickly find related information.

- **Make sure all the links work**   Like a good program, a good help file should be thoroughly tested. Users can get very annoyed if they click on a link and get the message "Topic does not exist."

This is far from an exhaustive list of the things that should go into a help file, but these tips should help to get you started in the right direction.

Getting Help with F1

Microsoft ✓ *Exam* *Objective*	**Implement Help features in an application.**

The primary means by which most people access the help system is by pressing the F1 key. For simple programs, such as a game, pressing F1 will access the contents page of the help system. For more complex programs, users expect to be able to click on a particular function or control and press F1 to get help specific to the current control or function. You get this kind of help when you click on a control and press F1 to get information about the properties, methods, and events of the control.

Microsoft ✓ ***Exam*** ***Objective***   **Set properties to automatically display Help information when a user presses F1.**

Like many other parts of the programming adventure, Visual Basic makes it relatively easy to provide not only help, but also context sensitive help for your programs. There are two things that you must do to provide the context-sensitive help for a program:

- Identify the Help file that will be used with the program.

- Assign context IDs to the controls that will access context sensitive help.

Determining Which Help File to Use

Once you have created a help file for your application, the first step to making it available to your users is linking it to the program. The easiest means of linking the help file to the program is through the Project Properties dialog box. The General page of the dialog box, shown in Figure 20.5, lets you enter the name of the help file to be associated with your program. If you are not sure of the name, you can click the browse button to open a file dialog box that lets you look for the file and select it. Exercise 20.1 walks you through the steps of associating a help file with a project.

F I G U R E   20.5

Project Properties lets you identify the help file for your project.

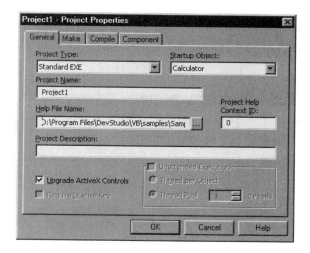

EXERCISE 20.1

Linking a Help File with a Project

1. Start a new project.

2. Open the Project Properties dialog box by choosing the Properties item from the Project menu.

3. Click the General tab of the properties to get to the proper page.

4. Click the Browse button on the General page to open the file dialog box so you can select the file.

5. Select the Test.hlp file that is located on the enclosed CD.

6. Close the Properties dialog box.

7. Run the program and press the F1 key. The index page of the Help system should appear.

You may have noticed as you worked through Exercise 20.1 that using the Properties dialog box specifies the full path to the help file, which may work fine on your machine, but can cause problems for your users if they do not have the same directory structure as you do (which it is safe to assume that they don't). Therefore, you need another method to set the help file for your project.

You can enter the name of the help file without the path information and Visual Basic will default to the current path, typically the folder where the application is located.

Microsoft ✓ *Exam* *Objective*

Use the HelpFile property to set the default path for help files in an application.

The best method of setting the HelpFile for your program is through code placed at the start of your program. All Visual Basic programs support the App object, which allows you to set and retrieve information about the currently running program. The specific property that identifies the help file for your application is the HelpFile property. Using the App object, you can specify the help file using a line of code like the following:

```
App.HelpFile = App.Path & "\Test.hlp"
```

This code specifies that the application should use the Test.Hlp file located in the same directory as the application itself. Using this technique, the directory structure of your user does not matter, as long as the executable and the help file are located in the same directory. You can make sure that they are located in the same place through the setup routine for your program.

You can learn more about creating setup programs in Chapter 21, "Creating Setup Disks with the Setup Wizard."

Context Sensitive Help

Setting the HelpFile property, or identifying the help file in the Project Properties, allows you access to the help file, but it does not allow the user to get context sensitive help. For context sensitive help, you need to identify the topic within the help file to be associated with each form or control in your program.

You do not have to link every control in your program with a specific topic. You only need to link those controls for which you wish to provide context sensitive help. However, it is a good idea to have a help topic for each form in your program.

Setting the Help ID for a Control or Form

Each topic that you create in a help file is identified by a specific tag. This tag is a numeric ID that enables you to associate the topic with a specific item in your program. The corresponding ID in your program is the HelpContextID property of a control or a form. By setting this property, either in the design mode or through code statements, you create a link between the control and the specific help topic.

For forms and most controls, the easiest way to set the HelpContextID is through the Properties window in the design mode. Figure 20.6 shows the setting of the HelpContextID property for a form.

FIGURE 20.6

Setting the Help-ContextID in the Properties window

NOTE

Controls such as the Label, Timer, Shape, and Line do not have a Help-ContextID property. Because the user cannot place the focus on these controls while the program is running, there is no way to get context sensitive help for them, nor should there be a need for it.

If you want to set the HelpContextID from code in your program, you can do it by using an assignment statement to set a value for the property. The following code statement sets the property for a text box:

```
txtName.HelpContextID = 220
```

Exercise 20.2 shows you how to set the HelpContextID to enable context sensitive help.

EXERCISE 20.2

Creating Context Sensitive Help

1. Start with the project you created in Exercise 20.1.

2. Add two command buttons to the form. Name the buttons **cmdFile** and **cmdAnalyze**. Set the Captions of the buttons to Open File and Analyze Database respectively.

3. Set the HelpContextID property of the cmdFile button to 220.

4. Set the HelpContextID property of the cmdAnalyze button to 240.

5. Run the program.

6. Move the focus to the "Open File" button and press F1. The help page shown in the next illustration should appear. Close the help window.

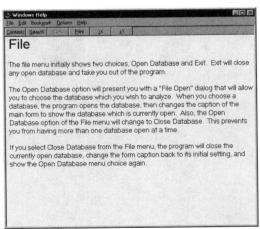

7. Move the focus to the "Analyze Database" button and press F1. You will see that a different help page is displayed.

One other element of your programs that you might want to associate with specific help topics is the menu. You can assign a help topic to each item in your menu. Like the other controls on your form, you can use an assignment statement to set the HelpContextID for the menu item, or you can set the value while you are in the menu builder as shown in Figure 20.7.

F I G U R E 20.7

Setting the Help-
ContextID for a menu

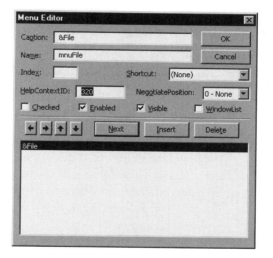

Default Help

At this point, you can create context sensitive help for your programs. But what happens if the user presses the F1 key on a control for which no Help-ContextID has been defined?

The user will not get an error message. When the user presses F1 on a control, Visual Basic does the following search:

1. Check for a HelpContextID for the control and if found, use it.

2. If there is no HelpContextID for the control, check the HelpContextID of the control's container, such as a frame, picture box, or form. If a Help-ContextID is found, use it.

3. Repeat step two until the top-level container has been accessed.

4. If no HelpContextID is found, display the Index page of the Help system.

If you specify a HelpContextID that does not exist in your help file, the user will encounter an error.

Displaying Help with the CommonDialog

Microsoft Exam Objective

Use the CommonDialog **control to display the contents of a Help file.**

Using the F1 key is the primary method through which users access the help system, but most programs also have Help options as part of the main menu. These options allow the user to view the Help contents and the Help index. The functionality for implementing these menu choices is not an integral part of Visual Basic, but it is a capability of one of Visual Basic's controls, the Common Dialog.

The Common Dialog control provides you with a means of using a variety of dialog boxes that are used in all Windows programs:

- File Open

- File Save

- Font Selection

- Color Selection

- Printer Control

- Printer Setup

- Help

The key dialog box we are concerned with in this chapter is the Help dialog box. Using the Common Dialog, you can invoke help from anywhere in your program, allowing your users to access help using menu choices or command buttons on dialog boxes that you build.

Accessing help from the Common Dialog requires the completion of three tasks—setting the HelpFile property, setting the HelpCommand property, and invoking the ShowHelp method. The HelpFile property of the Common Dialog is the same as the HelpFile property of the App object. The name of the file can be set using an assignment statement. The Help-Command property determines what action will be taken when the ShowHelp method is run; therefore, this property must be set before the method is invoked. The HelpCommand property has a variety of settings, as summarized in the following table.

Help Action	Common Dialog Constant
Execute a Help macro.	cdlHelpCommand
Display the contents page of the help system.	cdlHelpContents
Display a specific topic. (You must also set the HelpContext property).	cdlHelpContext
Display a topic in a pop-up help window.	cdlHelpContextPopup
Display help for a particular keyword.	cdlHelpKey
Display help for a keyword starting with a specific letter.	cdlHelpPartialKey

There are other settings of the HelpCommand property; however, these are the most commonly used values. You can find the description of all the settings in Visual Basic's help system.

To run a specific help command, you enter two lines of code in your program. The first line specifies the action to be taken and the second line invokes the ShowHelp method. The following code illustrates the code for this task:

```
getfile.HelpFile = App.Path & "\ArcHelp.hlp"
getfile.HelpCommand = cdlHelpContext
getfile.HelpContext = 220
getfile.ShowHelp
```

Displaying Help Contents

As mentioned above, the contents page of the help file is typically accessed from a menu item on your form. Exercise 20.3 takes you through the process of creating the menu and setting it up to access help.

EXERCISE 20.3

Accessing the Contents of Help with the Common Dialog

1. Start a new project.

2. Add the Common Dialog to your Visual Basic toolbox, by adding the control in the Components dialog box. You can access the Components dialog box by choosing the Components item from the Project menu.

3. Add an instance of the common dialog box to your form. Name the control **cdlHelp**.

4. Open the menu editor of the form. Create a top-level menu named **mnuHelp** and set the Caption of the menu to &Help. As a sub-menu of the Help menu, create an item named **hlpContents** and set the Caption property to Help &Contents.

5. Close the Menu Editor to build the menu.

6. Open the Click event of the Help Contents menu item.

7. Place the following code in the Click event procedure:

```
cdlHelp.HelpFile = "C:\Program Files\"&_
"DevStudio\VB\Help\VB5.hlp"
cdlHelp.HelpCommand = cdlHelpContents
cdlHelp.ShowHelp
```

8. Run the program and choose the Help Contents menu item. Your program should display the contents page of Visual Basic's help system.

Displaying the Help Index

The other item that is typically on a help menu is the search item. This item is usually coded to bring up the Index page of the help system to allow the user to search for a particular topic. Exercise 20.4 extends Exercise 20.3 by adding another menu item and setting up the code to display the Help index.

EXERCISE 20.4

Adding a Menu Item and Displaying the Help Index

1. Start with the project created in Exercise 20.3.

2. Open the Menu Editor and add another item under the help menu. Name the item **hlpIndex** and set the Caption property to Help Topics.

3. Close the Menu Editor and open the code window for the Click event of the Help Topics menu.

4. Add the following code to the Click event procedure:

```
cdlHelp.HelpFile = "C:\Program Files\"&_
"DevStudio\VB\Help\VB5.hlp"
cdlHelp.HelpCommand = cdlHelpKey
cdlHelp.HelpKey = ""
cdlHelp.ShowHelp
```

5. If you run the program and select the Help Topics item, you will see the Index page of Visual Basic's help system as shown in the following illustration.

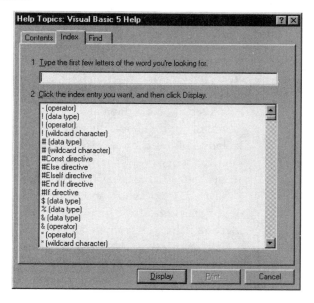

Creating Help Files

In the exercises in this chapter, we have used help files that already existed on your system, or were supplied on the CD that accompanies the book. For your programs, you will need to create your own help files, a very tedious task, but much easier than it used to be. Microsoft has introduced some new tools to help you with the creation of the files, and several third-party programs exist that provide complete solutions for creating help files.

To create a help file for you program, you need to perform four tasks:

- Create the Help topic information files.

- Create the Help project file that maps the help file information.

- Create the Help contents file.

- Compile the Help file from the text files and the Help project file.

After you create the help file and know all the context IDs for the topics, you will need to insert the topic IDs in the HelpContextID properties of the appropriate forms and controls.

Using the Help Workshop and a Word Processor

Prior to version 5 of Visual Basic, you had to not only understand how to create the topic information for a help file, but you also had to understand the intricacies of the Help compiler and learn how to create help project files. Version 5 didn't do anything about the complexity of creating the topic information files, but it did do something about the rest of the help file process. Included with version 5 of Visual Basic is the Help Workshop. You can install the Help Workshop from the Visual Basic CD by running the Setup.exe program located in the \tools\hcw folder of the CD.

The Help Workshop, shown in Figure 20.8, helps you organize the topics of your help file. The program also creates the help project file, the contents file, and helps you compile and test the actual help file.

The main effort in creating the help file for your program is creating the topic files. The full scope of this effort is beyond the scope of this book, but to create help topic files on your own, you will need to use a word processor that can create RTF files. You will also need to understand several formatting options of the word processor that are required to encode the help topic jumps, pop-ups, and context IDs. You can find more information about creating help files in Visual Basic's help system and VB Books Online.

F I G U R E   20.8

Help Workshop for cre-
ating help files

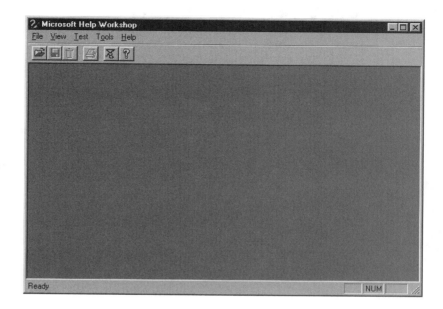

FIGURE 20.8

Help Workshop for creating help files

Using Other Help Products

Programmers try to find tools that help them to be more productive, so they can concentrate on creating the unique routines and interfaces for their programs, particularly in the case of creating help files. Fortunately for VB programmers, there are several products that make it fairly easy to create help files without having to worry about all the custom formatting required when using a word processor.

Several of these products are also designed to work specifically with Visual Basic. These products will search your forms for any control that has a HelpContextID and use this control as the first cut at the topics for the help file. When you have finished creating the help file, these same products will go back through your project and set the correct values of the HelpContextID properties for the forms and controls. Several of these products are:

- WinHelp Office by Blue Sky Software
- ForeVB by ForeFront Technologies
- VB HelpWriter by Teletech Systems

Other Ways of Providing Help

The Help system is, of course, the main method of providing help to your users; however, there are several other means of providing the user with timely information about the tasks they are performing:

- **Tooltips**   The little boxes that pop up when the user rests the mouse on a control for a few seconds. Typically, these tips are used to provide a brief description of the function of a control. You can include tooltips for many controls by entering a string of text in the ToolTipText property of the control.

- **Status Bars**   The status bar at the bottom of a form is often used to provide information to the user about a particular task, which is particularly useful in a data entry application where the status bar can be used to describe the information that should be input into the current control. To learn more about the status bar control, refer to Chapter 3, "Windows 95 Custom Controls."

- **Message boxes**   These boxes are usually reserved for warnings or confirmation of an action, but you can use a message box to provide help to a user on demand or when a problem occurs.

Summary

This chapter covered the two main means of displaying help in your Visual Basic programs. Specifically, we covered how to create context sensitive help and how to use the common dialog box to display help items.

The review questions cover the following exam objectives that were discussed in this chapter:

- Implement Help features in an application.

- Set properties to automatically display information when a user presses F1.

- Use the HelpFile property to set the default path for Help files in an application.

- Use the CommonDialog control to display the contents of a Help file.

Review Questions

1. HelpFile is a property of which object? Check all that apply.

   A. Form

   B. Common Dialog

   C. Project

   D. App

2. How do you make a specific topic appear when the user presses F1 on a control?

   A. Pass the control name to the Common Dialog.

   B. Set the value of the HelpContextID property of the control.

   C. Set the value of the Index property of the control.

   D. Set the ToolTipText property of the control.

3. What happens if there is no specific topic for a control when the user presses F1?

   A. The "Topic not Found" error is displayed in the help file.

   B. Help is not accessed.

   C. The HelpContextID of the control's container is used.

   D. Windows 95/NT help is shown.

4. What happens if the topic assigned to a control is not in the help file?

   A. The "Topic not Found" error is displayed in the help file.

   B. Help is not accessed.

   C. The HelpContextID of the control's container is used.

   D. Windows 95/NT help is shown.

5. What two properties of a Common Dialog must be set before trying to display help?

   A. HelpFile

   B. HelpContext

   C. HelpCommand

   D. HelpKey

6. What method of the Common Dialog is used to display help information?

   A. Help

   B. OpenHelp

   C. ShowHelp

   D. Assist

7. What files are created by the Help Workshop? Check all that apply.

   A. Help topic files

   B. Help file (.hlp extension)

   C. Help project file

   D. Help contents file

8. What groups of controls can be linked to a specific help topic?

   A. Any control that is visible on the screen

   B. Only controls with a HelpContextID property

   C. All controls

   D. Only menu items

CHAPTER

21

Distributing Your Applications

Microsoft Objectives Covered in This Chapter:

- Use the Setup Wizard to create an effective setup program.

- Create a setup program that installs and registers ActiveX controls.

- Edit the Setup.inf file.

- Edit the Vb5dep.ini file.

- Manage the Windows system registry.

- Edit the registry manually.

- Register components by using the Regsvr32.exe utility.

- Register a component automatically.

- Use the GetSetting function and the SaveSetting statement to save application-specific information in the registry.

Y ou have finally gotten through with that next killer application. You finished the design, all the tests ran perfectly, and you have compiled the application. You even included a help file to assist the users of your program. You're done with the application, right? Not quite yet. It used to be said that the program wasn't finished until the documentation was written, but there is also another part of the puzzle. The program isn't really finished until you have created setup disks or files to distribute your program and have tested the operation of the setup program.

Like many other parts of the programming process, Visual Basic provides you with a number of tools to make it easier for you to create setup programs and distribution disks. However, there are still decisions that you will have to make and customizations of the setup that you may have to perform. For example, will your program be distributed on disks, on CD, or over the Internet?

In addition to creating the setup disks, you will need to handle the registration of components on your users' systems. And, you will need to write application specific information to the Windows Registry to allow each user to customize the application to their liking.

This chapter will cover many of the issues related to distributing your applications. Specifically, we will look at the following certification exam objectives:

- Use the Setup Wizard to create an effective setup program.

- Create a setup program that installs and registers ActiveX controls.

- Edit the Setup.inf file.

- Edit the Vb5dep.ini file.

- Manage the Windows system registry.

- Edit the registry manually.

- Register components by using the Regsvr32.exe utility.

- Register a component automatically.

- Use the GetSetting function and the SaveSetting statement to save application-specific information in the registry.

Creating Setup Programs

When you begin to create setup programs and distribution disks (or files) for your programs there are a number of tasks that you need to accomplish:

- Compile your program.

- Determine the files that must be distributed with the program. These files include the VB runtime libraries, any other required DLL files, and any files required by your program (help files, databases, documents, or ReadMe files).

- Create a setup program for copying files to the user's machine and uncompressing the files.

- Compress the files that will be included on the distribution disks. Compression is necessary to minimize the number of disks needed for a standard installation or to minimize download time for an Internet installation.

- Identify the location where files should be installed on the user's machine. For example, most DLL or OCX files should be installed in the Windows\System folder on the user's machine. Other files should be installed in an application directory specified by the user.

- Create the actual disks or download files that will be used to distribute the program.

- Test the setup program. A setup program is like any other program; it must be tested to ensure that it works correctly. Nothing turns a user off faster than an installation program that doesn't work. Preferably, you should test the program on a machine other than your development machine to make sure all the proper components have been installed.

To make the creation of setup programs easier for you, Visual Basic provides you with the Setup Toolkit located in the Setupkit folder of Visual Basic. This toolkit provides you with:

- A setup program for copying and expanding compressed files from the setup disks to the user's hard drive.

- A compression program for compressing the files to be distributed with your application.

- A program to make cabinet files for Internet distribution.

- Dependency files to determine what components are needed with specific applications, such as Data Access Object files.

You can use the Toolkit programs directly, or you can make things even easier on yourself by using the Setup Wizard. This wizard automates the tasks of creating the setup program and the distribution disks for your programs. For most of your applications, whether standard programs, automation servers, or Internet programs, the Setup Wizard will handle the entire process of creating distribution media for you. Rarely will you need to handle setup tasks by hand.

Creating Setup Disks for Standard Programs

Microsoft **Use the Setup Wizard to create an effective setup program.**
Exam
Objective

The Setup Wizard is a great tool for creating setup programs and distribution disks for standard programs. You simply start the Setup Wizard, select the project to be processed, and follow the prompts. The wizard does the rest of the work. Well, almost. There are a few other steps that you have to perform, but the Setup Wizard makes the process quite easy.

The first step is to start the Setup Wizard. The wizard is a program separate from Visual Basic and is not available directly from the development environment. You start the Setup Wizard from the Windows Start menu. If you are using a typical Visual Basic installation, the Setup Wizard is located under the Microsoft Visual Basic 5.0 group and is named the Application Setup Wizard. When you start the wizard, you are presented with a start-up screen that introduces the wizard. If you move to the next screen of the wizard, you will see the project selection page shown in Figure 21.1.

F I G U R E 21.1

Selecting the Project to be set up

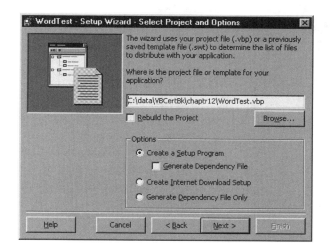

From this page of the wizard, you specify the project for which the setup files are to be created. You can enter the project name in the text box or click the Browse button to locate the project using an Open File dialog box. This page also allows you to set the options for creating your setup program. The first option determines whether to Rebuild the Project. If you choose this option, Setup Wizard will fire up Visual Basic and recompile the selected project. If you are sure that you have not made any changes in your project since the last time you compiled it, you can leave this option unchecked.

The other options on the page allow you to determine the type of setup to create. These options specify whether you will:

- **Create a Setup Program**   Specifies that you are creating a program to distribute your application using floppy disks, a CD, or over an internal network.

- **Create Internet Download Setup**   Specifies that you want to create a setup program that allows users to download your program over the Internet. This option is only available for ActiveX Control, EXE, or DLL projects that contain either Public classes or a UserDocument object.

If you want to distribute a standard program over the Internet, you would create a setup program with files written to a single directory. These files can then be downloaded by users, and the program can be set up from their local drive.

- **Generate Dependency File Only**   Specifies that setup should only create a .dep file that identifies all the program dependencies for your application. The dependencies are links to other files required by your program such as ActiveX control OCX files, DLL files for parts of the application, such as Data Access Objects, or ActiveX servers that are required by the application. You can create a dependency file when you create a setup program by checking the appropriate box on the page.

The second page of the Setup Wizard, shown in Figure 21.2, determines how you want to distribute the application. You can choose to distribute your application via:

- **Floppy disks**   Suitable for small applications.

- **Single Directory**   Typically used for CD or local network distribution.

- **Disk Directories**   Typically used if others will download the files over the Internet. The reason for breaking the setup into multiple files is to prevent problems with downloading a single large file.

F I G U R E 21.2

Distribution
Method page

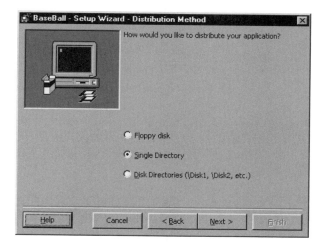

The third page of the Setup Wizard depends on the option you chose for the Distribution method. The page will request the following information depending on the option chosen:

- **Floppy Disk**   You will need to specify the location and size of the disks to use for the distribution. Figure 21.3 shows this option of the Setup Wizard.

- **Single Directory**   You will need to specify the location of the directory where the setup files will be written.

- **Disk Directories**   You will need to specify the location of the directory where the files will be written and the maximum size of each file. The size will be the space available on a typical floppy disk format, allowing files to be distributed via Internet or other online method, or copied to floppy disks later.

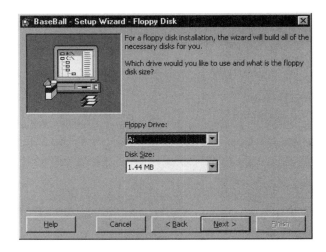

The next page of the Setup Wizard, shown in Figure 21.4, specifies any ActiveX server components that your application needs. Setup tries to determine if any are required and presents you with a list of the servers that it finds are needed. If necessary, you can add local or remote servers to the list by clicking the appropriate button and specifying the file location.

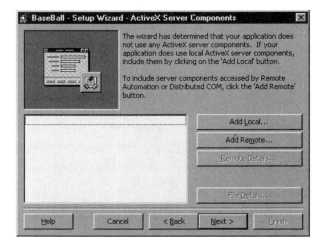

The next page of the wizard, shown in Figure 21.5, shows other file dependencies that the wizard has found for your application. These files are typically custom controls that are required by your application. If you feel that a file has been added in error, you can remove it by clearing the check box next to the file name.

FIGURE 21.5

File dependencies

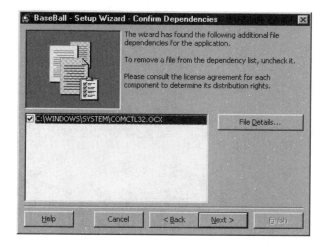

 If you remove a required file, your application will not run correctly on your user's machine.

When you click the Next button from the dependencies page, the Setup Wizard will analyze your project to determine what files are required to be distributed with the program. The wizard will almost always include the MSVBVM50.DLL file, which is the Visual Basic runtime library. In addition, there are typically several other OLE related files that are required for a program. Also, your application's EXE file will be added to the list. When the analysis is complete, you will see the list of required files, as shown in Figure 21.6. You can add other files to this list, such as help files or database files, by clicking the Add button and selecting the files from an Open File dialog box.

FIGURE 21.6

File Summary

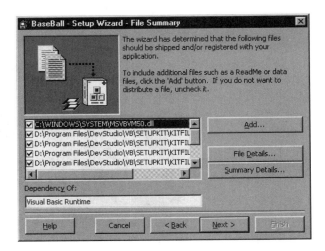

If you select a file from the list and click the File Details button, you will see detailed information about the file, as shown in Figure 21.7. The key reason for using this dialog box is to change the installation parameters for the file. When the Setup Wizard creates the file list, it makes assumptions about where a file should be placed on the user's drive. Typically, system files are placed in the Windows\System folder, and other files are placed in the Application folder chosen by the user. If you wish to change this behavior, you can open the File Details dialog box for the file and select the Destination Directory from the drop-down list. The values you see in the list are actually variable names that are used by the setup program. These names are used instead of specific directories so that the setup program can determine the actual directory structure of the user's machine and place the files accordingly. The other option you can set on this dialog box is to install the file as a shared file, which allows multiple programs to use the same copy of the file. Most DLL and OCX files will be installed as shared files.

After adding any necessary files, you can click the Next button, which will take you to the final page of the wizard and enable the Finish button. When you click the Finish button, the Setup Wizard starts the process of compressing the files required for the installation and copying the files to the specified location. If you are using floppy disks, setup will prompt you when to insert each disk needed for the setup. Exercise 21.1 walks you through the creation of setup disks for one of the programs created earlier in the book.

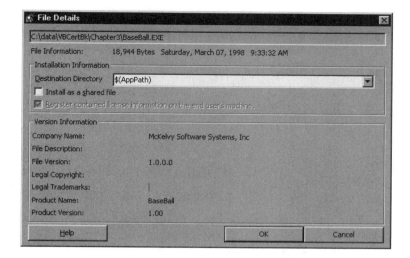

Microsoft Exam Objective

Create a setup program that installs and registers ActiveX controls.

EXERCISE 21.1

Creating a Typical Setup for an Application

1. Start the Application Setup Wizard.

2. On the Project selection page of the wizard, choose the BaseBall.vbp project created in Chapter 3, "Creating User Interfaces with Windows Common Controls." This file is located on the CD accompanying the book.

3. Because the executable for the project has not been created, check the Rebuild the Project option.

4. Choose the Create a Setup Program option and click the Next button on the page.

5. Select the Floppy Disk option from the Distribution Method page. Then, click the Next button.

6. Specify the size and location of your floppy disk. Then, click the Next button.

7. This project does not require any ActiveX server components. Therefore, you can click the Next button to move to the Confirm Dependencies page.

8. The Dependencies page should show the ComCtl32.Ocx file. This file is required for the BaseBall program, so do not clear the check box. Click the Next button.

9. The File Summary shows all the files needed for the BaseBall program. You do not need to add any files to the list. You can click the Next button.

10. Click the Finish button to allow setup to compress the files and copy them to floppies. When prompted, insert the correct floppy disk in your drive.

Creating Setup Disks for ActiveX Servers

Creating setup programs for ActiveX servers that you create is very similar to creating setup programs for other applications. Like other programs, you can use the Setup Wizard to create the setup program for the server. The key difference in the setup comes after you have confirmed the dependencies for the program. The Setup Wizard will display the Shared ActiveX Application page shown in Figure 21.8. This page allows you to define:

- Whether the application will be installed as a shared component or a stand-alone application

- Whether the ActiveX server will be accessed on a remote server through remote automation

FIGURE 21.8

Shared component options

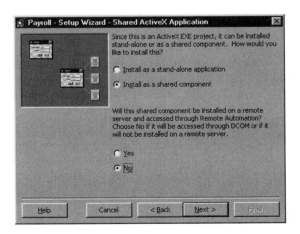

After setting these options, the Setup Wizard will proceed as it does for other programs. Exercise 21.2 shows you how to create the setup program for the Payroll server created in Chapter 11, "Creating and Running ActiveX Servers."

Creating a Setup Program for an ActiveX Server

1. Start the Application Setup Wizard and proceed to the project selection page.

2. Select the Payroll.vbp project and select the Create a Setup Program option. Click the Next button.

3. Specify Floppy disk as the Distribution Method and click the Next button.

4. Specify the size and location of the floppy disk and click the Next button.

5. Because the Payroll program uses database access, you will be shown the Data Access page as shown in the following graphic. There are no additional database formats that need to be specified, and the application uses the default of Jet workspaces. You can look at the page and click the Next button.

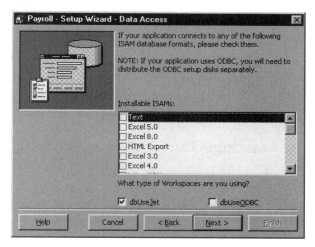

6. There are no server components required for the project. Click the Next button.

7. The Confirm Dependencies page should show the DAO350.DLL file, which is needed for accessing Jet databases. Click the Next button.

8. On the Shared ActiveX Application, select the Install as stand-alone application option and the No option. Click the Next button.

9. After the project is analyzed, you will see the File Summary page. There are no additional files required for the setup. You can click the Next button, then the Finish button to complete the setup. Insert disks as prompted by the wizard and your setup will be complete.

Modifying Setup Information

While the Setup Wizard works well for most programs, you will find from time to time that you need to create a custom setup program to handle special needs. For example, if you need to copy files to the application directory and to another directory on the user's drive, you will need to create a custom program. Another example would be if you wanted to allow the user to select portions of your program to be installed, similar to the way you can install portions of Visual Basic or Word.

To create a customized setup, you will need to perform the following tasks:

- Create the custom executable that performs the setup.

- Modify the Setup.lst file that contains the list of files required for installation.

- Modify the VB5dep.ini file to change the file dependencies for the application. (This is an optional step.)

Creating a Custom Setup.exe Program

Fortunately, creating a custom program is not as difficult as it sounds. When used in the default manner, Setup Wizard uses a stub program called Setup.exe to start the setup process. This program in turn calls Setup1.exe to handle copying files and performing other setup tasks. The Setup1.exe is compiled from the Setup1.vbp project contained in the Visual Basic setup folder. For most custom setups, you can modify this program to include the new features that you require, then compile it and replace the original Setup1.exe program with your modified program. You can then run the Setup Wizard as before to create distribution disks.

For most custom setups, you can create any new forms that you need, then tie these into the Setup1.vbp. The project even has comments that show you where to place code to customize the setup procedure. Figure 21.9 shows a customized setup form that could be used in the setup program.

FIGURE 21.9

A customized
setup form

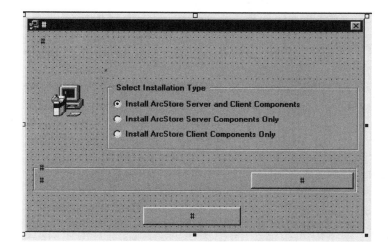

After you create the form(s) you need, you will have to modify the code in the setup program to utilize the new forms. In the Setup1 project is a form named frmSetup1. The code in the Load event of this form displays other forms of the Setup program. To display your form, look for the string "ShowOptionsDialog," the predefined location in the program where you can insert code to display your custom forms. If you need to copy groups of files to other directories besides the Windows or Application directories, you can use the code routines already created in Setup. Again, the Setup program has a location predefined for this task. Look for the string "MySection" in the Load event of the frmSetup1 form. The sections used by the CopySection procedure are defined in the Setup.lst file. To copy files in other sections, you create the sections in the Setup.lst file and use the CopySection procedure as indicated.

After you have made the necessary changes to the Setup1 project, you can compile it and use it as your setup program.

Modifying the Setup.lst File

***Microsoft
Exam
Objective***

Edit the Setup.inf file.

Modifying the Setup.lst file is the second part of customizing the setup program. If you need to copy files in multiple sections, you will need to create these sections and add the appropriate files to the section in the Setup.lst file. The Setup.lst file is a text file that can be modified by any text editor, such as Notepad. Figure 21.10 shows a modified Setup.lst file that adds a new section of files.

FIGURE 21.10

Modifying the Setup.lst file in Notepad

```
Setup.lst - Notepad
File   Edit   Search   Help
File5=1,,olepro32.dl_,olepro32.dll,$(WinSysPath),$(DLLSelfRegister),
File6=1,,msvcrt20.dl_,msvcrt20.dll,$(WinSysPathSysFile),,,7/11/1995,
File7=1,,msvcrt40.dl_,msvcrt40.dll,$(WinSysPath),,$(Shared),1/12/199
File8=1,,ctl3d32.dl_,ctl3d32.dll,$(WinSysPathSysFile),,,1/12/1996,27

Rem New Sections Added to List
[Client]
File1=1,,StKit416.DL_,StKit416.DLL,$(WinSysPath),,$(Shared),8/15/199
File2=1,,COMDLG32.OC_,COMDLG32.OCX,$(WinSysPath),$(DLLSelfRegister),
File3=1,SPLIT,MFC40.DL1,MFC40.DLL,$(WinSysPath),$(DLLSelfRegister),$
File4=2,,MFC40.DL2,MFC40.DLL
File5=2,,TABCTL32.OC_,TABCTL32.OCX,$(WinSysPath),$(DLLSelfRegister),
File6=2,,DBLIST32.OC_,DBLIST32.OCX,$(WinSysPath),$(DLLSelfRegister),
File7=2,,OC30.DL_,OC30.DLL,$(WinSysPath),,$(Shared),2/18/1995,638464
File8=2,,THREED32.OC_,THREED32.OCX,$(WinSysPath),$(DLLSelfRegister),
File9=2,,GAUGE32.OC_,GAUGE32.OCX,$(WinSysPath),$(DLLSelfRegister),$(
File10=2,,SSDATB32.OC_,SSDATB32.OCX,$(WinSysPath),$(DLLSelfRegister)

[Server]
File1=5,,Archelp.hl_,Archelp.hlp,$(AppPath),,,7/25/1997,38453
File2=5,,arcstr32.ex_,arcstr32.exe,$(AppPath),$(EXESelfRegister),,8/
File3=5,,labr32.re_,labr32.res,$(AppPath),,,7/31/1997,34324
File4=5,,DBUTIL32.ex_,DBUTIL32.exe,$(AppPath),$(EXESelfRegister),,7/
File5=5,,dbutil32.re_,dbutil32.res,$(AppPath),,,7/10/1997,1320

[Setup]
Title=ArcStore
DefaultDir=$(ProgramFiles)\arcstr32
Setup=setup132.exe
```

The Setup.lst file is referred to as the Setup.inf file in the Visual Basic certification exam objectives.

Changing the Vb5dep.ini File

Microsoft ✓ Exam Objective

Edit the Vb5dep.ini file.

The Vb5dep.ini file is another text file that contains information needed by Setup in order to properly install programs. The information in this file specifies dependencies of particular components. For example, the file will specify that applications using DAO 3.5 require the MSJTER35.DLL and MSJInt35 .DLL files. Like the Setup.lst file, you can modify the Vb5dep.ini file to reflect other dependencies that occur in your programs. When you add a new dependency, you will need to create a section name [enclosed in brackets], followed by the files required and the location of the files. Figure 21.11 shows a portion of the Vb5dep.ini file. You can find the file in the Setupkit folder of Visual Basic.

F I G U R E 21.11

Modifying the Vb5dep.ini file in Notepad

```
Vb5dep.ini - Notepad
File  Edit  Search  Help
Protocol6=ncacn_spx,SPX
Protocol7=ncadg_ip_udp,Datagram - UDP
Protocol8=ncacn_nb_ipx,Netbios over IPX

[DAO2535.tlb]
Dest=$(MSDAOPath)
Uses1=DAO350.dll
CABFileName=MSDAO350.cab
CABDefaultURL=http://activex.microsoft.com/controls/vb5
CABRunFile=MSDAO350.exe -Q

[MSJet35.dll]
Register=$(DLLSelfRegister)
Dest=$(WinSysPathSysFile)
CABFileName=MSJet35.cab
CABDefaultURL=http://activex.microsoft.com/controls/vb5
CABINFFile=MSJet35.inf
Uses1=MSJtEr35.dll
Uses2=MSJInt35.dll
Uses3=VBAJet32.dll
Uses4=VB5DB.dll
Uses5=MSRD2x35.dll
Uses6=MsRep135.dll
Uses7=ODBCJt32.dll
```

Working with the Windows Registry

Microsoft ✓ *Exam* *Objective*

Manage the Windows system Registry.

When users run your setup program to install your software, two key things happen:

- Files are copied to the user's hard drive.

- Components are registered for use in Windows.

The setup program places entries in the Windows Registry that specify the location of components. For most components, this is handled automatically for you. In some cases, however, it will be necessary for you to modify the Registry yourself. Also, you may want to store information specific to your application in the Registry, so users can customize your program and have the settings used each time the program is run. In this section, we will look at what the Registry is and how you can manipulate the information in the Registry.

Understanding the Registry

The Registry is a system database that is used with Windows 95 and Windows NT. This database contains information about the programs and components that are installed on a machine. The information that can be stored for a component includes:

- Description of the component

- Location of the component's file

- Version number of the component

- Class ID of the component, if applicable

All this information is stored in a hierarchical structure in the Registry. The information of the Registry can be displayed and edited in programs like

RegEdit; however, extreme caution should be used when editing the Registry because modifying or deleting Registry entries can cause programs not to run or cause your system to crash.

Microsoft Exam Objective

Edit the Registry manually.

If you do need to modify the settings of the Registry, you will need to follow these steps:

- Start RegEdit (or another tool designed to edit the Registry).

- Make a backup of the Registry before making any modifications.

- Find the Registry key you wish to edit using the Find dialog box in RegEdit.

- To edit the value of a key, double-click on the key and enter the new value in the editing dialog box.

- To delete a key, highlight it and press the Delete key.

Figure 21.12 shows the RegEdit utility being used to edit a Registry entry.

F I G U R E 21.12

Editing the Registry

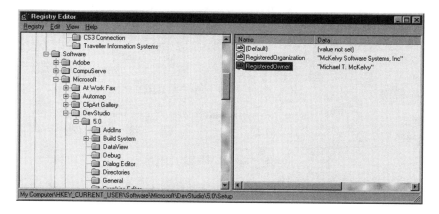

Registering Components

When you use a setup program to install an application on your machine, the setup program usually handles the registration of all the components that are required for the application. There are times, however, when you need to register components by other means. One example of this is when you simply copy a component to a new machine instead of using an installation program. In this case, the component will not be recognized by your system until the component is registered.

If you need to register a component on your system, there are two ways to do this:

- Use the Regsvr32.exe program.

- Automatically register the component by running it.

Using the Regsvr32.exe Program

Microsoft
✓ ***Exam***
Objective

Register components by using the Regsvr32.exe utility.

You use the Regsvr32 program by running it from the Run dialog box available on the Start menu. When you need to register a component, you enter Regsvr32 followed by the name of the file to be registered. There are also two optional switches that you can use with the program:

- **/s**   Suppresses messages during the registration process.

- **/u**   Used to un-register the server.

The following statement can be used to register a DLL component named MyDLL:

```
Regsvr32 C:\MyDll.Dll
```

Automatically Registering Components

Microsoft
✓ ***Exam***
Objective

Register a component automatically.

You can automatically register an out-of-process component, ActiveX EXE server, by running the program. This action will load the program, place information about the components of the program in the Windows Registry, and run the program. If you want to register the program without actually running it, you can simply run the program from the Run dialog box and use the /regserver option. This action loads the information about the server into the Registry, but does not execute the program. The following code will register the Payroll server created in Chapter 11.

```
Payroll.exe /regserver
```

Working with Application Specific Information

Microsoft ✓ **_Exam_** **_Objective_**

Use the GetSetting function and the SaveSetting statement to save application-specific information in the Registry.

The final thing that you need to know about working with the Registry is how to save and retrieve user information for your specific application. This information can allow the user to customize the program and have the program work according to their specification each time they run it. Some examples of information that you might store about a program are:

- Size and position of the main form of the program
- Buttons included on a customizable toolbar
- Most recently used files
- Font and color preferences

To work with the settings in the Registry, Visual Basic uses three commands—GetSetting, to retrieve information from the Registry; SaveSetting, to save information to the Registry; and DeleteSetting, to remove information from the Registry.

If you have worked with Windows INI files in the past, the Registry serves the same purpose, but the GetSetting and SaveSetting commands make handling the information much easier.

Saving Settings to the Registry

Obviously, before you can retrieve information from the Registry, the information must be saved. You can save any information to the Registry for almost any purpose using the SaveSetting command. To use this command, you specify the following:

- **Application name** The name by which the application will be known for registry settings. This information is passed as a string.

- **Section name** A string that identifies the section of the application information in which the setting will be stored. Using sections allows you to specify the same key name for multiple purposes. For example, you might want to specify the Top, Left, Height, and Width properties of several key forms in your program. By creating a section for each form, you can use the same property names without having them overwrite each other.

- **Key name** A string specifying the name of the specific property to be stored.

- **Value** A string that sets the value of the Key. Any values that are not strings need to be converted before storing them in the Registry.

When you use the SaveSetting command, your program will write a value to the specified location (specified by the Application, Section, and Key arguments) in the Registry. If the location does not exist, it will be created and the value will be stored. If the location exists, the value specified in the SaveSetting command will replace the current value. The following code line illustrates the use of the SaveSetting command.

```
SaveSetting "RegTest", "Main", "State", Str(Me.WindowState)
```

Retrieving Registry Settings

To retrieve information from the Registry, you use the GetSetting function. The GetSetting function retrieves a specific value from the Registry based on the location specified by the Application, Section, and Key parameters. The function also has an optional parameter that specifies a default value to use if the particular key is not found in the Registry. If the key is not found and no default is specified, a zero length string is assumed to be the default. Any value returned by the GetSetting function is in the form of a string. If you need a value other than a string, you will have to convert the value returned by the GetSetting function to the proper data type. The following code line shows the use of the GetSetting function.

```
Me.WindowState = Val(GetSetting("RegTest", "Main", _
    "State", "0"))
```

Deleting Registry Settings

The final command for manipulating Registry data is the DeleteSetting command. This command is used to remove a specific key from the Registry or to remove a section with all its associated keys. The DeleteSetting command uses the following arguments:

- **Application**   The name of the application whose settings will be deleted.

- **Section**   The name of the section to be deleted or the section containing the key to be deleted.

- **Key**   An optional argument. If the Key is specified, only the single key will be deleted from the section. If the Key argument is omitted, the specified section and all its keys will be deleted.

The following code could be used to delete the State key for the main form.

```
DeleteSetting "RegTest", "Main", "State"
```

To illustrate how these commands would be used in an actual application, exercise 21.3 shows how to save the WindowState, size, and position of a form.

EXERCISE 21.3

Working with Registry Settings

1. Start a new project in Visual Basic. Name the form **frmRegTest** and set the Caption property to "Registry Demonstration Application."

2. Add a command button to the form and name it **cmdSave**. Set the Caption property to Save Settings.

3. Add the following code to the Click event of the command button. The code first saves the WindowState property of the form. Then, if the form is not minimized or maximized, the position and dimensions of the form are saved. Note that the Str function is used to convert the numeric values to strings to pass to the SaveSetting command.

```
SaveSetting "RegTest", "Main", "State", _
Str(Me.WindowState)
If Me.WindowState <> 0 Then Exit Sub
SaveSetting "RegTest", "Main", "Top", Str(Me.Top)
SaveSetting "RegTest", "Main", "Left", Str(Me.Left)
SaveSetting "RegTest", "Main", "Height", Str(Me.Height)
SaveSetting "RegTest", "Main", "Width", Str(Me.Width)
```

4. Add the following code to the Load event of the form. This code retrieves the settings for the size and position of the form. The code first retrieves the WindowState information. Then, if the WindowState is normal, the code retrieves the size and position information. If you try to set the size or position with the form maximized or minimized, an error will occur. The code uses the Val function to convert the string information returned by the GetSetting function into numbers that are required for the property settings. The code also specifies default values for the GetSetting function calls.

```
Me.WindowState = Val(GetSetting("RegTest", "Main", _
"State", "0"))
If Me.WindowState <> 0 Then Exit Sub
Me.Top = Val(GetSetting("RegTest", "Main", "Top", "100"))
Me.Left = Val(GetSetting("RegTest", "Main", "Left", _
"100"))
Me.Height = Val(GetSetting("RegTest", "Main", "Height", _
"2500"))
Me.Width = Val(GetSetting("RegTest", "Main", "Width", _
"2500"))
```

5. Save the project. Then run it. You can resize the form and move it. Then click the Save Settings button. If you then exit the program and restart it, the program will start in the same position and size you specified. The following graphic shows this simple but illustrative program in action.

Summary

As you can see, even after the design, coding, and testing of the program are completed, there are several other tasks to attend to. It is not difficult to create an effective setup program, but it is an important part of the overall programming process. This chapter showed you how to create a setup program using the Setup Wizard. You also saw how you could modify the setup program and its associated files to provide a more customized installation for your users.

The other key topic of this chapter was working with the Registry. You saw how to register components using manual means when it is not possible to register them with a setup program. These skills are part of the certification exam objectives:

- Use the Setup Wizard to create an effective setup program.

- Create a setup program that installs and registers ActiveX controls.

- Edit the Setup.inf file.

- Edit the Vb5dep.ini file.

- Manage the Windows system registry.

- Edit the registry manually.

- Register components by using the Regsvr32.exe utility.

- Register a component automatically.

- Use the GetSetting function and the SaveSetting statement to save application-specific information in the registry.

Also part of the objectives, and possibly more important from a programming viewpoint, you saw how to store and retrieve information from the Registry information that is specific to your application. This capability lets you provide customization features for the users of your programs.

Review Questions

1. What does the Setup Wizard do?

    A. It installs a program on your local drive.

    B. It automatically creates an installation program for your application.

    C. It assists you in creating an installation program for your application.

    D. It allows you to modify your Visual Basic development environment.

2. Why would you need to modify the Setup.lst file?

    A. To customize the installation of an application

    B. To specify which program to install

    C. To add forms to the setup program

    D. None of the above

3. How do you register a component without using an installation program? Check all that apply.

   A. Use the Regsvr32.exe program.

   B. Run the ActiveX EXE server.

   C. Open the registry with a text editor and enter the information.

   D. You must use an installation program to register a component.

4. What type of data can be stored in the Registry?

   A. Any type of data is allowed.

   B. Only strings and numbers may be stored.

   C. Only strings may be stored.

   D. Any data except pictures.

5. Which command do you use from your program to replace a specific value in the Registry?

   A. GetSetting

   B. GetAllSettings

   C. DeleteSetting

   D. SaveSetting

6. What happens if you do not specify a default value for the GetSetting function and there is no entry in the Registry?

   A. An error occurs in your program.

   B. No value is returned.

   C. The function returns an empty string.

   D. The function returns the value of the last key in the registry.

7. What will the statement DeleteSetting "RegTest", "Main" do?

    A. Delete all keys in the Main section of the RegTest application.

    B. Delete the first key in the Main section of the RegTest application.

    C. Nothing. You must specify a key to be deleted.

    D. Delete all keys for the RegTest application.

8. What is the Regsvr32.exe program used for?

    A. To edit the Registry

    B. To register or un-register a component

    C. To only register a component

    D. Regsvr32 is not used with any programs you create.

APPENDIX

A

Answers to Review Questions

Chapter 1 Answers

1. What is the sequence in which the following events are triggered when a form is loaded?

    A. Initialize, Resize, Paint, and Load

    B. Load, Initialize, Resize, and Paint

    C. Initialize, Load, Paint, and Resize

    D. Initialize, Load, Resize, and Paint

    Answer: D

2. What is the sequence of events when a form is unloaded?

    A. Unload, QueryUnload, and Terminate

    B. QueryUnload, Unload, and Terminate

    C. Unload only

    D. QueryUnload and Unload

    Answer: D

3. How can you keep the user from exiting a form using the Close item on the Control menu or by clicking the Close button?

    A. Place code in the Unload event.

    B. Place code in the QueryUnload event.

    C. This can only be done using a Windows API call.

    D. This cannot be done in Visual Basic.

    Answer: B

4. How do you create a read-only property in a form?

    A. Create a Property Let procedure.

    B. Create a Property Get procedure.

    C. Create both a Property Get and Property Let procedure.

    D. Declare a Public variable in the declarations section of the form.

    Answer: B

5. Given the following code segment, how many instances of the form are created and displayed?

```
Dim frmVar1 As frmPerson, frmVar2 As frmPerson
Set frmVar1 = New frmPerson
Set frmVar2 = frmVar1
Load frmVar1
frmVar2.Show
```

A. None

B. 3

C. 1

D. 2

Answer: C

6. Given the following code, what happens when the frmPerson.Show method is called?

```
Dim frmVar1 As frmPerson, frmVar2 As frmPerson
Set frmVar1 = New frmPerson
Set frmVar2 = frmVar1
Load frmVar1
frmPerson.Show
```

A. The current instance of the form is displayed.

B. A second instance of the form is created and displayed.

C. An error occurs.

D. Nothing.

Answer: B

7. Which event(s) allow you to determine which key was pressed by the user? (Check all correct answers.)

A. Click

B. KeyPress

C. KeyDown

D. KeyUp

Answer: B, C, D

8. Which event(s) allow you to determine if a control or Shift key was pressed by the user? (Check all correct answers.)

   A. Click

   B. KeyPress

   C. KeyDown

   D. KeyUp

   Answer: C, D

9. When is the Terminate event of a form triggered?

   A. When the user moves to another form or program

   B. When the form is unloaded

   C. Never

   D. When all references to the form are deleted

   Answer: D

10. Which event is triggered when the user moves to another form?

    A. Unload

    B. Deactivate

    C. Terminate

    D. Load

    Answer: B

Chapter 2 Answers

1. How can you create an integer variable in your program? Check all that apply.

   A. Assign an integer value to a variable.

   B. Use the As Integer clause in the declaration statement for the variable.

   C. Make sure the variable's name begins with int.

   D. Add the % symbol to the end of the variable name.

   Answer: B, D

2. All of the following statements are true about variable names except:

   A. Names must start with a letter.

   B. Names can be any length.

   C. Names cannot include a period.

   D. Names must be unique within the scope of the variable.

   Answer: B

3. What are the advantages of using variable naming conventions? Check all that apply.

   A. The name of the variable forces its data type.

   B. The name indicates the data type of the variable.

   C. The variable names help with code documentation.

   D. The names indicate the scope of the variable.

   Answer: B, C, D

4. How do you create a global variable?

   A. Declare the variable with the Public statement anywhere in the program.

   B. Use the Dim statement to declare the variable in a standard module.

   C. Use the Public statement to declare the variable in a standard module.

   Answer: C

5. What are different types of procedures? Check all that apply.

   A. Sub

   B. Public

   C. Function

   D. Property

   Answer: A, C, D

6. Which of the following are true of creating an optional argument for a procedure? Check all that apply.

   A. You must include the Optional keyword.

   B. You must pass the argument ByVal.

   C. You cannot specify the data type of the variable.

   D. The argument must follow all required arguments.

Answer: A, D

7. Which of the following is the proper declaration for a procedure to which an array is to be passed?

   A. Sub ArraySort(sArray As Array)

   B. Sub ArraySort(sArray)

   C. Sub ArraySort(sArray() As Array)

   D. Sub ArraySort(sArray())

Answer: D

Chapter 3 Answers

1. Which control lets you display information in a hierarchical structure?

   A. TreeView

   B. ListView

   C. ListBox

   D. StatusBar

Answer: A

2. Which style of StatusBar panel can be modified by your program? Check all that apply.

   A. sbrText

   B. sbrCaps

   C. sbrNum

   D. sbrIns

Answer: A

3. How do you update the status of a sbrCaps style panel?

   A. It is handled for you automatically by the control.

   B. You need to place code in the KeyPress event of the form.

   C. You must place code in the KeyPress event of the StatusBar.

   D. Use a Windows API call to find out when the key is pressed.

Answer: A

4. Name the two techniques for identifying a Panel object in the Panels collection.

   A. Refer to it by the Index property.

   B. Refer to it by the Text property.

   C. Refer to it by the Style property.

   D. Refer to it by the Key property.

Answer: A, D

5. What property of the ProgressBar determines how much of the bar is filled?

   A. Min

   B. Max

   C. Value

   D. All of the above

Answer: D

6. What is the purpose of the ImageList control?

   A. Display bitmaps for the user to view.

   B. Provide a repository for images used by other controls.

   C. Allow easy editing of icons.

   D. Both A and B.

Answer: B

7. What are valid methods of adding a picture to the ImageList control? Check all that apply.

   A. Select a picture using a dialog box in the Property Pages.

   B. Set the Picture property of the ImageList control to the name of a PictureBox control.

   C. Set the Picture property of the ListImage object to the Picture property of another control.

   D. Set the Picture property of the ListImage object using the Load-Picture command.

Answer: A, C, D

8. What does a button of a button group on a toolbar do?

   A. Shows you the current status of an option.

   B. Allows you to select one option from several.

   C. Simply starts a function of the application.

   D. Provides a space in the toolbar.

Answer: B

9. All of the following statements are true about toolbars except:

   A. You can only have one toolbar on a form.

   B. Toolbars can be positioned anywhere on the form.

   C. Toolbars can be customized by the user.

   D. Toolbar buttons can display both text and images.

Answer: A

10. What do you have to do to allow the user to customize the toolbar?

   A. Write code to add buttons or remove buttons based on the user selection.

   B. Set the AllowCustomize property to true and the control takes care of the rest.

   C. You cannot do this with Visual Basic toolbars.

Answer: B

11. How many root nodes can a TreeView control have?

  A. 1

  B. Up to 5

  C. Maximum of 2

  D. No limit

Answer: D

12. What must you specify to make a new node the child of another node? Check all that apply.

  A. The Key value of the node to which it is related

  B. The text of the related node

  C. The Relationship must be specified as tvwChild

  D. The image to be associated with the new node

Answer: A, C

13. What property determines whether lines are drawn between parent and child nodes? Check all that apply.

  A. Appearance

  B. Style

  C. Indentation

  D. LineStyle

Answer: B, D

14. What advantages does the ListView control have over the standard ListBox? Check all that apply.

  A. ListView can display multiple columns of data.

  B. ListBox is limited in the number of items that are allowed.

  C. Only the ListView can be sorted.

  D. ListView allows you to sort on different fields and specify the sort order.

  E. ListView can display headers over columns of information.

Answer: A, D, E

15. Which of the following views displays the Text property of the List-Item objects? Check all that apply.

   A. Icon view

   B. Small icon view

   C. List view

   D. Report view

   Answer: A, B, C, D

16. Which views display the detail information of a ListItem that is contained in the SubItem array? Check all that apply.

   A. Icon view

   B. Small icon view

   C. List view

   D. Report view

   Answer: D

17. Which property of the ListView control determines which field a sort is based on?

   A. Sorted

   B. SortOrder

   C. SortField

   D. SortKey

   Answer: D

Chapter 4 Answers

1. What properties are required to be specified for a menu item? Check all that apply.

   A. Checked

   B. Index

C. Name

D. Caption

Answer: C, D

2. How can you enable the user to access a menu item from the keyboard? Check all that apply.

   A. Define an access key by designating a letter in the Caption property.

   B. Define a shortcut key by setting the Shortcut property in the menu editor.

   C. The user can press F10 and use the cursor keys.

   D. Define a shortcut key by setting the Shortcut property in code.

   Answer: A, B, C

3. All of the following statements about access keys are true except:

   A. You can have items on different menus with the same access key.

   B. The user must hold the Alt key while pressing the access key to open a top level menu.

   C. All top level menus must have a unique access key.

   D. Access keys are indicated to the user by an underlined letter in the caption.

   Answer: C

4. Which of the following statements about pop-up menus are true? Check all that apply.

   A. A pop-up menu can be used as a main menu.

   B. A pop-up menu can be created from a sub-level menu.

   C. A pop-up menu can have multiple levels.

   D. A pop-up menu can be activated by any event the developer chooses.

   Answer: A, B, C, D

5. Which form event would you use to activate a pop-up menu when the user clicks the right mouse button? Check all that apply.

   A. MouseDown

   B. Click

   C. MouseUp

   D. MouseMove

Answer: A, C

6. What is the proper syntax for activating the pop-up menu fmtFormat?

   A. Popup = fmtFormat

   B. Set PopupMenu = fmtFormat

   C. Me.PopupMenu fmtFormat

   D. Me.PopupMenu = fmtFormat

Answer: C

7. Which menu item properties can you change at run-time?

   A. WindowList, Caption, Index, Checked

   B. Name, Caption, Index

   C. Caption, Checked, Enabled, Visible

   D. Caption, Checked, Visible, Shortcut

Answer: C

8. What does the WindowList property do?

   A. Maintains a list of all forms in your program

   B. Allows you to add menu items to any menu at run-time

   C. Keeps a list of MDI child windows

   D. Works with any application

Answer: C

9. What is the proper syntax for adding an item to a menu array?

   A. filMRUFile.AddItem 1

   B. filMRUFile.Load 1

   C. Load filMRUFile(1)

   D. Load New filMRUFile

Answer: C

10. Which command is used to remove an item from a menu array?

   A. Delete

   B. RemoveItem

   C. Drop

   D. Unload

Answer: D

11. When removing items from the menu array, which of the following statements is true?

   A. You can remove all elements of the array.

   B. You must keep at least one element of the array.

   C. You cannot remove any elements that were created at design time.

Answer: C

Chapter 5 Answers

1. Which of the following properties determines how a control initiates a drag-and-drop operation?

   A. DragMode

   B. DragIcon

   C. DropMode

   D. Drag

Answer: A

2. What event can be used to indicate where a control in a standard drag-and-drop operation can be dropped?

A. DragDrop

B. DragOver

C. OLEDragDrop

D. Drag

Answer: B

3. A single control can be used as which of the following? Check all that apply.

A. The source of a standard drag-and-drop operation

B. The target of a drag-and-drop operation

C. The source of an OLE drag-and-drop operation

D. The target of an OLE drag-and-drop operation.

Answer: A, B, C, D

4. OLE drag-and-drop can be used for which of the following purposes?

A. Transferring information between applications.

B. Transferring information within an application.

C. Both A and B.

D. OLE drag-and-drop can only be used with OLE container controls.

Answer: C

5. Which of the following are advantages of OLE drag-and-drop over standard drag-and-drop operations? Check all that apply.

A. Allows you to move information between applications

B. Allows you to drag multiple controls simultaneously

C. Allows automatic handling of the drop operation

D. Allows you to use the same control as the source and target of an operation

Answer: A, C

6. How do you create the first element of a control array?

   A. Set the Index property of a control while in the design mode.

   B. Use the Load statement to load a control with an index value of 0.

   C. Use the CreateObject statement to create an instance of the control.

   D. Change the Index property of a single control at run time.

Answer: A

7. Which of the following restrictions apply to adding a control to a control array at run-time? Check all that apply.

   A. The form must be visible when the control is added.

   B. The control array must already exist.

   C. The Index value must be the next sequential number after the upper bound of the array.

   D. The Index of the new control must be unique.

Answer: B, D

8. Which of the following are properties of a control array?

   A. Count, Type, and Name

   B. Count, Item, LBound, and UBound

   C. Count, Name, and Index

   D. Index, LBound, and UBound

Answer: B

9. Which of the following statements can be used to change the value of a property in an element of a control array?

   A. txtMember.Top = 120

   B. txtMember(0).Top = 120

   C. txtMember.0.Top = 120

   D. txtMember0.Top = 120

Answer: B

10. What are the restrictions on removing controls from a control array? Check all that apply.

  A. The control must have been created in design mode.

  B. The control must have been added at run time.

  C. The control element must exist.

  D. All data must have been unloaded from the control.

Answer: B, C

11. Which of the following statements removes a control from an array?

  A. Delete txtMember(5)

  B. Remove txtMember(5)

  C. Unload txtMember(5)

  D. Load txtMember(5) vbRemove

Answer: C

Chapter 6 Answers

1. What three methods does the Collection object support?

  A. Load, Unload, Count

  B. Add, Remove, Item

  C. Add, Delete, Index

  D. Add, Remove, Sort

Answer: B

2. What method is common to all collections?

  A. Add

  B. Delete

  C. Remove

  D. Item

Answer: D

3. What is the only property supported by a collection?

   A. Name

   B. Index

   C. Count

   D. Type

   Answer: C

4. What does the Forms collection contain?

   A. A list of all forms in a project

   B. A list of all currently loaded forms

   C. A list of all visible forms

   D. All the child forms of an MDI application

   Answer: B

5. How are forms added to the Forms collection?

   A. By adding a form to a project

   B. Using the Add method of the Forms collection

   C. Using the Load statement

   D. Activating a form

   Answer: C

6. What does the Controls collection contain?

   A. A list of all controls on a form

   B. A list of all the controls used by your program

   C. A list of visible controls

   D. The names of all control arrays on the form

   Answer: A

7. What are key differences between the Controls collection and a control array? Check all that apply.

 A. A control array contains controls of a single type, the Controls collection contains controls of many types.

 B. The elements of a control array all have the same name, the elements of the Controls collection can have different names.

 C. The elements of a control array do not share any events, the elements of the Controls collection do.

 D. A control array is simply a subset of the Controls collection.

 Answer: A, B

8. How do you determine what the type of a control is?

 A. Use the IsType function.

 B. Use the TypeOf clause.

 C. Check the Type property of the control.

 D. Use the prefix of the control name.

 Answer: B

9. Why is it important to determine the type of a control?

 A. Process only controls that support a given property.

 B. Some control types are not included in the Controls collection.

 C. For programmer information only.

 Answer: A

10. What are the two methods of referencing an element of a collection?

 A. Using the name value or the index value

 B. Using the index value and the Key value

 C. Using the name and type

 D. Using name and Key

 Answer: B

11. Which of the following code segments can be used to process all the controls on a form? Check all that apply.

A. ```
For I = 0 To Controls.Count
    Debug.Print Controls(I).Name
Next I
```

B. ```
For All Controls
    Debug.Print Control.Name
Next Control
```

C. ```
For Each chgControl In Controls
    Debug.Print chgControl.Name
Next chgControl
```

D. ```
For I = 0 To Controls.UBound
    Debug.Print Controls.Item(I).Name
Next I
```

Answer: A, C

Chapter 7 Answers

1. What are the three types of property procedures that can be created for a class?

A. Add, Retrieve, Remove

B. Item, Add, Remove

C. Let, Set, Get

D. Let, Get, Object

Answer: C

2. Which property procedure is used to retrieve the value of a property?

A. Retrieve

B. Get

C. Item

D. Value

Answer: B

3. How do you create a method for a class?

A. Use a Method procedure declaration.

B. Use a Property Set procedure.

C. Create a Public procedure in the class module.

D. Create a Private procedure in the class module.

Answer: C

4. What command triggers an event created in a class?

A. RaiseEvent

B. SetEvent

C. Trigger

D. FireEvent

Answer: A

5. How do you create a Public class in a standard executable?

A. Set the Public property to True.

B. Set the Instancing property to SingleUse.

C. No special requirements.

D. You cannot create a Public class in a standard executable.

Answer: D

6. What does the Friend declaration do?

A. Makes a class available for use by any program

B. Makes the methods of the class usable by other parts of the program in which the class is defined

    C. Limits your program to creating a single object from the class

    D. Keeps you from having to specify the object name to reference the methods of the class

Answer: B

7. What is the Instancing property for?

    A. Sets the number of objects that can be created from the class

    B. Determines whether the class inherited properties from another class

    C. Specifies how the class in an ActiveX server can be used by other programs

    D. Specifies how the class in a standard program can be used by other programs

Answer: C

8. How do you use a class in your program?

    A. Simply call the methods and properties like any other procedure.

    B. Create an object based on the class using the Set statement or New keyword.

    C. Use the Call statement to access the class directly.

Answer: B

9. Which of the following statements can be used to create an object based on a class? Check all that apply.

    A. Set oUser = New cUser

    B. oUser = cUser

    C. Dim oUser As New cUser

    D. CreateObject("cUser")

Answer: A, C

Chapter 8 Answers

1. In setting up the data control, which property do you use to specify the database that the control will link to?

    A. DatabaseName

    B. RecordSource

    C. Connect

    D. RecordsetType

    Answer: A

2. What is a valid setting for the RecordSource property? Check all that apply.

    A. The name of a Table in the database

    B. The name of a Query in the database

    C. A valid SQL Select statement

    D. The name of another data control

    Answer: A, B, C

3. Which RecordsetType setting would you use if you wanted to create a read-only recordset?

    A. Table

    B. Dynaset

    C. Snapshot

    D. Read-only

    Answer: C

4. In setting up a text box as a bound control, which property specifies the field of the recordset to be displayed?

    A. Name

    B. DataSource

    C. DataField

    D. Text

    Answer: C

5. Which list controls let you create the selection list from a table in a database? Check all that apply.

   A. Standard ListBox

   B. DBList

   C. Standard Combo Box

   D. DBCombo

   Answer: B, D

6. Which of the following grid controls allow you to display data by linking to a data control? Check all that apply.

   A. Microsoft Grid control

   B. MSFlexGrid

   C. DBGrid

   D. None of the above

   Answer: B, C

7. Which of the following grid controls allow you to edit data by linking to a data control? Check all that apply.

   A. Microsoft Grid control

   B. MSFlexGrid

   C. DBGrid

   D. None of the above

   Answer: C

8. Which property of the DBList specifies the display field for the list?

   A. RowSource

   B. ListField

   C. DataSource

   D. DataField

   Answer: B

9. Which property of the DBList control specifies where the list information comes from?

   A. RowSource

   B. ListField

   C. DataSource

   D. DataField

Answer: A

10. How do you handle adding and deleting records in a database program using the data control?

   A. Set the appropriate properties of the data control (AllowAddNew, AllowDelete).

   B. Write program code to invoke recordset methods (AddNew, Delete).

   C. Either A or B can be used.

   D. Neither A nor B is correct.

Answer: B

11. How do you handle record addition and deletion when using the DBGrid control?

   A. Set the appropriate properties of the data control (AllowAddNew, AllowDelete).

   B. Set the appropriate properties of the DBGrid control (AllowAddNew, AllowDelete).

   C. Write program code to invoke recordset methods (AddNew, Delete).

   D. All of the above will work.

Answer: B

12. What items must be specified as part of the criteria for the Find methods?

   A. Field name, comparison operator, comparison value

   B. Field name, database name, comparison value

C. Data control, bound control name, comparison value

D. Field name, comparison operator, bound control name

Answer: A

13. Which methods can be used to locate a specific record in a dynaset-type recordset? Check all that apply.

   A. Seek

   B. FindFirst

   C. FindLast

   D. Search

   Answer: B, C

14. What must you do with literal dates in a search criteria for the Find methods?

   A. Enclose the date in single quotes.

   B. Enclose the date in double quotes.

   C. Enclose the date in # symbols.

   D. No special treatment is required.

   Answer: C

Chapter 9 Answers

1. Which object handles the connection to a specific database?

   A. DBEngine

   B. Workspace

   C. Database

   D. Recordset

   Answer: C

2. Which object provides the link to specific data?

A. DBEngine

B. Workspace

C. Database

D. Recordset

Answer: D

3. Which object is responsible for handling transaction processing?

A. DBEngine

B. Workspace

C. Database

D. Recordset

Answer: B

4. Which of the following is a valid data source for the OpenRecordset method? Check all that apply.

A. The name of a table

B. The name of a stored query

C. A SQL statement

D. The name of a data control

Answer: A, B, C

5. What type of recordset must you use if you want to use a SQL statement as the data source?

A. Table

B. Dynaset

C. Snapshot

D. Both the Dynaset and Snapshot can be used.

Answer: D

6. What is the proper method of referring to a field in a recordset in order to retrieve the value of the field? Check all that apply.

   A. RSProd!ProductName

   B. RSProd(ProductName)

   C. RSProd("ProductName")

   D. RSProd.Fields(3)

Answer: A, C, D

7. Which statement is valid for setting the ProductName field to a new value?

   A. Set ProductName = "Syrup"

   B. RSProducts!ProductName = "Syrup"

   C. SetFieldValue "ProductName", "Syrup"

   D. RSProducts.Fields(3).Set "Syrup"

Answer: B

8. In order to modify the value of a field, what is the proper sequence of commands?

   A. Assign the value of the field, then invoke the Edit and Update methods.

   B. Invoke the Edit method, then assign the value of the fields. The Update method is not needed.

   C. Invoke the Edit method, assign the values of the fields, then invoke the Update method.

   D. Invoke the Edit method, assign the values of the fields, then invoke the Commit method.

Answer: C

9. What is the proper method to use to add a record to the recordset?

   A. Edit

   B. NewRecord

   C. Add

   D. AddNew

Answer: D

10. Which method would you use to locate the first record in a dynaset-type recordset?

   A. FindNext

   B. Seek

   C. Search

   D. FindFirst

Answer: D

11. Which method would you use to locate the first record in a table-type recordset?

   A. FindNext

   B. Seek

   C. Search

   D. FindFirst

Answer: B

12. Which of the following are advantages of using the Find method instead of the Seek method? Check all that apply.

   A. Find is always faster than Seek.

   B. Find allows you to specify multiple criteria.

   C. Find lets you search for a range of values.

   D. Find works with all recordset types, Seek doesn't.

Answer: B, C

13. Which of the following are criteria for using the Seek command? Check all that apply.

   A. You must have an active index that contains the field to be searched.

   B. You must be working with a dynaset-type recordset.

   C. You must be working with a table-type recordset.

   D. You must specify the name of the field to be searched in the method call.

Answer: A, C

Chapter 10 Answers

1. What property of the Remote Data Control determines the database accessed by the control?

A. SQL

B. ResultsetType

C. DataSourceName

D. Connect

Answer: C

2. What property of a bound control must be set to work with a Remote Data Control?

A. UseRemoteData

B. DataSource

C. DataField

D. You cannot bind controls to the RDC.

Answer: B

3. What tool do you use to set up a data source for remote data access?

A. Remote Data Control

B. Remote Data Objects

C. ODBC Data Source Administrator

D. Visual Basic's Data Form Wizard

Answer: C

4. Which object of the RDO model provides the link to the database being accessed?

A. rdoEngine

B. rdoEnvironment

C. rdoConnection

D. rdoResultset

Answer: C

5. Which of the following methods is **not** supported by RDO?

   A. FindFirst

   B. MoveLast

   C. AddNew

   D. Update

   Answer: A

6. Which object of the RDO is used to retrieve specific data from a database?

   A. rdoEngine

   B. rdoEnvironment

   C. rdoConnection

   D. rdoResultset

   Answer: D

Chapter 11 Answers

1. Which of the following is **not** true of In-Process servers?

   A. An ActiveX DLL is an In-Process server.

   B. They are faster than Out-of-Process servers.

   C. They can run as a stand-alone application.

   D. They run in the same process space as the client.

   Answer: C

2. Which of the following is an advantage of an Out-of-Process server? Check all that apply.

   A. It can run as a stand-alone application.

   B. There are more multithreading options than for an In-Process server.

   C. It can handle more objects in a single project than an In-Process server.

   D. It is faster than an In-Process server.

Answer: A, B

3. Which of the following settings of the Instancing property apply only to Out-of-Process servers? Check all that apply.

   A. Private

   B. Public Not Creatable

   C. MultiUse

   D. SingleUse

Answer: C

4. Why use multithreading?

   A. It allows a single object to execute on more than one processor.

   B. It significantly speeds up any server operations.

   C. Multiple objects can run in separate threads and avoid blocking each other.

   D. There is no advantage to multithreading.

Answer: C

5. Which of the following multithreading models uses the most resources?

   A. Apartment model

   B. Single Threaded

   C. Thread Pool

   D. Thread per Object

Answer: D

6. Which setting of the Instancing property creates all client objects from the same instance of the server object?

   A. Private

   B. Public Not Creatable

   C. MultiUse

   D. SingleUse

Answer: C

7. How do you create a property for a server object?

   A. Declare a variable as Public.

   B. Use Property Procedures.

   C. Create a Friend variable.

   D. Use a Sub Procedure.

Answer: B

8. What statement is used to trigger an event?

   A. LoadEvent

   B. Trigger

   C. RaiseEvent

   D. Event.Raise

Answer: C

9. How do you display a server form from a client application?

   A. Use the Show method and specify the form name.

   B. Call a method of the server object that creates and displays an instance of the form.

   C. Use a server event to show the form.

   D. You cannot create forms in a server project.

Answer: B

10. What is the advantage of asynchronous processing?

    A. There is no advantage.

    B. The server can accomplish other tasks while the requested task is running.

    C. The client can accomplish other tasks while the requested task is running.

    D. It allows the client to display a server form.

Answer: C

11. What keyword must be used in a declaration statement to allow an object to respond to events?

    A. Notify

    B. New

    C. WithEvents

    D. UseEvents

Answer: C

Chapter 12 Answers

1. Which statement or function do you use to create an object variable?

    A. Dim oWord As Word.Application

    B. Set oWord = Word.Application

    C. Set oWord = CreateObject("Word.Application")

    D. Dim oWord As String

Answer: A

2. How is early binding set up in an application?

    A. Declare a variable as Object.

    B. Declare a variable as Variant.

    C. Use the CreateObject Function.

    D. Declare a variable as a specific object type.

Answer: D

3. How do you declare an object variable for late binding?

   A. Declare a variable as Object.

   B. Declare a variable as Variant.

   C. Use the CreateObject Function.

   D. Declare a variable as a specific object type.

   Answer: A

4. Which of the following statements creates an instance of an object? Check all that apply.

   A. Dim oWord As Object

   B. Dim oWord As New Word.Document

   C. Set oWord = New Word.Document

   D. Set oWord = CreateObject("Word.Document")

   Answer: B, C, D

5. What are advantages of early binding? Check all that apply.

   A. Objects are created faster.

   B. You can use an early bound variable with any object.

   C. Information about properties and methods is available while you program.

   D. There is no advantage.

   Answer: A, C

6. What are advantages of late binding? Check all that apply.

   A. Objects are created faster.

   B. You can use a late bound variable with any object.

   C. Information about properties and methods is available while you program.

   D. There is no advantage.

   Answer: B

7. Which of the following statements show the proper use of the New keyword? Check all that apply.

A. Dim oWord As New Object

B. Dim oSheet As New Excel.Sheet

C. Set New oSheet = CreateObject("Excel.Sheet")

D. Set oWord = New Word.Document

Answer: B, D

Chapter 13 Answers

1. Which statement is used to identify an external procedure to Visual Basic?

A. Declare

B. Dim

C. Public

D. DLLProc

Answer: A

2. Why would you use an Alias with a DLL procedure? Check all that apply.

A. When you need to use a DLL with the same name as a Visual Basic keyword

B. When you want to keep the real name a secret

C. When you need to use two or more procedures with the same name in separate DLLs

D. To shorten the name of the procedure to avoid typing

Answer: A, C, D

3. How do you pass a null pointer to a DLL procedure?

A. Create an empty string with a statement like sPassStr = " ".

B. Use the Space function to create a zero length string.

C. Pass a numeric value of 0.

D. Use the vbNullString constant.

Answer: D

4. What is a null-terminated string?

A. An empty string

B. A string with an ASCII 0 appended to the end of the string

C. Any fixed length string

D. A string with the character 0 in it

Answer: B

5. What value of the Instancing property should be used in creating a DLL for your own functions?

A. Global MultiUse

B. MultiUse

C. Public Not Creatable

D. Private

Answer: A

6. What does the AddressOf operator do?

A. Specifies a memory location where information from the procedure can be placed

B. Passes the pointer for a user-defined function to a DLL procedure

C. Generates a pointer for a string

D. Nothing

Answer: B

7. What is a callback procedure?

    A. A procedure in your program that is called by a DLL procedure

    B. A recursive procedure that repeatedly calls itself

    C. Part of a modem protocol

    D. A specific DLL procedure in the Windows API

Answer: A

Chapter 14 Answers

1. Which of the following statements is true about creating ActiveX controls?

    A. You must create the control completely from scratch.

    B. You can only use a single standard control in the creation of an ActiveX control.

    C. You cannot add properties to a standard control to enhance its capabilities.

    D. You can use multiple standard controls as well as drawing methods to create the interface of your control.

Answer: D

2. What statement is used to trigger an event in your ActiveX control?

    A. LoadEvent

    B. RaiseEvent

    C. FireEvent

    D. Trigger

Answer: B

3. Which property statement is required for a read-only property?

    A. Property Get

    B. Property Let

    C. Property Set

    D. Property Read

Answer: A

4. How do you create a method of a control?

    A. Use a Method declaration statement.

    B. Create a Sub or Function procedure and declare it as Public.

    C. Create a Sub or Function procedure and declare it as Private.

    D. Creation of the method is automatic because all procedures in a control are public.

Answer: B

5. What does the Control Interface Wizard do for you? Check all that apply.

    A. Designs the visual interface of your control.

    B. Helps you create properties, methods, and events for your control.

    C. Lets you assign properties of the control to properties of the constituent controls.

    D. Handles the code for storing property changes.

Answer: B, C, D

6. What is the purpose of Property Pages?

    A. To make it easier for you to create properties of your control

    B. To provide a developer with easy access to the properties of your control

    C. To automatically test the property settings of your control

Answer: B

7. Which of the following programs can use ActiveX controls that you create? Check all that apply.

    A. Visual Basic

    B. Microsoft Office

    C. Microsoft Visual FoxPro

    D. Internet Explorer 3.0

Answer: A, B, C, D

8. Which event is used to store developer settings for your control?

   A. WriteSettings

   B. StoreProperties

   C. WriteProperties

   D. Save

Answer: C

9. What is a PropertyBag?

   A. Another name for Property Pages

   B. An object used to store developer settings for a control

   C. A term we made up

   D. A list of properties that can be included in a UserControl

Answer: B

10. What method is used to retrieve developer settings for your control?

   A. The Read method of the UserControl object

   B. The Retrieve method of the PropertyBag object

   C. The ReadProperty method of the PropertyBag object

   D. The ReadProperty method of the UserControl object

Answer: C

11. What type of file is created when you compile an ActiveX control?

   A. EXE

   B. CTL

   C. OCX

   D. CAB

Answer: C

12. Which HTML tag is needed to insert an ActiveX control in a Web page?

A. control

B. object

C. bold

D. ActiveX

Answer: B

Chapter 15 Answers

1. Which control would you use to display a rendered Web page?

A. WebBrowser

B. Internet Transfer Control

C. WinSock

D. Picture Box

Answer: A

2. Which control would you use to retrieve HTML text?

A. WebBrowser

B. Internet Transfer Control

C. WinSock

D. Picture Box

Answer: B

3. What method of the WebBrowser control lets you move to a specific Web page?

A. GoForward

B. Navigate

C. GoBack

D. OpenURL

Answer: B

4. Which methods of the WebBrowser control work with the History list? Check all that apply.

A. GoForward

B. GoHome

C. GoSearch

D. GoBack

Answer: A, D

5. Which event of the WebBrowser control lets you know when you have successfully moved to another web page?

A. DownloadComplete

B. NavigateComplete

C. BeforeNavigate

D. ProgressChange

Answer: B

6. What port number should be used for the RemotePort property of the Internet Transfer Control for an Internet connection?

A. 1

B. 100

C. 80

D. 65

Answer: C

7. When do you use the UserName and Password property of the ITC?

A. For all Internet access

B. For access to secured sites

C. For access to FTP sites only

D. For access to HTTP sites only

Answer: B

8. Which method of the ITC allows you to retrieve HTML text from an HTTP site?

   A. OpenURL

   B. GetHeaders

   C. Navigate

   D. Retrieve

   Answer: A

9. How do you copy a file from an FTP site?

   A. Use the OpenURL method.

   B. Use the Execute method with a GET operation.

   C. Use the Execute method with a PUT operation.

   D. Use the Copy method.

   Answer: B

Chapter 16 Answers

1. What is the primary object used in creating ActiveX documents?

   A. UserControl

   B. Form

   C. UserDocument

   D. Class Module

   Answer: C

2. How many documents are allowed in a single project?

   A. 1

   B. Maximum of 5

   C. There is no set limit.

   D. Maximum of 10

   Answer: C

3. Which of the following is not allowed in an ActiveX document?

   A. Custom controls

   B. User created controls

   C. OLE container control

   D. Database controls

Answer: C

4. How do you store information from an ActiveX document so it is available when the document is reloaded?

   A. Write the information to a file.

   B. Use the methods of the PropertyBag object.

   C. It cannot be done.

   D. Specify the initial settings in the HyperLink object.

Answer: B

5. What does the Document Migration Wizard do for you?

   A. Helps you move documents to another folder.

   B. Helps you create an ActiveX document from an existing program.

   C. Creates a file that lets you distribute your document over the Internet.

   D. Lets you move from one document to another.

Answer: B

6. Which of the following can run an ActiveX document? Check all that apply.

   A. Internet Explorer

   B. Visual Basic development environment

   C. Windows Explorer

   D. Office Binder

Answer: A, B, D

7. Which file do you load to run an ActiveX document?

A. dob

B. vbd

C. cab

D. vbp

Answer: B

8. Which file is downloaded over the Internet to install and register an ActiveX document?

A. dob

B. vbd

C. cab

D. vbp

Answer: C

9. How are multiple documents handled when you compile your project?

A. All documents are compiled into a single file.

B. Each document is created in a separate file.

C. You cannot create multiple documents in a single project.

D. Files with links to each other are grouped together.

Answer: B

10. How do you display one document from another?

A. Use the Show method of the document.

B. Use the NavigateTo method of the HyperLink object.

C. Use the Display method of the document.

D. Use the Navigate method of the UserDocument object.

Answer: B

11. How do you pass information from one document to another?

  A. Set the value of a property in the target document.

  B. Use a global variable to contain the data.

  C. Use the PropertyBag.

  D. You cannot pass data between documents.

Answer: B

Chapter 17 Answers

1. Which of the following statements is used to turn off error handling in a procedure?

  A. On Error GoTo line

  B. On Error Resume Next

  C. On Error GoTo 0

  D. Error Off

Answer: C

2. Which of the following statements tells Visual Basic to retry the statement that caused the error?

  A. Resume Next

  B. Resume

  C. Retry

  D. Resume line

Answer: B

3. Which statement is used with deferred error handling?

  A. On Error GoTo line

  B. On Error Resume Next

  C. On Error GoTo 0

  D. On Error Defer

Answer: B

4. Which of the following are drawbacks of deferred error handling? Check all that apply.

   A. It runs slower than immediate error processing.

   B. Errors may occur between the original error and your error handler.

   C. Your error code is spread throughout your procedure instead of being located in a single place.

   D. If multiple errors occur, your program will crash.

Answer: B, C

5. What does the Clear method of the Err object do?

   A. Transfers error handling to the next higher procedure.

   B. Generates a runtime error.

   C. There is no Clear method.

   D. Resets the properties of the Err object.

Answer: D

6. Which of the following is a required argument of the Raise method?

   A. Description

   B. Number

   C. Source

   D. Helpfile

Answer: B

7. What is the purpose of the Raise method?

   A. Transfer error handling to the next higher procedure.

   B. Generate a runtime error.

   C. Trap errors that occur in your program.

   D. Reset the properties of the Err object.

Answer: B

8. What happens if you use a Resume statement outside of an error handling routine?

   A. Your program retries the statement that generated the error.

   B. Nothing happens.

   C. An error occurs as the Resume statement is not allowed to be used outside an error handler.

   D. Your error handler enters an infinite loop.

   Answer: C

9. What are some ways that you can centralize error handling? Check all that apply.

   A. Write a class to encapsulate functions and include the error handling in the class.

   B. Place an On Error GoTo procedure statement as the first line of your program and write an error procedure.

   C. Have the error handling code in each procedure call a function that identifies the error and indicates the appropriate action.

   D. Place your function in a public procedure that includes error handling capabilities.

   Answer: A, C

Chapter 18 Answers

1. Which of the following tools helps you avoid errors in your programs? Check all that apply.

   A. Auto Syntax Check

   B. Require Variable Declaration

   C. Call Stack

   D. Immediate Window

   Answer: A, B

2. Which of these tools will display the value of a variable? Check all that apply.

   A. Immediate Window

   B. Watch Window

   C. Call Stack

   D. Locals Window

Answer: A, B, D

3. Which of these tools will show you the properties of a form and its controls?

   A. Watch Window

   B. Immediate Window

   C. Auto Data Tips

   D. Locals Window

Answer: D

4. Which of these tools allows you to change the value of a variable?

   A. Watch Window

   B. Immediate Window

   C. Auto Data Tips

   D. Locals Window

Answer: B

5. How can you cause a program to pause execution? Check all that apply.

   A. Set a Breakpoint in code.

   B. Set a watch to break when the value changes.

   C. Insert the Stop command in your program.

   D. Right click the mouse on the program while it is running.

Answer: A, B, C

6. How are the scope of a variable and the scope of a watch related?

   A. The scope of the variable determines the scope of the watch.

   B. The scope of the watch determines the scope of the variable.

   C. The scope of the watch and scope of the variable are set independently and are, therefore, unrelated.

   Answer: C

7. Which command do you use to skip over a procedure when you are stepping through a program?

   A. Step Into

   B. Step Out

   C. Run to Cursor

   D. Step Over

   Answer: D

8. What Visual Basic element must you use to debug an ActiveX DLL?

   A. Call Stack

   B. Immediate Window

   C. Project Group

   D. The Compiler

   Answer: C

9. When is the program code of a User Control running and able to be tested? Check all that apply.

   A. When the control is being built

   B. When the control is being added to another project and the properties are being set

   C. When a project containing the control is running

   D. During compilation of the control

   Answer: B, C

Chapter 19 Answers

1. Which compilation option typically produces the smaller executable file?

   A. Compile to native code.

   B. Compile to P-code.

   C. Both options produce the same size file.

   Answer: B

2. Which compilation option typically produces the faster executable?

   A. Compile to native code.

   B. Compile to P-code.

   C. Both options produce equally fast programs.

   Answer: A

3. Which compiler options would be a benefit for a program to be run on a Pentium Pro machine? Check all that apply.

   A. Favor Pentium Pro

   B. Create Symbolic Debug Information

   C. Assume No Aliasing

   D. Remove Safe Pentium FDIV Checks

   Answer: A, D

4. How can you set the value of conditional compilation arguments? Check all that apply.

   A. Use the #Const directive.

   B. Use the Const statement.

   C. Use an assignment statement in your program.

   D. Use the Project Properties dialog box.

   Answer: A, D

5. What are reasons for using conditional compilation? Check all that apply.

A. To maintain multiple versions of a code

B. To incorporate debug information

C. To compile a single module for testing

D. To create demonstration programs

Answer: A, B, D

6. What compiler options can lead to unexpected results from your program? Check all that apply.

A. Remove Integer Overflow Checks

B. Remove Floating Point Error Checks

C. Create Symbolic Debug Info

D. Favor Pentium Pro

Answer: A, B

7. How can you access version information about your program that is input in the Make dialog box?

A. It is unavailable while your program is running.

B. Through the properties of the App object

C. Through the properties of the Program object

D. Read the header information in your code files.

Answer: B

Chapter 20 Answers

1. HelpFile is a property of which object? Check all that apply.

A. Form

B. Common Dialog

C. Project

D. App

Answer: B, D

2. How do you make a specific topic appear when the user presses F1 on a control?

   A. Pass the control name to the Common Dialog.

   B. Set the value of the HelpContextID property of the control.

   C. Set the value of the Index property of the control.

   D. Set the ToolTipText property of the control.

   Answer: B

3. What happens if there is no specific topic for a control when the user presses F1?

   A. The "Topic not Found" error is displayed in the help file.

   B. Help is not accessed.

   C. The HelpContextID of the control's container is used.

   D. Windows 95/NT help is shown.

   Answer: C

4. What happens if the topic assigned to a control is not in the help file?

   A. The "Topic not Found" error is displayed in the help file.

   B. Help is not accessed.

   C. The HelpContextID of the control's container is used.

   D. Windows 95/NT help is shown.

   Answer: A

5. What two properties of a Common Dialog must be set before trying to display help?

   A. HelpFile

   B. HelpContext

   C. HelpCommand

   D. HelpKey

   Answer: A, C

6. What method of the Common Dialog is used to display help information?

   A. Help

   B. OpenHelp

   C. ShowHelp

   D. Assist

Answer: C

7. What files are created by the Help Workshop? Check all that apply.

   A. Help topic files

   B. Help file (.hlp extension)

   C. Help project file

   D. Help contents file

Answer: B, C, D

8. What groups of controls can be linked to a specific help topic?

   A. Any control that is visible on the screen

   B. Only controls with a HelpContextID property

   C. All controls

   D. Only menu items

Answer: B

Chapter 21 Answers

1. What does the Setup Wizard do?

   A. It installs a program on your local drive.

   B. It automatically creates an installation program for your application.

   C. It assists you in creating an installation program for your application.

   D. It allows you to modify your Visual Basic development environment.

Answer: C

2. Why would you need to modify the Setup.lst file?

   A. To customize the installation of an application

   B. To specify which program to install

   C. To add forms to the setup program

   D. None of the above

Answer: A

3. How do you register a component without using an installation program? Check all that apply.

   A. Use the Regsvr32.exe program.

   B. Run the ActiveX EXE server.

   C. Open the registry with a text editor and enter the information.

   D. You must use an installation program to register a component.

Answer: A, B

4. What type of data can be stored in the Registry?

   A. Any type of data is allowed.

   B. Only strings and numbers may be stored.

   C. Only strings may be stored.

   D. Any data except pictures.

Answer: C

5. Which command do you use from your program to replace a specific value in the Registry?

   A. GetSetting

   B. GetAllSettings

   C. DeleteSetting

   D. SaveSetting

Answer: D

6. What happens if you do not specify a default value for the GetSetting function and there is no entry in the Registry?

    A. An error occurs in your program.

    B. No value is returned.

    C. The function returns an empty string.

    D. The function returns the value of the last key in the registry.

Answer: C

7. What will the statement DeleteSetting "RegTest", "Main" do?

    A. Delete all keys in the Main section of the RegTest application.

    B. Delete the first key in the Main section of the RegTest application.

    C. Nothing. You must specify a key to be deleted.

    D. Delete all keys for the RegTest application.

Answer: A

8. What is the Regsvr32.exe program used for?

    A. To edit the Registry

    B. To register or un-register a component

    C. To only register a component

    D. Regsvr32 is not used with any programs you create.

Answer: B

APPENDIX

B

Glossary of Terms

Access key   A key combination (such as Alt+F) that allows the user to open a main menu, or a single key that allows the user to select a menu item.

ActiveX documents   A specialized Visual Basic application that can run within a Web Browser.

ActiveX Server   Any program that exposes objects to other programs for use.

Alias   Another name by which a procedure is identified for use in an application.

Asynchronous operation   Program execution where multiple instructions can be run simultaneously.

Bookmark property   An identifier for a specific record in a recordset.

Breakpoint   A debugging tool that pauses the execution of the program at a specific point.

Callback procedure   A procedure in an application that can be called by a function in a DLL routine.

Child form   A form that is contained within a parent form.

Class modules   The code structures that implement classes in Visual Basic.

Class   A structure that provides a definition of an object. A class defines the data (properties), tasks to perform (methods), and notifications (events) of an object.

Collection   A grouping of similar objects, such as forms, recordsets, controls, and so on.

Common Dialog   A control that enables the programmer to easily create Open, Save, Help, and Print dialogs for a programs.

Conditional compilation   Visual Basic only compiles parts of a program as they are needed.

Control array   A group of controls of the same type that have the same name. Members of the array are identified by the Index property. Arrays are used for easier processing of multiple controls.

Controls collection   A special collection that provides a reference to every control on a given form.

DAO   Data Access Objects is the object model that allows the programmer to work with databases in a program.

Database   An object that provides a link to a single database file (that is, Biblio.mdb).

DBEngine   The top level object of the DAO model. The DBEngine object provides the main link to the DAO model.

Dynamic Link Library (DLL)   A file that contains object definitions for use by client programs. A DLL works as an in-process ActiveX server.

Dynaset   A recordset that returns a series of pointers to information in the tables of a database. These pointers allow a program to access the data in the table and even to modify it, but it does not give direct access to the tables themselves.

Early binding   Declaring a specific object type is known as early binding of the object.

Encapsulation   The data about an object and the code used to manipulate the data are contained within the object itself. The data is stored as the properties of the object and the code as the methods of the object. Encapsulation allows the object data and code to stand alone, independent of outside routines.

Explicit declaration   A means of defining the data type of a variable by specifying the type in the declaration statement.

Forms collection   A special collection that provides a reference to every loaded form in an application.

Friend declaration   Allows the programmer to make a property or method available to other modules in the current project (the one in which the class is defined), without making the routine truly public.

Global variable   Another name for Public variable.

HyperLink A string that identifies a link to another document or Web page.

Implicit declaration A means of defining the data type of a variable by placing a particular symbol at the end of the variable name.

In-Process server An ActiveX server that is contained in a DLL file and runs in the same process (memory) space as the client application.

Inheritance Allows one object to be created based on the properties and methods of another object. With inheritance, it is not necessary to code the properties and methods that are derived from the parent object. The programmer only has to code new or modified properties and methods.

Invalid value error An error that occurs when the programmer tries to assign a value to a variable that the variable is not capable of handling.

Jump A link between two topics in a help file.

Late Binding Declaring a generic object variable is known as late binding of the object.

Local variable A variable that is usable only in the procedure in which it is defined.

Logic error An error that does not cause the program to crash, but does cause the program to yield incorrect results.

Method A procedure that provides an object with the ability to perform a task.

Modal form A form that must be exited before other forms of the application may be accessed.

Module level variable A variable declared at the beginning of a form or code module that is available to all procedures in the module, but not outside the module.

Multithreading Processing multiple parts of an application in separate threads (typically on multiple processors).

Native code Machine level instructions that make up an application.

Object Browser   A Visual Basic tool that lets the programmer see the properties, methods, and events of an object.

Open Database Connectivity   A specification that provides a consistent means to communicate with many types of databases.

Out-of-Process server   An ActiveX server that is contained in an EXE file and runs in a separate process (memory) space from the client application.

P-code   An interpreted code that is between the "English-like" commands that programmers enter and the machine code that a computer uses.

Parent form   A form that provides a container for other forms of the application.

Polymorphism   Relates to the use of the same method name in various objects; for example, a Print method for the printer, a form, or a picture box. While the name of the method is the same, the actual code for the method in each object can be different. However, because the code for the method is encapsulated in the object, each object knows how to perform the correct task when the method is called.

Pop-up   A small window that contains additional information about a topic. The window "pops up" in response to a mouse click on a particular style of text.

Procedure   A self-contained segment of code that performs a specific task.

Programming interface   The structure by which programs communicate with one another.

PropertyBag   A storage device for maintaining information for an ActiveX document or ActiveX control.

Public variable   A variable that can be accessed from anywhere in the program.

Query   A SQL statement that is used to retrieve or modify data.

Recordset   An object that contains the actual information used by an application.

Remote data Data located in a database server such as Oracle or SQL Server.

Runtime error An error that occurs while the program is running.

Shortcut key A key combination that directly invokes a menu option.

Snapshot A read-only look at the information in the database at the time the recordset was created.

Status bar A bar at the bottom of a form that provides the user with additional information about the application.

Synchronous operation Program execution where one instruction must be completed before the next instruction can be started.

Syntax error An error in the "wording" of a line of program code.

Table The physical location of the data in a database. Also, a type of recordset that directly accesses the database tables.

The Registry A database in Windows 95 and Windows NT that contains information about the settings of the computer.

Thread pooling A method of multithreading where a specific number of threads are allocated for processing. Objects will use these threads in a "round-robin" fashion.

Tooltip A small window that provides additional information about a control. The tooltip pops up when the user rests the mouse cursor on the control for a few seconds.

Trapping an error Handling an error within an application so the user does not see the original error information, and so the program does not crash.

Watch A debugging tool that tracks the value of a variable or expression.

Workspace An object in DAO that handles security and transactions for database operations.

Index

Note to the Reader: Throughout this index **boldfaced** page numbers indicate primary discussions of a topic. *Italicized* page numbers indicate illustrations.

W

X

Y

Z

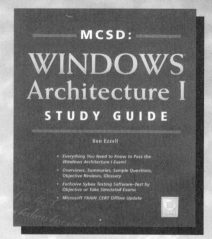
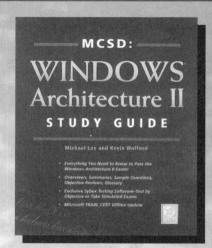

MCSD: Visual Basic® 5 Study Guide

Exam 70-165: Objectives

OBJECTIVE	PAGE
Design Issues	
Design and create forms. Skills include: Create an application that adds and deletes forms at run time; Use the Forms collection.	11, 184
Implement drag-and-drop operations within the Microsoft Windows® shell.	151, 160
Determine when to use a specific event. Skills include: Add code to the appropriate form event, such as Initialize, Terminate, Load, Unload, QueryUnload, Activate, and Deactivate.	16
Add a menu interface to an application. Skills include: Dynamically modify the appearance of a menu; Add a pop-up menu to an application; Create an application that adds and deletes menus at run time.	121, 133, 129, 139
Implement user interface controls in an application. Skills include: Display data by using the TreeView control; Display items by using the ListView control; Provide controls with images by using the ImageList control; Create toolbars by using the Toolbar control; Display status information by using the StatusBar control; Create an application that adds and deletes controls at run time; Use the Controls collection.	73, 96, 103, 84, 89, 75, 139, 188
Coding Issues	
Declare a variable. Skills include: Define the scope of a variable by using the Public, Private, and Static statements; Use the appropriate declaration statement.	41, 44, 50
Write and call Sub and Function procedures. Skills include: Write and call Sub and Function procedures by using named arguments or optional arguments; Write and call Sub and Function procedures that require an array as an argument; Call procedures from outside a module.	62, 64, 65
Create and use a class module. Skills include: Add properties to a class; Add methods to a class; Identify whether a class should be public or private; Declare properties and methods as Friend; Set the value of the Instancing property.	201, 204, 212, 223, 216
Access data by using the data controls and bound controls. Skills include: Add data to a table by using the DBList or DBCombo control; Add data to a table by using the standard ListBox control; Display information by using the DBGrid control; Display information by using the MSFlexGrid control.	235, 249, 248, 260, 258
Access data by using code. Skills include: Navigate through and manipulate records in a Recordset; Add, modify, and delete records in a Recordset; Find a record in a Recordset; Use the Find or Seek method to search a Recordset.	269, 281, 284, 290, 254, 293
Incorporate dynamic-link libraries (DLLs) into an application. Skills include: Declare and call a DLL routine; Identify when it is necessary to use the Alias clause; Create a DLL routine that modifies string arguments; Pass a null pointer to a DLL routine; Pass an argument by value and by reference; Pass a function pointer to a DLL by using a callback function; Pass a string to a DLL.	384, 388, 395, 393, 390, 394, 391
Build a Microsoft ActiveX™ client. Skills include: Use the Dim statement to reference an object; Use the Set statement to create an instance of an object; Use the CreateObject function to create an instance of an object.	369, 371, 365, 367, 368
Create an Automation server that exposes objects, properties, methods, and events. Skills include: Define properties for objects by using property procedures; Create a method that displays a form; Create a multithreaded component; Use App object properties to control server behavior; Call an object server asynchronously by using a callback mechanism; Create, use, and respond to events.	330, 336, 342, 349, 333, 353, 337

NOTE Exam objectives are subject to change at any time without prior notice and at Microsoft's sole discretion. Please visit Microsoft's Training & Certification Web site (www.microsoft.com/Train_Cert) for the most current listing of exam objectives.